D1707529

China's Minority Cultures: Identities and Integration Since 1912

China's Minority Cultures: Identities and Integration Since 1912

Colin Mackerras

 LONGMAN

ST. MARTIN'S PRESS
NEW YORK

Longman Australia Pty Ltd
Longman House
Kings Gardens
95 Coventry Street
Melbourne 3205 Australia

Offices in Sydney, Brisbane, Perth, and associated companies throughout the world.

Typeset by Kimberly Ellen
Set in Palatino 10/12 pt
Produced by Longman Australia Pty Ltd
Printed in Singapore through Longman Singapore

National Library of Australia
Cataloguing-in-Publication data

Mackerras, Colin, 1939- .

China's minority cultures : identities and integration since 1912.

Bibliography.

Includes index

ISBN 0 582 80671 2.

1. Minorities - China - Social conditions. 2. China - Civilization - 1912–1949.

3. China - Civilization - 1949–   . 4. China - Social conditions - 1912–1949.

5. China - Social conditions - 1949-   . I. Title

951.05

CHINA'S MINORITY CULTURES: INDENTITIES AND INTEGRATION SINCE 1912

St. Martin's Press, Scholarly and Reference Division.

175 Fifth Avenue, New York, N.Y. 10010

First published in the United States of America in 1995

Printed Singapore through Longman Singapore

Library of Congress Cataloging–in–Publication Data

Mackerras, Colin.

China's minority cultures : identities and integration since 1912/Colin Mackerras.

296p.23.4 x 15.6cm.

Includes bibliographical reference and index.

ISBN 0-312-1582-1 (cloth)

1. Ethnology--China--History--20th century. 2. China--Ethnic realtions.   I. Title

DS730.M338   1996

305.8'00951--dc20   95-20956

CIP

Contents

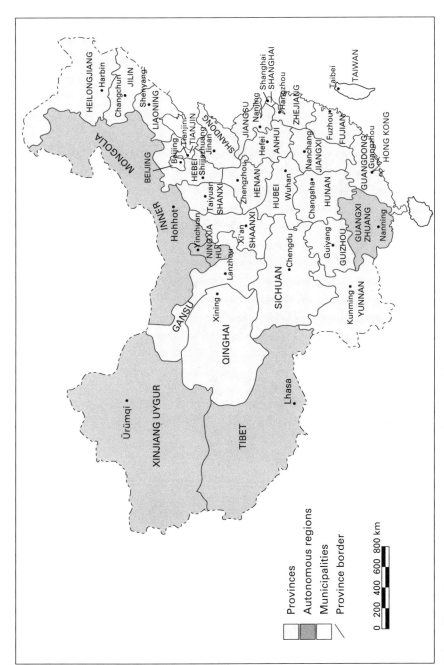

Map 1 China: Provinces, autonomous regions and municipalities.

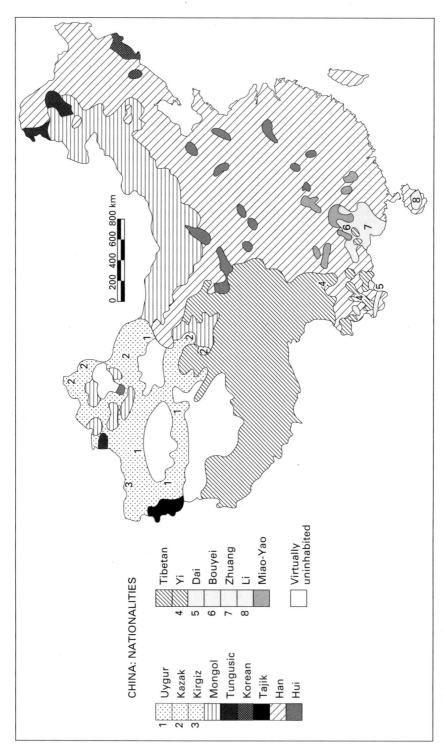

CHINA: NATIONALITIES

1 Uygur
2 Kazak
3 Kirgiz
  Mongol
  Tungusic
  Korean
  Tajik
  Han
  Hui

  Tibetan
4 Yi
5 Dai
6 Bouyei
7 Zhuang
8 Li
  Miao-Yao

☐ Virtually
  uninhabited

0 200 400 600 800 km

Map 2 China's nationalities.

Preface

This book has arisen out of a long-term project which I am carrying out on the minority nationalities of China. This has already resulted in several publications, the main ones of which are included in the list of works cited. It is based on the principle that, while the study of individual nationalities is very valuable — and quite a few scholars have already carried out excellent research of this type — it is also both valid and indeed necessary to examine China's minorities as a whole.

I should like to thank the Australian Research Council for grants which it gave me to carry out the research upon which this book is based. To Professor Stevan Harrell of the University of Washington and to Dr David Schak of the Faculty of Asian and International Studies, Griffith University, I owe a debt of gratitude for reading and commenting extensively, on the whole typescript and on Chapters 4 and 8 respectively. Other individuals deserving of my gratitude are too numerous to mention. I confine myself to noting that there are many colleagues, ethnologists and other professionals in China, belonging to the Central University for Nationalities and many other organisations, who have helped me enormously by facilitating my various visits and by offering me advice and friendship and by making their expertise so readily available to me. Finally, those many members of the minorities — scholars, officials and ordinary people — who talked to me either in interview or in quite informal ways are the primary souce of the knowledge on which this book is based. I stand in their debt more than they can possibly know.

One problem affecting the study of China's minorities is romanisation. For those minorities which lacked their own writing scripts at the time the Chinese Communist Party came to power in 1949, I have used the standard Chinese *pinyin* system. There are several major languages in the PRC for which internationally recognised romanisation systems exist, even if they are not universally accepted. These include Tibetan, Mongolian, Korean and Russian. For Korean I have adopted the McCune–Reischauer system and for Tibetan the Wylie system used in such scholarly works as the English translation of Tucci's *The Religions of Tibet*.[1] With the exception of the Mongols, the names of almost all nationalities follow standard practice in English-language works published in the PRC.[2] Place names are normally romanised according to standard practice in the PRC, which more often than not means the *Hanyu pinyin*. Other cases where it has proved rational and sensible to use *pinyin* are, first, personal names of people belonging to nationalities without their own writing systems in 1949; second, book and article titles in the Chinese language, and the names of their authors, including those belonging to a minority nationality; and third, terms applying to several different nationalities. Book and article titles of works in languages using the Roman alphabet, as well as the authors' names, are given exactly as they appear on the title page.

All the photographs used in this book were taken by the author, the great majority in 1990, 1992 and 1994, but a few in the 1980s.

Notes

1 See Giuseppe Tucci, trans. Geoffrey Samuel, *The Religions of Tibet*, Routledge & Kegan Paul, London and Henley, 1980, p. xii.

2 Any member of the Mongol nationality is called a Mongolian in the PRC. To avoid confusion, I have adopted the term Mongol to refer to members of the Mongol nationality, regardless of place of residence, and Mongolian to a citizen of the Mongolian People's Republic or, since 1991, the State of Mongolia.

1 Introduction

The disintegration of the Soviet Union, Yugoslavia and Czechoslovakia brought with it revivals in the cultures of those nationalities which had formed the larger states. In each case, these expressed themselves, among numerous other factors, in the form of a resurgence of traditional religions and insistence on the use of their own languages coupled with renewed affection for national literatures and arts. There was a political aspect to these disintegrations, with the members of the minorities in the larger states harbouring feelings of resentment because they felt themselves to be the victims of ill-treatment or discrimination.

There can be no doubt about the importance of ethnic cultural resurgence internationally in the last two decades of the twentieth century, or that this resurgence carries with it implications for the political integration of those nation-states with ethnic minorities. Even in nation-states which are not threatened with strong secessionist movements, the rise of ethnic cultures has posed a major political challenge to governments, democratic and authoritarian alike. In the United States, calls for the 're-empowerment' of ethnic minorities against the discrimination and marginalisation they claim to have suffered have been especially strong,[1] with the year 1992 being commemorated as the fifth centenary not of the 'discovery' of North America by Chrisopher Columbus but as the starting point of European domination and marginalisation of once proud peoples. Among the world's states, China ranks high for its large population and area, and for the number and significance of its minorities.

The scope of the present book is ethnic identities and integration in the histories of the cultures of China's minority nationalities from 1912 to 1995.

The reason for the former date is that it was the year in which the Republic of China came into being, and for the latter that it was when this book was completed. The period covers two main Chinese states, those being the Republic of China (1912–49) and the People's Republic of China (PRC, founded in 1949). The place is those territories which, as of the mid-1990s, make up the PRC. While it is true that the cultural changes wrought by the PRC do not look nearly as fundamental in the mid-1990s as they did in the mid-1970s, it remains sensible to use the year 1949 as a dividing point for the chapters throughout this book, if only because that was the year of the establishment of a new state ruled by a different political party with an ideology separate from that of its predecessor.

Two important points associated with identities should be stated as outside the scope or aims of the present book. One is to describe or analyse the various minorities of China, including their cultures.[2] The other is to explore how the minorities in China have come to play a significant role in the establishment of a Han or Chinese identity.[3]

Instead, my objective here is to focus on two general themes which appear to me to have gained some currency and importance in dealing with minorities. One is the relationship — and possible tension — between the identities of the minorities on the one hand and their integration into China on the other. A related but subordinate theme is the tension between tradition and change in the cultures of the minorities. The more extensive the change that takes place, the more the traditional culture of any people is likely to come under threat. It is also my objective to comment on the factors which bring about or restrain change in the cultures of the minorities.

Culture

The term 'culture' can be used in various ways, covering a range of descriptive definitions from those devised in the nineteenth century by such scholars as the German Gustav Klemm and the British Sir Edward Bennett Tylor to more modern interpretive conceptions such as that of Clifford Geertz, in which its emphasis is on meaning as distinct from description. Tylor defined 'culture' as 'that complex whole which includes knowledge, belief, art, morals, law, custom, and any other capabilities and habits acquired by man as a member of society'.[4] Although Tylor's book was originally published as early as 1871, his notion still retains currency for the *descriptive*, as opposed to *interpretive*, understanding of culture and has been described as a 'classic definition'.[5] A more contemporary, but still very similar, conception of culture advanced by Marvin Harris defines it as 'the total socially acquired life-way or life-style of a group of people', adding that it 'consists of the patterned, repetitive ways of thinking, feeling, and acting that are characteristic of the members of a particular society or segment of a society'.[6]

Culture being such a broad phenomenon under these definitions, it is necessary to select certain sites which may be regarded as representative of the whole. In this book, these belong to three broad categories of 'culture'. The first comprises those relating to the mind, such as religion and education, which come under the general headings of 'knowledge', 'belief' and 'morals' in Tylor's definition or 'thinking' in Harris's. The second is several areas of artistic life — specifically literature, the performing arts and theatre — belonging generally to the sphere of 'art' in Tylor's definition or 'thinking' or 'feeling' in Harris's. The third category is courtship, marriage, divorce and other gender issues, which belong to the realms of 'morals', 'custom', 'law' and 'other habits' in Tylor's notion and of 'feeling' and 'acting' in Harris's.

The minorities

In this book, the term 'minorities' means those people identified as minority nationalities (*shaoshu minzu*) by the government of the PRC since the 1980s. The Chinese term *minzu*, designating a nation or nationality, was first used late in the nineteenth century. Although the specific attributes of a *minzu* have been a subject of controversy, there has been general agreement that the territory making up China is home to various nationalities, not only the majority Han who constitute about 92 per cent of the population, but also a range of others, including Manchus, Tibetans, Hui and Mongols. In the PRC, a nationality is believed to be defined and identified by its history, language, economic life, common territory and culture. Since the late 1970s, the PRC government has recognised 55 minority nationalities, among which the most populous is the Zhuang, with some 15.5 million people, and the least is the Lhoba, with 2312.[7]

It should be emphasised that identification as a nationality in the PRC is determined by a range of factors, including national politics, the research and recommendations of ethnologists sponsored by the state and the feelings and self-awareness of individual groups and people.[8] Ethnicity is known by anthropologists to be a somewhat elastic concept, because the boundaries between different ethnic groups and even the ethnic identity of an individual are often very difficult to establish. In the sense that the PRC government has identified a precise number of minority nationalities in China and every PRC citizen is designated as belonging to a particular nationality, it could be argued that there is something fixed about the current official view of ethnicity in China. Officials of the Nationalities Affairs Commission whom I interviewed in 1990 informed me that they did not expect any further groups to be accepted as *minzu*. On the other hand, the four censuses held in China since 1949 show very clearly that individuals and groups can change their nationality — in other words, that it is possible for people to cross ethnic boundaries.[9]

Apart from the size of their population, there are many other respects in which the minorities vary sharply from one another. Their living places range from the very high and dry plains of Tibet to the jungles of southern Yunnan, from the far northeast cold areas to the tropical regions of Hainan.

Although they take up only a small proportion of the total population, the territories they inhabit are about five-eighths of China's total area. Their territories are thus on the whole very much less densely populated than those inhabited by the Han. The western half of China is overwhelmingly minority territory. In addition, the vast bulk of China's border areas are home to particular minorities; during the Republican period, it was very common to equate 'border areas' with 'minority territories'.

The languages spoken by China's minorities range widely.[10] The minorities of southwestern China speak languages in the Sino-Tibetan or Tai-Kadai families, with very few exceptions, such as the Va of Yunnan whose language belongs to the Austro-Asiatic family. The Sino-Tibetan family of languages has several subfamilies like the Tibeto-Burman, itself with many subdivisions. Minorities in China speaking Tai-Kadai languages include the Zhuang, Bai, Bouyei and Dai. There is disagreement over whether Miao-Yao languages belong to the Sino-Tibetan or constitute their own separate family. The minorities of northern China speak languages belonging to the Altaic branch of the Ural-Altaic family, which is also divided into subfamilies. The Turkic subfamily of the Altaic branch includes Uygur, Kazak, Kirgiz, Uzbek and others and is prevalent in Xinjiang in the northwest. Other subfamilies of the Altaic branch further east are the Mongolian languages, of which Mongol is by far the most important, and the Manchu-Tungus, spoken by most of the minorities of northeast China. The classification of Korean remains extremely controversial.[11] The Hui are the only minority of China without their own language. They are almost entirely Chinese-speaking, although there are some exceptions to this pattern.[12] The Manchus have their own language, but it is no longer widely used, the great majority of Manchus now speaking not their own language, but Chinese.[13] On the other hand, the language of the Xibes of Xinjiang, which is closely based on Manchu and very similar to it, continues in use to this day, both in its spoken and written forms.[14]

In terms of cultures also, the minorities vary very greatly. Some are very close to the Han — for example, the Manchus, the Zhuang and the Bai. Others are extremely different, such as the Turkic peoples of Inner Asia (for example, the Uygurs, Kazaks and Kirgiz) or the Tibetans. Some have very rich literatures and traditions, among which the Tibetans, Mongols and Koreans are pre-eminent, while others have generally lacked written scripts, even though that has not prevented them from developing their own literatures using Chinese characters (for example, the Bai people of Western Yunnan). At the other end are a series of minorities which are quite small in population and lack scripts or strong cultures.

Definitions

To establish the identity of a person, group or nationality means to determine those features which can define them and serve to distinguish them from others. 'Who am I?' and 'How am I different from others?' are questions which loom large in a world where large-scale government or multi-national corporations appear to determine how people should think, what attitudes they should hold, what arts they should like and what lifestyle they should observe and follow. In Alice Walker's novel *Possessing the Secret of Joy*, the central character Tashi is even prepared to have herself genitally mutilated in order to establish an African identity she believes has been robbed from her through white colonisation. While Tashi is a fictional character, she represents the realities of black women and their sufferings. It is obvious from her experience that identity is a matter over which emotions can run very high indeed.

As a concept, identity is psychological and social. It applies not only to individual people but also to groups or nationalities. In *Possessing the Secret of Joy*, Tashi speaks not only as an individual person, but also as a representative of a social group: black women. It was as a member of this minority that she felt her identity had been subverted. Identity refers not only to ethnic groups but to various other classifications — for example, by sexual preference (e.g. homosexuals 'coming out' in many Western societies).

Just as the identity of a person — who that person is — can be defined to a large extent according to experience or biography, so a nation can be identified by its history. As Benedict Anderson puts it, from somebody's experiences 'comes a conception of personhood, *identity*'. In the same way, it is what he terms 'the biography of nations' which largely defines what they are; it is their experience which 'engenders the need for a narrative of "identity"'.[15]

In historical terms, ethnic identities in the contemporary world are quite commonly rediscovered or even reinvented on the basis of imagined past identities. In many parts of the world, including China, it has become fashionable or advantageous either politically or socially to establish identity as an ethnic or other minority. For that reason, many groups have used history to find again an identity which may have been lost or invent one which was rather hazy or nonexistent in the first place. David Wu has proposed that the Bai minority of Yunnan province are among those with 'reinvented' cultural traditions. He argues that their reassertion of their ethnic and cultural identity is based almost entirely on cultural traits accepted over thousands of years from the Han, including from Han immigrants over the past four centuries.[16]

It is thus clear that feelings of identity can change. Communities may feel hardly any allegiance to an ethnic group, but rather to a religion or to a leader at one time, but come to feel ethnic identity at another. Moreover, the particular nationality to which they feel adherence may itself change over time. Improvements in communications may well produce the effect, among remote communities, of strengthening feelings of consciousness of belonging to an ethnic group.

History includes a host of factors: economic structure — that is, how the community produced what it needed to survive and thrive; its political nature; who held power; its social customs; patterns of family life. Among many nationalities, their origin often bears strongly on their identity, because it can define in the realm of myth what distinguishes them from larger neighbours or rivals. That is why the quest for 'roots' has become so fashionable among minorities which feel themselves to be have been marginalised by more powerful neighbours.

One aspect of the history and current circumstances of nationalities which frequently defines their identity is pride in belonging. This is a feature common to nationalisms of all kinds, whether the 'nation' has its own independent government or is a minority within a larger nation-state. We saw it earlier as marking identity for groups other than ethnic minorities, such as homosexuals. Thus it is that people feel pride because they belong to a particular nationality and point to its attributes or accomplishments. This frequently occurs even when other people within the same nationality or members of other nationalities are not so enthusiastic about particular attributes.

An opposite mark of identity to pride is struggle, especially against enemies, with dislike or hatred of 'otherness' taking a prominent place. Erik Erikson has written as follows:

> In its individual and collective aspects, psychosocial identity strives for ideological unity; but it is also always defined by that past which is to be lived down and by that potential future which is to be prevented. Identity formation thus involves a continuous conflict with powerful negative identity elements. In times of aggravated crises these come to the fore to arouse in man a murderous hate of 'otherness,' which he judges as evil in strangers — and in himself.[17]

The ideological unity to which Erikson refers is assumed to be secular. But in the last decade and more, religions have reassumed social and even political importance in many parts of the globe. Islam has reasserted itself as a symbol of the identity in quite a few of the newly independent states of what used to be the Soviet Union, in particular those of Central Asia. In part, religion's role in defining identities follows directly from the failure of other ideologies, especially Marxism-Leninism, but to some extent even from the materialism of liberal capitalism which is so sacred to the West. In China, quite a few of the minorities have cultures which are much more religious than that of the majority Han, whose tradition of Confucianism makes their civilisation notable for its secularity. Certainly religion has played a crucial role in the emerging sense of identity found among China's minorities.

A factor of national identity over which debate has raged is whether it necessarily implies the right to sovereignty as an independent state. Most of the nationalists whose actions tore the Soviet Union and Yugoslavia apart certainly thought that the right to statehood followed automatically from their own feelings of national identity. Such a opinion has become very fashionable in Western countries.

However, there is an alternative view. One contemporary observer has written that 'states have no obligation to change their boundaries to accommodate the wishes of a minority community that may nonetheless predominate in a region'.[18] He warns against confusing national identity with state citizenship, since national identity 'is a political and cultural phenomenon', whereas citizenship is legally determined by specific nation-states.[19] A conference on minority discourse held at the University of California, Berkeley, in 1986 featured papers arguing passionately for political action against the marginalisation of minorities in the United States, but did not advocate secession.[20] Although the participants may have supported the independence of the East Timorese, Tibetans or Eritreans, the major parallel drawn with their own struggle was not with those of peoples overseas but with the women's movement in their own country because of its concern with changing the world towards the empowerment of marginalised groups.[21]

The distinction between national identity and statehood brings us to the term 'integration'. The term is explored in greater detail elsewhere as it applies to minorities, and there is no need to embark upon it again.[22] Here it is sufficient to observe that integration can refer to one or other of two distinct but related notions. One of these concerns the relationships between a majority and minority peoples, the other the patterns by which the different parts of a large nation-state cohere. In the first of these two senses, integration implies a political, cultural, social and economic structuring of a larger state which sees the minorities maintaining their own cultures and identities, but influenced by the majority and not seeking secession in a new sovereign state with its own independent government.[23] In the second sense, integration means the 'manner and degree to which parts of a social system (its individuals, groups and organs) interact and complement each other'.[24]

Terms applying to the relations between peoples living in the same nation-state range from 'pluralism', denoting a situation where peoples of varying cultures coexist, to 'assimilation', which implies that minorities are compelled by a majority to give up their own cultures. In terms of culture, one interesting term is 'acculturation'. As early as 1935, Robert Redfield and others proposed that 'acculturation comprehends those phenomena which result when groups of individuals having different cultures come into continuous first-hand contact, with subsequent changes in the original cultural patterns of either or both groups'.[25] It refers generally to a long-term coexistence of various peoples resulting over centuries in a common culture which incorporates elements from all earlier ones, including those of the minorities.

The particular topics chosen under the heading 'culture' do not necessarily point in the same direction when applied to the overall tension between ethnic identities and integration. Thus, as will be examined more fully in later chapters, questions of marriage and education have not worked nearly as strongly in favour of national identity as those of religion, but on the other hand they have assisted the processes of integration better. But I would argue that all the topics chosen are indeed criteria for cultural identity and integration because they are very important aspects of culture itself, as defined above. The topics are selected for their importance in cultures, not for the conclusions they would point towards in assessing the tension between the ethnic identities of China's minorities and their integration with each other, with the Han and into the Chinese state over the period 1912–95.

A note on sources

The material in this book is based largely on field research. This writer has visited a number of minority areas in many parts of China, ranging from Tibet in the southwest to Yanbian, Jilin province, in the northeast, and from Xinjiang in the northwest to Guangxi, Yunnan and Guizhou in the south-east. These visits took place over twelve years spanning the period 1982–94. They have already resulted in other publications on the minorities, the most substantial being *China's Minorities*, which takes up a range of political, for-eign policy, economic and demographic issues.[26] The present book differs sharply in its focus on several sites of culture, as defined above.

The fieldwork is supplemented by written sources, almost all of them either in the Chinese or English languages. There has been an explosion of publications on minorities by Chinese scholars over the 1980s and 1990s, many of them dealing with aspects of cultures, although issues of identity have not received the attention they have deserved. While it is true that the-oretical issues are raised in this material, the general thrust is descriptive. The immense volume does not of course guarantee either quality or accu-racy. Much of this material is based on very limited fieldwork, or even none at all. On the other hand, it should be added in fairness that much of it results from extensive and reasonably well organised fieldwork by com-petent scholars. In any case, it is often the only material available in a field which has still not been examined nearly as fully as it warrants.

There has also been a substantial and growing quantity of excellent research carried out in the West, especially the United States, the largest in scale among a range of such works being Dru Gladney's *Muslim Chinese* on the Hui people.[27] This particular work is based on detailed and extensive fieldwork in a limited number of places but over a long period of time. It deals with one minority only. Although the Western studies are in general very much fewer in number and smaller in scope than the Chinese, they are considerably stronger from a theoretical point of view and issues of identity are among those they take up.

Policy background, 1912–1995

Although politics is not central to the present book, some material on pol-icy is necessary as background to those cultural matters which do constitute the focus. This is because politics have weighed heavily upon China as a whole and its policies on minorities have varied greatly over the period 1912–95, producing markedly different effects on the minorities themselves.

The Guomindang governments recognised essentially five nationalities in China, those being the Han, the Tibetans, the Manchus, Mongols and Hui or Muslims. These categorisations, which were shared by Sun Yat-sen and Chiang Kai-shek, took no account of the numerous peoples of southern China, such as the Miao, the Bai and the Zhuang, or of some of those of the north — for example, the Koreans of Yanbian in Jilin province. On the other hand, social scientists with links to the government had some definite notions of the linguistic variations existing in China and categorised the various peoples on the basis of the language they spoke.

Sun Yat-sen's policies in the latter part of his life were based rather closely on those of the Soviet Union, which meant that he was inclined to accept notions of self-determination and autonomy for the minorities. However, Chiang Kai-shek was strongly against such ideas on the grounds that they reeked of communist influence. In a major debate over Mongolia in the late 1920s he refused any hint of autonomy for the Mongols of Inner Mongolia. The basic ground for his stand was that autonomy had the potential to threaten Chinese unity, which he regarded as of the highest importance in his struggle for a modern China. It is true that Chiang Kai-shek softened his view in his later years, the Constitution of 1946 articulating quite a liberal policy on the minorities. But by that time Chiang's government was too exhausted by the war against Japan, corruption and economic disintegration to be able to implement any of its central ideas, let alone those on the minorities.

In practice, the control which the warlord governments and that of Chiang Kai-shek exercised over those territories they all claimed as part of China was quite limited. Tibet behaved very much like an independent state, even though it was not recognised as such either by China or the international community. The territories where the Japanese set up their puppet state of Manchoukuo from 1932 to 1945 contained a substantial population of China's minorities, including almost all the Koreans, a high proportion of the Manchus and some of the Mongols. The Japanese had taken over Korea itself as a formal colony in 1910, expanding their military and other influence into China after that.

In Xinjiang a succession of Han-dominated governments held sway for the whole of the period 1912–49. Although these governments were clear that Xinjiang was indeed part of China, in fact the central authorities had little control. The most important of the rulers in Xinjiang during the Republic was Sheng Shicai, who came to power in 1933. The following year he proclaimed his 'Six Great Principles', the first three being anti-imperialism, kinship to the Soviet Union, and equality among the nationalities. This policy clearly showed powerful Soviet influence and signalled Sheng's Xinjiang as a Soviet client. Sheng even joined the Soviet Communist Party at Stalin's suggestion. However, the Soviet Union overdid itself in trying to assert its control in Xinjiang, as a result of which there was a firm rupture in relations late in 1942, with Sheng submitting himself to Chiang Kai-shek.

Despite his policy of equality among nationalities, Sheng tried to suppress Islamic influence. The region had been noted for anti-Chinese rebellion since early in the nineteenth century and Sheng's anti-Muslim activities merely inflamed an already volatile situation. During the time Sheng was leader of Xinjiang, he was responsible for putting down several secessionist rebellions by the Muslim minorities of the region. Relations hardly improved after his final departure from Xinjiang in September 1944, with yet another secessionist rebellion, which established a state called the East Turkestan Republic, breaking out later the same year.

In the Constitution of the Chinese Soviet Republic adopted in 1931, the CCP followed a policy of allowing the secession of those minorities which wanted it. However, for a variety of reasons mainly connected with the need to resist Japanese aggression in the Mongolian areas of China, Mao Zedong had this policy reversed. Secession was firmly excluded but in its place Mao was prepared to allow autonomy in the minority areas. In contrast to the Guomindang, the CCP recognised as minorities not only the Manchus, Tibetans, Hui and Mongols, but also a range of southern peoples and the Koreans of the northeast.

When the CCP came to power in 1949, it immediately declared a policy towards the minorities based on the notion of China as a multinational unitary state. China did not consist of united republics, as the Soviet Union conceived itself, but was one republic with numerous nationalities. The 'multinational unitary state' involved two notions in balance against each other: that the minorities would enjoy a degree of autonomy, but must remain part of China, secession being absolutely forbidden under any circumstances.

Autonomy meant that the minorities would enjoy the right to some political control over their own areas, with members of the relevant minority holding positions of political power. In cultural terms, the minorities had the right to use their own languages and to preserve their traditional literatures and arts. Within the basic policies of the PRC, concessions and exemptions were made in certain social areas, including the sphere of family life.

The most serious crisis for the policy of autonomy came in Tibet. The Guomindang had regarded Tibet as part of China, but in fact exercised virtually no control over it. When the CCP came to power, it sent troops to re-establish control in the region and in May 1951 the central government signed an agreement with the local authorities with two main provisions: that Tibet would return to the PRC but that its social system would be left intact, with the Tibetans exercising regional autonomy. During the 1950s there was a series of rebellions against Chinese rule in the eastern Tibetan areas. The climax came with a major rebellion in March 1959 in Lhasa. This was suppressed by Chinese troops with considerable bloodshed and great bitterness on the part of the Tibetans. The Fourteenth Dalai Lama fled from Tibet to India, where he became the focus of a lasting attempt to revive an independent Tibet. One of his arguments against China has been his claim that China is attempting to destroy Tibetan culture.

The Cultural Revolution decade of 1966–76 saw a continued policy of autonomy in theory, but in practice a rather drastic reversion towards assimilation of the minorities. The reason for this was that Mao Zedong became totally obsessed with the idea of class struggle, which he encouraged China to regard as 'the key link'. The result was that differences among the nationalities were swept under the carpet so that everything could be seen in terms of class struggle. Religions of all kinds were subject to savage persecution, while the traditional literatures, theatres and other arts were suppressed to make way for revolutionary models.

It was not long after Mao Zedong died in September 1976 that his brainchild, the Cultural Revolution, was discontinued. In June 1981 the Central Committee of the CCP moved to the formal denunciation of the Cultural Revolution and virtually everything connected with it. Naturally, the Cultural Revolution's notions of the minorities were discarded and the policies of autonomy revived and strengthened. The 1982 Constitution has a good deal to say on the subject of autonomy for the minority areas, including not only in the political and economic but also in the cultural spheres. It lays down that the government head of all such areas must be a member of the relevant nationality. In addition, it stipulates the right of minorities to use their own spoken and written languages, including in government and the law.

In 1984 the Chinese government adopted a Law on the Autonomy of Nationality Areas, which in essence followed, expanded and strengthened the 1982 Constitution's views on autonomy. This law allocates quite a bit of space to matters of concern to the present book in the field of culture. One of the 'general principles' laid down is freedom of religion. In Article 11, the law adopts the standard PRC principle that 'no state organ, social group or individual may compel a citizen either to believe in religion or not to believe in religion, and may not discriminate among citizens on the basis of their belief, or otherwise, in religion'. It also goes on to forbid the use of religious activity to disrupt social order.

The chapter on 'the rights of autonomy of the autonomous organs' devotes several articles to education and literature and the arts. Article 36 declares that these organs may determine the education system at all levels within the areas under their jurisdiction, including the content of the curriculum, the language of instruction and the methods of student recruitment, provided that they follow the state's general educational direction and stay within PRC law. Article 38 asks the autonomous organs to develop literature and arts 'in the forms and with the features special to the nationalities'.[28]

In the late 1980s and early 1990s, the policies of autonomy came under strain for political reasons when several attempts at secession were made in the minority areas. The most serious of these were in Tibet, where from 1987 to 1989 major demonstrations, mostly led by monks, erupted in the capital Lhasa and elsewhere. They reached a climax in March 1989, when demonstrations recalled the uprising of March 1959 in Lhasa. These were crushed brutally by the Chinese authorities, with heavy casualties being suffered by the Tibetans. The demonstrations and the Chinese reaction produced a very deleterious impact on relations between Han and Tibetans, and also brought the question of Tibet into the international arena as a foreign policy issue. However, it did not result in a backtracking by the Chinese government in its policy on autonomy.

Despite the variations in policy among the Guomindang, CCP and others, in one area they have been in striking agreement. All have wished to retain the unity of China. The Guomindang struggled at length against the secession of northern — or what it called 'Outer' — Mongolia. Not until 1945 did Chiang Kai-shek agree to acknowledge the independence of the Mongolian People's Republic, and he rescinded his agreement as soon as he was forced to retreat to Taiwan in 1949. In Taiwan's magnificent Imperial Palace Museum even as late as the mid-1990s, maps of China show it as including northern Mongolia, where in October 1991 the Mongolian People's Republic was replaced by the State of Mongolia.

The PRC early recognised the Mongolian People's Republic and accepted the transition to the State of Mongolia. However, the CCP has been just as keen as the Guomindang to retain the unity of the remaining territories which the Republic of China had inherited from the Qing dynasty. Like the Guomindang before it, it has insisted that Tibet, Xinjiang and Inner Mongolia are integral parts of Chinese territory. On the record so far, it will fight against any attempts at secession on the part of any of its territories, including Tibet and Xinjiang.

In general, China has — albeit at a cost — consolidated its hold over its minorities during the course of its history. And the process of national integration and of the integration of minorities within the Chinese state has accelerated in the second half of the twentieth century. Yet the issue of China's national unity and integration will continue to conflict at certain points with the feelings of consciousness or identity of certain of those peoples it currently defines as nationalities.

Although this book is not concerned primarily with the political arena which issues of secession bring out so forcefully, there is inevitably tension between the national identities of minorities and China's integration, which sometimes expresses itself in violent clashes, because the stronger the feelings of national consciousness and identity become among the minorities, the more they have the potential to threaten China with disintegration and fragmentation.

Economic background, 1912–1995

Apart from the policies which various governments adopted towards the minorities, it is necessary also to consider the economies of the minorities, however briefly. This is because of the influence which economic development and systems exert on societies and cultures. Although specialists may disagree on the extent of this influence, none would wish to ignore it altogether.

With very few exceptions, such as the Koreans, the minorities of China have traditionally been considerably poorer than the Han Chinese. This remains the case today. At the same time, not many live in the low-lying plains, the most important exceptions being the Koreans, the Manchus and some Hui. One major reason is that the Han have tended for centuries to take over the territory of the minorities, ensuring that they retreated ever more deeply into the mountains.

Before the CCP's accession to power in 1949, the minorities had a wide range of ways of producing what they needed to survive, with the vast majority of the population being forced to cope with exceedingly scarce resources. Many were like the Han in being agriculturalists, and thus sedentary, including the more populous of the southwestern minorities such as the Zhuang, Bouyei, Miao, Yi and Bai, but also some in the northeast like the Manchus and Koreans. The northwest and north have enormous areas of land suitable for pasture and minorities like the Kazaks, Kirgiz and Tajiks are traditionally pastoralists and hence nomadic. A few peoples were still hunting and fishing — for example, the Tungus peoples of the northeast, like the Oroqens and Ewenkis. Quite a few practised more than one economic mode, populous examples being the Tibetans, Mongols and Uygurs, many communities of which were pastoral, others agricultural. A few southwestern nationalities combined slash and burn agriculture with fishing and hunting or gathering; the Drung, Nu, Lisu and Va, all of Yunnan, were among those in this category.[29]

The modernisation of the minorities' economies made very slow progress down to the middle of the twentieth century, taking industrialisation as the main index of modernisation. Only in about 20 of the minorities had industry developed even to an embryonic extent. Those with the most advanced industrial development were the minorities living in territories with special political factors. Examples include the Uygurs of Xinjiang, where the Soviet-supported Sheng Shicai made some efforts towards industrialisation, and the Manchus and Koreans of the northeast, where Japanese control pushed a measure of modern economic growth.

The economies of the minorities were overwhelmingly rural and self-sufficient. They had to be, because communications were extremely poor. Roads were few and very bad in all but a few minority areas, while railways and telephones were virtually nonexistent except for areas in the northeast of China. The Japanese-built railway linking Manchuria with Korea passed through Yanbian in Jilin province, home to the Koreans, the area being known at that time as Jiandao province.[30]

In most of the agricultural minorities, the basic class division was landlords and peasants, with the landlords owning most of the land and property. In those minorities believing in religions with powerful clergies, such as Islam, these constituted an important power-holding group very similar to a class. There were also secular officials and rulers at the top of the society, such as tribal chiefs or, in a few cases, princes.

The feudal serf system was practised by most communities of the Dai in Yunnan province. Manors were established for feudal lords, with serfs working the land. The Tibetan system is labelled 'feudal serf' by PRC writers —

a label which is very controversial, with two translations of the same Tibetan word, 'tenant' or 'serf', being used in the literature. However, it is not my purpose to examine this issue here.[31] What is clear, however, is that the landowners, exercised great power over those under them. Sir Charles Bell, a British official who visited Tibet in the 1920s, wrote that the nobility 'are a class apart' with 'a great gulf fixed between them and ordinary folk who bow down low before them'.[32] Senior monks and government officials also wielded enormous power, both politically and socially.

One minority to practise a slave system was the Yi, formerly known by the pejorative term the Lolo, who live in the Liangshan area of what is today Sichuan. The highest caste was termed the Black Lolo and made up about 7 per cent of the population. The Black Lolo owned most of the land and property and monopolised political power. The property included not only animals, but even the members of castes other than their own. The slave-owners bought and sold members of the lower classes freely and had the power of life and death over many of them. Mobility between the slave-owning and slave classes did occur, but it was very rare indeed.[33]

In addition, there were some minorities among which remnants of primitive communalism persisted. These included the Drung, Nu, Lisu, Jingpo and Va of Yunnan, as well as the Oroqens and Ewenkis of the northeast of China. By the middle of the twentieth century, private ownership and individual production had begun to develop to a greater or lesser extent among these minorities. At the same time, there were still communities among which the means of production, such as land, animals and tools, were publicly owned, with labour being carried out collectively and the social product being distributed more or less equally —[34] or at least considerably more so than under the other systems discussed here.

In line with its aim of carrying out a revolution in China, the CCP after 1949 attempted to eradicate the economic systems of the old order in all the minority areas, including Tibet, and to establish a socialist one based on Marxism-Leninism. Among other factors, this meant taking over the landed estates and many other properties of the rich classes as well as those of the monasteries, temples or mosques. However, because of local resistance and respect for autonomy, the process of setting up the socialist economic system was a phased one in the minority areas, with some like the Mongols, Zhuang and Koreans responding very much more quickly than others, such as the Yi and Tibetans. It was not until 1958 that the slave system of the Yi people of Liangshan was eradicated, while the old Tibetan system remained more or less intact until after the suppression of the March 1959 rebellion. Although the movement towards setting up communes began in 1958 in the Han and some minority regions, it was much slower in others. At the same time, certain tax and other economic exemptions were given to the minorities.

With the Cultural Revolution came an obsession with class struggle in economic matters, as in all others. This meant the withdrawal of certain forms of autonomy like most of those in the taxation area. The commune movement was pushed with greater vigour and extended to all those minorities which had previously been spared them. In the late 1960s, communes were established among the Yi of Liangshan, the Nu and the Dai, though the process was not completed in Tibet until 1975.

With the period of reform since 1978, economic autonomies of various kinds have been restored in several areas, including taxation. Autonomous places are now allowed control over their own budgets. Just as everywhere else in China, free enterprise has mushroomed and flourished in the minority areas. This writer has seen numerous examples of vibrant free markets in minority areas and in general found a very favourable response to economic reform among those many people consulted on the subject during interviews.

Over the period of the PRC, production has expanded enormously in the minority areas. Industry has been introduced into most of them and communications have improved out of sight. There is a network of roads throughout the minority areas, though it must be added that many are still extremely rough. There are railways linking the major eastern coastal cities with a great many of the minority areas, even including the Xinjiang capital Ürümqi. Lhasa, however, is still reachable from Beijing only by air or road, but not all the way by rail. In the last few years, direct trade between Xinjiang and the newly independent Central Asian countries which once formed part of the Soviet Union has increased greatly. The standard of living has risen greatly in virtually all minority areas, by comparison with what it was in the days before 1949.

Very serious problems remain, however. In the late 1980s and the 1990s, government authorities have expressed that they are alarmed at the widening inequalities between the Han and most minority areas, and among the minority areas themselves. In 1988, a Korean leader revealed that the 20 per cent of people at the bottom of the economic heap among the minority nationalities were still finding difficulty 'keeping their bellies full and their backs warm'. He added that many members of the minorities were prevented by traditional values from recognising how desirable it was to make money[35] — in other words, to follow government policy. Two points are clear from the statement: the first is that quite a high proportion of people are still desperately poor despite all the improvements which have taken place, and the second is that the clash between modern and traditional thinking is still very much alive in many, and possibly most, minority areas.[36]

Notes

1 See especially Abdul R. JanMohamed and David Lloyd, 'Introduction: Toward a Theory of Minority Discourse: What Is To Be Done?', in Abdul R. JanMohamed and David Lloyd (eds), *The Nature and Context of Minority Discourse*, Oxford University Press, New York, Oxford, 1990, pp. 1–2.

2 One compendium which attempts such a task of descriptive ethnography, with respect to China, in English is Ma Yin et al. (eds), trans. Liu

Qizhong et al., *China's Minority Nationalities*, Foreign Languages Press, Beijing, 1989, itself a translation, summary and updating of an earlier Chinese-language book.

3 See Dru C. Gladney, 'Representing Nationality in China: Refiguring Majority/Minority Identities', *The Journal of Asian Studies*, vol. 53, no. 3, February 1994, pp. 92–123. Gladney argues (p. 93) that much is to be learned 'about the construction of majority identity, known in China as the "Han" nationality' through 'reading the representation of minorities'.

4 Edward B. Tylor, *Primitive Culture: Researches into the Development of Mythology, Philosophy, Religion, Language, Art, and Custom*, J. Murray, London, 1871 , vol. 1, p. 1.

5 John B. Thompson, *Ideology and Modern Culture, Critical Social Theory in the Era of Mass Communication*, Polity Press, Cambridge, 1990, p. 128. Milton Singer, 'The Concept of Culture', in David L. Sills (ed.), *International Encyclopedia of the Social Sciences*, 18 vols, The Macmillan Company and The Free Press, New York, 1968–79, vol. 3, p. 539 states that Tylor's definition is 'still the basis of most modern anthropological theories of culture'. For a detailed discussion of the descriptive, symbolic and structural conceptions of culture, see Thompson, *Ideology and Modern Culture*, pp. 127–45.

6 Marvin Harris, *Culture, People, Nature, An Introduction to General Anthropology*, 2nd edn, Harper & Row, New York, 1975, p. 144. See also the very similar definition in Grant Evans (ed.), *Asia's Cultural Mosaic, An Anthropological Introduction*, Prentice Hall/Simon & Schuster [Asia] Pte Ltd, Singapore, 1993, p. 420.

7 Questions of identification are discussed in some detail, amongst other places, in Colin Mackerras, *China's Minorities: Integration and Modernization in the Twentieth Century*, Oxford University Press, Hong Kong, 1994, pp. 140–45, while population issues are covered on pp. 119–34, for the period 1900–49, and on pp. 233–59 for the period 1949–92. The population figures given here are from the 1990 census. Figures for all four censuses for the nationalities are given on pp. 238–40.

8 David Y.H. Wu, 'Chinese Minority Policy and the Meaning of Minority Culture: The Example of Bai in Yunnan, China', *Human Organization*, vol. 49, no. 1, Spring 1990, p. 3.

9 On reregistration among the minorities, see Mackerras, *China's Minorities*, pp. 243–45.

10 The minority languages are dealt with in great detail in S.A. Wurm et al., *Language Atlas of China*, Longman on behalf of the Australian Academy of the Humanities and the Chinese Academy of Social Sciences, Hong Kong, 1987, especially p. A-4 and map A-4. See also Amara Prasithrathsint, 'The Language Mosaic', in Grant Evans (ed.), *Asia's Cultural Mosaic, An Anthropological Introduction*, pp. 76–78.

11 See ibid., p. 78, where other sources are cited.

12 In Tibet I learned that the Hui there speak Tibetan. According to He

Liyi, the Muslims of the Bai county of Jianchuan in Yunnan 'speak our local Bai language'. See He Liyi, with Claire Anne Chik, *Mr China's Son, A Villager's Life*, Westview Press, Boulder, San Francisco, Oxford, 1993, p. 218.

13 Wu, 'Chinese Minority Policy and the Meaning of Minority Culture', p. 3 claims that 'only a few hundred elderly Man [Manchu] residing in the northernmost villages of China can still speak the Manchu language'. Wurm et al., *Language Atlas of China*, p. C-5, puts the number of Manchu speakers at only 70.

14 The Xibes were sent from the northeast to Yili by the Manchu government in 1764. To this day, the main concentrated community of Xibes in China is in Yili.

15 Benedict Anderson, *Imagined Communities, Reflections on the Origin and Spread of Nationalism*, Verso, London, New York, 1983; rev. edn, 1991, pp. 204–5.

16 See Wu, 'Chinese Minority Policy and the Meaning of Minority Culture', especially pp. 4, 10–11.

17 Erik H. Erikson, 'Identity, Psychosocial', in David L. Sills (ed.), *International Encyclopedia of the Social Sciences*, vol. 7, pp. 61–62, copyright 1968 Crowell Collier and Macmillan Inc. See also JanMohamed and Lloyd, 'Introduction: Toward a Theory of Minority Discourse: What Is To Be Done?', p. 1: 'Cultures designated as minorities have certain shared experiences by virtue of their similar antagonistic relationship to the dominant culture, which seeks to marginalize them all.'

18 Gidon Gottlieb, 'Nations Without States', *Foreign Affairs*, vol. 73, no. 3, May/June 1994, p. 110.

19 ibid., pp. 108–9.

20 See Jan Mohamed and Lloyd, 'Introduction: Toward a Theory of Minority Discourse: What Is To Be Done?', pp. 1–16.

21 See Nancy Hartsock, 'Rethinking Modernism: Minority vs Majority Theories', in Abdul R. JanMohamed and David Lloyd (eds), *The Nature and Context of Minority Discourse*, especially pp. 17, 36.

22 See, for instance, Mackerras, *China's Minorities*, pp. 8–10.

23 See also June Teufel Dreyer, *China's Forty Millions, Minority Nationalities and National Integration in the People's Republic of China*, Harvard University Press, Cambridge, Mass., and London, 1976 , p. 1.

24 James D. Seymour, *China, The Politics of Revolutionary Reintegration*, Thomas Y. Crowell, New York,1976 , p. 6.

25 Quoted in Edward H. Spicer, 'Acculturation', in David L. Sills (ed.), *International Encyclopedia of the Social Sciences*, vol. 1, p. 22.

26 For a discussion of the circumstances of the various visits to minority areas, see *China's Minorities*, pp. 14–16.

27 Dru C. Gladney, *Muslim Chinese, Ethnic Nationalism in the People's Republic*, Council on East Asian Studies, Harvard University, Cambridge, Mass., 1991.

28 See the full text of the law, among other places, in *Zhonghua renmin*

gongheguo falü huibian, 1979–1984, Renmin chubanshe, Beijing, 1985, pp. 538–53. Articles 36 and 38 are on pp. 547 and 548 respectively. The political ramifications of autonomy are discussed in much more detail in *China's Minorities*, pp. 145–66.

29 For formation on the pre-1949 production patterns of the minorities, see, for example, Chang-tu Hu, in collaboration with Samuel C. Chu, Leslie L. Clark, Jung-pang Lo and Yuan-li Wu, ed. Hsiao Hsia, *China, Its People, Its Society, Its Culture*, HRAF Press, New Haven, 1960, pp. 73–85 or Ma (ed.), *China's Minority Nationalities*, pp. 4–5 *passim*.

30 I have discussed the minorities' economies in the first half of the twentieth century in far more detail in *China's Minorities*, pp. 105–19.

31 Among the many scholars to reject the term 'feudal serf' system outright is Franz Michael. See 'Non-Chinese Nationalities and Religious Communities', in Yuan-li Wu, Franz Michael et al., *Human Rights in the People's Republic of China*, Westview Press, Boulder and London, 1988, pp. 278–79.

32 Sir Charles Bell, *The People of Tibet*, Clarendon Press, Oxford, 1928, p. 64.

33 See Ma (ed.), *China's Minority Nationalities*, pp. 6–7 and Hu et al., *China*, p. 82.

34 Ma (ed.), *China's Minority Nationalities*, p. 7.

35 Cited in Gao Shi, *China Daily*, 7 October 1988, p. 4.

36 I have considered the economy of the minority areas in China in some detail in *China's Minorities*, pp. 198–232.

2 Religion, 1912–1949

Although the modernisation process had already begun among some of China's minority nationalities in the first half of the twentieth century, there was a strong tendency for religion to be highly traditional. In terms of the concepts of integration and identity, the influence of religion — with some significant exceptions — militated strongly in favour of national identities, but against the integration of the minorities, not only with the Han, but also with other nationalities espousing different religions and with the various Chinese states holding power.

The main forms of religion among China's minority nationalities in the first half of the twentieth century were Islam, Buddhism of various kinds, and polytheistic nature- or ancestor-worship. Daoism was found among the Yao, as well as some of the minorities most strongly influenced by the Han, such as the Zhuang or Bai. A religion which grew in influence greatly at that time was Christianity; except among the small Russian community in Xinjiang, this was due to missionaries from Western countries.

This chapter aims to focus on the role of religion among the minority nationalities from 1912 to 1949. Its approach is social rather than theological, and there is no attempt to consider the precise tenets of the religious beliefs to which the various nationalities adhered. Important a subject though that is, it is totally different from the social function of religion and lies outside the scope of the present study.

Islam

Most of the peoples of Xinjiang were Muslim, including the Uygurs, Kazaks, Uzbeks, Kirgiz and Tajiks. The Hui, who had concentrations in the north-

west but lived all over China, were the most populous of the Islamic nationalities. In general, Islamic political and spiritual influence was substantial
among these nationalities as the Republic dawned; it had declined only
slightly, if at all, by 1949.

Sufi mysticism had produced a very large impact on Chinese Islam from
the mid-Qing on, especially in the northwest. On the other hand, Chinese
Muslims were quite resistant to the kind of modernising reforms which so
changed Islam in the nineteenth-century Ottoman Empire and some other
Muslim countries. As one scholar has written, 'Modern Islamic reforms in
Arabia, Egypt, and India in the nineteenth century had no counterpart in
China.' Although Sufi mysticism had some hold in the northwest, its influence in other parts of China was weak in the nineteenth and early twenti-
eth centuries and China produced not a single Sufi mystical poet.[1]

The establishment of the Soviet Union in 1917 exercised a social influence in Xinjiang, especially in the northwestern areas nearest the border.
The ruler of Xinjiang in the first years of the Republic of China was the
intensely conservative Han Yang Zengxin. Despite his attempts to prevent
it, a trend emerged among progressive Muslims from the northwest of
Xinjiang, and even from the south, to visit the Soviet Union. Some got temporary jobs there and were much impressed with the new and modernised
life they found. Yang Zengxin's reaction was to increase surveillance. His
measures included ordering his officials to check carefully on those who
wanted to go to the Soviet Union, censoring mail, and banning publications
in Turkic languages. Signs forbidding political discussion were stuck up on
restaurants throughout Xinjiang.[2]

For most of the 1930s and the early 1940s, Xinjiang was under the rule of
a Han from Manchuria called Sheng Shicai, who for most of his tenure of
office followed very pro-Soviet policies. Some mosques were closed down
or were converted into clubs or theatres, women were encouraged to appear
in public unveiled, the Islamic clergy was publicly ridiculed and clubs promoting Soviet practices and ideas were established.

Sheng Shicai sponsored a vigorous campaign in favour of atheism,
inevitably bringing him into conflict with the Muslims who still believed
in their own right to determine state decisions. In the later years of his government, especially 1937–41, his anti-Muslim purges became more widespread and savage, the reasons being the outbreak of a Muslim-led rebellion
in the south in 1937 and the Stalinist purges in both the Soviet Union and
Xinjiang. Sheng Shicai targeted the Muslims with particular severity, because
he saw them and their religion as sources of secessionist and nationalist
opposition to his rule — in the terms of this book, as conducive to feelings
of national identity, but also as hostile to the integration of China and its
nationalities. Many Muslims were arrested and imprisoned, especially the
landowners, petty officials and clergy, but even anybody caught reading
religious books. Some were summarily shot, while others were sent to work
in the gold mines of the Altay region.[3]

The reaction of Islamic leaders against Sheng Shicai's innovations and purges was, not surprisingly, fierce. The series of rebellions against his rule is ample testimony to their feelings. Resistance to Sheng's attempts to impose social change and reduce religious influence was considerably greater among the Kazaks of northern Jungaria than among those of Yili. But in general Muslim life was both stricter and stronger in the south, where the Uygurs predominated, and the Islamic clergy and landowners were considerably more powerful than was the case in the north. What ordinary people thought about the turmoils and religious persecution is much more difficult to gauge. Lattimore claims that Uygurs of the poorer classes held a low opinion of the clergy,[4] and it would come as no surprise that the main targets of Sheng's purges should also be the ones most resented by them. Yet it cannot have escaped the notice of the average Uygur, Kazak or Kirgiz that Sheng Shicai was a Han and that his principal backers were foreigners. Religious sentiment was inevitably bound up with ethnic loyalties to a large extent.

Although Islam had become very strong in Xinjiang by the twentieth century, it was not nearly as exclusive as it was in Southwest Asia. Among the Uygurs, Islam retained many features of the old Uygur folk religion. Muslim shrines were found everywhere and showed 'in their names association with the older ancestral cult'. Witchdoctors were among the main medical practitioners and the Muslim celebration retained elements of pre-Islamic festivals.[5] It is worth noting, also, that Islamic rules were not observed with equal rigidity among the various nationalities. Despite the retention of pre-Islamic customs, the Uygurs were somewhat stricter in their Islamic practice than the Kazaks. Owen Lattimore even describes the Kazaks as 'lax' in the observance of many of the rules of Islam, such as details of the Muslim dietary laws other than the prohibition against pork. He writes that 'they do not adhere strictly to the house of prayer or the seasons of fasting, and frequently neglect to circumcise their sons',[6] practices generally taken for granted among Muslims. Aitchen Wu, a Han Chinese official in Xinjiang in the 1930s, puts forward a very similar view, although in less polite language: the Kazaks 'are by no means strict in their religious observances, being wild and utterly undisciplined nomads'.[7]

According to Dru Gladney, the Islam of the Hui underwent a revival at the end of the nineteenth and in the early decades of the twentieth century. It was caused by 'accelerated exchange between China and the outside world', with Chinese Muslims beginning to travel extensively in the Islamic centres of Southwestern Asia.[8] There was a small growth of Muslim education (see Chapter 3) and a flowering of Muslim associations and periodical press. The first of the associations was the Chinese Muslim Mutual Progress Association (*Zhongguo Huijiao jujin hui*), set up in 1912 by Wang Haoran (1848–1918), who had returned in 1908 from a period of study in the Islamic countries of Southwestern Asia.[9]

Intensive debate took place among Hui Muslims over such issues as the integration of Islam with Chinese culture. At one extreme were those who saw the two as mutually hostile and advocated a return to the 'pure' Islam of the Arab countries. This school refused to use Chinese language in association with Islam and preferred the architecture of Southwest Asian mosques to the Chinese style, which was very similar to that of Han Buddhist temples. At the other extreme was a school of thought which stressed that the two cultures were entirely compatible, and was perfectly happy with mosques in Chinese architectural style or to read the *Koran* in Chinese. On the whole, Hui Islam during the Republican period tended towards reformism and modernism.[10]

Islam retained its political and social influence among the Hui more or less intact right down to the end of the Republican period. The Hui Muslims of Ningxia, Gansu and Qinghai maintained their strictness in religious taboos, such as that concerning the eating of pork, they generally refrained from drinking or smoking and observed the fasting month of Ramadan universally. The mosque was the centre of religious activities, with the clergy retaining very substantial, or even dominant, authority within society. Among almost all the sects, the head cleric of the mosque was elected at a meeting by his co-religionists, adopting an age-old 'democratic style'.[11] However, clashes could occur over disagreements among the sects. Relations between Hui and Han were, if not very good, at least 'relatively friendly and peaceful' by comparison with earlier times. In the villages, there was not very much ethnic communalism or friction.[12] It is likely that inter-ethnic tensions were no more intense than among the various sects of Hui Islam.

This brings us to another trend of great significance: namely, that the Hui came to support Chinese nationalism. The old animosity between the Hui and other Chinese began to break down. According to one scholar, a growing number of Muslims came to consider themselves as the same race as other Chinese and even resented 'being classified as a racial minority'. Politically they came to identify themselves with Chinese national life, with some joining the army and a few even becoming involved in the country's main organs of political power. Hui soldiers helped defend China against the Japanese.[13]

It is thus clear that, in terms of integration and ethnic identities, Islam operated very differently in Xinjiang and among the Hui in the first half of the twentieth century. In Xinjiang it militated against integrating Muslim nationalities with China or with the Han and in favour of retaining national identities. On the other hand, Hui Islam does not seem to have opposed the integration of the Hui with the Han and with China as a whole, nor does it appear to have been conducive to the retention of Hui identity at that time.

Buddhism

Buddhism, although far less uniform in teaching and practice than Islam, was also an important and powerful religion amongst the minority nationalities. Of the various forms of minority Buddhism, the most important was Tibetan or lama Buddhism.[14] Apart from the Tibetans, the nationalities adhering to this religion included the Mongols, Tu, Yugurs, Monba, Primi and a part of the Naxi.[15]

The dominant sect of Tibetan Buddhism was called the dGe lugs pa, founded by the great Tsong kha pa (1357–1419). According to one of the greatest of all twentieth-century Tibetologists, 'the entire political and cultural history of Tibet was dominated by the monasteries'.[16] In the first half of the twentieth century, the Tibetans were among the most profoundly religious of all peoples in Chinese territory. As it had for centuries, Tibetan Buddhism ran through virtually every aspect of their life. Prayer flags atop houses and rosary beads were a normal part of everyday existence. Most houses had religious books kept respectfully, whether the inhabitants could read them or not, and the best room was often used as a chapel. An annual procession around a village, with the people carrying sacred texts, was a means of praying for a good harvest. Villagers and nomads sometimes made long pilgrimages to holy places, offering butter lamps and burning incense before the temple images and repeatedly walking around the sacred buildings.[17] According to Sir Charles Bell, religion lay 'deep down in the hearts' of all classes of Tibetan society. Even the nomad tribes 'that rob and raid' could 'often be controlled by religious influences'.[18]

The government was a theocracy in the sense that religious officials held political power and the supreme state ruler was the same person as the highest religious leader, the Dalai Lama. Tibet was ruled by the Dalai Lama or a regent acting for him through a bureaucracy which included both monks and laymen. The 'Bras spungs, Se ra and dGa' ldan Monasteries in and near Lhasa, which together with the bKra shis lhun po in Xigaze were the four greatest centres of the dominant dGe lugs pa sect, held enormous political authority.

Whereas the Ninth to Twelfth Dalai Lamas had all died young, the Thirteenth (1876–1933), who came to full power in 1895, not only enjoyed a reasonably long reign but exercised real personal authority.[19] Although the death of the Thirteenth Dalai Lama saw a hiatus in his line and a reversion of power to regents, the first half of the twentieth century can hardly be accounted a period of decline for the political power of religion or the theocracy in Tibet. Indeed, the system of government, which had been founded by the great Fifth Dalai Lama of the seventeenth century, 'lasted with little change' beyond the middle of the twentieth century.[20]

The main centres of religion were the monasteries, which were also centres of scholarship and repositories of tradition. The major monasteries were large communities with numerous buildings, more like towns than institutions. Some 'monastic towns' had semi-independent monasteries within them 'each separately endowed and correspondingly different in size and splendour'.[21] In sharp contrast to Islam, Tibetan Buddhism was highly flamboyant, Tibetan monasteries and temples being crowded with beautiful images and decorations.

It was possible to enter the monastic order at any stage of life, from the age of 7, or even earlier, to 70. Novices were under the control of teachers and discipline was very rigid and severe. In the main monasteries of the dGe lugs pa sect, monks spent a great deal of their time learning the scriptures by heart, but although reading was thus central to literacy, writing was not. 'Learning to write and compose good Tibetan was regarded as the work of clerks and officials, and so positively harmful to the acquisition of true religious knowledge.'[22] Many a monk who could recite enormous religious tracts by heart could hardly write his name.

Monks occasionally helped with the harvest, but otherwise did no farm labour or herding of cattle. It was herdsmen who looked after the considerable numbers of livestock owned by the monasteries, such as yaks, goats and sheep. On the other hand, some monks undertook non-religious work. Some were responsible for supervising the peasants and nomads who belonged to their monastic estates. The kitchen was a major part of the monastery, and members of the community were responsible for providing food and tea. Some of the monks went in for business and trade, while others made substantial sums of money by lending to private individuals. Some monks actually left the monastery and ran restaurants. Permission to go outside was not hard to obtain. Like so many aspects of Tibetan life, the monasteries were extremely conservative, life within them changing very little over time.[23]

Buddhism in Tibetan areas such as Qinghai was very similar to that found in Tibet itself. Several of Qinghai's monasteries were very large, with 1000 monks or more in the mid-1930s, although the great majority were relatively small, having less than 100 monks.[24] It was possible to enter a monastery at any stage as an adult or a child and religious life was hardly different from that found in the Tibetan heartland. Monks engaged readily in non-religious work. A Han Chinese who surveyed the monasteries of Qinghai in the late 1940s was struck by the fact that, for the monks, 'engaging in commerce and agriculture are both regarded as perfectly legitimate'.[25]

The Mongols were believers in shamanism, as well as worshipping their own folk pantheon, but conversion to Tibetan Buddhism, begun in the thirteenth century, gathered momentum from the sixteenth. Although shamanism suffered serious persecution, it did not die out completely, but camouflaged itself by such means as adopting gods from the lamaistic pantheon and the phraseology of lamaistic prayers. The folk pantheon, which included protective deities in the form of armed heroes on horseback such as Chinggis Khan and the mythical Ge sar Khan, maintained its following. Yet Tibetan Buddhism became so overwhelmingly the dominant religion of the Mongols that its imprint on Mongol culture and political economy simply replaced that of any rivals.[26]

In the first half of the twentieth century, belief in Tibetan Buddhism remained very strong among the Mongol masses. Yet there were powerful political pressures against the religion in the Mongol areas, especially in the Mongolian People's Republic. Alternative forms of belief, including socialism, became considerably stronger among the Mongols in the first half of the twentieth century than among the Tibetans. By the middle of the century, the hold of Tibetan Buddhism among the Mongols had weakened greatly.

In Inner Mongolia, the Mongol princes and aristocracy maintained tight links with the main monasteries. Many of the most powerful lamas were in fact from the princely families. The lamas and monks performed useful rituals on their behalf, such as chanting scriptures for rain or aid against a natural disaster.[27] Yet the first half of the twentieth century saw the destruction of the Mongol theocracy so by the time the Chinese Communist Party came to power in China, Tibetan Buddhism was politically very much weaker among the Mongols than among the Tibetans.

As in Tibet, the Mongolian monasteries were major landowners and economic and trading centres. However, in contrast to those of Tibet, the economic functions of the Inner Mongolian monasteries declined sharply in the first half of the twentieth century. One of the reasons was that the Han people continued to take over land formerly in the hands of Mongols. The Japanese economic assertiveness in the Mongolian Xing'an provinces in the west of their puppet state of Manchoukuo produced an adverse effect on the monasteries' economic power.[28] The processes of modernisation remained very rudimentary among the Mongols, but they were considerably stronger than among the Tibetans.

The reasons why people entered monasteries varied enormously. In two sample Mongol monasteries the motives ranged from the faith of the monk's parents or himself to the poverty of lay life or escape from a personal misfortune. In some cases the aristocracy designated specific men to enter a monastery, presumably to serve their interests there.[29] The reasons for entering Tibetan monasteries were no doubt very similar.

The number of males entering the monastic estate in the Tibetan and Mongol areas was very high indeed. In both cases, all families were expected to contribute at least one son to the religious life. Among both peoples, the proportions remained extremely high in the first half of the twentieth century and may even have increased in some places.

A Chinese government count of 1737 showed 316 231 monks and lamas in the Tibetan areas concentrated in 3477 monasteries. This was nearly one in three of the total population of about one million — a quite staggering proportion.[30] A British encyclopedia of the late nineteenth century gave Lhasa's population as 25 197, of whom 7540, or about 30 per cent, were monks or lamas.[31] Some decades later, the great 'Bras spungs Monastery by itself had between 8000 and 10 000 monks and, together with the Se ra and dGa' ldan monasteries, the number of monks was over 20 000.[32] Down to the middle of the twentieth century and beyond it is estimated that from 30 to 50 per cent of the total Tibetan male population was in the monastic order at any one time, and it was more than half in a few individual counties.[33]

In the Tibetan areas of Qinghai province, the proportion of the total population in monasteries was high but appears to have been somewhat lower than in the Tibetan heartland. A survey of Tibetan monasteries in Qinghai published in 1948 found a total of 26 534 lamas concentrated into 276 monasteries, and 58 others for which no detailed populations were available.[34] There are no accurate data on how many Tibetans and Mongols there were in Qinghai at the time, but there were far more Tibetans than Mongols and the total of both is most unlikely to have exceeded 600 000 by much, probably being a good deal less.[35] What this means is that the proportion of males in the clerical order may have been more than one in ten, but was probably less than one in five. It was practice in Qinghai, as in other Tibetan Buddhist areas, for families to be generous in giving sons to the monasteries: 'if there are two sons in the family, one must leave the family to become a lama, and if three then two will do so'.[36]

Concerning the Mongolian areas, a British military diplomat, Lieutenant-Colonel P.T. Etherton, claimed in the mid-1920s that the proportion of men who were monks was at least 45 per cent and rising; and that the Chinese government fostered lamaism 'as the best means to restrict the population and so avert the possible resuscitation of the Mongol race'. His view is based on a highly critical view of lama Buddhism which he believed responsible for the degeneration of a great nation.[37] Yet figures from the 1930s and 1940s suggest that he might not have been too far out in parts of Chinese-controlled Inner Mongolia. In Ulanqab League to the north of Hohhot and Yih Ju League to its southwest, the proportions of the male Mongol population in the monastic order were claimed as respectively 44 and 42 per cent.[38] However, more precise 1934 figures for the whole of Suiyuan province, of which Huhhot was the capital, show 27 203 monks out of a total Mongol population of 224 522, or 12.12 per cent;[39] and although the proportion of the male population would be about double that of the total, this would still leave the figure at approximately one-quarter, or considerably less than the proportions found in Ulanqab and Yih Ju Leagues.

Overall, there appear to have been considerably fewer monks and lamas in the Xing'an provinces of Japanese-controlled Manchoukuo. Certainly the Japanese did not encourage lama Buddhism, because it was anti-Confucianist and unproductive. They estimated the proportion of the the entire male Mongol population in the monastic estate at 25 to 30 per cent. This estimate is in sharp contradiction to their own more precise figure for the number of priests in the Xing'an provinces. They claimed that there were 17 876 priests in the Xing'an provinces in the mid-1930s with the total Mongol population there in September 1934 being 439 277, so the monastic order took up about 4 per cent of all Xing'an's Mongols or 8 per cent of the males.[40]

Etherton believed the Mongol lamas to be uneducated and to lead 'a life of indolence and ease, with no incentive to work' because they could get what they wanted for the asking.[41] The Japanese saw them as not only well esteemed in their own communities but as 'well-lettered, erudite men'. Although more favourably impressed than Etherton in terms of education, the Japanese were in some ways very caustic about the lamas all the same, as the following comment makes clear:

> The Lamas were originally in a strict sense of the term celibates, but they are at present a degenerate class. Venereal diseases are more rampant among them than the secular population. Their temples are in many cases filthy dens where unnatural and extravagant forms are indulged in. Lamas may as often be seen in quarters where female attendance is procurable at any hour of the day. Retaining little of value as a religion in its pure form, Lamaism is thought destined to fall in decay unless the priesthood be morally and religiously regenerated in time.[42]

In most of mainland Southeast Asia, the prevalent form of Buddhism is Theravada. There were four Chinese minorities adhering to Theravada Buddhism: the Blang, De'ang and Achang, but especially the Dai. All these four minorities live in Yunnan province near the borders with Burma or Laos.

Like their co-nationals in Thailand, the Dai have an extremely religious tradition: In the Republican period, Theravada Buddhism was tightly woven into the everyday life of the people, and it is probably fair to say that, apart from the Tibetans and a few of the Islamic minorities, they were the most deeply religious of all China's more populous nationalities. Every village had at least one Buddhist temple, even those with only 20 or 30 families, and the great majority had several. The largest of the temples was virtually always the finest building in the village. They had a great deal of money invested in them and were the economic and social focus of the community.

All Dai males spent much of their boyhood in the temples, where they were looked after by an adopted father, himself a monk. While in the temple they learned the Dai language in order to be able to read and chant the Buddhist sutras. At about 15 or 16 the boys either left the temple to return to the lay life or decided to remain. In that case they took a vow to remain celibate and observe the 'ten abstinences', which included any taking of life, lying, drinking alcoholic liquor, and singing, dancing or watching dramas. It was against the religious principles of monks to engage in production. The highest rank of monks commanded enormous respect wherever they went and also held great political power. In any village they occupied the highest social status and shared political power with the headman.

The general populace contributed quite a bit of its money to support religion. All people had an obligation to contribute to the upkeep of the temples and, since the monks did not produce anything, they depended on the people for their livelihood. In a small village with one temple and 30 families, each one might take it in turns to provide the monks with meals. Frequently the people gave their best food to the monks, even at the cost of going without themselves. It has been calculated that at least one-fifth of the average family's expenditure was given over to the support of religion.[43]

Among the Han Chinese, Buddhism meant the Mahayana form. Minorities with believers in Mahayana Buddhism included the Gin of Guangxi (the same as the Vietnamese) and the Lahu of Yunnan, but above all the Bai, also of Yunnan. However, it is worth stressing that other faiths exercised some influence over all three minorities. All believed in nature- and ancestor-worshipping faiths while Christianity had begun to create greater or lesser impact among them. Daoism found adherents among both the Gin and the Bai.

Buddhism among the Bai dates from about the first half of the ninth century. For them the principal deity was Guanyin, the Goddess of Mercy and the patron of women and mothers, as well as of fishermen, with others like Amida Buddha generally taking on a lesser importance. It was to Guanyin that Buddhist temples were dedicated, while Amida Buddha and other deities were relegated to a shrine within the Guanyin temples.[44]

Bai Buddhist monks dedicated themselves to chanting sutras in honour of Guanyin and other deities. Ordinary peasants could take on work as Buddhist monks or masters on a semi-professional basis. This role could be hereditary, being handed on in some cases over numerous generations. Some married women formed societies which took a vow of partial or total abstinence from meat and alcoholic beverages. Such women met on the many festival days to chant sutras or repeat the name of Guanyin and Amida in the temples, with the aim of acquiring individual merit.[45]

It emerges from this account that the Tibetans and Mongols shared a single religious faith which in each case made for a strong sense of identity in opposition to the Han and jointly with each other. In the case of the Mongols, Japanese opposition to their religion no doubt spurred a sense of identity as well. The Dai religion was in marked contrast with the Han and the learning of Dai language to read Buddhist sutras by boys and young men can only have intensified a sense of national consciousness. On the other hand, the Bai religion was heavily influenced by the Han. Differences may have remained, but it is very doubtful that Bai identity was helped by their religion. On the contrary, the interchange of Han and Bai religious elements was among the factors bringing the Bai close to assimilation with the Han by the time the Guomindang fell.

Other religious forms

Polytheism, nature and ancestor worship and shamanism in various forms were practised by some northern nationalities like the Manchus, Ewenkis, Oroqens and Daurs, as well as by a great many of the southwestern minorities such as the Zhuang, Yi, Shui, Bouyei, Dong, Yao, Tujia, Miao and Naxi. Among some of these minorities, the influence of Han folk religion was strong. For instance, many of the spirits in which the Bouyei believe are common also in Han folk religion.[46]

Nature worship derived from the belief that non-material forces direct-ed those natural phenomena which were a part of everyday life, or that spir-its actually resided within them. The Oroqens were typical in their worship of night and day, the four seasons, wind, rain, thunder, lightning, drought, birds and beasts and so on.[47] One ethnologist, himself from Western Hunan, wrote after an investigation of the Miao of his area in the late 1920s or early 1930s that 'among heaven and earth, the sun and the moon, the wind, clouds, thunder and rain, mountains and rivers, anything supernatural, there is nothing that they do not respect as a god'.[48] Miao religion was heavily influ-enced by the Han in the sense that, of the 40 or so gods accorded special rit-ual observations, over half were of Han derivation. These rituals were often quite elaborate, involving a long succession of activities and including ani-mal sacrifice.[49] Among some Zhuang communities, women cutting cogongrass would plait a cogongrass person before opening their sickles and would then worship the image. This was to avoid irritating the spirits within the grass who might otherwise thwart its growth in future years.[50]

A very good example of a polytheistic nature-worshipping minority of the south was the Yi. A Western missionary living in southwest China in the Republican period wrote of them:

> The sun, the moon, rivers, mountains, and many other inanimate things are regarded as living, sentient beings that can talk, marry, and have children. These, along with trees, rocks, animals, and insects are often regarded as gods. There are magical horses that in an incredibly short time fly up into the sky or cover long distances from one place to anoth-er. Men and gods have marvellous powers. Thunder, rain, hail, and the wind are great beings that are regarded as powerful gods.[51]

Because the spirit within things did not die, the soul of a person went on living after death. Among the Yi, for instance, almost all people were believed to become gods after death if good, or demons if bad, both of them having supernatural power. Consequently, ancestor worship shared a very significant place with nature worship among a great many of the national-ities, both of the north and the south.[52] Confucianism and Han influence added further impetus to the strength of ancestor worship.

Among the northern nationalities like the Manchus, Oroqens, Daurs, Ewenkis or Hezhens, there was a group of male or female specialists who carried out the shamanistic rituals, involving trances, spirit dances, curing the sick and other functions. The English word 'shaman' takes its origin from the Manchu-Tungus tongues in which it means 'an agitated, frenzied person or dancer'.[53] There were religious specialists also among the nature-worshipping nationalities of the southwest, in Chinese termed *wu*. The Zhuang were a typical example. The specialists functioned as intermedi-aries between ancestors or spirits and living people. They carried out reli-gious ceremonies or sacrifices, performed ritual dances and music and tried to cure the sick. Just as in the north they could be either male or female.[54]

Another typical nature-worshipping minority was the Miao of whom one ethnologist wrote: 'if somebody was ill, then they would say it was due to a spirit and invite in a sorcerer (*wu*) to exorcise it, or they might sacrifice to heaven or to their ancestors ...'[55]

The Austrian-American botanist and student of many of China's south-western peoples, Joseph Rock, found a distinct cultural identity among the Naxi of Lijiang in Yunnan. They are a people who for many centuries had been ruled by their own kings until 1723, when the Qing dynasty took control sending Chinese officials to administer their area. A major feature of the Naxi society was a polytheistic religion which 'seemed to combine elements of tribal shamanism with *Bon*, the heterodox religion of Tibet', where it had antedated lama Buddhism by many centuries. The religious specialists were called *tomba*, a term which Rock translates into English as 'wizards'. One of their main functions was to perform ceremonies aimed to cure people of disease through dance accompanied by a gong, cymbal and drum which they played themselves. They also enjoyed great control over the knowledge of Naxi society through their mastery of the written language. They were able to chant from manuscripts which were passed from one generation of 'wizards' to the next.[56]

The social influence of the *tomba* could be very negative. Peter Goulart, whose account of the 'forgotten kingdom' in and around Lijiang in the 1940s is generally very flattering, claims that, among the Naxi there, the *tomba* influenced young lovers to commit suicide as a refuge from marriages forced on them by their parents. According to his account, the *tomba* of Lijiang stood to profit from these suicides because they got rich emoluments from the ceremonies which the suicides occasioned. For this reason, they 'kept up a subtle and cunning propaganda' among affected young Naxi lovers. The origin of this tradition, according to Goulart, lay in the fact that the Naxi followed the custom of the free mixing of the sexes at courtship gatherings, but had been forced by their own rulers influenced by Chinese Confucian morality into the system of arranged marriages. The method usually followed was by taking the poisonous root of black aconite boiled in oil which, though very painful, was swift.[57]

Christian missionaries were active in a great many parts of China, including the nationality areas from places as widely varied as Xinjiang or Yanbian. Although the number of converts which they gained was not large by comparison with the whole population, their overall influence was considerable, because they were part and parcel of the Western impact on China. At the same time, their effectiveness varied sharply from region to region. C.P. Fitzgerald, who carried out some pioneering research on the Bai of western Yunnan in the late 1930s, wrote that their conviction of holding a monopoly on truth was a strongly inhibiting factor for the Christian missionaries. 'The idea of an exclusive creed, the one true way distinct from all others which are false, is so unfamiliar to their mental habits as to be barely comprehensible.'[58] Although he was referring specifically to the Bai people, the same comments would hold true for many other Chinese nationalities, including the Han. Another very different obstacle in the path of the missionaries was the local clergies of religions such as Islam and Tibetan Buddhism, who exercised powerful social influence. Goulart described the Naxi and Tibetans of Lijiang as 'inconvertible', with Catholic and British Protestant missions proving equally unsuccessful. The main reason he suggests is the influence of the local clergy, especially the monks and lamas of the Tibetan Buddhist monasteries. 'Any Tibetan who embraced Christianity became automatically an outcast, was driven away from his home and his very life was in jeopardy,' concludes Goulart.[59]

Yet the missionaries did enjoy some signal successes. From the beginning of the twentieth century, Western missionaries converted some Bouyei peasants and traders in Guizhou.[60] Among the Miao of the same province, an American missionary enterprise, begun in Anshun in 1897, gained quite a few converts in the villages and resulted in the setting up of a school network. Even more important was the British Protestant missionary base established in 1904 in Shimenkan, Weining county. In addition to spreading Christian influence, the Shimenkan base devised a romanised script for the Miao language to be used as a vehicle of instruction. By the eve of the war against Japan, some 50 schools had been established in the Miao border regions near Weining which had graduated a substantial number of students. However, after the outbreak of the war, General Yang Zisen, who held effective power in Guizhou, ordered that the management of the schools be transferred to the Weining county government. Later the government money supply for the schools dried up and they were forced to close down.[61]

Women and religion

Men held the power in most of the religions of the minorities. This was true above all of Islam, noted for its male domination in its powerful clergy, but also of Tibetan, Dai and other Buddhism, as well as Christianity. A partial, but by no means total, exception to this overall pattern of male domination in religions was shamanism. Mongol shamans could be either male or female. The shamans of the Tungus and other northeastern peoples were initially female, and surveys among Oroqen communities referring to the period 1900–45 showed that women were still in a fairly clear majority among shamans.[62] Yet this does not prove that religion favoured women. By the twentieth century, women among the Tungus and other shamanistic peoples of the northeast were considered 'unclean' from the religious point of view and subject to various taboos. Even the female shamans who continued to function into the twentieth century were exempt from the taboos and the notion that they were unclean only when they wore their ritual dress and were actually on the job.[63]

Among the Yi or Lolo, there was a priestly profession of wise men who held great moral and other power. Their work included repeating the sacred books, training future members of their class, exorcising demons, healing diseases and divination. They were the only ones with education or the ability to read and understand the sacred books. Below them were a group of magicians who could perform ceremonies and sacrifices, as well as heal diseases and exorcise, but who were not allowed access to the sacred books. Lower still were a group of fortune-tellers or palmists, with hardly any status at all. What is significant is that, whereas the highest of the three classes was entirely male, the middle one comprised mostly men but included some women and the lowest was mainly, although not exclusively, female.[64]

The 'wizards', or *tombas*, of the Naxi of Lijiang showed one highly distinctive feature of religion, namely that although this was of all China's nationalities possibly the one with the highest degree of female influence, its religious specialists were male. The *tombas* were mainly hereditary, descending from father to son. Only in recent times did they begin passing on their specialisation to disciples who, though not their sons, were also male.[65] Even the priests who were related to the *tombas* and could carry out religious ceremonies were male.[66]

The Koreans

Although religious influence among the Koreans was much slighter than among the Islamic or main Buddhist nationalities during the Republican period in China, there was a range of religious beliefs which exerted some impact on them. In religion, as in several other respects, the Koreans constitute a special case in themselves, but also provide an example illustrating Mahayana Buddhism and Christianity, both Catholic and non-Catholic.

Buddhism is a very ancient religion in Korea itself. However, when the Koreans went to Yanbian in Jilin province, Buddhism tended to be the religion of the rich, who tried to use it to control those less well off than themselves. As a result, it did not gain much of a following among ordinary poor people. Not only was it never as strong in Yanbian as in Korea itself, but the number of its adherents dwindled in the twentieth century.

In 1913 the Jiandao Confucian Association was set up in Yanbian to support Yuan Shikai's attempt to make Confucianism the state religion. Although thus extremely conservative, some Confucianists were also very patriotic and set up some anti-Japanese groups around the time of the great March First Movement of 1919 in Korea. This great nationalist movement aimed at ousting the Japanese, who had taken over Korea itself as a colony in 1910. Later, the Japanese were able to take control of Confucianism in Yanbian, in part because this was the official belief of their puppet state of Manchoukuo, formally set up in March 1932.[67]

An originally Korean faith was the Doctrine of the Heavenly Way (*Ch'ondo-gyo*). In Korea itself this was a new name for the *Tonghak* (Eastern Learning), the egalitarian ideas of which had, in the second half of the nineteenth century, produced an enormous rebellion in Korea in many ways analogous to the Taipings in China. Its influence spread to Yanbian very early in the twentieth century. In both Korea and Yanbian, the adherents of the Doctrine of the Heavenly Way were initially extremely anti-Japanese, but split into two factions, one of them supportive of the Japanese. In Yanbian the split occurred in the 1920s, somewhat later than in Korea. By the time the state of Manchoukuo was actually set up, there were some 4000 believers in this religion.[68]

Christianity has played a significant role in the nationalism and modernisation of Korea. In Yanbian both Catholicism and Protestantism were introduced through foreign missionaries in the last years of the nineteenth or first of the twentieth century. Both gained some influence, especially Protestantism. Figures for 1936 show some 38 900 Korean Protestants in Manchoukuo, including 22 100 Presbyterians and 4000 Methodists. The number of Korean Catholics in the same year was about 12 500. In 1942, the Japanese compelled all Korean Protestant churches to unite into the Manchoukuoan Korean Protestant Church.[69]

The Protestant and Catholic missionaries never enjoyed good relations with one another. The Protestants focused more attention on charitable work among the Koreans than did the Catholics. Perhaps more important was the fact that the Catholic missionaries were German, whereas the Protestant ones were North American or British. The Japanese tried to win over as many Christians as they could, but made far more headway with the Catholics than the Protestants. With the outbreak of the Pacific War, the Japanese expelled the foreign Protestant missionaries, but because Germany was a country friendly to them, allowed the Catholic missionaries to stay.[70]

Conclusion

The fact that religion was such a conservative force among the minorities in the first half of the twentieth century is not to say that nothing changed. But the extent of change was slight if the comparison is with such phenomena as education or politics. Moreover, religion tried to prevent change in other areas of society — and to some extent succeeded. The Tibetans, among the most religious of the nationalities, were also among the most conservative. The Thirteenth Dalai Lama found to his cost that even the most insignificant of reforms encountered opposition from the great monasteries of Lhasa.

In terms of religious beliefs and practices, there were enormous variations among the various minorities. Religion played a rather slight role in Korean life compared with Tibetan, even though the range of religious beliefs found among Koreans was very much wider. While some of the nationalities practised exclusive religions such as Islam, others were quite eclectic and quite prepared to adopt any religious belief with the potential to help them in the present world.

Many of the minorities shared religious factors with the Han, usually introduced from Han to minority rather than the other way around. In addition to Daoist impact on minorities such as the Bai, many of the pantheons had much in common with those of the Han. This did not necessarily mean that the relevant nationality got on well with the Han. For instance, some Yi communities, especially in Yunnan, worshipped quite a few originally Han gods as their own, and yet remained very much apart from the Han and on bad terms with them, politically and in other ways.[71] But it did mean that religion played a slighter part in the promotion of identity than it might otherwise have done.

With the exception of the Hui, whose Islam underwent reform, the stronger the clergy of any minority, the more powerful its religion was likely to be in promoting national identity, simply because the clergy itself acted as a bulwark dividing the people from non-Islamic peoples, especially the Han. It follows that those religions without strong clergies, such as nature or ancestor worship, were far less likely to promote national identity.

The secessionist rebellions in Xinjiang emphasise the role of Islam and the Islamic clergy in opposing integration in either of its two senses, that between the Han and the minorities on the one hand and the national integration of China as a single country on the other. The Tibetan clergy was more interested in preserving tradition and the de facto independence of Tibet than in any form of integration with China. The situation with the Mongols was similar but more complicated, because the clergy was weaker politically and — largely because of the Japanese occupation — the status of Inner Mongolia more questionable. The Mongol clergy there favoured its own people's nationalism where China was concerned, but does not seem to have been especially active either in supporting or opposing Japanese rule in the Xing'an provinces of Manchoukuo. Generally speaking, the more strongly a religion or its clergy furthered a sense of national identity among the minorities, the more they acted as a force in opposition to integration in either of its two senses.

Notes

1 Wing-tsit Chan, *Religious Trends in Modern China*, Columbia University Press, New York, 1953; Octagon Books, New York, 1969, p. 187.

2 Andrew D.W. Forbes, *Warlords and Muslims in Chinese Central Asia, A Political History of Republican Sinkiang 1911–1949*, Cambridge University Press, Cambridge, 1986, pp. 18–19; Xinjiang Social Sciences Academy's Nationalities Research Institute, *Xinjiang jianshi, dier ce*, Xinjiang Renmin chubanshe, Ürümqi, 1980, pp. 393–94.

3 See Forbes, *Warlords and Muslims*, p. 155.

4 Owen Lattimore, et al., *Pivot of Asia, Sinkiang and the Inner Asian Frontiers of China and Russia*, Little, Brown and Co., Boston, 1950, AMS, New York, 1975 reprint, pp. 127–28.

5 See Chang-tu Hu, in collaboration with Samuel C. Chu, Leslie L. Clark, Jung-pang Lo and Yuan-li Wu, ed. Hsiao Hsia, *China, Its People, Its Society, Its Culture*, HRAF Press, New Haven, 1960, p. 77.

6 Lattimore, et al., *Pivot of Asia*, p. 132.

7 Aitchen K. Wu, *Turkistan Tumult*, Methuen, London, 1940, p. 221.

8 Dru C. Gladney, *Muslim Chinese, Ethnic Nationalism in the People's Republic*, published by Council on East Asian Studies, Harvard University, and distributed by Harvard University Press, Cambridge, Mass., and London, 1991, pp. 53–54.

9 Chan, *Religious Trends in Modern China*, pp. 202–5.

10 Gladney, *Muslim Chinese*, pp. 55–61.

11 Ma Fulong, 'Yisilan zai Ningxia', in Gansu Provincial Library Bibliography Department, comp., *Xibei minzu zongjiao shiliao wenzhai (Ningxia fence)*, Gansu sheng tushuguan, Lanzhou, 1986, p. 219. The article is drawn from *Xibei tongxun*, vol. 2, nos 8 and 9, 1948.

12 A. Doak Barnett, *China on the Eve of Communist Takeover*, Frederick A. Praeger, New York, 1963, pp. 182–84. See also Ma Cibo, 'Huijiao yu Huizu bian', in Gansu Provincial Library Bibliography Department, comp., *Xibei minzu zongjiao shiliao wenzhai (Gansu fence)*, Gansu sheng tushuguan, Lanzhou, 1984, pp. 231–32. This article is abstracted from *Xin xibei*, vol. 3, no. 3, 1940.

13 Chan, *Religious Trends in Modern China*, pp. 210–12. In his 'debate on Islam and the Hui nationality', Ma Cibo writes that Sun Yat-sen's 'nationalism is not at all the republic of five nationalities . . . because we [the Chinese nation] are for the most part only one nationality'. See Ma, 'Huijiao yu Huizu bian', p. 234. It should be noted, however, that although most writers believed that the Hui shared Chinese nationalism, an alternative view can be found. For instance, writing in the late 1940s, Ma Fulong, 'Yisilan zai Ningxia', pp. 226–27, believed that a problem still existed between Han and Hui and that 'mutual hatred' had been worsened by Hui soldiers being forced into mainly Han units during the war against Japan.

14 For a detailed account of this religion, in English, including its doctrines, practices and rituals, see Giuseppe Tucci, trans. Geoffrey Samuel, *The Religions of Tibet*, Routledge & Kegan Paul, London and Henley, 1980, pp. 29–162 and R.A. Stein, trans. J.E. Stapleton Driver, *Tibetan Civilization*, Faber and Faber, London, 1972, pp. 165–91.

15 See Michael Aris, with the assistance of Patrick Booz and contributions by S.B. Sutton and Jeffrey Wagner, *Lamas, Princes, and Brigands, Joseph Rock's Photographs of the Tibetan Borderlands of China*, China House Gallery, China Institute in America, New York, 1992, pp. 85, 89–91 for brief description and photographs relevant to Tibetan Buddhism among the Naxi.

16 Tucci, trans. Samuel, *The Religions of Tibet*, p. 110.

17 David Snellgrove and Hugh Richardson, *A Cultural History of Tibet*, George Weidenfeld and Nicolson, London, 1968, p. 257.

18 Sir Charles Bell, *The People of Tibet*, Clarendon Press, Oxford, 1928, p. 26.

19 Snellgrove and Richardson, *A Cultural History of Tibet*, p. 237.

20 Thubten Jigme Norbu and Colin M. Turnbull, *Tibet, Its History, Religion and People*, Chatto & Windus, London, Simon & Schuster, NY, 1969;

Penguin, Harmondsworth, 1987, p. 251.

21 ibid., p. 257.

22 Snellgrove and Richardson, *A Cultural History of Tibet*, p. 239.

23 See especially Tucci, trans. Samuel, *The Religions of Tibet*, pp. 158–62 and Snellgrove and Richardson, *A Cultural History of Tibet*, pp. 238–45.

24 See the list in Ma Hetian, 'Qinghai zhi zongjiao', in Gansu Provincial Library Bibliography Department, comp., *Xibei minzu zongjiao shiliao wenzhai (Qinghai fence)*, Gansu sheng tushuguan, Lanzhou, 1986, vol. 2, pp. 622–27. The article is abstracted from an original published in 1935.

25 Wang Wenhan, 'Qinghai Meng Zang renmin zhi zongjiao xinyang', in Gansu Provincial Library Bibliography Department, comp., *Xibei minzu zongjiao shiliao wenzhai (Qinghai fence)*, vol. 2, p. 636. The article is abstracted from one published originally in *Bianjiang tongxun* vol. 5, no. 1, 1948.

26 See Walther Heissig, trans. Geoffrey Samuel, *The Religions of Mongolia*, Routledge & Kegan Paul, London and Henley, 1980, especially pp. 2–3, 24–35, and 84–101.

27 Inner Mongolian Autonomous Region Editorial Group (ed.), *Menggu zu shehui lishi diaocha*, Nei Menggu Renmin chubanshe, Hohhot, 1985, pp. 182–83.

28 The Mongolian area of the Japanese-controlled state of Manchoukuo was divided into four provinces: North, South, East and West Xing'an.

29 Inner Mongolian Autonomous Region Editorial Group (ed.), *Menggu zu shehui lishi diaocha*, p. 163.

30 Wang Duanyu, 'Lama jiao yu Zangzu renkou', *Minzu yanji*, no. 2, 20 March 1984, pp. 44–45; Zhang Tianlu, *Xizang renkou de bianqian*, Zhongguo Zangxue chubanshe, Beijing, 1989, pp. 8–9.

31 J.T. Walker and A. Terrien De Lacouperie, 'Tibet', in *The Encyclopædia Britannica, A Dictionary of Arts, Sciences, and General Literature, Ninth Edition, Volume XXIII*, Adam and Charles Black, Edinburgh, 1888, p. 344.

32 Snellgrove and Richardson, *A Cultural History of Tibet*, p. 237; Norbu and Turnbull, *Tibet*, p. 257.

33 Wang, 'Lama jiao yu Zangzu renkou', p. 45. Further detailed figures on the population of monasteries in Tibet, which supplement but do not conflict with those given above, can be found in Stein, *Tibetan Civilization*, pp. 139–40.

34 Wang, 'Qinghai Meng Zang renmin zhi zongjiao xinyang', p. 633. The list in Ma, 'Qinghai zhi zongjiao', pp. 622–27, referring to the mid-1930s, lists 231 monasteries, with 15 313 monks in 187 monasteries, but with no figures given for the population of 44 of the monasteries.

35 The unreliability of the figures is clear from two rather irreconcilable sets of statistics. A 1931 government count puts the total population of Qinghai at 2 490 000, but with Tibetans taking up only 200 000, or 8 per cent, and Mongols 50 000–60 000, that is 2 per cent: Sun Hanwen, 'Qinghai minzu gaiguan', in Gansu Provincial Library Bibliography Department, comp., *Xibei minzu zongjiao shiliao wenzhai (Qinghai fence)*,

vol. 1, p. 313. This article is drawn from *Xibei lunheng*, vol. 5, nos 4 and 5 [1937]. On the other hand, late-1940s government statistics claim a total Qinghai population of 1 346 310, with about 600 000 Tibetans: Wang, 'Qinghai Meng Zang renmin zhi zongjiao xinyang', pp. 632–33.

36 Sun, 'Qinghai minzu gaiguan', p. 311.

37 P.T. Etherton, *In the Heart of Asia*, Houghton Mifflin, Boston and New York, 1926, pp. 202–3.

38 Zhang, *Xizang renkou de bianqian*, p. 29.

39 Song Naigong, et al. (eds), *Zhongguo renkou, Nei Menggu fence*, Zhongguo caizheng jingji chubanshe, Beijing, 1987, pp. 57–58.

40 See *The Japan–Manchoukuo Year Book 1936, Cyclopedia of General Information and Statistics on the Empires of Japan and Manchoukuo*, The Japan–Manchoukuo Year Book Co., Tokyo, pp. 895 and 886.

41 Etherton, *In the Heart of Asia*, p. 202.

42 *The Japan–Manchoukuo Year Book 1936*, p. 895.

43 On Buddhism among the Dai before 1949, see Jiang Yingliang, *Daizu shi*, Sichuan Minzu chubanshe, Chengdu, 1983, pp. 528–48.

44 C.P. Fitzgerald, *The Tower of Five Glories, A Study of the Min Chia of Ta Li, Yunnan*, The Cresset Press, London, 1941; Hyperion Press, Westport, Connecticut, 1973, p. 112. For a discussion of Bai religion, see also Colin Mackerras, 'Aspects of Bai Culture, Change and Continuity in a Yunnan Nationality,' *Modern China, An International Quarterly of History and Social Science*, vol. 14, no. 1, January 1988, pp. 54–61.

45 Fitzgerald, *The Tower of Five Glories*, p. 114; see also Yunnan Provincial Editorial Committee of the *Five Series on Nationalities Problems* (ed.), *Baizu shehui lishi diaocha*, Yunnan Renmin chubanshe, Kunming, 1983, p. 70.

46 Hu et al., *China*, p. 85.

47 Qiu Pu, trans. Wang Huimin, *The Oroqens, China's Nomadic Hunters*, Foreign Languages Press, Beijing, 1983, pp. 99–100.

48 Shi Honggui, 'Xiangxi Miaozu kaocha ji (zhailu)', in Zhang Ermu et al., eds, *Xiangxi wenshi ziliao, di shijiu ji, Miaojiang guzhen, Xiangxi wenshi ziliao* bianji bu, Jishou, 1990, p. 144.

49 Hu et al., *China*, p. 81.

50 Huang Xianfan, Huang Zengqing and Zhang Yimin, *Zhuangzu tongshi*, Guangxi Minzu chubanshe, Nanning, 1988, p. 725.

51 David Crockett Graham, *Folk Religion in Southwest China*, Smithsonian Press, Washington, D.C., 1961, p. 82. In this comment Graham makes no distinction between the various Yi groups.

52 See, for instance, Manduertu, 'Zhongguo beifang minzu de saman jiao', in Jilin Provincial Nationalities Research Institute (ed.), *Saman jiao wenhua yanjiu, diyi ji*, Jilin Renmin chubanshe, Changchun, 1988, p. 3, referring specifically to the northern nationalities.

53 Qiu, trans. Wang, *The Oroqens*, p. 108; Morigendi, 'Dawoer zu zhi zongjiao xinyang', in Jilin Provincial Nationalities Research Institute (ed.), *Saman jiao wenhua yanjiu, diyi ji*, p. 140.

54 Huang, Huang and Zhang, *Zhuangzu tongshi*, p. 730.
55 Shi, 'Xiangxi Miaozu kaocha ji', p. 144. On shamans among the Miao of Western Hunan, see especially Shi Qigui, *Xiangxi Miaozu shidi diaocha baogao*, Hunan Renmin chubanshe, Changsha, 1986, pp. 567–70.
56 S.B. Sutton, 'Joseph Rock: Restless Spirit', in Aris, *Lamas, Princes, and Brigands*, p. 25. Peter Goulart, *Forgotten Kingdom*, John Murray, London, 1957, pp. 179–92 uses the romanisation *dtomba* for the Naxi term which Rock translated as 'wizard'. Other romanisations are *dobbaq* or *nto-mba*.
57 Goulart, *Forgotten Kingdom*, pp. 179–85.
58 Fitzgerald, *The Tower of Five Glories*, pp. 146–47.
59 Goulart, *Forgotten Kingdom*, pp. 97–100.
60 Hu et al., *China*, p. 85.
61 See, for instance, Liang Oudi, 'Guizhou de Miaomin jiaoyu', *Bianzheng gonglun*, vol. 3, no. 2, February 1944, pp. 54–55.
62 Qiu, trans. Wang, *The Oroqens*, pp. 108–9.
63 Manduertu, 'Zhongguo beifang minzu de saman jiao', in Jilin Provincial Nationalities Research Institute, *Saman jiao wenhua yanjiu, diyi ji*, Jilin Renmin chubanshe, Changchun, 1988, p. 3.
64 Graham, *Folk Religion in Southwest China*, pp. 78–80.
65 See Song Enchang et al., in Luo Zhufeng et al., *Zhongguo da baike quanshu, zongjiao*, Zhongguo da baike quanshu chubanshe, Beijing, Shanghai, 1988, p. 283.
66 See the photographs of *tombas* in Aris, *Lamas, Princes, and Brigands*, pp. 113–16. On p. 117 is a photograph of priests described as 'close cousins of the Naxi *tomba*' performing a 'burning of the demons' ceremony.
67 Interview with Professor Pak Changuk of Yanbian University 6 October 1990; *Brief History of the Koreans* Compilation Group, *Chaoxian zu jianshi*, Yanbian Renmin chubanshe, Yanji, 1986, pp. 223–24.
68 Han Woo-keun, trans. Lee Kyung-shik, *The History of Korea*, Eul-yoo Publishing Company, Seoul, 1970;1981, p. 458; *Chaoxian zu jianshi*, p. 220.
69 Bernard Vincent Olivier, *The Implementation of China's Nationality Policy in the Northeastern Provinces*, Mellen Research University Press, San Francisco, 1993, p. 96.
70 Interview with Professor Pak Changuk of Yanbian University 6 October 1990; *Chaoxian zu jianshi*, pp. 217–19.
71 Graham, *Folk Religion in Southwest China*, pp. 82; 88–89.

3 Pre-1949 Education

Like religion, education is a factor of strong relevance to attitudes and mind patterns. But, in contrast, it tended to point in more modern and somewhat less conservative directions in the first half of the century. Though still reluctant to accept change, education was somewhat more forward-looking in its texture than was religion.

The processes of change in education in the minority areas followed patterns similar to those in other parts of China. At the turn of the twentieth century, education in the minority areas of China was mainly traditional, but already the roots of Christian missionary and other schools following a nontraditional system more in line with modern patterns had been planted. During the Republican period, the traditional structures weakened, but essentially remained in place. The Christian missionary schools grew more numerous and stronger. But the most important development was the rise of a significant number of government-run schools which aimed to exercise an integrative influence over the minorities' children by pushing Han Chinese culture at the expense of that of the particular ethnic group. The governments hoped that their educational system would militate against feelings of minority national identity and hence integrate the country by encouraging a sense of loyalty to a unified China among the nationalities. These government schools tried to instil pride in national accomplishment and history into the students, but the relevant nation was China, certainly not the individual minorities.

Major change in the Chinese education system as a whole began before the Qing dynasty fell in 1911. The drift against Confucian education in China as a whole manifested itself most strongly in the abolition of the traditional examination system in 1905. Early in 1909, some Mongol and Tibetan nobles set up the Mongol and Tibetan School in Beijing. The aim of the school was to train officials to rule Mongolia and Tibet. That the training was to be a new approach to the old objective of keeping the distant peoples under control is shown through the Chinese name of the school: *Zhibian xuetang*, which means literally 'school to colonise the borders'.[1] Still, the emphasis had definitely moved away from the general moralism based on the classics which had characterised the Confucian system, and towards training local people to use local knowledge to control local people, although still in the interests of the central government.

Traditional and non-national government systems

The traditional education systems of the minorities differed enormously from one to the other, although a common thread was evident among those many nationalities with strong specialist clergies in that these constituted a dominant force in educating the people. Some of the minorities had no education system at all, and teaching and learning were informal parts of socialisation. Others simply followed the Han Chinese ways of education. Attachment to literacy also differed widely among the nationalities. But among those with education systems, however poorly developed, it was mainly or entirely the richer members of society who could enjoy access.

It is clearly impossible to detail the education of all nationalities. Consequently, a few vastly disparate examples are selected to represent the effects which some modernising processes produced on traditional systems. These are the Tibetans, the Islamic nationalities of Xinjiang, the Bai of Yunnan and the Koreans of Jilin, especially Yanbian. The impact of the National Government of Chiang Kai-shek and the issue of the education of girls are considered later.

The Tibetans

The dominance of religion among the Tibetans extended to education. The saying 'monasteries are schools, and religion is education' showed the pervasive way in which monasteries controlled education, monks being society's intellectuals.[2] It was possible for ordinary people to gain an education, but the commonest method was by entering a monastery and becoming a monk. The main monasteries contained printing presses, for they were centres of publishing as well as learning. Such secular literature as existed, like story-telling and drama, was mainly oral, and so did not need to be written down.

It was the function of two schools in Lhasa, the Peak and Ecclesiastical, to train monk employees for work in the government. Some graduates of the former, as well as sons of the hereditary aristocracy, could undertake study at the Ecclesiastical School. However, this institution 'passed into oblivion' with the death of the Thirteenth Dalai Lama at the end of 1933.[3] The main school for lay officials to enter administrative posts was the rTzi phrug pa in Lhasa. In addition, two schools operated there to teach specialist Tibetan subjects, one for medicine, the other astrology.

The largest proportion of schools in Tibetan regions were private. Apart from six or seven main private schools and quite a few lesser ones in Lhasa, there were also some in such cities as Xigaze and Gyaze. Their clients were mainly the sons of the aristocracy, although lower-class people were occasionally allowed to attend, while their curriculum included calligraphy, arithmetic, reading and learning the Buddhist sutras by heart.[4] A Tibetan writer gives some details of these schools:

> Examinations are held at the onset of every holiday. Only the first three students are rewarded. Beginning with the fourth student, the students are caned by each preceding student according to academic rank and the last student is compelled to cane a tin before the entire school. The modern system of promotion to a higher class was not prevalent in Tibet, but subjects taught included both temporal and ecclesiastical fields of knowledge. In Tibet, only those students with ambition and opportunity to proceed to administrative jobs studied for a longer period of time. The other students left school after a period of five or six years of study or until such time when they had learnt enough to conduct their daily lives. Academic fees were unknown in Tibet. On the school-leaving day, teachers and students were served Tibetan tea and sweetened rice. Rich students made cash donations and the teachers garlanded the outgoing students with ceremonial scarves as they departed to build lives of their own.[5]

Although the processes of modernisation began in Tibetan education from early in the twentieth century, they made only modest headway in the Tibetan areas, and hardly any in Tibet itself. The reforms of Zhang Yintang, the Han official sent to Tibet as Deputy Resident in 1906, were based on frankly assimilative policies, but they did include opening secular schools. However, neither he nor his reforms lasted long. One account credits the Thirteenth Dalai Lama with introducing a secular education system, superimposed on the foundation of religious education.[6] The Tibetan government paid for the establishment of an English school in Gyaze for the children of noble and middle-class Tibetan families. Set up in 1924, it closed down after only two years. The Thirteenth Dalai Lama's reforms, although extremely minor, came up against the implacable conservative opposition of the three great monasteries of Lhasa. According to Hugh Richardson, the 'threat to monastic supremacy was the key to the reaction against innovations and it showed that the Dalai Lama, although the summit and master of the system, was also its creature'.[7] The net result was the failure of the Thirteenth Dalai Lama's attempts at even the mildest of change, including any in the area of education.

Attitudes similar to those of the great monasteries in the 1920s have retained some currency even towards the end of the century. An account still popular in the West, written mainly by a former Tibetan abbot and the elder brother of the Fourteenth Dalai Lama, concedes that the lack of attention given to organised education was the major fault of old Tibet, called 'the most fortunate of lands',[8] but goes on to argue that secular education was not really necessary.

> A secular education corresponds only to secular needs, and in Tibet these are minimal. The son of a nomad knows all there is to know about the life before him by the time he is nine or ten years old. So with the son or daughter of a farmer . . . Reading and writing are virtually unnecessary for there is no such thing as secular literature in Tibet.[9]

In Tibetan areas such as in the Sichuan border regions and Qinghai, the introduction of modern and reformed education was much more extensive and effective than in Tibet itself. There were two main reasons for this. One was that the various Chinese governments which influenced Tibetan areas like those in the Sichuan border regions and Qinghai were keener to use education as a means of integration and Chinese control, as well as for their own version of progress, and thus to oppose the use of education by traditional ruling elites for the furthering of Tibetan national identity or pride in Tibetan culture and tradition. The other was that Christian missionaries were more active in such places than in Tibet itself.

One example suffices to illustrate each point. One of the measures the energetic reformer Zhao Erfeng carried out in the first decade of the twentieth century in western Sichuan was to attempt the introduction of compulsory education. While he did not achieve this aim, the number of schools in the Tibetan areas of what are now the Sichuan border regions did grow very rapidly indeed. In 1907 there were only two primary schools with 60 students, but by 1911, within only four years, the number of schools had risen to exceed 200 while that of students had climbed over 9000.[10] The curriculum included ethics, Chinese language, history, geography, arithmetic and physical culture. In fact, it followed the patterns of the modernising Han Chinese of the time, certainly not those of traditional Tibet.

Western Christian missionaries had won permission to operate in the Chinese inland in the nineteenth century. But it was not until the early twentieth century that they established schools in the Tibetan areas. British, French and American missionaries ran schools in Xikang in substantial numbers, and while the courses contained plenty of Christian religion, they also ran to a good deal of the sort of modern material with the potential to be useful in the current world. An influential case in point was the Latin School in the Xikang capital Kangding (Dardo), run by French Catholic missionaries from the end of the Qing. It took in orphans and the children of converts and was heavily subsidised by the Catholic Church. The curriculum included Latin and religious (Catholic) knowledge, but also French, Chinese, history, geography and mathematics. The maximum period of study there was ten years, covering primary and secondary grades, but even that was very long indeed by comparison with the normal Chinese school. The best students were selected for further university study in Catholic theology with a view to a religious vocation. Such a school could be — and indeed was — accused of trying to turn Tibetans (or Han) into foreigners.[11] While its educational influence was thus hostile to a sense of Tibetan, or even Chinese, national identity, it could nevertheless claim to have contributed to reform and modernity in terms of Tibetan education.

The Islamic nationalities

While the Tibetans have always shown much attachment to study and their monasteries have been centres of learning and printing, the same was never the case in Xinjiang. Colonel P.T. Etherton, who was British Consul-General at Kaxgar from 1918 to 1922, claimed that 'nothing intellectual has emanated' from Xinjiang and that the people of Kaxgar showed 'no tendency towards advancement'.[12] The phraseology is perhaps unnecessarily harsh and born of a rather *de haut en bas* attitude which, in company with their quite extraordinary perceptiveness and energy, was typical of British power-holders of those days. Yet it is true that the culture of Xinjiang's peoples was very derivative and that, even in the 1920s and 1930s, virtually all printed books in Kaxgar came from outside Xinjiang.[13]

Education in Xinjiang before the 1930s was mainly Islamic. Numerous local schools operated, although the fees there closed access to all but the well-to-do. They were controlled by mullahs who ensured that the curriculum was heavily Islamic. In addition, there were schools attached to the mosques where boys were taught to read, write and recite the *Koran*. Muslim conservatives opposed any challenge to their monopoly of education.

However, from the second half of the nineteenth century, a 'new education' began to appear in parts of Xinjiang. It maintained the role of the *Koran* and Islamic doctrine, and its schools were virtually always near mosques. But it differed in that the emphasis on modern science and mathematics was greater than in the old Islamic schools and the dominance of the *Koran* was slighter.

As in some Tibetan areas, the Qing government in its last years attempted to impose compulsory education, of the 'new' kind in Xinjiang. In the Kaxgar area, at least, both Han Chinese and Muslim children received free education and almost all the villages had a school. The curriculum included Chinese, physical drill and the *Koran*, but even the last item did not ease the strenuous opposition of the Muslims, who hated state-run education. One Muslim millionaire merchant from near Kaxgar, who had himself founded a charitable organisation to build libraries and schools to educate both boys and girls, made known his view 'that the new educational policy was making boys disrespectful to their elders; they were losing their faith and were joining the ranks of the gamblers'.[14] The result was that the experiment aimed at popularising a reformed education system failed. With the overthrow of the Qing, the local regime led by Yang Zengxin wanted to continue a Chinese system of education under the Republic. However, according to Etherton, in his time the Chinese-style schools were deserted, and interest in them had waned to vanishing point, even on the part of the Chinese officials whose job it was to lead a revival in enthusiasm for them.[15]

In the early years of the Republic, the main foreign influence on Xinjiang education came from the Turkish Ottoman Empire, which was finally overthrown in 1922. This was significant in that it showed education as furthering not Chinese, but Turkish, national identity, almost all the minorities of Xinjiang being ethnically and culturally Turkic. During World War I, an Ottoman subject set up a school in Kaxgar where the curriculum was based on the Turkish model and the children were encouraged to recognise the Sultan of Turkey as their spiritual and temporal leader. Yang Zengxin, fearing the impact of any allegiance to a Turkish identity, had the school closed down and all those associated with it put in prison. Later he allowed its reopening, but only on condition that the symbols of subordination to Turkey be removed and Chinese language and military drill be taught. With the defeat of the Ottomans in the war, the perceived threat from Turkey disappeared, only to be replaced by one from the newly established Soviet Union.[16]

From the start, Soviet influence was strongest in the Yili region in the northwest of Xinjiang. In April 1918, over 1000 teachers, students and workers demonstrated for four hours in the Yili capital, Gulja, in support of the new Soviet government.[17] When Sheng Shicai came to power in 1933, his pro-Soviet and revolutionary policies created a substantial social impact in parts of Xinjiang, especially in the capital Ürümqi and in Yili and areas near the northwestern border with the Soviet Union. The education system his regime created was based on the Soviet model, including secondary and professional schools, as well as public primary schools in which students of various nationalities studied together, schools restricted to children of the local nationality, and kindergartens.[18] Soviet specialists were active in the education system. The curriculum reflected Soviet influence, with Russian replacing English as the main foreign language taught in Xinjiang's schools.[19] In addition, it was one of the main principles of Sheng Shicai's education system to train technical personnel of various sorts in order to promote the Xinjiang economy. To this end he had schools established with a focus on agriculture, pasture, veterinary surgery, engineering, accountancy and banking, as well as teacher training and other areas.[20]

From 1936 to 1942, Sheng Shicai adopted two three-year plans to promote and popularise education in Xinjiang. Figures show very dramatic expansion over the period. For example, there were only three ordinary middle schools in 1935, with 425 students, but seven with 2590 students in 1943. The total number of primary schools in 1937 was 215, with 33 045 students, but by the end of 1942 there were 556 public primary schools with 85 992 students in addition to 1883 primary schools restricted to children of the local nationality with 180 035 students, a total of 266 027 primary-school students.[21] It is very clear that the emphasis was on the primary sector, where Sheng Shicai and his advisers believed they could most readily achieve basic literacy and expand their own influence on society, which naturally they saw as progressive and desirable.

Sheng Shicai should certainly be given credit for expanding education among the minorities, as is amply shown in the figures given above for the general increase in school and student numbers during his tenure of office, and especially in the 1942 numbers of schools reserved for children of the local nationality and of the students attending them. One of the main principles of Sheng Shicai's policies was to encourage ethnic diversity. He recognised the different languages and cultures of the peoples of Xinjiang and in this respect promoted ethnic identities. At the same time, there were definitely limits to his tolerance, as shown by the fact that his efforts to eliminate the influence of the Islamic mullahs in society as a whole were felt most keenly in the education system.

Despite Sheng Shicai's achievements, three negative factors should be kept in mind. The first was the extreme lack of freedom in the education system, which derived from his Stalinist model. Uygurs nowadays look back on his regime with absolute horror: 'His spies were everywhere and he had any intellectuals massacred if they dared disagree with his line.' This comment, from a secondary school teacher in Gulja, was quite typical of what I heard during a visit to Xinjiang in October 1994.[22]

The second negative factor was that Sheng's policy, which was aimed at ethnic unity, appears to have had precisely the opposite effect. The Uygurs and others saw his propaganda and education as being aimed against them and saw no breadth of mind in the recognition he claimed to accord their different cultures. If anything, Sheng's policies inflamed rather than cooled down ethnic tensions in Xinjiang.[23]

Third, the Han remained more likely to attend school than most of the Islamic nationalities. Figures from 1942 show that the number of Uygurs in Xinjiang schools was 202 608, or 6.9 per cent of the total Uygur population, with Kazaks at 26 298 (7.6 per cent), Kirgiz at 2493 (3.8 per cent), Uzbeks at 1037 (13 per cent) and Tajiks at 229 (2.6 per cent), while the number of Han students was 24 250, or 12 per cent of the Han population.[24]

Islamic education among the Hui of Ningxia generally followed age-old practice, meaning that the mosques provided religious instruction to the male devotees, both boys and men. The principle was 'dual emphasis on moral character and learning' (*pinxue jianzhong*), the classes including worship, fear and respect for God and instruction in the *Koran*. Classes were not free: payment came from the relevant locality itself, and boys gave their teachers a monthly offering of grain or some other product, rather than money.[25]

Some pioneering work in the field of Hui educational reform was done by Wang Haoran (1848–1918). When he returned to China from study in Islamic countries in Southwestern Asia in 1908, he was accompanied by two Turkish scholars and quickly set up schools which departed from Chinese Islamic traditions. The first was a teachers' school in Beijing, which used both Chinese and Arabic, and the second, set up in 1909, a primary school for Muslim children, in which studies extended beyond the purely religious. Although other Muslim groups followed suit with schools reformist by the standards of that time, the total number of Islamic high schools in all China had reached only eleven by 1936, while in 1948 there were only 570 Muslim students in higher educational institutions. The Islamic Theological College, the only one of its kind, was opened in the Chongqing Mosque in 1945.[26] Most education of Hui people in the first half of the twentieth century belonged in the state sector discussed below.

The Bai

The Bai people, centred in Dali of western Yunnan province, are representative of the nationalities which by the early years of the twentieth century were already highly integrated with, and heavily influenced by, the Han. Their educational tradition in the twentieth century could easily be that of a Han community.

In Dali, the practice was for academies (*shuyuan*) to be set up in the prefectural and county towns, while the market towns and villages had *sishu*, which were the traditional private schools found all over China. These academies and schools taught mainly the Confucian classics and system of ethics. After the reform of 1898, a few modern primary and secondary schools were set up, the curricula of which included some scientific knowledge. Primary schools became popularised in every county. In the early years of the Republic there was a secondary school in Dali with five classes and over 500 students.[27]

Meanwhile, Protestant and Catholic missionaries set up their own schools, which charged low tuition fees or none at all. By government order from 1925 on, it was forbidden to make religious subjects compulsory, or to undertake study of religious propaganda in class.[28] This did not prevent strong attempts to use the schools for Christian missionary purposes, despite the heavy antagonism the various forms of Christianity felt for one another. The leaders of the schools were all foreign missionaries, while any Chinese who taught had first to become a Christian.[29]

C.P. Fitzgerald found two kinds of schools among the Bai: urban, maintained by the provincial and local government; and village schools run by the villagers themselves. The first type will be briefly considered in the section on the National Government below. For the peasants, it was the village school that mattered. It used the local ancestral temple for classes and village public lands provided the revenue which maintained it. In wealthy villages, tuition was often free or very cheap. The curriculum was dominated by instruction in reading and writing the Chinese language, but supplemented by elementary geography, arithmetic and Chinese history, as well as the outlines of anatomy and physiology, with the aim of improving public health and eliminating superstition. Although these schools were not government-run, political propaganda on behalf of the Nationalist Party was compulsory, the reason for this being to arouse patriotism and national consciousness or identity. A maximum period of study would see a child begin school at the age of 7 and leave at 14.[30]

The national consciousness imparted by the village schools was clearly Chinese, not Bai. This fact, together with the domination of the curriculum by the Chinese language, suggests very strongly that the Dali village schools were instruments of integration and Chinese national unity as far as the government was concerned. The Confucian system of instruction was undergoing substantial change: there was still a strong ethical emphasis, but Confucian ethics were yielding to the Three Principles of the People. Fitzgerald claims that 'the old methods of memorising Chinese classics' were giving way to more modern methods of teaching,[31] in which learning the classics by rote did not matter so much. The instruction in physiology in the interests of public health is yet another factor suggesting that these private village schools had changed quite a bit in the direction of modernity since the beginning of the twentieth century.

The Koreans

The Koreans represent the highly literate Confucianised nationality, the great majority of whom live in their own state, not in China. Among the nationalities singled out here for special attention, they were the only one seriously affected by the Japanese invasion. Not only was Korea itself a Japanese colony from 1910 to 1945, but the threat and reality of Japanese subjugation, as well as the struggle against it, loomed very large in the education of the Koreans of northeast China over the whole of the first half of the twentieth century until Japan's defeat in World War II.

In the late nineteenth century, most of the Koreans in Yanbian had been initially either refugees from their own country or those refugees' children. Since the Qing government did not formally relax its policy of excluding all but Manchus from the Yanbian area until the 1880s, no traditional educational infrastructure, either Korean or Chinese, existed in Yanbian before the 1880s. As the twentieth century dawned, there was a limited number of traditional Confucian schools and academies, but virtually nothing else.

The period from 1900 to the Japanese occupation of Manchuria in 1931 saw the continuation of the traditional institutions and the emergence of four new kinds of school in the Yanbian area. The first was the modern scientifically based school organised by Koreans themselves. The earliest of these, in Longjing, dates from 1906. They became fairly numerous and influential in the following years, becoming known as centres of progressive activities and ideas.[32]

The Korean schools were also noted for their hostility to the Japanese and their desire to keep Korean culture strong in the face of onslaught from Japan. Students and teachers took the lead and were the backbone among the 20 000 participants at an important mass meeting which took place on 13 March 1919 in support of Korean independence, a function supporting the March First Independence Movement which had just begun in Seoul. The mass meeting was followed by a large demonstration led by 320 school students and teachers. The Japanese suppressed the demonstration, killing thirteen people and wounding over 30 others, six of them so seriously that they later died. Most of the casualties were students.[33] When Japanese troops occupied Yanbian late in 1920, they attacked the Korean schools and destroyed some of them. This did not prevent a further growth of Korean schools in the following years, both at primary and secondary levels. By 1927, there were 191 schools run by Koreans, with a total of 7895 students.[34] Clearly the impact of these schools favoured Korean national identity and culture and strongly opposed the integration of the Koreans into the Japanese empire.

The second kind of school was that run by the Japanese. The first was the Kando Central School opened in Longjing in 1908. Just after the March First Movement of 1919 in Korea itself, the Japanese changed their policy away from direct military rule towards trying to strengthen their hold through cultural means. They set up schools in which the curricula glorified the Japanese Empire and subverted Korean nationalism.[35] The same approach was followed in Yanbian. Through extensive subsidies, they were even able to take over some of the Korean schools and change them from centres resisting the Japanese empire to those advocating it.

The last two kinds of school to develop in the first three decades of the twentieth century were the public schools run by the warlord governments and those by Protestant and Catholic missionaries from North America and Western Europe. Both of these enjoyed some currency as modernising agents, even though more in the interests of foreign powers than of the Koreans. In statistical terms, the public schools were at a clear advantage. In 1928 the number of Korean students attending them was 7529, while in 1932 the sixteen missionary schools enrolled 1526 Koreans.[36]

With the establishment of the Japanese puppet state of Manchoukuo in 1932, the new rulers simply took over the Korean schools. They forced Korean schools in Yanbian to use textbooks only in Japanese, not allowing the use of those in Korean.[37] The curricula were designed to promote the Japanese empire and the 'fusion of Japan and Korea into one entity', among other similar slogans. Japanese officers or their collaborators were sent to the schools to train the students in the Japanese military ways and values. In January 1939, the Japanese got the Manchoukuoan government to issue a proclamation compelling Korean students to substitute Japanese names for their original Korean ones. Those who dared to refuse were excluded from attending school.[38]

Many Koreans protested as vigorously as they could. The resistance, including that organised by the Chinese Communist Party (CCP), did what it could to compile its own teaching material and organise makeshift classes and schools which used Korean as the language of instruction, and in as many ways as possible kept Korean culture alive. The target students were not only children, but grown workers, peasants and anybody who could be reached.[39] Even in the Japanese-controlled schools there were those who refused to accept subjugation. In June 1939, students at a senior school in Longjing held a seven-day strike in protest against the Japanese education system imposed on them.[40]

The Japanese occupation aimed to crush Korean identity and integrate the Koreans of Manchuria — but into the Japanese empire, not into China. It failed on both counts. If pride in one's own nationality's history and culture, and hostility and hatred of 'otherness' are manifestations of identity, as suggested in the Introduction, then the Japanese appear to have produced precisely the opposite effect to the one intended — namely, to have provoked a feeling of national consciousness stronger than the one existing beforehand. On the other hand, Japanese influence and then occupation did have a progressive impact on the Koreans of Jilin in the sense that it uprooted traditional techniques of education and attitudes towards it, as well as provoking a greater desire for literacy, numeracy and the kind of knowledge useful in the modern world.

At the end of the war, Soviet troops occupied China's northeast and the CCP was able to take over Yanbian. It immediately abolished the Japanese schools and instituted its own policies, including encouraging the use of Korean as the language of instruction and the revival of Korean culture. It also tried to increase the number of schools at all levels in order to improve literacy, numeracy and the level of general knowledge of the people, as well as to instil its own values into the people. In April 1949, the Yanbian University was set up in Yanji, at that time using Korean as the medium of instruction. At the time of the proclamation of the People's Republic in October 1949 there were in Yanbian 31 secondary schools with 13 797 students and 647 primary schools with 129 800 students,[41] making the Koreans the best provided with educational facilities among China's minorities.

The National Government

Chiang Kai-shek's National Government did not exercise effective authority in all parts of China. Over the nationalities discussed above, it had either limited or no control for most of the period it held power. Yet it can reasonably claim to have been the first government in Chinese history to develop a formal and ostensibly nationwide education system for the minority nationalities.

On 17 June 1929, the Guomindang's Third Central Executive Committee took several decisions concerning the education of the minorities.[42] Apart from determining a budget for Mongol and Tibetan education, it set up the Mongol and Tibetan School in Nanjing, which was aimed to attract good young people from among the Mongols and Tibetans to Nanjing for training, and to research Mongol and Tibetan matters.[43] Most important of all, the Central Executive Committee decided that the Ministry of Education should establish a Mongol and Tibetan Education Section (*Mengzang jiaoyu si*). Shortly afterwards, the Ministry revised its 'Organic Law', first adopted in December 1928, to take account of the new Section, which was formally established in February 1930. Its functions concerned the furthering of education in the Mongol and Tibetan areas, including the training of Mongol and Tibetan teachers, and the instruction of the children of those two nationalities, and in addition covered 'other border education'.[44] In other words, although termed Mongol and Tibetan, the new section was actually intended to deal with the education of all the minority nationalities.

In 1929 the National Government set down some aims of Chinese education in general and on 1 June 1931 followed them up with a series of twelve educational guiding principles, of which the first was that 'the Three Principles of the People are the basis for the education of the Republic of China'.[45] In September 1931, the Guomindang's Central Executive Committee adopted a document on 'adopting the Three Principles of the People in Education', which included a section on 'Mongol and Tibetan education' — that is, education among the minorities. The section laid down three guiding principles of education as follows:

1 In obedience to the educational aims of the Republic of China and their principles of implementation, we must do all we can to popularise and develop Mongol and Tibetan education.
2 We must, according to their particular environments, try to raise the level of knowledge of the Mongol and Tibetan peoples and improve their livelihood; and pay attention to fostering their national consciousness, to training their capacities to practise autonomy, and to enhancing their production skills.
3 In obedience to Sun Yat-sen's principle of the equality among nationalities, we must use the power of education to strive for the unification of language and unity of purpose of the Mongol and Tibetan peoples, so as arrive at the achievement of a great nationalist country of the Republic of Five Nationalities.[46]

The section on Mongol and Tibetan education also had comments to make about the language of instruction and curricula. In practical terms, 'striving for the unification of language and unity of purpose of the Mongol and Tibetan peoples' meant that in textbooks for primary schools the Mongolian or Tibetan languages should be used alongside the Chinese, but in those for the secondary and higher levels only Chinese should be used. Teaching materials at all levels of the education system should take note of the history of the Chinese nation's amalgamation (*ronghe*) and the relationship between the geography of the border areas and 'inner regions' (*neidi*).[47]

Clearly, the National Government intended that the education system should contribute towards its general aims of development. In particular, education should assist the government to strengthen its tutelage and control over the minorities in the interests of national unity, but at the same time respect some of the main features of the minorities which differentiated them from the Han. The government wanted to integrate the minorities with the Han and into the Chinese state. Its education system certainly did not aim to foster the national identities of particular nationalities, but instead that of the Chinese nation as a whole.

After the 1945 victory in the War of Resistance against Japan, the Mongol and Tibetan Education Section was renamed the Office of Border Education (*Bianjiang jiaoyu si*) and the various educational bodies within the Mongolian and Tibetan Affairs Commission were reallocated to it.[48] Just as with its predecessor, the areas which came under the jurisdiction of this Office were 'all the border regions of China inhabited by tribespeople including Mongols, Tibetans, Mohammedans, Miaos, Lolos and other tribes',[49] not just Mongolia and Tibet.

The coherent ideas of the National Government on minority education were quite slow to express themselves in extensive action. It was not until the period of the war against Japan that more than halting measures were taken towards actually setting up a government educational structure among the minorities. A scholar of the People's Republic has claimed that 'in the modern educational history of the Tibetans, the period of the War of Resistance against Japan was the fastest for the development of the education of the Tibetans, as well as the period when it became to develop comprehensively'.[50] The same would hold true for most other minorities. It was in November 1941 that the Guomindang's National Government announced a comprehensive strategy for education among the minorities. The Ministry of Education called it 'the most important recent code of rules for border education'.[51]

It is well known that the war against Japan exercised a generally demoralising effect on the Guomindang government. However, in the field of education it had the effect of forcing some useful and effective measures. This was the case not only among the minorities, but generally throughout China as well. One sign was that the expansion of education into the remote villages of the interior, which had been planned for a long time, actually became a reality.[52]

Beginning from January 1940, or before the comprehensive strategy was completed, the National Government began setting up a 'national' education structure among the minorities. Ironically, it began in Tibet, where the local authorities were not even sure that they were part of China. It took over the Lhasa Municipal First Primary School and changed its name to the Tibetan Lhasa Primary School. By the end of 1947 there were just sixteen national primary schools in the nationality areas, virtually all of them headed by Han principals. Of these sixteen, eight were in Suiyuan, two in Ningxia, three in Xikang, and one in each of Tibet, Sichuan and Qinghai. Another six schools had been opened but were forced to close down, while a second was in preparation in Tibet. Those closed down included one in each of Guizhou and Yunnan, which were not represented at all among the sixteen schools. The total number of students at the sixteen schools was 2143, with 162 teachers and administrative staff.[53]

The rules of these schools were the same as elsewhere in China, but there were some special features due to the fact that they were in nationality areas and intended for minority students. Some of these features were laid down by a regulation promulgated on 3 September 1945. For example, all classes must accept students of any nationality and holidays and summer and winter vacations must follow local custom, as long as the number of teaching days did not fall below 295 per year.[54]

Following the principles of September 1931, these primary schools were supposed to use both the local language and Chinese as mediums of instruction. To cope with this plan, the Ministry of Education began in 1932 to create general knowledge textbooks in various languages, including Mongolian and Tibetan. The content was determined by the Ministry itself and was the same as that found elsewhere in China. For example, according to an official publication, 'speeches made by high government officials' were translated into various languages, such as Mongolian and Tibetan, and printed in the minority language side by side with Chinese,[55] indicating that the National Government placed a high priority on spreading its own propaganda through the liberal policy of using minority languages in primary schools. In 1947 books were issued containing some material, such as pictures, which was specific to the particular nationalities.[56] Despite such good intentions, one observer reported from the Xikang capital Kangding in July 1948 that 'all school classes in Tibetan areas, as elsewhere, are conducted in Chinese', suggesting that the plan to use minority languages in class had failed.[57]

In addition to the national primary schools, there was also a national structure of secondary, vocational, technical and normal (or teacher-training) schools. As of 1947, there were twelve institutions in this last category, with a total of 2777 students. Apart from a Mongol school in Suiyuan, which lasted only fourteen months, the first to be set up was the National Southwest Normal School in Zhaotong, Yunnan province, in September 1939.[58]

Another achievement of the war years which is well worth mentioning was the establishment of province-level schools for the minorities. In 1943, the Ministry adopted a three-year plan to set up many province-level schools over the years 1944–46. There had been a limited number before this time but, apart from in Xinjiang, very few indeed before the war broke out in 1937. The provinces involved included Jehol, Chahar, Suiyuan, Gansu, Qinghai, Xinjiang, Sichuan, Xikang, Yunnan, Guizhou and Guangxi. So although there were Tibetan areas included, Tibet itself was not one of them.

The province with the most extensive educational facilities was Xinjiang. In 1944 Sheng Shicai fell from power, and the National Government moved in. During his last years, Sheng had actually fluctuated violently in his attitude to the Soviets, and the National Government's policy towards them was ambivalent. In any case, it left the Xinjiang educational system essentially in place but carried out some alterations it believed necessary. It made some changes in the structure to accord with its own system, introduced textbooks used elsewhere in China, strengthened the examination system and, according to its own version, 'honoured the local culture and as appropriate increased the teaching time allocated to the *Koran*'.[59] Sheng had prided himself on honouring the local culture, but made no bones about his negative attitude towards the *Koran*. The National Government also sent some teachers to Xinjiang from other Chinese provinces. According to 1945 figures, the number of students at primary and secondary level had risen since 1942. The average number of class levels per school was 5.8 and of students 129, probably rather similar to the situation prevailing under Sheng Shicai.[60]

Apart from Xinjiang, the best-supplied province was Gansu: by 1947 there were about 130 primary schools there with more than 7200 students and over 310 teachers.[61] The figures show an average of about 55 students and nearly 2.5 teachers per school — in other words, the overwhelming majority were very small, and many had only one grade, which made it very difficult for students to stay for more than one year.

The contrast with Xinjiang in the average number of class grades and students per school is very striking indeed. It reflects very well on the efforts Sheng Shicai made towards spreading basic literacy and numeracy in Xinjiang, since a student who stays at school five or six years is much more likely to gain a lasting and useful education than one who leaves after completing only one or two grades. It is quite possible for a literate person to retreat into illiteracy, if the reading and writing skills are not properly grounded or consolidated.

The fact that the government spread educational facilities among the minorities did not mean that they were necessarily welcomed. Referring to Ningxia in 1948, a Hui writer drew attention to 'the Muslim psychology of opposition to reading "Han books"'.[62] One observer in Kangding in mid-1948 wrote somewhat more strongly about the Tibetans:

> In the case of the Tibetans, for example, there is passive resistance to the government's education policy . . . Although there are a few Chinese-educated Tibetan teachers, and a few of mixed Chinese–Tibetan blood, by far the majority are Chinese. According to Tibetans with whom I talked, their main objection is not to the language, however, but to the simple fact that they are forced to send their children to Chinese schools. They feel that a formal education is a useless waste of time and of no conceivable use to them . . . Education is looked upon as an onerous obligation to be avoided if possible, and the practice of paying substitutes to go to school in place of one's own children is said to be prevalent.[63]

Governmental attempts at the integration of China as a nation and of the minorities with the Han do not appear to have been particularly successful. Whether the feelings of identity of the Hui or Tibetans actually strengthened is doubtful, but nor do they seem to have weakened much.

The fact that the schools were government-run did not make them available to all. The government schools among the Bai of Dali serve as an example. Both primary and secondary levels charged fees, and although the former were well attended, only the wealthy could afford to educate their children to secondary level.[64] Apart from tuition fees, there were various kinds of other charges to be covered as well, such as book fees, physical exercise fees, medical fees and 'respect the teacher fees'. The breakdown of the family background of students at the Dali Girls' Secondary School was: landlord, 30 per cent; business, 33.4 per cent; military and political, 23 per cent; workers and peasants, 7.1 per cent; and others, 6.5 per cent. There were altogether 1340 graduates of the Heqing Secondary School from 1926 to 1949, of whom 80 to 90 per cent were the children of landlords, rich peasants or capitalists.[65]

Girls and education

In China as a whole, there was a quite clear rise in female participation in the education system during the period of the Republic. This was an important achievement, considering that education for girls was in its infancy in 1912, except for some Christian missionary girls' schools.[66] Although much less pronounced than among the Han, the trend towards more female participation in education extended also towards many of the minorities.

In general, Christian missionaries were at the forefront of pressing for and implementing education for girls. The Protestant and Catholic churches ran special schools for girls, many of them in the minority areas, with the numbers increasing substantially during the Republican period. There were even coeducational schools in some minority areas run by missionaries. In the Tibetan areas, two examples were the Boys' and Girls' Schools of Rongzha and Dawu, both in Xikang province.[67] Just as with other missionary schools, those teaching minority girls placed some emphasis on spreading Christianity and were not interested in promoting ethnic identities, but did play a modernising role.

Governments were generally willing to encourage education for girls, albeit of a very conservative kind. The policy of Chiang Kai-shek's National Government on education for girls was spelt out in April 1929 and applied to all the nationalities. It declared that opportunities in education should be equal for both males and females, but that for girls it should stress 'preserving the special qualities of motherhood' as well as improving family and social life.[68] In Japanese-occupied Manchoukuo policy dictated that 'the fair sex' should 'be taught to become first and foremost good wives and good mothers by giving them practical training while fostering in them the virtues for which Oriental women are noted'.[69] Although the emphasis for both governments reflected a strong Confucian influence, very few indeed of the minorities were likely to be offended by the ideas expressed.

In practice, girls received very little education among most of the minorities, even from the 1920s to the 1940s. In the country as a whole, minority girls were evidently even less well represented in the education system than their Han counterparts.[70] In Manchoukuo in the mid-1930s, there were hardly any government girls' schools in the Korean province of Jiandao or the Mongol Xing'an provinces, even though a few such schools had been set up in the Japanese client state as a whole.[71]

A few specific points about female education are worth noting. The Turkish initiative in education, which was felt in Xinjiang in the early Republican period and was noted in an earlier section, included the setting up of a school for girls in Kaxgar. The objective was to increase women's interest in social and political matters, with reading, writing, sewing and singing in the curriculum.[72] Non-government Korean schools in Jiandao province were in the forefront of the movement to educate girls. In the second decade of the century, Korean schools especially for girls were established in Yanji, Longjing and other towns, bringing girls up to about 5 per cent of all students.[73] The Korean hunger for education at that time, and in the succeeding decades, was mainly a male phenomenon, yet Korean women were probably keener to study in the period of Japanese domination than those of most nationalities.[74]

Among the Confucianised Bai of Dali, female education dates mainly from the May Fourth Movement of 1919.[75] For the peasants, the village schools were paramount and by the late 1930s they were attended by about 70 per cent of the boys and 30 per cent of the girls in the villages of Dali.[76] This was a surprisingly high proportion of the girls, considering that the national proportion of female students to the total number at primary level in the late 1930s was about 20 per cent,[77] but it must be remembered that not only did far fewer girls go to school than boys, but they stayed there for much shorter periods.

The progress towards education for girls was thus both very halting and uneven, but considering the background this was clearly an area of change and progress in the first half of the twentieth century. Opportunities for female education among the minorities were meagre in 1949, but considerably better than they had been in 1912. Among the great majority of minorities, credit for this result was due mainly to the Chinese state education system and to foreign Christian missionaries.

Conclusion

The period of the Republic may have seen the decline of old education systems, but certainly not their destruction. On the other hand, it did preside over at least the beginnings of new systems and structures among virtually all the minorities. At first the religions succeeded in impeding the growth of the new education systems, as happened in Xinjiang and some other places. However, the various attempts to establish state-run systems did eventually bear some fruit. Ironically, for most of the minorities, the years of the war against Japan were the period of greatest success in spreading education and literacy among most of the minority peoples, just as they were in China as a whole.

Comparing the Koreans and Tibetans, we find very important contrasts in the areas of concern to this chapter. The Koreans were enormously affected by the Japanese invasion; the Tibetans hardly at all. At the same time, the Korean education system was greatly transformed, while that of the Tibetans was considerably less affected, especially in the Tibetan heartland where change was probably slighter than among any other of the more populous nationalities. In this light it may not be surprising that the Tibetans proved resistant to what little communist influence came their way, whereas the Koreans were, of all minorities, the ones to give greatest support to the CCP.

In most cases, such change as occurred was due more to pressures from outside the minorities than within. It was the intervention of various Han Chinese governments, especially that of Chiang Kai-shek, and of the Japanese, which occasioned the substantial changes in the education systems. Among some minorities, especially the Koreans, there were significant forces at work within the nationalities themselves which favoured change, but these were the exception rather than the norm.

The various governments that ruled China between 1912 and 1949 faced insuperable problems in their attempts to modernise China and integrate its various peoples into a unity. Most of them tried to use education to those ends. None was nearly as successful as it wanted to be. But, with the major exception of Tibet, the local power-holders among the minorities exercised slighter authority over their own peoples in 1949 than they had done in 1912. And education was one important factor in bringing about this change.

Notes

1 Ding Zhipin, *Zhongguo jin qishi nian lai jiaoyu jishi*, Guoli bianyi guan, Nanjing, 1933, p. 25.

2 Zhu Jielin, *Zangzu jinxiandai jiaoyu shilüe*, Qinghai Renmin chubanshe, Xining, 1990, p. 2.

3 Tashi Dorjee, trans. K. Dhondup, 'Education in Tibet', *The Tibet Journal*, vol. 2, no. 4, Winter 1977, p. 32.

4 Zhu, *Zangzu jinxiandai jiaoyu shilüe*, pp. 19–20.

5 Dorjee, 'Education in Tibet', p. 37.

6 Thubten Jigme Norbu and Colin M. Turnbull, *Tibet, Its History, Religion and People*, Chatto & Windus, London, 1969; Penguin, Harmondsworth, 1987, p. 322.

7 H.E. Richardson, *A Short History of Tibet*, E.P. Dutton, New York, 1962, p. 130.

8 Norbu and Turnbull, *Tibet*, p. 30.

9 ibid., p. 335.

10 Zhu, *Zangzu jinxiandai jiaoyu shilüe*, pp. 50–54.

11 ibid., pp. 116–17.

12 P.T. Etherton, *In the Heart of Asia*, Houghton Mifflin, Boston and New York, 1926, p. 77.

13 Cyril E. Black, Louis Dupree et al., *The Modernization of Inner Asia*, M.E. Sharpe, Armonk, New York and London, 1991, pp. 149–50.

14 C.P. Skrine and Pamela Nightingale, *Macartney at Kashgar, New Light on British, Chinese, and Russian Activities in Sinkiang, 1890–1918*, Methuen, London, 1973; Oxford University Press, Hong Kong, Oxford, 1987, p. 162.

15 Etherton, *In the Heart of Asia*, p. 78.

16 See Andrew D.W. Forbes, *Warlords and Muslims in Chinese Central Asia, A Political History of Republican Sinkiang 1911–1949*, Cambridge University Press, Cambridge, 1986, p. 18.

17 Xinjiang Social Sciences Academy's Nationalities Research Institute, *Xinjiang jianshi, dier ce*, Xinjiang Renmin chubanshe, Ürümqi, 1980, p. 392.

18 *Dierci Zhongguo jiaoyu nianjian*, Ministry of Education, Nanjing, 1948, vol. 4, p. 1245.

19 See Forbes, *Warlords and Muslims*, p. 137.

20 See Fu Xiruo, 'Lun Xinjiang sheng jiaoyu', in Gansu Provincial Library Bibliography Department, comp., *Xibei minzu zongjiao shiliao wenzhai (Xinjiang fence)*, Gansu sheng tushuguan, Lanzhou, 1985, vol. 2, p. 952. The article is abstracted from *Xibei luntan*, vol. 1, no. 5, 1948.

21 The figures are from Fu, 'Lun Xinjiang sheng jiaoyu', p. 951 and, for those for the end of 1942, *Dierci Zhongguo jiaoyu nianjian*, vol. 4, p. 1245.

22 See also the view of Sheng Shicai put forward in the secondary schools and higher in the 1990s in Xinjiang Uygur Autonomous Region Education Commission Higher Education History Teaching Material Compilation Group, *Xinjiang difang shi*, Xinjiang daxue chubanshe, Ürümqi, 1992, pp. 271–83, 297–98, 305. This view is quite positive about Sheng in his early years of rule but savagely critical of his actions in the period from 1937 to 1942, when among other crimes he arrested and killed progressive personalities, and destroyed the anti-Japanese national united front, p. 305.

23 For example, see Fu, 'Lun Xinjiang sheng jiaoyu', p. 955.

24 For these figures and proportions, see ibid., p. 954. The population of Xinjiang and the ethnic breakdown in the early 1940s are discussed in Colin Mackerras, *China's Minorities, Integration and Modernization in the Twentieth Century*, Oxford University Press, Hong Kong, 1994, pp. 124–26, the proportions of the total ethnic populations given by Fu tallying very well with other available data noted there.

25 Ma Fulong, 'Yisilan zai Ningxia', in Gansu Provincial Library Bibliography Department, comp., *Xibei minzu zongjiao shiliao wenzhai, Ningxia fence*, Gansu sheng tushuguan, Lanzhou, 1986, pp. 222–23.

26 Wing-tsit Chan, *Religious Trends in Modern China*, Columbia University Press, New York, 1953; Octagon Books, New York, 1969, pp. 198–202.

27 Yunnan Provincial Editorial Committee of the *Five Series on Nationalities Problems* (ed.), *Baizu shehui lishi diaocha*, Yunnan Renmin chubanshe, Kunming, 1983, p. 215.

28 Colin Mackerras, 'Education in the Guomindang Period, 1928–1949', in David Pong and Edmund S.K. Fung (eds), *Ideal and Reality, Social and*

Political Change in Modern China, 1860–1949, University Press of America, Lanham, New York, London, 1985, pp. 164–65, 182.

29 *Baizu shehui lishi diaocha*, p. 214.

30 C.P. Fitzgerald, *The Tower of Five Glories, A Study of the Min Chia of Ta Li, Yunnan*, The Cresset Press, London, 1941; Hyperion Press, Westport, Connecticut, 1973, p. 84.

31 ibid.

32 *Brief History of the Koreans* Compilation Group, *Chaoxian zu jianshi*, Yanbian Renmin chubanshe, Yanji, 1986, pp. 192–93.

33 Jin Donghe, *Yanbian qingnian yundong shi*, Yanbian Renmin chubanshe, Yanji, 1989, p. 249.

34 *Chaoxian zu jianshi*, p. 194.

35 See Han Woo-keun, trans. Lee Kyung-shik, *The History of Korea*, Eulyoo Publishing Company, Seoul, 1970; 1981, p. 480.

36 *Chaoxian zu jianshi*, pp. 194–96.

37 *General Account of the Yanbian Korean Autonomous Prefecture* Compilation Group, *Yanbian Chaoxian zu zizhi zhou gaikuang*, Yanbian Renmin chubanshe, Yanji, 1984, p. 50.

38 Jin, *Yanbian qingnian yundong shi*, p. 90.

39 *Chaoxian zu jianshi*, pp. 198–200.

40 Jin, *Yanbian qingnian yundong shi*, p. 267.

41 Bernard Vincent Olivier, *The Implementation of China's Nationality Policy in the Northeastern Provinces*, Mellen Research University Press, San Francisco, 1993, p. 91.

42 Ding, *Zhongguo jin qishi nian lai jiaoyu jishi*, p. 193.

43 Zhu, *Zangzu jinxiandai jiaoyu shilüe*, p. 134.

44 Ministry of Education Advisers' Room, *Jiaoyu faling*, Jiaoyu bu, Chongjing, Nanjing, 1946, p. 2; *Dierci Zhongguo jiaoyu nianjian*, vol. 4, p. 1214.

45 *Jiaoyu faling*, p. 33. See also Mackerras, 'Education in the Guomindang Period', pp. 155–56.

46 *Dierci Zhongguo jiaoyu nianjian*, vol. 4, p. 1211.

47 Border Education Section of the Ministry of Education, *Bianjiang jiaoyu gaikuang*, Jiaoyu bu Bianjiang jiaoyu si, Chongqing, 1943, p. 149.

48 Wulanshaobu, 'Zhongguo Guomindang de dui Meng zhengce, 1928–1949', in CCP Inner Mongolian Regional Party History Research Institute of the Inner Mongolian University and Inner Mongolian Recent and Modern History Research Institute of the Inner Mongolian University (eds), *Nei Menggu jindai shi luncong, di sanji*, Nei Menggu Renmin chubanshe, Huhhot, 1987, pp. 208–9.

49 *China Handbook, 1937–1944, A Comprehensive Survey of Major Developments in China in Seven Years of War*, Chinese Ministry of Information, Chungking, 1944, p. 245.

50 Zhu, *Zangzu jinxiandai jiaoyu shilüe*, p. 130.

51 *Dierci Zhongguo jiaoyu nianjian*, vol. 4, p. 1211.

52 See Mackerras, 'Education in the Guomindang Period', pp. 173–77.

53 *Dierci Zhongguo jiaoyu nianjian*, vol. 4, pp. 1222–23.

54 *Jiaoyu faling*, p. 663.

55 *China Handbook, 1937–1944*, p. 246.

56 *Dierci Zhongguo jiaoyu nianjian*, vol. 4, pp. 1221–22.

57 A. Doak Barnett, *China on the Eve of Communist Takeover*, Frederick A. Praeger, New York, 1963, p. 225.

58 *Dierci Zhongguo jiaoyu nianjian*, vol. 4, pp. 1229–30.

59 ibid., p. 1245.

60 ibid.

61 ibid., pp. 1237–51.

62 Ma, 'Yisilan zai Ningxia', p. 224.

63 Barnett, *China on the Eve of Communist Takeover*, p. 225.

64 Fitzgerald, *The Tower of Five Glories*, p. 83.

65 *Baizu shehui lishi diaocha*, p. 216.

66 See Mackerras, 'Education in the Guomindang Period', pp. 170–73. The Qing Ministry of Education's first encouragement of female education at government level was in August 1906. On 24 January 1907 it adopted sets of regulations for the running of primary and teacher-training schools for girls. See also Ding, *Zhongguo jin qishi nian lai jiaoyu jishi*, p. 21.

67 Zhu, *Zangzu jinxiandai jiaoyu shilüe*, p. 117.

68 *Jiaoyu faling*, p. 34.

69 *The Japan–Manchoukuo Year Book 1939, Cyclopedia of General Information and Statistics on the Empires of Japan and Manchoukuo*, The Japan–Manchoukuo Year Book Co., Tokyo, p. 674.

70 National figures show that the proportion of girls in primary schools rose from over 6 per cent in the early 1920s to 25.57 per cent in 1945. See Mackerras, 'Education in the Guomindang Period', p. 171. Overall figures specifying minority female participation in education are rare. Figures for 1941 by province covering examinees and enrolled students at training college level and above are given in *Dierci Zhongguo jiaoyu nianjian*, vol. 4, p. 1420. Provinces with serious under-representation of females include Suiyuan, Xinjiang, Gansu, Ningxia and Shaanxi in the north and Xikang, Yunnan and Guizhou in the south — almost all of them provinces with concentrations of minorities. Unfortunately, the specific nationality of the females concerned is not given.

71 See the figures in *The Japan–Manchoukuo Year Book 1939*, p. 674.

72 Etherton, *In the Heart of Asia*, p. 79.

73 *Chaoxian zu jianshi*, p. 193.

74 Interview with Professor Pak Changuk of Yanbian University, 6 October 1990.

75 *Baizu shehui lishi diaocha*, p. 215.

76 Fitzgerald, *The Tower of Five Glories*, p. 84.

77 *Dierci Zhongguo jiaoyu nianjian*,vol. 4, p. 1457.

4 Marriage and Divorce: Some Gender Issues Pre-1949

Although previous chapters have taken up gender issues briefly, such as those involved in religion and education, this chapter gives them far greater emphasis. The main site of examination of these issues is in the family, with a special focus on marriage and divorce. The aim is to cast light on the extent to which gender issues related to a sense of ethnic identity. Did they strengthen the distinctiveness of the minorities? Did they assist or impede the integration of China as a nation-state, or of the nationalities with one another and with the Han?

The first half of the twentieth century was the period when demands for a slackening of the rigidity of family life and improvement in the livelihood of women were beginning to make themselves felt in China as a whole. The May Fourth Movement of 1919, with its emphasis on a new culture and hostility to Confucianism, was undoubtedly of great importance in pushing the early stages of family reform and shifts in gender relations. One of the signs that Chiang Kai-shek's government was keen to advocate a less restrictive family system and a better deal for women came at the end of 1930, when, as part of the Civil Code of the Republic of China, it promulgated new Succession and Family laws, both coming into effect on 5 May the following year.[1] Although these were far more liberal than anything which had preceded them, their impact was less than spectacular, and they continued to be widely flouted right down to the time the Guomindang fell. The government intended that the laws should cover all nationalities equally, yet it was more interested in the Han than any of the minorities, and the effect on the latter was even weaker than on the Han. In contrast to the situation with education, the impact of the government on gender issues among the nationalities was very weak indeed.

Family questions

In his classic anthropological introduction to the subject of kinship and marriage, Robin Fox suggests that in many societies, 'both primitive and sophisticated', relationships to ancestors and kin 'have been the pivots on which most interaction, most claims and obligations, most loyalties and sentiments, turned'.[2] This is most certainly so of the Han Chinese and the most Confucianised of China's minorities. For many centuries, Han Chinese society has been noted for its family-centredness, with an extreme importance laid on filial piety (xiao). In the ideology which the West has for long known as Confucianism, filial piety is possibly the most highly rated of all moral virtues. Fox further notes that the search for ancestry is primary in giving people 'roots', no matter what their society.[3] Given the importance of roots for identity, his comment surely suggests that matters relating to family are relevant in discussions of that topic.

As explained in the Introduction, there was a wide range of ways by which the minorities attempted to produce what they needed to survive. Even within this variety of production patterns, however, the patrilineal family remained the fundamental productive unit within the overwhelming majority of the minorities. In most cases, it was the nuclear family which was the basic social unit, but in others the extended family was more important from the point of view of production. An example of a minority in which the extended family was the primary social and economic unit was the Mongols, though each nuclear family occupied a separate tent. The way each minority produced what they needed to survive had some bearing on their family patterns.

Although families exist as an institution among all the nationalities of China, and indeed virtually all other peoples as well, the nature of the family and its relationship with marriage, sexual relations and giving birth to and socialising children is far from consistent among the various peoples. Among the Tibetans and several other minorities of China, sexual relationships were available outside marriage. Among the Mosuo people in the areas around the Lugu Lake, which straddles a small central western part of the border between Yunnan and Sichuan provinces,[4] the practice of persons of different sexes actually living together under the same roof in one or more sexual relationships was unknown. Much of the socialisation of Tibetan children took place within a neighbourhood of co-operating families, rather than within one family.[5]

One of the great points of division in the family systems of the nationalities in China in the first half of the twentieth century was that between the Confucianised peoples, such as the Bai, Zhuang or Koreans, and those with little impact from traditional Confucianism, such as the Tibetans and the Islamic minorities, which formed a separate and distinct group. In most cases, it was minorities with cultures and societies most strongly influenced by the Han which adopted Confucian beliefs and practices most readily, but there were exceptions to this pattern. Thus the Muslim Hui are closer to the Han culturally and socially than are the Confucian Koreans. There was a very definite stamp in the family systems of those nationalities which practised the typically Confucian ideology and practice of ancestor worship, and it did not apply to those, like the Tibetans and Muslim minorities, which did not do so. Islamic nationalities were firmly opposed to ancestor worship. Even the Hui, who emphasised filial piety, resisted the rites associated with ancestor worship.

For Muslims, the *Koran* is the revelation of the will of God, or Allah, to his messenger Muhammad. It is a work which has a good deal to say on matters concerning family, marriage and divorce. Yet, because it derives from the social customs and values of Arab society at the time of Muhammad's life (c. 570–632), it inevitably reflects that society. Muslim peoples around the world respect and attempt to follow the *Koran*, making it a substantial influence in their lives. However, they do not all interpret either Islam or the *Koran* in precisely the same way, since the Koranic influences cannot possibly be the only ones operating on them. Some currently Muslim nationalities came into existence before Islam itself, a prime example being the Arabs, while many adhered to other religions before being converted to Islam. The Uygurs embraced Manicheism in the eighth century, later abandoned it in favour of Buddhism and then, in a long process lasting several centuries from the tenth century on, were converted to Islam.

The present discussion of family issues focuses on marriage, arranging the topic by stage, and its possible aftermath, divorce. It begins with the prelude to marriage.

Finding a spouse

Courtship among most of the nationalities of Yunnan, Guizhou and Guangxi took place largely through gatherings on festival days, at which folk songs and music played an important role. The boys played reed-pipes (termed *lusheng* in Chinese) to girls dressed in their best clothes. It was essential that young people, either male or female, be good singers in order to be able to do well in the love stakes. Like many other southwestern nationalities, the Miao were relaxed in love matters, and the musical gatherings could lead to sexual relations.[6] Courtship through such gatherings initially implied that the young people chose their own partners, but in the course of time such freedom declined, due mainly to the influence of Confucianism. The Han Chinese, with their restrictive Confucianism, were generally horrified by the practices of the Miao and other minorities of the southwest, leading them to judgmental misinterpretations — for instance, confusing premarital sex with promiscuity and courtship through singing and dancing with orgies.[7]

Courtship for the Jingpo of Yunnan included communal houses, where young people would go, sing songs with each other and live together. However, in contrast to practice among other nationalities, the father of a resultant child did not necessarily marry the mother, but preferred to escape the obligation by the traditional sacrifice of a buffalo. Marriage itself was generally arranged by the parents. Another common type of marriage was by capture. At the behest of a man who was proposing such a marriage, the local sorcerer declared whether it would be propitious, and if the signs were positive everybody agreed, including the girl, so that the capture was really just a ceremony. But in many cases the girl, and even her parents, were kept in ignorance about the abduction until it actually took place.[8] Like the Jingpo, the Yi often practised marriage by capture, but by prearrangement, with the bride's relatives taking her to the appointed field, whence she could be taken away. The most prevalent form of Yi marriage was by arrangement through go-betweens.

Like many of the other minorities of the south and southwest, the Zhuang had once left the choice of marriage partner for their children to decide. However, from very early times, Han Confucian influence led to the introduction of the system of arranged marriages, and by the end of the Qing the old forms persisted only in remote mountain districts.[9] On the other hand, the Yao resisted Han influence more successfully so that, as late as the twentieth century, the great majority of marriages were not arranged by parents but determined by the young people themselves through courtship gatherings. The contrast between these two minorities in this matter is an example of the correlation between ways of finding a spouse on the one hand and the overall extent of integration on the other.

There were two ways leading to marriage among the Miao. One was the arranged marriage; the other was through the free choice of the partners themselves. Although the two forms coexisted, the arranged marriage system was more prevalent in some Miao areas than others, and had become considerably stronger during the Qing dynasty than the Ming, because of the strengthening influence of the Han people at that time. Miao areas where free marriage was most common included southeast, central and western Guizhou, as well as Yunnan.[10]

In the case of the arranged marriages, a normal process was for the man's parents to spot an appropriate girl at a reed-pipe gathering, then if they did not know the family to look into its circumstances; if all the indications were positive, a matchmaker would then undertake the necessary arrangements. In the case of the free marriages, the man would follow up his friendship at a reed-pipe gathering by going to his partner's village and calling her out for further courting by whistling. If all went well, he would later, after several meetings, go with some friends at night to the girl's house and take her to his own home. If the parents raised no objection, the young couple would regard them as having given consent. This was necessary whether the marriage was an arranged or free one.[11]

To a far greater extent than their Miao counterparts, the young of the nearby Shui minority of Guizhou and Guangxi depended on their parents and matchmakers to find them a marriage partner. The free love marriages which had prevailed during the Song dynasty were gradually replaced by the more restrictive system.[12] As in the case of the Miao, the reason for this was the growing impact of, and integration with, the Confucian Han. Although many young Shui men continued to look for partners at festivals or song gatherings, they usually tried to keep any further meetings secret from the girl's father and brothers. And even if the pair agreed to marry, they had to go through the ritual of matchmaker involvement and parental decision or face social condemnation.[13] It is not surprising that the clash between the freedom of the song gatherings and the restrictiveness of the arranged marriages often led to great anguish. We already saw in Chapter 2 that suicide pacts were frequent among the Naxi of Lijiang in Yunnan for this very reason.

Courtship gatherings were a feature of Bai society, but this did not mean that marriage was free. According to C.P. Fitzgerald, no Bai marriage was 'arranged by the free choice of the bride and groom . . . and consequently affection and companionship, though these may happily come after marriage, are not pre-determining reasons for a marriage'.[14] Despite Fitzgerald's optimistic tone, companionship and affection were not by any means invariable after marriage. The contradiction between the freedom of the courtship gatherings and the compulsion implied in arranged marriages created sharp social contradictions among the Bai — and indeed many other nationalities. One very prominent ethnologist of the People's Republic of China (PRC) claims quite plausibly that some women caught in the trap of unhappy arranged marriages 'had no recourse other than suicide',[15] but does not give any indication of how widespread such a tragedy might be.

Among the Islamic and the great majority of other minorities of the north and northwest, courtship was not a normal or expected part of finding a spouse, because of the tradition whereby parents arranged marriages with the aid of a matchmaker. As regards the Muslim minorities, arranged marriages were the norm among the Hui, Uygurs, Kazaks, Kirgiz and Uzbeks. Marriages were sometimes arranged many years before the wedding itself, while the bridal couple were still children or infants. Among the Kirgiz and a few others, it was possible to arrange a marriage even for an unborn foetus.[16]

The Koreans are an example of a Confucian minority. They were quite conscientious followers of the famous Southern Song dynasty Neo-Confucianist philosopher Zhu Xi (1130–1200), who laid down very conservative rules concerning the family. Young people married a spouse selected by their parents through a matchmaker without regard to their own opinions. These Confucian customs began to decline in the 1920s due to the 'cultural enlightenment movement' in Jiandao (Yanbian), but remained strong throughout the period of Japanese occupation.[17]

According to S.C. Das, an Indian traveller of the late nineteenth century, marriages in Tibet were at that time normally arranged through a matchmaker, with the man's parents taking the initiative.[18] Sir Charles Bell claims that in the 1920s a son was 'consulted by his father as to the bride proposed for him', but on the other hand, 'the parents consult a daughter hardly at all', suggesting that arranged marriages remained the norm, with the bride-groom having somewhat more say in the choice than his bride. However, Bell adds that gradually the strict rule forbidding marriage to be contract-ed in defiance of the parents' wishes was breaking down in his time, with more and more young men choosing their own brides. This freedom was commoner among the peasants and the traders than among the landed gen-try.[19] By the 1940s, there was evidently some change in the direction of free-choice marriage: Heinrich Harrer states that the young people chose their own spouses, irrespective of their parents.[20]

While PRC sources frequently acknowledge freedom of marriage among ordinary Tibetans in the past, they insist that this did not extend to the low-est classes. One Tibetan writer of the PRC has it that '[a]s chattels of their masters in the feudal-slave society, serfs' and slaves' marriages were decid-ed first and foremost by the feudal lord, and parents had only second say in the matter. The couple themselves, of course, had no choice.'[21] These var-ious accounts do not contradict each other, although they do present a some-what different slant, with Harrer's being, not surprisingly, more positive about old Tibetan society than those of the PRC writers.

The Tibetans of Qinghai followed a similar marriage system to that of the Tibetan heartland. A Han Chinese writer of the mid-1930s calls it 'rather free', implying a comparison with the Han but making no direct reference either to arranged marriages or to class variations. He adds, with obvious disapproval, that in Qinghai a Tibetan woman can live together with a man and even raise a family extramaritally, 'without consulting her father'.[22]

Mongol marriages were generally arranged by the parents, sometimes through the aid of a matchmaker. In one Mongol community in northern Manchuria in the early 1930s, the practice was for the boy's father to send a middleman, usually a close male relation of the boy, to the girl's family. He would give presents of food and drink and ascertain whether the girl's family was in favour of the match, but he did not discuss financial matters such as bride-price.[23] In another Mongol community in southern Chahar province, marriages were similarly arranged by the parents. One researcher found in about 1930 that 'informal child engagements were common and sometimes even unborn children were engaged: two pregnant women would agree to have their offspring marry each other if of opposite sex'.[24]

Marriage taboos

The wide range of processes by which China's peoples found spouses is matched by differences in taboos. Confucianism and Islam again turn out to be restrictive, which does not mean they have a monopoly on taboos.

The *Koran's* main proscription concerning marriage is that Muslims may not marry those who do not accept Islam: 'Do not marry Unbelieving women (idolaters), Until they believe: A slave woman who believes Is better than an unbelieving woman' who can only 'Beckon you to the Fire'.[25] In general,

China's Islàmic minorities followed this taboo strictly. Muslims normally married only within their own nationality and hardly ever with a Han. It was even the case that people of a particular Islamic sect rarely married a Muslim of a different sect. The Bonan and Dongxiang peoples, both of Gansu province, are Muslims, but in each minority there are believers in several sects divided so sharply that disputes sometimes erupt into violence. Since the whole point of the Koranic ban on marrying unbelievers is to ensure spiritual harmony between husband and wife, it is not surprising that believers in one of the sects were forbidden to marry anybody adhering to another.[26]

Although class affected the choice of a marriage partner among the great majority of China's nationalities, there was none which laid heavier emphasis on it than the Yi of Liangshan in Xikang province. A highly warlike people fiercely resistant to Chinese rule, the Yi of Liangshan practised a rigid slave caste system according to which no member of the slave-owning class, which constituted about 10 per cent of the population, could marry or hold sexual relations outside their own caste. The penalty for an offending woman of this class was death, and for a man a heavy fine.[27] Peter Goulart, who has written of the minorities of Lijiang, Yunnan and surrounding areas from his work there in the 1940s, paints quite a positive picture of Yi life — for instance, he denies seeing signs of cruelty by masters against slaves.[28] Yet he acknowledges the importance of caste in gender and other relations, even within relative freedom for women in other respects. 'Any girl may marry or have as many romances as she likes, provided it is within the caste.'[29]

Virtually all sectors of practically all societies at more or less all times avoid, and usually ban on pain of punishment to offenders, sexual relations, and hence marriage, between primary kin — that is, an individual's mother, father, son, daughter, brother and sister.[30] The very few exceptions allowing brother–sister marriages include only such highly stratified states such as ancient Egypt or the Incas, and then only among the ruling class.[31] However, wider incest taboos apply variously in different societies, and there are some sharp distinctions among the nationalities of China.

The Chinese Family Law of 1931 banned blood relations within the eighth degree for people with the same surnames, but allowed for marriage between cousins with different surnames.[32] The emphasis on the same surname as a sign of incest was in accordance with the Confucian tradition and made the Han rather contemptuous of practice among some minorities with a different focus. According to one ethnologist from Western Hunan who had investigated the Miao of his area in the late 1920s or early 1930s, 'of old they had no aversion to marriage among two people of the same surname', but were gradually abandoning the practice, under the benign influence of the Han.[33] A study of the custom in the 1940s among the southwestern peoples found that it was indeed prevalent among the Miao, but with exceptions in quite a few places 'where the extent of Sinicisation (*Hanhua*) was comparatively deep'.[34] The Bouyei were very similar to the Miao in this regard. Another nationality with marriages between people of the same surname was the Yi of Liangshan, but this was specifically among the aristocracy.

Because the Yi were notable for status barriers between the aristocracy and slave castes, they would prefer to marry a close relative with the same surname or somebody from another nationality than outside their own caste. Among the Yao, marriage between people of the same surname was common only in communities with very small populations where it was impossible to find a suitable partner with a different surname.[35]

It should be added that the original society of the Miao and some of the Tibeto-Burman speaking groups of southwest China gave no place to the surname. Finding this offensive, Han officials or school teachers often conferred surnames on members of the minorities, being more likely to follow their own usage than that of the minorities in the choices they made. Moreover, several clans were often arbitrarily given the same Chinese-language surname. It is also worth noting that among the great majority of the southwestern minority peoples, bilateral cross-cousin marriages were common. Although the issue of marriage betweeen people of the same surnames would in this case be totally irrelevant, the practice shows that their societies had no problem with marriages between cousins.

The Jingpo of Yunnan were totally unconcerned with the Family Law of 1931, and probably hardly any of them even knew about it. They were, however, bitterly opposed to any sexual relationships between people of the same surname, who did not go to the communal houses where free love was practised. Love songs would elicit the name of partners in order to make sure the proscriptions against incest were being followed. In the case of sexual relations between brother and sister, both were punished by death, and if between the children of two brothers the man was executed.[36]

The *Koran* and Islamic tradition both forbid any sexual relations, let alone marriage, between a man and his mother, daughters, sisters, aunts, nieces and several foster categories, but not including first cousins.[37] Islam thus puts the focus less on the surname than on the blood or foster relationship. Aitchen Wu, a Confucian Han who worked in Xinjiang in the 1930s, writes that the Uygurs permitted no union 'between those reared on the same milk, but close lateral relationship is not in itself an obstacle',[38] with a very similar comment on the Kazaks. By 'close lateral relationship' he may, with his strong Confucian beliefs, have meant mainly first cousins with the same surname.[39]

Tibetan law forbade matrimonial alliances with anybody related within seven degrees. When he visited Tibet in the late nineteenth century, Das found that alliances within only three or four degrees were quite common, and among the Khampas, marriages were 'promiscuously contracted', including between brother and sister, or nephew and aunt. Rockhill disagrees with Das concerning the Khampas, claiming that though they may once have practised customs he would have regarded as incestuous, Chinese influence had led to their near-disappearance, and since his experience was mainly with the Khampas, his account can be preferred. Marriage between classes was generally possible. The exception was that the aristocracy or royal family did not marry commoners, although the men did occasionally marry the daughters of people outside the noble classes.[40]

The tradition among the Mongols was to forbid marriages among people of the same patrilineal common descent group. In one community in southern Chahar province, it was permissible for people of the same descent group to marry provided they were separated by more than five degrees of collaterality. Marriages between maternal first cousins were permitted but not considered desirable, and they were rare. In addition to kinship, territory was also a factor in marriage. Just as marriage with close relations was considered socially undesirable, so women often went long distances for marriages.[41] Another Mongol community in northern Manchuria followed similar prohibitions on incest but with some striking differences. It allowed but discouraged marriages between first cross-cousins — those whose parents were siblings of alternative gender — but placed no restriction on marriage between the children of first cross-cousins — that is, between second cross-cousins. Marriages between third cross-cousins, specifically the children of male second cross-cousins, were highly regarded because they reunited two family lines which had been separated by incest rules.[42]

Marriage

The age of marriage among the minority nationalities, especially the women, was very young. As in most poor societies or those with traditional economies, high death rates in most places and lack of good birth control methods gave incentive for high birth rates and early marriage. The average age of women at the time of first marriage in 1935 was 16.46 among minority nationalities and 17.11 among the Han. The trend was upwards under the Guomindang, reaching a high point of 18.6 years for minority women and 18.58 for Han in 1948.[43] In general, the average age of first marriage was slightly lower among minority women than among Han.[44] There were variations among the nationalities and among regions. Contemporary PRC scholars estimate the age of first marriage of minority nationality women in Xinjiang before 1949 to have been about 15.[45] Korean women married on average at 16.06 years of age in the 1930s, with 95.4 per cent of women marrying for the first time between the ages of 15 and 18, but in the 1940s they married on average when they were 17.1 years old.[46] According to Das, Tibetans married at any age between 15 and 25, with the bride frequently being older than the bridegroom.[47] Harrer puts the normal marriage age of girls at 16, and of boys at 17 or 18 at the latest,[48] while, with specific reference to the Tibetans of Qinghai province, a mid-1930s Han Chinese source estimates the age of first marriage for women at 15 or 16.[49] Traditionally Mongol men married at an odd-numbered age, especially 17 or 19, but like the Han they were regarded as being one year old at birth.[50]

The great majority of minorities, and indeed all but a few of the Han, followed virilocal or patrilocal residence patterns — that is, the woman went to live with her husband upon marriage, rather than the other way around. However, the practice of delayed patrilocal residence, known in Chinese as *buluo fujia* (literally 'not moving into the husband's family'), was practised among most of the minorities of southwest and south China, with only minor differences among the various nationalities. The bridegroom sent people to the bride's house to welcome her and she would go, accompanied by a retinue of her brothers and sisters, and related girls of the same generation, to the bridegroom's house for the wedding celebrations which lasted for up to three days. During that time, sexual relations between bride and groom were forbidden as a mark of respect to the guests and to both families. After the celebrations, the bride went back to her own family. On festival days and a few other occasions the bridegroom sent somebody to get his bride and they could live together for a few days. Among the Dong people, the wife dressed as a bride whenever going to the man's house. Only after the bride got pregnant did she move into her husband's house, and only after the baby was born did they count as a formally married couple. In some areas, land or oxen allocated to them as wedding gifts were not actually given until the first baby was born.[51]

The 1931 Family Law established monogamy as the norm and laid down penalties for bigamy. It thus outlawed polygyny and stripped concubinage of its legal status, but made no mention of concubines.[52] The great majority of nationalities were mainly monogamous, but with rich or aristocratic men practising polygyny despite the law. A typical example is the Miao. An agricultural people, among whom land was family-owned and scarce, the nuclear family was the primary social unit with concubines being restricted to the very rich and kept in separate household establishments.[53] In two Mongol communities, one in southern Chahar, the other in northern Manchuria, the family was based on monogamous marriage, with polygyny occurring only when the first wife was sterile.[54]

According to tradition, Muslim men were allowed four wives at any one time,[55] and this rule was generally followed by rich Hui, Kazaks or Kirgiz, to name but three examples. Aitchen Wu remarked that all Uygurs who could afford it practised polygyny and it 'appears in practice to work very well'. Although four was the normal limit, his experience was that ways were available 'to evade the prohibition, and it is not uncommon to find a rich man enjoying the pleasures of the seraglio'.[56] Very few came into this category. It was normal even among those who could afford two or more wives to keep them in separate houses, or even different towns. Generally speaking, wives did not readily tolerate rivals.[57]

The central motivation for polygyny among the nomadic Kazaks becomes clear from a Chinese comment of the late 1940s:

> The status of women is equivalent to that of a slave among the Kazaks and there is no way they can resist the men. Consequently, a polygamous family system on a semi-slave pattern has been formed. Many wives can bring in wealth. You can say that the more slaves there are, the more the master can win for himself. Because women are producers, to marry many wives is in order to increase production in the family.[58]

What mattered to rich Kazak men was less 'the pleasures of the seraglio' than property.

Among the Tibetans, about 70 per cent of marriages were monogamous. Approximately one in 20 was polygamous. Among poor families, sisters could take in a single husband; when a woman was widowed and remarried a younger man for economic reasons, she might share him with her daughter when the latter grew up. Officials and nobles took in a plurality of wives if the first or second failed to produce a son.

The custom of polyandry was followed both among the Tibetans and the Monba. 'Relevant departments' under the PRC claim that about 24 per cent of all Tibetan marriages were polyandrous,[59] but much fewer among the Monba.[60] The great Tibetologist Giuseppe Tucci acknowledges that it existed in every part of Tibet but added that 'it was not as common as is generally believed'.[61] It is likely that the figure of 24 per cent is an exaggeration. The Tibetans had three forms of polyandry: the sharing of a wife in common by two or more brothers, friends, or father and son. Only the first two of these patterns existed among the Monba.[62]

The first was much the commonest of these three forms. Its main purpose among land-owning families was to avoid 'fragmentation of the estate upon which family status depended'.[63] However, though to a lesser extent, polyandry did exist also among poor families which held no inheritable land. Reasons included the fear that the children would be too numerous to support and the wish to keep the sons together.[64] The eldest brother was the head of the family and his brothers simply shared his wife. Each brother had his own room and the wife had hers. The brother who went into her room at night would hang a sign on the door to warn the others away. The children all referred to the eldest brother as their father and the others as uncle.[65] Tibetan society praised this kind of polyandrous woman for her ability to maintain good relations among her husbands. 'Some old people even cited her as a model to educate the younger generation.'[66] On the other hand, despite the social approbation, one PRC investigation found that husbands 'were not happy with this kind of life'.[67]

Once a Tibetan man was widowed, he might agree with his son to share a wife if the son was of marriageable age. The aim was to avoid a second family which would split the property inheritance. In such cases, the resultant children referred to the elder man as 'grandfather' and to his son as 'father'.[68] At least in some parts of Tibet, other people often looked down on this kind of polyandrous family, even though its members made no attempt to hide its situation.[69] In other words, it was not nearly as acceptable socially as brothers sharing a wife, even though the aim was actually very similar.

Of the various marriage forms found among the minorities, one that stood out as unusual, either in China or elsewhere,[70] was the matrilocal 'walking marriage' (zoufang hun), the principal marriage pattern among the Mosuo people. The essential feature was that a man would spend the night with a woman at her house but return to his maternal relatives at dawn. In other words, the couple never lived together or organised themselves as a family. This arrangement began when men were 17 or 18 and women 15 or 16. The couple might meet in the course of their work, at a festival or during religious activities. There were no obstacles in terms of class differences between the man and woman, but there were strict rules against a liaison between people with a blood relationship through the mother's line. In general, the couple were of a similar age, but in rare cases it was possible for their ages to differ by 20 years or even more.

In practice, the criteria which men regarded as important in such a partner were physical beauty, good household management and devotion to himself, whereas women emphasised intelligence, ability and wealth, for although inheritance was through the female, her husband could contribute to her family. The walking marriage involved no ceremony or wedding and could be discontinued at any time at the wish of either party. Reasons for discontinuation might include getting sick of one another, the man's home being too far away from the woman's, shifting attention to another partner, or opposition from relatives. To change frequently endowed social prestige, since it appeared to show a person as desirable and in demand.

The visits of the walking marriages were at first secret, but made public after a period ranging from about ten days to two months. The marriages could last from several months to well over a decade, with the number of partners per person ranging from just a few to as high as one hundred in exceptional cases. The children were brought up by the mother and her sisters, whose own children she herself shared, and who might not even know who their father was. In any case, the children regarded their mother's current partner as her brother and their uncle, even if he was in fact their father.[71]

Infidelity and divorce

The Mosuo were among those peoples for whom female infidelity lacked relevance. Those southwestern minorities with liberal views on sexual freedom had to some extent shared such an attitude, but the impact of Confucianism made any act of female infidelity an increasingly serious misdemeanour with the course of time, although it should be added that the degree of condemnation for offenders varied from people to people, and sometimes even within different branches of the same people. Jeffrey Kinkley claims that, among the Miao, extramarital affairs were frequent and, as the influence of Confucianism waxed, elopements and litigation were common. He concludes that 'marriage was not quite so permanent among the Miao as among the Chinese'.[72]

The moral power-holders of the great majority of the nationalities, as among most peoples around the world, took a very serious view of such behaviour as female infidelity. Tucci notes that, despite the preponderance of women in the population, a Tibetan husband had the right to cut off the tip of an unfaithful wife's nose, with her trying to heal the wound with a black covering.[73] However, Harrer claims that he did not hear of a case where this punishment was actually carried out.[74] The murder of a Tibetan wife for infidelity 'was not infrequent', says Tucci, but according to law 'the culprit had to pay blood-money'.[75]

As Tucci notes, there were more females than males among the Tibetan population, an extremely unusual phenomenon at that time among China's peoples.[76] Moreover, a high proportion of the male population was in the monasteries and thus committed to celibacy. If we then add in the factor of polyandry, it becomes obvious that there were not nearly enough men to go around. It was husbands who were at a premium, not wives. All this makes it perfectly credible, as claimed by a Tibetan PRC writer, that many women 'formed casual attachments when and where they could', cases of rural and nomadic unmarried women with two or three children being 'common'.[77] It would also no doubt make female infidelity a very widespread temptation and phenomenon, but not necessarily render it acceptable to husbands.

According to Etherton, an unfaithful Uygur wife risked being seated upon a donkey facing its tail, her face blackened, and then being led through the bazaars to be exposed to the ridicule and 'missiles of all kinds' of the crowds.[78] However, very much harsher treatment was meted out in some cases. Etherton recalls the case of a 'border tribesman', the nationality of whom he does not make clear other than that it was Muslim, who 'hacked off' the head of his young and pretty wife for 'holding converse with a neighbour across the wall'.[79] Etherton is fond of relating such bloodthirsty stories, and while this particular one could easily be true, it is worth noting that the general punishment of being led through the bazaars is somewhat less savage than the hundred lashes ordained by the *Koran* for adulterers,[80] or the death by stoning which tradition prescribes for unfaithful wives in some parts of the Islamic world.

One option for the husbands of unfaithful wives was divorce. Divorce has always been rare in China and was almost unknown in most Han communities.[81] Despite some significant exceptions, it had in general always been very much less difficult for men than for women in China. While it is true that the minorities might follow different norms from the Han, many were quite Confucianised by the time the Republic was born. Moreover, Islamic law is like Confucianism in being one-sided on the subject of divorce. Although the *Koran* bans unfair or cruel treatment against divorced women, it allows men to pronounce the wish to repudiate their wives without giving reasons or going to court.[82] The 1931 Family Law applied to all nationalities and granted women equal treatment in regard to divorce. On the other hand, its failure to give any consideration to their low social and economic position made it no more than a formal equality.[83] The net result was that, even in the first half of the twentieth century, such advantages as divorce might bring were, in the great majority of the minorities, open very much more to men than to women.

The Uygurs, Tajiks, Uzbeks and several of the other Muslim nationalities were apparently considerably less family-oriented than most of their faith in South and Southwest Asia. Several Chinese writers expressed themselves quite shocked at how easy divorce was in Xinjiang.[84] In the 1920s, Etherton found temporary marriages quite common, and a bit like a form of legalised prostitution. Any Muslim man could find a temporary wife through a go-between, preparing the divorce at the same time as the marriage. Even in theory, the wife needed only to wait 100 days before remarrying, but in practice she could move to another town and find another husband more quickly.[85] Writing a little later, Lattimore commented that the Uygur family was 'unstable to a degree unsurpassed' among other Muslims, with casual and temporary relations between the sexes and divorce easy.[86]

It is important to add that traditional Islamic law had since the beginning allowed for the temporary 'marriage of pleasure' for men who were away from their wives for a long time — for example, on religious campaigns.[87] This provision may have been a kind of legalised and moral prostitution which, while changing in the way it operated over the centuries, came to exercise some impact on the marriage systems of some of the Muslim peoples, including the Uygurs. It comes as no surprise that this system was much more to the benefit of men than women, since they had much more freedom of action in making choices and could divorce much more easily. Despite the obvious anti-Muslim bias in such sources, it does not seem either implausible or insulting to the Uygurs for a PRC writer to allege that Uygur women, 'humiliated and with nobody to turn to, often retreated into prayer'.[88]

In contrast to the Uygurs, divorce was considered 'disgraceful' among the Kazaks. Together with the Tatars, Kirgiz and Uzbeks, the Kazaks insisted on marriage as being a lifetime arrangement. With the Uygurs, the father kept the sons and the mother the daughters in the case of divorce, but with the Kazaks the father kept all children.[89] The variations among nationalities which were both Turkic and Islamic may derive from the differing impacts created by the combination of cultural tradition and Islam.

Although divorce among the Mongols was generally freer than among the Kazaks, there were enormous differences prevailing from place to place. In the northern Manchurian community mentioned earlier, divorce was rare and occurred only when sexual misconduct, such as premarital unchastity or adultery, was discovered. Such misdemeanours were regarded much more seriously for the woman than the man, but if a wife divorced her husband over an affair, his reputation suffered tremendously and bitter wrangling might ensue between the two families. Usually the middleman who had arranged the marriage in the first place was made responsible for divorce proceedings.[90] In the southern Chahar Mongol community, divorce was comparatively common and often preceded by separation. One researcher found that separation mostly 'resulted from incompatability, or dislike of the girl by her husband's parents'.[91] As in the northern Manchurian community, the middleman who had originally arranged the marriage usually also brought about its end, but it was not unknown for a lama to check the signs and recommend dissolution.

Turning to the southwestern minorities, we find that although a Bai husband could divorce his wife for adultery, in fact he rarely did so, since the crime was hard to prove and would bring unwanted scandal. It was usually preferable to take a concubine, in addition to his wife, so that the latter 'would remain the recognised, but neglected mistress of her husband's home'. A wife could in theory leave her husband in case of cruelty or depravity, and return to her father's home, but scandal was certain to ensue, so few fathers welcomed a returning daughter, and there was little chance that she would be able to remarry.[92]

In Yi society, divorce was actually more difficult for the husband than the wife. Bride-prices were high, and the family of a woman who initiated the divorce had to repay it to the husband's family. Men rarely initiated divorce. According to one Western missionary, 'The reason given is that when women are irritated they may commit suicide, whereupon the groom and his family must pay to the wife's mother, and generally in addition to the grandmother on her mother's side, a sum of money or make a gift equal in value to the original bride-price.'[93]

In contrast, divorce for the Miao was comparatively easy, with men and women enjoying equal rights to propose it. There were a number of recognised grounds for divorce, including a love affair involving either party, childlessness after a period of marriage, decrepitude or illness. The side making the first suggestion of divorce had to make compensation, which was very substantial in some places.[94] Whether it was actually common or not may have depended on the community. One writer, referring specifically to Western Hunan, states that 'divorce is absolutely free, and the Miao have long since practised it',[95] his wording conveying perhaps a strong hint of disapproval. But while the sources agree that divorce was easy among the Miao, they differ on the actual extent of its occurrence.[96]

According to Das, the conditions of divorce among the Tibetans of the late nineteenth century depended on the innocence or guilt of the relevant parties. If there were children, the husband retained the boys and the mother the girls, and if either held property a certain share was given for the maintenance of the children kept by the other. 'In cases of marriage between slaves or serfs, the owner decides their separation or continued union.'[97] Tucci describes divorce in Tibet as 'not uncommon' and usually by mutual consent.[98] On the other hand, Harrer claims that divorce was rare and had to be approved by the government.[99] It is quite possible that it became more difficult in the course of time, being more so in the 1940s than it had once been. But it is also quite likely that Harrer, who is generally extremely defensive about the old Tibetan society, has underestimated the extent of divorce. The predominance of available women, referred to earlier, could point to a high divorce rate and an even higher remarriage rate for men not in monasteries.

Further gender issues

Much of the material so far suggests that the position of women among the minorities was somewhat better than among the Han people, or, in the case of the Islamic nationalities, less fettered than their sisters in many other parts of the world — particularly in Arab communities. Evidence of protest based on gender is extremely sparse. Yet, as is obvious from the material both in this and earlier chapters, there were very few minorities in which the status of women came anywhere near that of men.

The attitude expressed in the Chinese phrase *zhongnan qingnü* ('making much of the male but light of the female') was found among a great many of the nationalities. One ethnologist writing in the 1930s describes the notion of 'making much of the male but light of the female' as a 'disease running through the society' of the Miao of Western Hunan. He predicts the gradual demise of the idea due to the advocacy of equal rights between the sexes current in his time.[100] However, we shall see in later chapters that his expectations have proved far too optimistic.

One of the main implications of the idea of *zhongnan qingnü* was a preference for sons over daughters. This attitude was shared by almost all nationalities from the Koreans to the Mongols or Tibetans, from the Miao to the Islamic nationalities of the northwest. The most prominent exception was the Mosuo of the Lugu Lake region, among whom 'giving birth to a daughter was more important than to a son'.[101]

One of the most severe forms of discrimination against women among the Han was the practice of foot-binding, which not only caused great deformity and pain, but severely restricted their ability to undertake productive labour. Although banned by the Qing court in February 1902, foot-binding was still very widely practised when the Republic of China was established in 1912, but had gone a long way towards disappearing by the time the Chinese Communist Party (CCP) rose to power.[102] Very few indeed of the minorities adopted this practice, even those most heavily influenced by the Han. In other words it was one rather important respect in which the minorities were able to maintain their identities against the Han, although not against each other.

There were some exceptions to the general principle that the minorities resisted foot-binding for their women. French travel accounts from the beginning of the twentieth century state that the feet of Hui women 'were mutilated like those of the Chinese women'.[103] A portion of the Bai adopted foot-binding in an attempt to show themselves more Han than the Han, but the practice remained anathema to the main communities even of this nationality.[104]

The early Manchu tradition was to give women considerably greater freedom than did the Han Chinese. Manchu women never bound their feet, despite becoming highly integrated with the Han. In Beijing, Manchu women adopted the practice of wearing a kind of shoe which made their feet appear to be bound. In Manchuria, by contrast, Han women very early began to abandon the practice of foot-binding to accord with local custom. This was in sharp contrast to the situation along the Mongolian frontier, where Han women persisted tenaciously in binding their feet. Owen Lattimore attributes this different behaviour in the two places 'to the ready amalgamation between Chinese and Manchus, as contrasted with the profound cleavage' between Mongols and Han Chinese.[105]

Property inheritance and political power

A vital issue concerning the status of women is the ownership of property and its transfer to the next generation. Among the majority of nationalities, property was held by men and only males had rights of inheritance. The traditional practice among the Han was to divide inheritance equally among brothers, and this was very slow to change in the first half of the twentieth century, even though the inheritance laws of 1931 put daughters on an equal footing with sons.[106]

Inheritance custom varied among the Mongols. Two PRC accounts have it that practice was to give the entire property to one son — among richer families the eldest, but among poorer more often the youngest. This was due to anxiety that he would be able to cope less well than his elder brothers.[107] Jagchid and Hyer, referring clearly to richer families, state that 'in cases of polygamy [polygyny], the sons of the first wife usually have a more privileged position in receiving . . . shares of inheritance, than the sons of the other wives'.[108] However, all agree that daughters did not normally receive inheritance. Among the Miao, land, living quarters, animals, money and debts were divided equally among the sons. At the time of allocation, which was before the death of the father, both parents discussed the means of allocation with the sons, and if disputes arose, elder male relations were invited to take part in arbitration.[109]

Although many of the nationalities generally restricted inheritance to males, a substantial number conceded a portion to females. The most striking group was the Muslim nationalities, for although Islam has the reputation of being against certain kinds of women's rights, in fact the *Koran* cites God as directing that males should receive a 'portion equal to that of two females', with daughters being able to take a substantial share of the inheritance if there are no sons.[110] In other words, the *Koran* far from excludes females from inheritance altogether.

In general, China's Islamic nationalities followed the Koranic principles in matters of inheritance. A work of the late Qing about Xinjiang in general, and making no distinction among the various minorities, writes that 'in the case of those with sons property goes to the sons, with the daughters getting one half that of the sons of the former wife'. It goes on to specify that 'in the case of those with daughters but no sons, then the property succeeds to the daughters'.[111] Among the Uzbeks, a daughter got half the inheritance of a son, just as stipulated in the *Koran*, but handed over the inheritance to her husband for safekeeping when she married.[112] The Kazak practice was for parents to hand over some animals or other property to a daughter upon her marriage, but only the sons could receive inheritance upon their parents' death.[113]

The Dong and Bouyei family property was inherited by the sons, but land which the mother brought in as part of her dowry could succeed only to daughters.[114] In Tibet, daughters could inherit, provided there were no sons. In such cases, the husband joined her family upon marriage, taking her name.[115] The chieftains of the Dai bequeathed everything to the eldest son. Ordinary people of that minority left their house to their eldest son, dividing most of their other property among all sons; however, though married daughters could not inherit, those still unmarried when their parents died could do so.[116]

The women of the Yi of Xikang, southwest Sichuan and Yunnan were able to inherit equally with the men. Among the slave-owning castes of the Yi of Liangshan, both daughters and sons inherited slaves as well as animals and silver. In this extremely violent society, men spent more time fighting and squandered their wealth more freely than did the women. As a result, women often ended up with more property than men. This gave them considerable social status. Peter Goulart claims that men and women were completely equal among the Yi and even that elderly or important ladies took precedence over their husbands when receiving guests or sitting down to a feast.[117]

In terms of inheritance, females did best among the Mosuo of the Lugu Lake region. The dominant family structure was based on the residence of the female, rather than the male, and inheritance was matrilineal. On the other hand, in most families property was shared out rather than being held only by the women, and all children inherited, not just the daughters.[118] Although women enjoyed a relatively high social status and influence, the minority could not be classified as matriarchal.[119] Another matrilineal minority was the Lahu of southwestern Yunnan, among which many families lived together in the same public house and produced and owned communally, with inheritance going to all children but through the mother.[120]

Political power among all the minorities was entirely or largely the preserve of men. The Muslim nationalities were especially strict in excluding women from political affairs. Other minorities which were in general somewhat better disposed towards giving women a say in social or family life were also rather rigid when it came to politics. The laws of the Tibetan government specifically forbade women to take part in, or even discuss, state affairs or to participate in military matters.[121] The minorities of Guangxi, Guizhou and Yunnan, among which women did relatively well socially and economically, allowed them very little or no political power. The Dai of Yunnan were prepared to allow women some economic possessions, but gave overwhelming preference to men when it came to political power. Although the historical records speak of 'female chieftains', in fact the twentieth century, let alone the Republican period, did not bring any forth any, and political power for women was restricted to an advisory role. The mother could succeed to headship of the family on the death of her husband, yet the Dai was like almost all the other minorities in placing the father as head.[122] Even the Mosuo people, although highly exceptional in that they were matrilineal and matrilocal in family and social life, preferred males as headmen or chiefs. Queens and other female leaders of the minority nationalities can be found in the Republican period, an example being a female Tibetan leader of south-eastern Qinghai in the mid-1930s who threatened to boil anyone alive who helped the Communists during their Long March, but they are notable for their rarity.

The monopoly of male power among pre-industrial societies is an anthropological issue which relates to the function of women in bearing and raising children and the consequent importance of the mother–child bond.[123] The fact that men are usually the main property-owners merely reflects and strengthens their political power. It is hardly surprising that women held more political power than men in not a single one of China's minorities. What is perhaps more noteworthy is the strikingly different degrees of their subordination among the various minorities, due among other factors to different descent practices, economic patterns and religions.

Conclusion

It follows from virtually all the above material that, with minor exceptions, the women of China's minority nationalities suffered considerably greater discrimination and marginalisation even than their menfolk. This is not at all surprising. What is perhaps more worth saying is that, despite its severity, among most of the minorities it was somewhat less savage than that inflicted on Han women, especially those of the countryside. Even more remarkable is the comparison between the Muslim women of Xinjiang and those of Southwest Asia. In Lattimore's words, they 'generally enjoy[ed] more freedom than their sisters in Islamic countries of the Near East',[124] with a generally better social status. In particular, their fate as wives was less unenviable than their counterparts in many Muslim countries.

The period 1912–49 was one of very gradual change in gender relations in China. One of the factors influencing the rate of change was the extent of urbanisation. With some notable exceptions such as the Koreans, this was very much less among most of the minorities even than the Han. What this signifies is that change was, on the whole, even slower among the minorities than among the Han.

An ideology such as Confucianism or religion like Islam inevitably affected relations between people of the two genders. Both have been very restrictive in their impact, in the sense that they lay greater emphasis on what may not be done than on what is permissible. Some of the peoples of Guangxi, Guizhou and Yunnan, such as the Miao, Yao, Gelao and Dai, allowed young people of opposite sexes to play together not only in childhood but even after puberty. In the first half of the century, the Miao were increasingly influenced by Confucianism, but were still resisting it in many respects. For instance, a Miao widow might begin experimenting with alternative men or seek a new partner not long after the death of her husband, a fact very shocking to Han Chinese.[125]

As far as the female sex was concerned, the relevance of ethnic identities in the first half of the twentieth century was evident in the differing attitudes towards women found among at least some of the minorities as compared to the Han. The Yi, Miao and Mosuo were distinct from the Han in their attitude towards women, while for the Islamic minorities what mattered in determining the status of women was much more religion than any Han ideas. Part of the resistance of southern minorities like the Miao and Yao to the Han Chinese was unwillingness to adopt the Confucian code of ethics surrounding relations between the sexes.

The fact that men began to wear manufactured clothes reduced the relevance of women in their own communities as weavers and embroiderers. The result was the beginnings of integration of the minority economies into those of the Han and of China as a whole. However, it should be added that the integration process developed at a crawling pace and had made only a small impact by 1949.

Marriage forms and attitudes towards courtship, female infidelity and divorce differed substantially among the nationalities, with some being very restrictive and judgmental but others notable for their comparative or even extreme freedom. Clearly there were aspects of the family system which could be regarded as particular to one minority or to a group of them and hence as possible sources of national identification or identity, even if they were not necessarily interpreted in such terms. Certainly, matters of marriage and divorce allowed many of the minorities to differentiate themselves sharply from the Han.

The issues of marriage and divorce raised in this chapter were among those factors which gave the Han the excuse to look down on the minorities, or at least some of them. They despised the Miao and many other minorities of Guizhou, Guangxi, western Hunan and Yunnan for what they believed was freedom in love amounting to gross immorality. They regarded the Tibetan practice of polyandry as disgusting and any view of incest other than their own as repulsive. For centuries officious Han Chinese had been keen to eliminate such practices and induce wayward minorities to follow their own Han morality, with its strong Confucian overtones.

Han contempt was a source of resentment and antagonism on the part of the minorities, a fact which would have provoked pride or at least defensiveness about a particular nationality's customs. Although such hostility against those who treat a people with contempt and defensive pride in their own practices readily leads to feelings of national identity, the evidence that family matters were a major factor producing such sentiments during the Republican period is very patchy at best.

Three broad groups of minorities are perceptible. One was those minorities like the Miao, Bai and Bouyei who, reluctantly or willingly, had accepted Confucian impact over the centuries and continued to do so during the Republic. They may have continued resenting having their courtship, marriage and divorce practices criticised, but it is doubtful if this was a major factor in producing feelings of identity. A second group is those nationalities in which family morality was closely bound up with religion, such as most of the Islamic peoples. In these cases, any feelings of identity resulted much less from differences from the Confucian nationalities in family matters than from the Islamic religion itself. Finally, there is that group with which the Han, and indeed most of the minorities, maintained very little or even no contact. For this group, which included the Jingpo and Yi, Han or Confucian impact in family matters was largely irrelevant.

To interfere with the social practices of the minorities was usually beyond the capacity of the various governments of the Republican period, especially since control in those areas was uneven at the best of times, extremely weak in Tibet and completely nonexistent in Manchuria during the period of Japanese occupation. The Chinese government may have wanted to strengthen national integration, and even integration between the Han and the minorities, through such methods as introducing nationwide rules on marriage and divorce, but such a consideration was very low indeed on the agenda with the passage of the 1931 Family Law. It was the Han people who were in the forefront of the leaders' minds when they brought in rules concerning the family. The government never really tried very hard to implement such regulations among more than a very few of the minority communities and such attempts as it made met with very limited success.

Notes

1 *China Handbook, 1937–1944, A Comprehensive Survey of Major Developments in China in Seven Years of War*, Chinese Ministry of Information, Chungking, 1944, p. 189. For detailed commentary, see Olga Lang, *Chinese Family and Society*, Yale University Press, New Haven, 1946, pp. 115–19.

2 Robin Fox, *Kinship and Marriage, An Anthropological Perspective*, Penguin Books, Harmondsworth, 1967; 1976, p. 13.

3 ibid.

4 In the PRC, the Mosuo are regularly classified as a branch of the Naxi nationality. See, for instance, Yan Ruxian, trans. Xing Wenjun, 'A Living Fossil of the Family — A Study of the Family Structure of the Naxi Nationality in the Lugu Lake Region', *Social Sciences in China*, vol. 3, no. 4, December 1982, p. 60. However, the Mosuo themselves do not necessarily accept this classification. The issue of Naxi and Mosuo identification is discussed in some detail by Charles F. McKhann, in 'The Naxi and the Nationalities Question', in Stevan Harrell (ed.), *Cultural Encounters on China's Ethnic Frontiers*, University of Washington Press, Seattle and London, 1995, pp. 46–62.

5 Clark W. Sorensen, 'Asian Families, Domestic Group Formation', in Grant Evans (ed.), *Asia's Cultural Mosaic, An Anthropological Introduction*, Prentice Hall/Simon & Shuster [Asia] Pte Ltd., Singapore, 1993, pp. 89–90.

6 See also the discussion in Jeffrey C. Kinkley, *The Odyssey of Shen Congwen*, Stanford University Press, Stanford, 1987, pp. 139–45.

7 Norma Diamond, 'The Miao and Poison: Interactions on China's Southwest Frontier', *Ethnology, An International Journal of Cultural and Social Anthropology*, vol. 27, no. 1, January 1988, p. 23.

8 Alan Winnington, *The Slaves of the Cool Mountains, The Ancient Social Conditions and Changes Now in Progress on the Remote South-Western Borders of China*, Lawrence & Wishart, London, 1959, pp. 178–80.
9 Huang Xianfan, Huang Zengqing and Zhang Yimin, *Zhuangzu tongshi*, Guangxi Minzu chubanshe, Nanning, 1988, p. 701.
10 *Brief History of the Miao Nationality* Compilation Group, *Miaozu jianshi*, Guizhou Minzu chubanshe, Guiyang, 1985, pp. 320–21.
11 For a detailed account of the processes in one part of Kaili county in Southeastern Guizhou in the early years after liberation, before any major changes had occurred, see Guizhou Provincial Editorial Group, *Miaozu shehui lishi diaocha, Er*, Guizhou Minzu chubanshe, Guiyang, 1987, pp. 262–69.
12 *Survey of the Sandu Shui Autonomous County* Compilation Group, *Sandu Shuizu zizhi xian gaikuang*, Guizhou Renmin chubanshe, Guiyang, 1986, p. 59.
13 *Brief History of the Shui Nationality* Compilation Group, *Shuizu jianshi*, Guizhou Minzu chubanshe, Guiyang, 1985, p. 111.
14 C.P. Fitzgerald, *The Tower of Five Glories, A Study of the Min Chia of Ta Li, Yunnan*, The Cresset Press, London, 1941; Hyperion Press, Westport, Connecticut, 1973, pp. 150–51.
15 Song Enchang, *Yunnan shaoshu minzu yanjiu wenji*, Yunnan Renmin chubanshe, Kunming, 1986, p. 540.
16 Ma Yin et al. (eds), trans. Liu Qizhong et al., *China's Minority Nationalities*, Foreign Languages Press, Beijing, 1989, p. 167.
17 *Brief History of the Koreans* Compilation Group, *Chaoxian zu jianshi*, Yanbian Renmin chubanshe, Yanji, 1986, p. 229.
18 Sarat Chandra Das, edited by W.W. Rockhill, *Journey to Lhasa and Central Tibet*, Murray, London, 1902, p. 247.
19 Sir Charles Bell, *The People of Tibet*, Clarendon Press, Oxford, 1928, p. 175.
20 Heinrich Harrer, trans. Richard Graves, *Seven Years in Tibet*, Rupert Hart-Davis and the Book Society, Britain, 1953; J.P. Tarcher, Los Angeles, 1982, p. 197.
21 Tiley Chodag, trans. W. Tailing, *Tibet, The Land and the People*, New World Press, Beijing, 1988, p. 228.
22 Sun Hanwen, 'Qinghai minzu gaiguan', in Gansu Provincial Library Bibliography Department, comp., *Xibei minzu zongjiao shiliao wenzhai (Qinghai fence)*, Gansu sheng tushuguan, Lanzhou, 1986, vol. 1, p. 311.
23 Herbert Harold Vreeland III, *Mongol Community and Kinship Structure*, HRAF Press, New Haven, 1962; Greenwood Press, Westport, Connecticut, 1973, p. 245.
24 ibid., p. 167.
25 Abdullah Yusuf Ali (trans. and ed.), *The Holy Qur-an, Text Translation and Commentary*, Khalil Al-Rawaf, Riyadh, Saudi Arabia, 1946; The Islamic Center, Washington, 1978, ii, 221, p. 87.
26 Zhang Tianlu, Song Zhuansheng and Ma Zhengliang, *Zhongguo Musilin renkou*, Ningxia Renmin chubanshe, Yinchuan, 1991, pp. 29–30.

27 David Crockett Graham, *Folk Religion in Southwest China*, Smithsonian Press, Washington DC, 1961, pp. 77–78.

28 Peter Goulart, *Forgotten Kingdom*, John Murray, London, 1957, p. 141.

29 ibid., p. 143.

30 One of Robin Fox's four basic principles governing human society is that 'primary kin do not mate with each other'. See *Kinship and Marriage*, p. 31. He discusses 'the incest problem' at some length on pp. 54–76.

31 Marvin Harris, *Culture, People, Nature, An Introduction to General Anthropology, Second Edition*, Harper & Row, New York, 1975, p. 327.

32 Lang, *Chinese Family and Society*, p. 116.

33 Shi Honggui, 'Xiangxi Miaozu kaocha ji (zhailu)', in Zhang Ermu et al. (eds), *Xiangxi wenshi ziliao, di shijiu ji, Miaojiang guzhen, Xiangxi wenshi ziliao* bianji bu, Jishou, 1990, p. 143.

34 Yang Hanxian, 'Xi'nan jizhong zongzu de hunyin fanwei', *Bianzheng gonglun*, vol. 3, no. 6, June 1944, p. 50.

35 ibid., pp. 48–51.

36 Winnington, *The Slaves of the Cool Mountains*, pp. 179, 181.

37 See *The Holy Qur-an*, iv, 23, p. 186; H.A.R. Gibb and J.H. Kramers, *Shorter Encyclopaedia of Islam*, Cornell University Press, Ithaca, NY, 1953, p. 447.

38 Aitchen K. Wu, *Turkistan Tumult*, Methuen, London, 1940, p. 217.

39 See also Feng Jiasheng et al. (comp.), *Weiwuer zu shiliao jianbian, xiace*, Minzu chubanshe, Beijing, 1981, pp. 456–57 where the comment is made that Islamic custom does not forbid 'marriage between people of the same surname'.

40 Das, ed. Rockhill, *Journey to Lhasa*, p. 251. See also Harrer, *Seven Years in Tibet*, p. 198.

41 Vreeland, *Mongol Community and Kinship Structure*, pp. 161–62.

42 ibid., p. 237.

43 Arthur P. Wolf and Chieh-shan Huang, *Marriage and Adoption in China, 1845–1945*, Stanford University Press, Stanford, 1980, pp. 134–35 give some localised figures for the age of marriage of both men and women born between the late nineteenth and the second decade of the twentieth century. They suggest that the age of first marriage tended to rise for both men and women in the Republican period, with men marrying a few years later than women.

44 See the figures comparing the ages of first marriage among minority nationality and Han women in all years from 1935 to 1982 in Zhang Tianlu, 'Zhongguo shaoshu minzu renkou', in Deng Zhixian (ed.), *Minzu renkouxue sanlun*, Guizhou Minzu chubanshe, Guiyang, 1990, p. 52.

45 Zhou Chongjing et al. (eds), *Zhongguo renkou, Xinjiang fence*, Zhongguo caizheng jingji chubanshe, Beijing, 1990, p. 270.

46 Zhang, 'Zhongguo shaoshu minzu renkou,' pp. 51, 53.

47 Das, *Journey to Lhasa*, p. 250.

48 Harrer, *Seven Years in Tibet*, p. 198.

49 Sun, 'Qinghai minzu gaiguan', p. 311.

50 See Sechin Jagchid and Paul Hyer, *Mongolia's Culture and Society*, Westview Press, Boulder, 1979, p. 82.
51 Ye Dabing, Wubing'an et al. (eds), *Zhongguo fengsu cidian*, Shanghai cishu chubanshe, Shanghai, 1990, p. 110.
52 Lang, *Chinese Family and Society*, p. 117.
53 Chang-tu Hu, in collaboration with Samuel C. Chu, Leslie L. Clark, Jung-pang Lo and Yuan-li Wu, ed. Hsiao Hsia, *China, Its People, Its Society, Its Culture*, HRAF Press, New Haven, 1960, p. 80.
54 Vreeland, *Mongol Community and Kinship Structure*, pp. 151, 219.
55 *The Holy Qur-an*, iv, 3, p. 179 allows for marriage with 'two, or three, or four' wives but adds 'if ye fear that ye shall not Be able to deal justly (with them), Then only one'.
56 Wu, *Turkistan Tumult*, pp. 217–18.
57 Hu et al., *China*, p. 76.
58 Zuo Yingfan, 'Hasake lisu', in Gansu Provincial Library Bibliography Department, comp., *Xibei minzu zongjiao shiliao wenzhai (Xinjiang fence)*, Gansu sheng tushuguan, Lanzhou, 1985, vol. 2, p. 993. The original article was published in *Xibei tongxun*, vol. 2, no. 1, 1948.
59 Tiley Chodag, *Tibet*, pp. 229–30.
60 Tibetan Social and Historical Investigation Materials Series Editorial Group, *Menba zu shehui lishi diaocha, Er*, Xizang Renmin chubanshe, Lhasa, 1988, pp. 120–21.
61 Giuseppe Tucci, trans. J.E. Stapleton Driver, *Tibet, Land of Snows*, London, Elek, Stein and Day, New York, 1967, p. 159.
62 See *Brief History of the Menba Nationality* Compilation Group, *Menba zu jianshi*, Xizang Renmin chubanshe, Lhasa, 1987, pp. 71–73.
63 Sorensen, 'Asian Families', p. 114.
64 Tibetan Social and Historical Investigation Materials Series Editorial Group, *Zangzu shehui lishi diaocha, Er*, Xizang Renmin chubanshe, Lhasa, 1988, pp. 96–97 and Tibetan Social and Historical Investigation Materials Series Editorial Group (ed.), *Zangzu shehui lishi diaocha, San*, Xizang Renmin chubanshe, Lhasa, 1989, p. 13.
65 Ye, Wubing'an et al. (eds), *Zhongguo fengsu cidian*, p. 118.
66 *Zangzu shehui lishi diaocha, Er*, p. 96. See also, for example, Sorensen, 'Asian Families', p. 114.
67 *Zangzu shehui lishi diaocha, San*, p. 13.
68 Ye, Wubing'an et al. (eds), *Zhongguo fengsu cidian*, p. 113.
69 *Zangzu shehui lishi diaocha, Er*, p. 97.
70 See Harris, *Culture, People, Nature*, pp. 345–46. One of the few peoples, other than the Mosuo, to have followed this pattern were the Nayar of Kerala in India.
71 See Yan Ruxian and Song Zhaolin, *Yongning Naxi zu de muxi zhi*, Yunnan Renmin chubanshe, Kunming, 1983, pp. 93–107; Lin Xinnai (ed.), *Zhonghua fengsu daguan*, Shanghai Wenyi chubanshe, Shanghai, 1991, pp. 453–54.

72 Kinkley, *The Odyssey of Shen Congwen*, p. 140.

73 Tucci, *Tibet*, p. 163.

74 Harrer, *Seven Years in Tibet*, p. 198.

75 Tucci, *Tibet*, p. 163.

76 For a discussion of this question see Colin Mackerras, *China's Minorities: Integration and Modernization in the Twentieth Century*, Oxford University Press, Hong Kong, 1994, pp. 131–34.

77 Tiley Chodag, *Tibet*, p. 230.

78 P.T. Etherton, *In the Heart of Asia*, Houghton Mifflin, Boston and New York, 1926, p. 89.

79 ibid., p. 81.

80 *The Holy Qur-an*, xxiv, 2, p. 896 says: 'The Woman and the man Guilty of adultery or fornication, — Flog each of them With a hundred stripes'.

81 See Wolf and Huang, *Marriage and Adoption in China, 1845–1945*, p. 178.

82 On the various forms of divorce in Islamic law, see Gibb and Kramers, *Shorter Encyclopaedia of Islam*, pp. 564–71.

83 Lang, *Chinese Family and Society*, pp. 40–41, 117.

84 See Wang Shunan, *Xinjiang tuzhi*, quoted from Feng et al. (comp.), *Weiwuer zu shiliao jianbian, xiace*, p. 459.

85 Etherton, *In the Heart of Asia*, pp. 88–89.

86 Owen Lattimore et al., *Pivot of Asia,Sinkiang and the Inner Asian Frontiers of China and Russia*, Little, Brown and Co., Boston, 1950, AMS, New York, 1975 reprint, p. 127.

87 Gibb and Kramers, *Shorter Encyclopaedia of Islam*, p. 449.

88 Ma et al. (eds), *China's Minority Nationalities*, p. 149.

89 Wu, *Turkistan Tumult*, pp. 217, 222. See also Zhang, Song and Ma, *Zhongguo Musilin renkou*, pp. 45–46 and Luo Jiansheng, *Wuzibieke zu*, Minzu chubanshe, Beijing, 1990, p. 45.

90 Vreeland, *Mongol Community and Kinship Structure*, p. 248.

91 ibid., pp. 170-1.

92 Fitzgerald, *The Tower of Five Glories*, pp. 163–64.

93 Graham, *Folk Religion in Southwest China*, p. 78.

94 Shi Qigui, *Xiangxi Miaozu shidi diaocha baogao*, Hunan Renmin chubanshe, Changsha, 1986, p. 179.

95 Shi, 'Xiangxi Miaozu kaocha ji', p. 143.

96 *Miaozu jianshi*, p. 320 claims that divorce was actually quite rare in practice, whereas Kinkley, *The Odyssey of Shen Congwen*, p. 140, states that there were 'many divorces, followed by remarriages'.

97 Das, *Journey to Lhasa*, pp. 250–51.

98 Tucci, *Tibet*, p. 163.

99 Harrer, *Seven Years in Tibet*, p. 198.

100 Shi, *Xiangxi Miaozu shidi diaocha baogao*, p. 179. Shi's investigation was actually undertaken in the mid-1930s and drafted in 1940, although not published until much later.

101 Yan and Song, *Yongning Naxi zu de muxi zhi*, p. 65.

102 See Lang, *Chinese Family and Society*, pp. 45–46, 156.

103 See Jacques Waardenburg, 'Islam in China: Western Studies', in Shirin Akiner (ed.), *Cultural Change and Continuity in Central Asia*, Kegan Paul International, London, 1991, p. 311.

104 Colin Mackerras, 'Aspects of Bai Culture, Change and Continuity in a Yunnan Nationality', *Modern China, An International Quarterly of History and Social Science*, vol. 14, no. 1, January 1988, p. 53.

105 Owen Lattimore, *Manchuria, Cradle of Conflict*, rev. edn, Macmillan, New York, 1935, AMS, New York, 1975 reprint, p. 269.

106 Lang, *Chinese Family and Society*, p. 117.

107 *Brief History of the Mongol Nationality* Compilation Group, *Menggu zu jianshi*, Nei Menggu Renmin chubanshe, Huhhot, 1985, p. 321; Inner Mongolian Autonomous Region Editorial Group, *Menggu zu shehui lishi diaocha*, Nei Menggu Renmin chubanshe, Huhhot, 1985, pp. 186–87.

108 Jagchid and Hyer, *Mongolia's Culture and Society*, p. 253.

109 *Miaozu shehui lishi diaocha, Er*, pp. 260–61.

110 *The Holy Qur-an*, iv, 11, p. 181.

111 Wang, *Xinjiang tuzhi*, quoted from Feng et al., comp., *Weiwuer zu shiliao jianbian, xiace*, p. 460.

112 Luo, *Wuzibieke zu*, p. 38.

113 Jiahefu Mierzhahan, trans. Nabijian Muhamudehan and He Xingliang, *Hasake zu*, Minzu chubanshe, Beijing, 1989, p. 77.

114 *Brief History of the Dong Nationality* Compilation Group, *Dongzu jianshi*, Guizhou Minzu chubanshe, Guiyang, 1985, p. 147. Ye, Wubing'an et al. (eds), *Zhongguo fengsu cidian*, p. 156.

115 Bell, *The People of Tibet*, pp. 87–88.

116 Jiang Yingliang, *Daizu shi*, Sichuan Minzu chubanshe, Chengdu, 1983, p. 508.

117 Goulart, *Forgotten Kingdom*, p. 143.

118 See Yan Ruxian and Song Zhaolin, *Yongning Naxi zu de muxi zhi*, Yunnan Renmin chubanshe, Kunming, 1983, p. 42. See also Yan, 'A Living Fossil of the Family', pp. 61–64, 67.

119 Robin Fox, *Kingship and Marriage*, pp. 112–13, suggests three types of matrilineal organisation, the first being that based on the mother–daughter–sister roles and matrilocal residence. This is the one which best describes the Mosuo of the Lugu Lake area. Fox considers that in such societies 'women have higher prestige and influence than in the others', but he denies that 'power and authority were in the hands of women in such a system'.

120 Yan, 'A Living Fossil of the Family', pp. 79–80.

121 Tiley Chodag, *Tibet*, p. 226.

122 Jiang, *Daizu shi*, pp. 494–95.

123 The third of Robin Fox's four basic principles of human society is that 'the men usually exercise control' and he goes on to give his reasons, which are based on 'primate nature'. See *Kinship and Marriage*, pp. 31–32.

124 Lattimore, *Pivot of Asia*, p. 142.

125 See Kinkley, *The Odyssey of Shen Congwen*, pp. 139–40.

5 Literature and the Performing Arts, 1912–1949

The minorities of China have produced a significant body of traditional arts, including some long recognised as world masterpieces. In the field of architecture, the Potala Palace in Lhasa certainly counts among the the great buildings of the pre-twentieth-century world, as well as being one which establishes Tibetan identity and of which Tibetans all over the world are extremely proud. In the arts of the minorities, the Republican period was generally one of continuing strong tradition with only minor modernising beginnings, but certainly it was not without its achievements.

It is the aim of this chapter to relate the minorities' arts of the Republican period — a factor far too important for culture for us to ignore without serious distortion — to the themes of ethnic identities and integration. However, because it is not possible to cover all branches of the arts of China's many minorities in a short space, this chapter focuses on the main genres of just two artistic forms: literature and the performing arts. The two are actually connected quite closely, since the librettoes of drama performances are generally considered a branch of literature, and the performance of epics and other poetry through song is both a kind of literature and one of the performing arts.

It is necessary to point out the problems in original source material in studying minorities' literature and theatre in China. The fact is that, for all but a few of the minorities, we are forced to rely on materials collected by ethnologists of the People's Republic. They deserve immense credit, in my opinion, for their work, and the quantity of material published since the early 1980s has been enormously impressive. However, published materials are usually translated into Chinese and there is no guarantee that changes have not been made for political or other reasons. One American scholar cites an example of a Miao creation epic which was altered in publication to avoid insulting or offending members of another minority.[1] Censorship of this kind is nowadays found also in Western countries. Yet that does not alter the possibility that any published version of a poem, story or drama is quite likely to be 'purer' politically or socially than the original.

Literature

There are many branches of literature. For the purposes of this chapter, two are selected for treatment, namely fiction and poetry. Although certainly not the only forms of literature produced by the minorities, they are important branches which held an important socialising influence within their communities.

Among China's minorities, only a few had their own scripts at the time the Republic came into existence, including the Tibetans, Mongols, Koreans and Yi, while the Uygurs and other Turkic peoples used Arabic script. Among these nationalities, a few had produced significant written literatures using their own languages, the Tibetans and Mongols being good examples.

Tibetan written literature was almost entirely religious,[2] and although a tradition of high-culture Tibetan tracts for the educated, which were similar to novels, arose towards the end of the eighteenth century, it was already moribund by the end of the nineteenth.[3] Lama Buddhism also exercised a very deep influence on written Mongolian literature. One particularly distinguished writer was Injannashi (1837–92), a novelist and poet who lived in the Ordos in Inner Mongolia and thus in that Mongolian territory which is still part of China. His most famous work is a fictionalised account of Mongolian history entitled *The Blue History* (*Köke-sudar*),[4] which Heissig describes as 'the first Mongolian historical romance'.[5] There was a high-culture written language called Chagatai which was shared by the Turkic peoples of the Central Asia such as the Uygurs, Kazaks and Kirgiz; and from the fourteenth to the eighteenth centuries, 'Chagatai literature' produced notable poetic and philosophic writers.[6] Written Korean literature was, naturally enough, influential among China's Korean population, but more or less entirely created in Korea itself.

Of all minorities, the Manchus were probably the one which produced the most voluminous literature during the Qing dynasty when they actually ruled China, but most of it was not in Manchu. That language was used for official documents, political affairs, historical records and other such material. However, Manchu aristocrats who wrote literary forms such as poetry and novels used Chinese right from the start of the Manchu dynasty, and copied the Han genres of literature.[7] The pre-eminent Manchu literary figure of the Qing dynasty was Cao Xueqin (1715–63), the main author of *A Dream of Red Mansions* (*Honglou meng*), possibly China's most celebrated novel.[8] But in fact he wrote in Chinese and the novel belongs as much to Chinese as to Manchu literature. The Hui used Chinese both as their written and spoken language and such Hui literary figures as Pu Songling hardly showed a significant Hui identity.

Some of the minorities with their own spoken language but not scripts did in fact produce written literatures, but used Chinese characters to write their own languages. A good illustrative example is the Bai. By the Qing period, even what literary identity remained to the Bai was severely threatened by the influence of the official examination system on their intellectuals. On the one hand, the system 'led them to a dead end in terms of literary creativity', but on the other forced any with pretensions to entry into the bureaucracy to master the official Chinese language demanded for the examinations.[9]

In traditional times and right down to the middle of the twentieth century and beyond, the main literary expression among the minorities was oral. Short lyric and long poems were the favoured forms, with the content of the former being love, home, physical environment, labour and everyday life and of the latter focusing on myths, love and other stories, national heroes, and episodes in the history of the minority or of its national origin. With their emphasis on the heroes and history of the nation, these poems are very much exponents and representative of the national identities of the minorities. They were composed over a long period by artists who were themselves very much part of the people. Some of them are still known by name, such as the nineteenth-century folk poet and singer Lu Dayong of the Dong people of northern Guangxi, southeastern Guizhou and western Hunan.[10] However, since records were rarely kept about the folk arts, the great majority lived and died much loved by the people, but leaving no name to posterity. The folk poems were the main method of artistic communication within society, a major way of spreading that kind of knowledge and education necessary to socialise its members. Such poems, whether short or long, were performed through song and, because of their rhythmic nature, were frequently themselves the accompaniment for dance.[11] The poems were oral literature in the sense that it was through performance, rather than reading, that they were appreciated, but this did not preclude their being written down. In the case of the Yi people, quite a few oral folk historical poems, legends and stories were written down by clerics and used for religious purposes.[12] Even those minorities without scripts could record examples of oral literature. For example, from about the seventeenth century, Dong songs were increasingly written down with Chinese characters expressing Dong language.[13]

In terms of the number of heroic long epic poems, the most productive minority group was the Mongols, the story of Jangghar being particularly famous and popular. In Xinjiang a long epic poem celebrates the struggle of the Kirgiz hero Manas against the Kalmuck Mongols and their Chinese overlords, portraying it as an Islamic fight against the infidel.[14] The con-

clusion of the epic shows Manas and his forces capturing the Chinese capital Beijing, but then being forced to retreat, with Manas and most of his
army perishing on their way back home. Although Manas is the central figure, the epic is a kind of encyclopedia for the myths, folk-tales and legends
of the Kirgiz.[15]

Of all heroic long poems, not only in China but elsewhere, the one claimed
in China to be the world's longest is that believed to be created by the Tibetans
about Prince Ge sar.[16] Tibetan scholars nowadays believe that at least one
version — an early woodblock — may date back as far as the twelfth century.[17] There are surviving texts of this epic in several different Tibetan,
Mongolian, Turkic, Chinese and other languages.[18] However, as with other
folk literature, this is primarily an oral tradition. Most of the work consists of
long verse songs, but they are interspersed with narrative sections in prose,
chanted extremely rapidly on a single note. There are many versions of the
Prince Ge sar tale, differing in content, length and dialect, but the basic story
is everywhere the same, concerning the exploits and eventual enthronement
and triumph over evil of the virtuous Prince Ge sar of Gling, a mythical kingdom probably in eastern Tibet.[19] The Prince Ge sar story is found all over the
Tibetan areas, and has spread also to the Mongolian.[20] In both Tibetan and
Mongolian cultures, Ge sar has not only become the subject of an epic, but has
also been deified and included in the folk pantheon.[21]

The long epic poem is special to the minorities in the sense that it was a
form which the Han people did not produce, for all their literary greatness.
On the other hand, the Chinese ballad form called *shuochang* (literally 'speak
and sing') was introduced among northern nationalities like the Manchus
and Mongols, northwestern nationalities such as the Uygurs, Kazaks and
Kirgiz and a few of the southern nationalities, such as the Zhuang and the
Dong, well before the nineteenth century. Despite its name it could be sung,
spoken or both. Individual nationalities adapted the content from their own
long folk poems, legends and stories, or took over items from Han novels
and stories, like the *Romance of the Three Kingdoms* (*Sanguo yanyi*).[22]

In the last few decades of the Qing and during the Republican period,
the traditional literary forms were supplemented among some of the minorities by others mainly from other Chinese peoples but in a few cases from
overseas. The Miao were among those to adopt, for the first time, the ballad form *shuochang*. Modern novels and literary criticism began to appear.
To take but one example of criticism, Mongol writers began to contribute to
the already extensive commentary on *A Dream of Red Mansions*.[23]

The traditional oral literature of the minorities continued to be popular
and performed during the late Qing and Republican periods. In terms of
style, change was slow and hesitant. Regarding content, the literatures of the
minorities not surprisingly reflected the developments among their own
peoples. This was an extremely unstable period all over China, characterised
by numerous rebellions, civil wars and foreign invasions, which affected
the minorities as they did the Han. The long Miao poem *The Song of Zhang
Xiumei* deals with the Miao rebellion centred on southeast Guizhou and led

by Zhang Xiumei which raged from 1856 to 1870.[24] Quite a few of the Uygurs' very short epics known as *kuchuk* mourn the martyrdom of those killed during Yakub Beg's revolt, which is portrayed as a holy Islamic war against the Chinese.[25] Some poems concern the Republican revolution which overthrew the Qing dynasty.[26]

In cultural terms, the Tibetans were among the most conservative of all the nationalities in the hundred and more years leading to the middle of the twentieth century. A major British account of Tibetan culture in the period of 'Manchu overlordship' (ending in 1911) describes it as beset by 'a certain sterility'.[27] Yet different adaptations of such items as the story of Prince Ge sar did arise, with the tradition remaining very much alive all over the Tibetan areas. Folk storytellers and singers continued to perform it. Such artists were illiterate and learned the story by heart at an early age, then adapting it as they wished. Some claimed to learn the whole item in a dream, as if by divine intervention.[28]

As oral literature, the poems of this period, like earlier ones, use the language of the relevant nationality. In style many are forthright, even robust, reflecting the spirit of combat and resistance inherent in their topics. On the other hand, a note of solemnity infuses much of the literature, for these were not times to bring humour to the foreground.[29]

Two specific items of minority literature which follow a traditional form, but use content and style characteristic of the modern age, are the Dong 'Song of 1911' ('in Dong 'Gal Xenh Hais') and the Mongolian long poem *Ghada Merin*. 'Song of 1911' is a Dong song of over 130 lines by Jie Hongyou (1864–1929) dealing with the changes in the Dong countryside over the period of the 1911 revolution. Its hero is a Dong performer who is also a military leader, and the song gives a very positive picture of the revolution. Although the author was literate and wrote the poem down in Chinese, it was through song and frequent performance in Dong language in Dong villages that it came to be appreciated by the Dong people.[30]

Ghada Merin deals with an uprising against the warlord Zhang Zuolin and the Mongol princes led by the poem's hero Ghada Merin (1892–1931). It relates how the uprising erupted in 1929 and spread to several Mongol banners and counties, but ended with the imprisonment and execution of its leader at the hands of Zhang Zuolin. Shortly after the uprising, short poems in its support began to emerge among the people, and later on a connected long poem appeared, describing the course of the rebellion, with the focus on the character of its leader.[31] One of the refrains of the long poem is: 'It was for the land of the Mongol people that Ghada Merin led his uprising',[32] suggesting that the issue of land deprivation and seizure by the Han loomed large in the consciousness of the Mongols. Like 'Song of 1911', this long poem used the form and language of its nationality, with a setting, theme and hero belonging to the particular minority. Both can thus claim to be representative of ethnic identity.

The Republican period continued to produce folk exponents of the traditional oral literature which had for so long been prevalent among the minorities. Just as in the past, most such artists still lived and died beloved by those who appreciated their art but unsung by those who might leave historical records.[33] However, several of the artists lived to see the People's Republic, which took much more trouble to record the careers of 'people's artists' than any earlier regime had done.

Among those whose names have survived are the Mongol Pajai (1902–62) and the Dai singer Kanglang Shuai, born in 1911.[34] Pajai was from a poor pastoral family and when very young was sent into a monastery, where he learned to perform the traditional poems of the Mongols. At the age of 18 he abandoned the monastic life and became a wandering performer, roaming around the grasslands of Inner Mongolia. His repertoire included items from classical Chinese novels like *The Romance of the Three Kingdoms,* which had long before been incorporated into the body of Mongol literature in translation.[35] In addition, he placed great weight on singing the traditional epic poems, such as the one about Ge sar Khan which, as earlier noted, had spread from the Tibetan to Mongolian regions. He also created and performed his own poems, often choosing content hostile to the Mongolian princes and lamas.[36] He was very anti-Japanese and during their occupation refused orders to go to the capital of their puppet state of Manchoukuo. When the Inner Mongolian Autonomous Region was set up in 1947, he became a member of a CCP professional troupe, becoming after that 'an official representative of this political direction'.[37]

Kanglang Shuai's career shows some similarities, but also differences. Like Pajai, he came from a poor family and when very young was sent into a monastery, there absorbing many stories from the Buddhist sutras and learning to perform. He returned to lay life at the age of 22 and became a peasant, performing during his spare time. When his fellow peasants built a house, married or had some other cause for celebration, they would invite him to sing, and he eventually became acknowledged as the best folk singer in the Dai area of Sipsong Panna. He was also invited to perform in the court of the local chieftain and travelled in Burma and Thailand. The items he performed included both those transmitted from the past and his own creations. Since he had known great poverty and oppression, the content of his songs tended to be mournful.[38]

Both Pajai and Kanglang Shuai were clearly representatives of their own minority, transmitting and contributing to their particular form of national folk art. That neither was famous in his own day outside his own narrow region does not detract from the role each played as a contributor to his own national identity. Pajai may have taken much of the content of what he performed from the Han, in the case of *The Romance of the Three Kingdoms,* or the Tibetans, in the case of Ge sar, but this does not alter the fact that the language, music, style and social context of his art were Mongol.

Both of these artists were exponents of oral literature and musical art. Although a few of the minorities had produced notable individual literary writers before 1911, the period of the Republic saw a great expansion in the number and range of such figures. Some of these contributed to the sense of identity of their own peoples, but it is extremely doubtful if the majority did so. By far the most important of the writers were the Manchu Lao She and Shen Congwen, whose Tujia and Miao ancestry justifies his categorisation among the minorities, even though his father regarded himself definitely as Han.[39] Both men rank among the finest literary figures in Republican China.

Lao She (1899–1966) was the pen-name of Shu Qingchun. He was brought up in Beijing, a city he came to know and write about more expressively than any other single author. He lived abroad, mainly in England, from 1924–30 and in the United States after the war against Japan. During the Republican period, he produced numerous novels and short stories and, during the war years, some spoken dramas. In some ways, Lao She went through processes of literary development similar to other Chinese writers of the period, experiencing the same anguish over China's failure to solve its problems and anger over the Japanese invasion. However, although he became very patriotic and his years in England in particular made him very nationalistic, his status as a Manchu does not loom at all large in his writings. He even appears to have been ashamed of his Manchu origins. Commenting on one of his early novels, one writer has charged that he lacked 'the courage to speak forth openly, that he was a Manchu, an alienated outsider', who yet 'because of his tremendous need to identify himself with the country of his birth . . . longed to be accepted as an insider'.[40] Lao She's love of nation meant that he thought of himself more or less entirely as Chinese, while hiding any positive emotions he might feel as Manchu.

Shen Congwen came from Fenghuang, which is in the Miao and Tujia area of western Hunan. There is a great deal of local colour in his works, and the novel *Frontier Town* (*Biancheng*), among his best-known stories, is set in a Miao town in Hunan at the point where its borders meet Guizhou and Sichuan. Although it is the west Hunanese locality, rather than the minorities, which looms largest in his writings,[41] the Miao also occupy a significant place and usually with a positive image. 'He expressed belligerent pride' in the culture of the Miao 'and sympathy for them as an oppressed people'.[42] While his frontier romances do set the 'tribespeople' apart from ordinary society, it is clear that Shen actually accepts their way of life, as if, in sharp contrast to most writers of the time and earlier, he was trying to render them 'human'.[43] Shen's autobiography, among the most prominent in its category in twentieth-century Chinese literature, begins with a reference to his home town, noting that the Manchus had sent troops there to suppress, torture and kill the Miao tribes.

Yet Shen's Miao identity is scarcely a prominent feature of his works. He preferred to depict himself as a champion of the downtrodden peoples than as one of them. One work sums up this issue by saying that, although 'Shen judged the larger Han culture from a regional or ethnic Miao perspective' in some of his works, yet 'he himself had a hushed-up Miao and Tujia ancestry', because he was, like Lao She, ashamed of his ethnic origins.[44] Only once in his writings, in 1931, did he directly acknowledge any Miao blood.[45]

The minority which underwent greatest change in terms of poetry and fiction during the first half of the twentieth century was probably the Koreans. Already before the Japanese took over Korea itself as a colony in 1910, the Yanbian Koreans were beginning to develop their own literature using the traditional Korean forms. Since at least the nineteenth century, the Koreans have enjoyed a literacy rate high by comparison with other nationalities of China, opening the way for a good potential readership of written literature.

The years from 1910–49 saw several major developments in the literature of the Chinese Koreans. One was the rise of a significant body of individual literary figures, including poets, novelists and short story writers. The outstanding example of the earlier generation was Kim Bong-yong (1850–1927), a prolific writer of poetry, biographies of historical figures and other forms of literature. Originally an official in the dying Yi dynasty of Korea itself, he fled to China in 1905 and settled in Nantong, Jiangsu province, where the great bulk of his work was published in Chinese, not Korean. Although he never lived in Yanbian, he was firmly anti-Japanese and anti-imperialist.[46] Of a later generation was Kim Ch'ang-gul, a short story writer whose works mainly reflect and oppose Japanese rule among the Koreans of China. One of them was *Dark Night* (*Am Ya*), published in 1939. Set in the 1930s in a Korean village in China, it attacks the rule of the Japanese and their local collaborators in simple but sharp language.[47]

The second major development is to some extent clear from the comments on the first: the strong political influences on both the oral and written Korean literature of the period. Possibly the most important factor was an emphasis on opposition to the Japanese occupation, both of Korea itself and later of Yanbian. During the Manchoukuo period of 1932–45 the Japanese tried to Japanise the Koreans in their puppet state of Manchoukuo by promoting literature advocating their conservative 'imperial way' (*wangdao*) and by trying to prevent the use of the Korean language as far as they could — for example, by cancelling Korean language classes in schools. Both Japanisation measures were to some extent successful, but also produced a tremendous backlash of opposition and resentment. Korean poets and novelists continued to write in their own language, many adopting anti-Japanese themes, despite the danger inherent in such a course. The other aspect of the politicisation of Korean literature was that the influence of the Chinese Communist Party (CCP) was stronger on the Koreans at this time than on any other minority. During the years between the end of the war and the establishment of the People's Republic of China, Korean poetry was produced in support of land reform and other communist causes, while writers such as Kim Ch'ang-hwal wrote short stories on the theme of participation by Koreans in the People's Liberation Army.[48]

The first notable Uygur literary figure of the modern era was Tajalli (1850–1930), who wrote poetry in four languages, Uygur, Arabic, Persian and Hindustani, and was read and published both in Xinjiang and in Turkic areas further west.[49] During the Republican period, which Tajalli lived to see only in the late stages of his career, the modernising process continued and intensified in Xinjiang, due mainly to the impact of the Soviet Union. From the 1920s, both the Uygurs and Kazaks produced quite a few Soviet-influenced poets of note, while among the Uygurs new forms, such as the novel, were introduced from the Soviet Union.[50]

One of the most politically active Uygur poets was the short-lived Lutpulla Mutallip (1922–45). Perhaps his most famous poem is 'Youth' ('Yashlik') which young Uygurs still learn by heart in the 1990s. Its thrust is to bemoan the rapid passing of time:

Youth is the best time of life,
But it passes all too rapidly.
Every day we tear a page from the calendar,
Like leaves falling from a tree.[51]

In 1938 Lutpulla wrote a poem against the Japanese occupation called 'China'. In 1943, while working in the *Xinjiang Daily*, he fell into disfavour with the current Sheng Shicai regime for his writings and was forced to leave the Xinjiang capital Ürümqi, going to Aksu, where he worked as a reporter in the local *Aksu News*. When the anti-Guomindang and separatist East Turkestan Republic was set up late in 1944 he supported it actively, and for this he was assassinated by a Guomindang agent on 18 September 1945. There is considerable irony in the fact that he could be an ardent pro-Chinese patriot when the opposition was Japan, but also a fervent pro-Turkestan, and hence anti-Chinese patriot, once Japan was cancelled as the main threat and the enemy was the Guomindang.[52]

Several other nationalities produced individual literary figures during the period of the Republic, including the Zhuang, Mongols and Bai, but on the whole their works show little interest in ethnic identities. A representative is the poet, historian and linguist Zhao Shiming (1870–1942), a Bai from Jianchuan county in Yunnan. He was one of the main authors of the Minguo edition of the regional gazetteer of Yunnan province, the *Yunnan shengzhi*. He took a lively interest in the affairs of the turbulent times through which he lived, commenting through poetry and in other ways on events and political leaders. However, although he clearly felt extremely strongly against the Japanese invasion, was very patriotic and wrote with warmth about the natural and human-made environment of his homeland, there is little that is specifically Bai either in the content or style of his output.[53]

Tibetan conservatism restricted literary growth in the first half of the twentieth century, the main written works being commentaries on Buddhist writings by lamas following the old style. There was a very limited number of 'literary rebels and innovators', all of them clerics. One of them was dGe 'dun chos 'phel, whose works include a history of the kings of Tibet and a translation of the *Karma-sutra* into Tibetan. The disciple of a lama who had once been a favourite of the Thirteenth Dalai Lama's, he became involved in political and literary disputation with the Tibetan Buddhist hierarchy,[54] as a result of which he was imprisoned and tortured. He was released in November 1950 but died the following year.[55]

The performing arts

There are several branches of the performing arts, ranging from very simple solo songs to complex dramas. This section will discuss only song, dance and drama. In a song and/or dance, there may or may not be a story. The epics discussed in the previous section were performed rather than read and in that sense were also a branch of the performing arts, including a story; on the other hand, a love song normally has no plot. For a drama, however, a story is not only normal but essential. In a dance or song, the performer might impersonate a character, but mostly will not do so, whereas it is central to a drama that more or less all those involved on stage are acting out a specified role. A drama almost always involves at least some interplay or dialogue between or among impersonated characters, but this is not normally the case with song or dance. There are of course types of dance which come close to being drama, and it is certainly possible for the action in a drama, as here defined, to consist largely or even entirely of dance.

Song and dance

Among the performing arts, song and dance are pre-eminent among the overwhelming majority of China's minority nationalities. These two forms very frequently went together, although songs without dance and vice versa were perfectly possible. The combination of song and dance was traditionally a folk form, performances being part of social and family life. What this meant was that ordinary people could perform as part of their socialisation.

Song and dance fulfilled several major social functions, which were easily combined in one occasion. National festivals were celebrated in part through song and dance, which were often also a means of courtship. The reed-pipe gatherings of the Miao and other minorities of Yunnan, Guizhou and Guangxi have already been discussed in Chapter 4.

Many festivals were specific to one or several nationalities, and some were shared by the great majority but, because of the vast range and diversity of China's minorities, none by all of them. For instance, the lunar New Year was widely celebrated in China not only by the Han, but by most of the minorities. Even in this case, however, there were quite a few exceptions, including the Tibetans, Dai, Miao and Yi, whose forebears developed their own calendars based on their own observation of the natural world, as well as most of the Muslim nationalities, who followed Islamic practices.

The Zhuang were entirely typical of the minorities in that song and dance, including forms used for courtship, were a regular companion of major festivals, such as the Chinese lunar New Year. Indeed, along with the third day of the third month and several other dates, the New Year was one of the possible times for a festival of song. People formed themselves into groups and carried on dialogues through song, which usually amounted to a kind of contest. The tone of the songs varied according to the event being marked or celebrated. There were love songs for courtship, wedding songs to celebrate a marriage, elegies for a funeral, or house-building songs to celebrate the completion of a new house.

The Republican period was not one of great change in the folk songs of the Zhuang. Yet, just as with the epic poems discussed in the previous section, Zhuang people created a few new short songs responding to political or other events. One, called 'The Song of the 1911 Revolution', explostulated on the miseries of the Qing dynasty for China and then went on to exult that the Wuchang uprising had 'hunted out the dog emperors of the Qing dynasty'. 'Only with the founding of "the Republic" can the masses look forward to eliminating despotism.'[56]

Although the Confucianised and Muslim minorities were less free in their courtship practices than such southern peoples as the Miao, they were not without musical gatherings for courtship. One major case in point is the *huaer hui*, or folk song gatherings. These were a custom of parts of Gansu and Qinghai and could involve large numbers of people who would sing folk songs in dialogue, largely for courtship purposes. The custom was found among several Islamic nationalities, including the Hui, Salar, Bonan and Dongxiang. Because Islamic law forbade love songs in the villages, young people would find a place outside and away from the Muslim clergy to meet for these gatherings.[57]

Religion was a major cause for celebrations, festivals, song and/or dance. The Muslim nationalities, such as the Hui, Uygurs, Kazaks, Kirgiz, Tajiks and Uzbeks, had several celebrations which derived their existence from religious practice. Principal among these was the end of the Ramadan month of fasting, the ninth in the Islamic calendar, during which adult Muslims eat only before sunrise or after sunset.

Among the nationalities adhering to Tibetan Buddhism, there were large-scale gatherings and celebrations with a decisively religious function. Of these, the most important was the two-week New Year festival established by the great Tsong kha pa, founder of the dominant dGe lugs pa sect, in Lhasa in 1408 as a rededication of Tibet to Buddhism. The festival's functions included exorcising evil influences, invoking a better era and calling up good fortune for the year just beginning. The Tibetan New Year festival had been primarily for the clergy, but in the course of time become a kind of national fesival for all Tibetans.

Central to the New Year celebrations were religious dance-dramas known as '*cham*, which were performed by trained monks acting out the roles of divinities and usually wearing awesome masks, with musical accompaniment from shawms, drums and cymbals. The function of these dance-dramas was to provide a physical manifestation of the protective spirits already invoked during the preceding ceremonies and to exorcise evil. The '*cham* were thus very serious rituals, but they were also very colourful and impressive and so excellent entertainment for the crowds of spectators who thronged to the monasteries for the festival.[58]

The Tibetan missionaries who strengthened Tibetan Buddhism in Mongolia in the sixteenth and seventeenth centuries also brought the 'cham masked dance-dramas to Mongolia, where they were performed annually in the main monasteries. In time, gods of the Mongol folk religion were introduced into the 'cham dances as appropriate victors over evil. Just as elements of the Mongol folk religion survived amid the general triumph of Tibetan Buddhism among the Mongols, so the masked dance-dramas of the Tibetans were able, while remaining essentially Tibetan, to take on some degree of distinctively Mongol flavour.[59] Just as Tibetan Buddhism itself declined markedly among the Mongols in the first half of the twentieth century, so did the masked dance-dramas. Yet, in Inner Mongolia at least, they were very far from dead by the time the CCP set up the Inner Mongolian Autonomous Region in 1947.

The example illustrates one of the principal trends of the minorities' song and dance forms during the Republican period: decline within continuity. The political instability of the period, together with the accompanying general social disintegration, could hardly assist such traditional arts. The song and dance courtship festivals of the Miao inevitably suffered through the large-scale civil wars which afflicted Guizhou in the late 1920s and first half of the 1930s. But the minorities to suffer the most serious decline of their traditions were those affected by the Japanese invasion, the most populous of which were the Manchus, Koreans and Mongols. The Japanese were keen to spread their cultural influence in the areas they occupied, and above all to Japanise Manchoukuo. They had little or no sympathy for cultures alternative to their own. It is true that the Japanese, like Sheng Shicai in Xinjiang, were to some extent responsible for the introduction of more modern forms of art, but the effect on the traditional was no less damaging for that.

Yet it should be noted that trends were not necessarily the same everywhere among the minority areas. In general, the weaker the modernising influences remained, the stronger the traditional arts, and especially song and dance, could remain. The enormous conservatism of the Tibetans, for instance, ensured that the decline of the traditional performing arts culture was slower than among most of the other more populous minorities.

It follows from the continuity of song and dance among the minorities during the Republican period that, as artistic forms, they retained elements characteristic of their own ethnic or regional group, or religion. This applied both to style and cultural context. What this means is that song and dance were prime art forms giving play to the identity and consciousness either of individual minorities or regions or religions. On the other hand, the identity was not a very creative one, being inherited from the past and handed down with relatively little or no change.

Drama

Despite the prevalence of song and dance among China's minorities, the number with a surviving drama tradition as the Qing dynasty fell was rather small.[60] The people with the oldest drama tradition, and the main one without roots deriving from the Han Chinese, were the Tibetans.[61] Other minorities with their own drama traditions included the Bai, Zhuang, Dong, Bouyei, Dai, Koreans, Manchus and Mongols. Other than the Mongols, whose drama tradition had been imported from Tibet along with Tibetan Buddhism, most of these traditions had derivations which made them scarcely different from a regional style of Han theatre. The Hui people lacked their own drama tradition separate from the Han, but Hui people did make substantial contributions to some forms of Han theatre. The best example to illustrate this point is the Hui actor Ma Lianliang (1902–67), who was undoubtedly the finest exponent of the Shanghai school of Peking Opera in the first half of the twentieth century.

In the dramas of the minorities, three main trends stand out for the period of the Republic. One was decline or stagnation of distinctive traditional forms. The second was that new forms which the Han Chinese adopted from elsewhere were rather slow to spread among the minorities, such forms including above all the spoken drama (*huaju*) introduced from the West through Japan in the first decade of the century.[62] Finally, Han influence on theatrical tastes was considerably stronger by the middle of the twentieth century than it had been when the Qing empire fell. The implication was that processes of acculturation had speeded up and the national identities of the minorities was expressed only rather weakly through the drama.

The Manchus at one time had their own traditional form of drama, which was made up of *shuochang* stories performed as drama through traditional songs and dances. The small-scale items generally had only two performers, but the larger casts in the longer and more elaborate pieces were divided in a way similar to the Chinese drama — that is, with *sheng* or male characters, *dan* or female, *jing* (painted face), *chou* (clown) and others. The stories concerned sacrifices to the gods or ancestors, Manchu historical figures and so on. At first the performances were entirely in Manchu, but during the Qing dynasty, the Manchu drama became more and more heavily influenced by the Han. As a result, Han traditional drama forms became increasingly prevalent among the Manchus, while their own tended to go out of fashion and, to the extent that it survived, to use Chinese language in preference to Manchu. There is evidence that isolated performances of the old Manchu drama still took place as late as the 1930s, but by that time Manchu tastes in drama were very little different from Han.[63] The main Manchu contributor to drama of the late Qing and early Republic was the dramatist and actor Wang Xiaonong (1858–1918), but the form in which he excelled was the Peking Opera,[64] a purely Han form, and his being a Manchu was incidental.

Although the drama of the Mongols was introduced from Tibet, their nomadic life severely hampered the development of a drama tradition. Yet they also developed their own tradition to some extent, based on performance at the monasteries. One example is the drama *Moon Cuckoo*, the story of an Indian prince, turned into a cuckoo, who defeats evil and continues to preach Buddhism to the birds. It was written about 1831 by the senior lama Rabjai, born in Inner Mongolia in 1803, and continued to be performed in many monasteries of Inner Mongolia and the eastern Gobi until early in the twentieth century, the roles being played less and less frequently by monks and more by laity, both male and female.[65]

The Mongolian People's Republic, which was established in 1924, gave rise to a revolutionary theatre characterised by its strong propaganda content and by the blending of traditional Mongolian, Western and Chinese patterns. It inevitably influenced the Mongols of Inner Mongolia, especially since it was a useful propaganda weapon against the Japanese occupation of the 1930s and 1940s. Students and other young people adopted modern forms of theatre like the spoken drama, forming themselves into amateur companies and performing items with strong anti-Japanese content for propaganda purposes,[66] their activities spanning the Mongolian areas of the Japanese puppet state of Manchoukuo and those areas which were still part of Chinese provinces. There was a group of Mongol playwrights in Yan'an which produced revolutionary propaganda items in the spoken drama and song drama forms.[67] The CCP set up the Inner Mongolian Autonomous Region in 1947 and among its early cultural actions was the introduction of drama reform and the establishment of formal drama companies.

Of all the minorities, the one with the drama that underwent the greatest change during the Republican period was the Koreans. Several forms of traditional Korean folk and ritual drama, including masked and puppet items, survived into the twentieth century. Early in the century, a new form of opera termed *changguk* (literally 'sung drama') was developed in Seoul, based on the traditional long sung narratives of the Koreans, and absorbing some particularities of Korean performing arts in terms of rhythm, melody and movement. Although this form was taken up in Yanbian, the Japanese were hostile to the Korean arts, which did not flourish under their military occupation.

In the 1920s, the Korean areas began to take a serious interest in the spoken drama, calling it the 'new school drama'. The performers were amateurs and, as in the early days among the Han, the content was social and political, with an emphasis on opposing the old system of arranged marriages. During the period when Yanbian was part of Manchoukuo (1932-45), drama performances were among the ways used to stir up Korean nationalist resistance against the Japanese. As in the Han areas, it was the communists who were most successful, as a result of which Marxist-Leninist ideas became intertwined with nationalist ones in the dramas. These anti-Japanese leftist items were performed by amateurs who carried out their activities mainly in the villages and away from the watchful eyes of the Japanese. In the period after the war, the CCP, which early in 1946 succeeded in filling the vacuum left by the defeated Japanese, established formal companies for the performance of drama, such as the Spark Troupe and the Yanbian Cultural Work Troupe, both in Yanbian. The CCP authorities promoted older Korean forms like the *changguk*, as well as the newer spoken dramas. The content was still extremely politicised, with many items set during the war and focusing on anti-Japanese propaganda.[68]

At the other end of northern China, in Xinjiang, the Islamic nationalities like the Uygurs and Kazaks all had superb song and dance and musical traditions, but not drama — no doubt at least in part because of the proscriptions laid on such performances by Islamic law. Because of Soviet influence, strongly supported in the policies of Sheng Shicai's regime, both artists and intellectuals were keen to produce new dramas, either spoken plays or operas, which blended the Marxist-Leninist Soviet style with the traditions of the relevant minority. One of the practitioners was the poet Lutpulla Mutallip discussed above. In the early 1930s, folk artists in parts of Xinjiang began experimenting with small-scale operas and musical plays and ballets. Later, in the 1930s, clubs promoting theatre and experimental play troupes were set up in Ürümqi, Kaxgar, Yili and other places. The first full-length Uygur opera, using a Uygur story and combining Western and Uygur musical instruments for accompaniment, dates from 1936. Entitled *Erip and Sanam*, it was two hours in length and based on the traditional love story of the same name. Introduced under Soviet influence it predated the premiere of the first full-length Han song drama (*geju*), *The White-Haired Girl* (*Baimao nü*) by nearly a decade.

Among the minorities of southern China, the one with the oldest style of drama is probably the Bai. Called *Chuichui qiang* (literally 'blow tunes'), it may date as far back as the fourteenth century.[69] However, although it does illustrate some Bai features, such as the poetic structure of the lyrics, it derives from Han regional theatre and its stories are taken mainly from Han novels and dramas. By the Republican period, it was quite static, with no major innovations occurring during that time. The main change to the drama diet of the Bai people in the first half of the twentieth century was the introduction of the spoken drama during the War of Resistance against Japan. Students of the Central China (Huazhong) University in Wuhan went to Dali, Yunnan province, to perform anti-Japanese items.[70] It is clear even from this limited material that the ethnic identity of the Bai gained hardly anything from drama between 1912 and 1949.

Another minority with a good drama tradition, and one which saw a definite development during the Republican period, was the Dong. The Dong drama came into existence in Guizhou in the 1830s, based on arrangements for the stage of Han stories translated into Dong language and Dong long epic poems. Three changes worthy of note took place during the second and third decades of the twentieth century. The first was that Dong drama spread from Guizhou to the Dong regions of Guangxi, in particular Sanjiang in the far north near the border with Guizhou and Hunan. The first Dong troupe in Sanjiang was set up after 1915 when two teachers moved from Guizhou to Sanjiang and there took on pupils. The second change was a trend in favour of using Dong epic poems, legends and stories as material for the Dong drama in preference to Han stories, the implication being that Dong drama became to some extent a more specific symbol of Dong identity than had earlier been the case.

The third development in Dong drama in the Republican period exemplifies the second, namely the composition of the item which has become the best known of all Dong dramas, *Julang and Nyangmui*. The two authors were Liang Shaohua (1893–1978) and Liang Yaoting, about ten years his senior. Liang Shaohua had already been an actor for several years when the collaborative composition began, in the second decade of the century, but Liang Yaoting died before the work was finished, so Liang Shaohua completed it and took his troupe on tour in various Dong areas performing it, to enthusiastic response. The drama is set in mid-nineteenth-century Dong society and concerns the love between Julang and Nyangmui. Because Nyangmui's parents have arranged an alternative marriage for her, the lovers elope to a village and take work there, but their landlord boss lusts after Nyangmui and kills Julang. In the original version Nyangmui escapes into the mountains and marries an invalid to whom she bears two sons. Having gained an education, one of them becomes an official, enabling him to take revenge on the landlord. The item was enormously long, taking up to seven days to perform in full.[71]

One general form of theatre which is common in the villages of southern provinces like Guizhou, Guangxi and Hunan is the *nuo* drama. It is a form of religious ritual theatre deriving originally from exorcistic dances found among the nationalities of the area, including not only the Han, but also the Bouyei, Yi, Tujia, Yao, Miao and others. The most striking shared feature of the numerous forms of *nuo* drama is the use of masks. These vary from nationality to nationality and enable particular characters, and their features, to be recognised immediately. The stories are generally strongly influenced by the Han and often come from classical novels such as *The Romance of the Three Kingdoms* — in other words, the content is not necessarily religious, even though the occasions for performance may be so.[72]

The *nuo* drama is ancient, masked theatre, being attested as early as the Song dynasty in Guangxi.[73] However, it certainly survived into the twentieth century, even in the cities. Moreover, there are particular types which are of twentieth-century origin, a probable example being the 'changing into people drama' (*bianren xi*) of the Yi of Weining in Guizhou. This concerns the origins of the Yi people, dramatising the change of monkeys into people.[74]

A form of minority drama said to be at least partly derived from *nuo* is Bouyei drama. Its origin is either late Qing or Republican period, but although it was popular among the Bouyei, in fact it was so strongly influenced by the Han that it differs little in style and character classification from a typical Han regional theatre style. The stories are either Han or Bouyei in origin. In the case of the Han plots, only the sung sections use Bouyei language exclusively, the other parts being partly or entirely in Chinese.[75]

Although in the early Qing period, it was the Tibetans among all China's minorities who had the strongest drama tradition, there appears to have been very little development in later periods. The number of items performed was traditionally quite limited, and none was added during the Republican period, suggesting that creativity had reached a dead end. According to Snellgrove and Richardson, performances were rare at that time, but the dramas were 'immensely popular' and would draw spectators from miles around.[76]

Tibetan drama is characterised by its masks, melismatic singing and the immensely important role of dance in the action. The stories are mythological and, although the drama is essentially a secular form of entertainment, heavily infused with religious ideas and characters. The items were extremely long, lasting up to several days. Performances took places under tents with the audience sitting or standing around in an almost complete circle.[77]

Conclusion

It is perhaps not surprising that not many of the literary or theatre figures of the minorities became recognised China-wide as pre-eminent. What is more striking is that a few of them did so. In the field of fiction these were mainly the Manchu Lao She and the part-Miao Shen Congwen, and in the theatre the Hui actor Ma Lianliang. On the other hand, these artists contributed very little or nothing at all to the identities of their own minorities, but rather to that of China as a whole. Lao She and Shen Congwen are both in the mainstream of twentieth-century Chinese fiction, meaning that their belonging to a minority was more or less irrelevant. As for Ma Lianliang, he achieved fame and distinction in a Han form of drama, in which it was very easy to forget that he was not himself Han. In this sense, the literature and drama of China in the first half of the twentieth century were assimilative in nature.

The impact of the Japanese on the literatures and performing arts of the minorities in the regions they occupied was substantial. What happened was that, at the same time as the occupation did great damage to the traditional arts, it provoked a nationalist backlash which, while not outstanding in the literature it produced, was creative in that it adapted national characteristics and settings to new forms imported from outside. The Korean and Mongolian languages could be used for a form such as the spoken drama which was new and not part of the traditional theatre.

Among those nationalities which retained their traditions and identities most strongly, few created anything new. Tibetan literature and performing arts and the oral literatures and dances of the Mongols, Miao, Dai and others persisted, resisting even mild change. The Dong drama was at first an exception to a pattern of overall stagnation and decline, but a period of unusual creativity in the first decade and more of the Republican period tended to peter out in the course of time. Other traditional forms, such as the Manchu drama, declined almost to the point of vanishing.

In terms of identities and creativity, the Republican period was not a good one for the literatures and performing arts of the minorities. While the traditional folk arts certainly retained national features, what change occurred was more integrative with China or Japan than giving prominence to the identity or consciousness of the individual nationality. Thus a Chinese national event such as the 1911 Revolution was cause for rejoicing among the masses of many peoples other than the Han. There was certainly nationalist reaction against the Japanese and, in Xinjiang, against the Soviet Union. Yet, in the arts, it was against an invasion or other onslaught that feelings of nationalist consciousness were focused. Positive feelings of consciousness of identity appear to have been directed more towards religion or region than nationality.

Notes

1 Mark Bender, 'Approaching the Literatures of China's Minority Nationalities', *China Exchange News*, vol. 21, nos 3 and 4, Fall–Winter 1993, p. 14.

2 For a brief English-language account of traditional Tibetan literature, see R.A. Stein, trans. J.E. Stapleton Driver, *Tibetan Civilization*, Faber and Faber, London, 1972, pp. 248–81.

3 See Mao Xing (gen. ed.), *Zhongguo shaoshu minzu wenxue*, Hunan Renmin chubanshe, Changsha, 1983, vol. 1, pp. 446–54. This work is a large-scale three-volumed account of the literatures of China's minorities, arranged by nationality and, within each, by form and chronologically. The overwhelming focus is on the tradition, but in some cases there is substantial material on the twentieth century.

4 See Sechin Jagchid and Paul Hyer, *Mongolia's Culture and Society*, Westview Press, Boulder, 1979, pp. 218–19. Some of the Mongols further north regard their conationals from Injannashi's home area as 'quite Sinicised' and thus 'tainted': ibid., p. 142.

5 Walther Heissig, *Geschichte der mongolischen Literatur*, Otto Harrassowitz,Wiesbaden, 1972, vol. 1, p. XI. On Injannashi and his works, including *The Blue History*, see also Mao (gen. ed.), *Zhongguo shaoshu minzu wenxue*, vol. 2, pp. 137–49.

6 This 'Chagatai literature' or 'literature of the Chagatai period' is discussed in some detail in Mao (gen. ed.), *Zhongguo shaoshu minzu wenxue*, vol. 1, pp. 95–128.

7 Zhang Juling, *Qingdai Manzu zuojia wenxue gailun*, Zhongyang minzu xueyuan chubanshe, Beijing, 1990, p. 10. This work gives a full account of authored Manchu literature during the Qing period.

8 Cao wrote virtually all the first 80 chapters of the total 120 which made up the first full printed edition of 1791.

9 Li Zuanxu, *Baizu wenxue shilüe*, Zhongguo minjian wenyi chubanshe [Yunnan ban], Kunming, 1984, p. 263. A major study of the written literature of the Bai people from the Yuan to the Qing periods can be found on pp. 220–326.

10 On Lu Dayong and his work, including excerpts from two of his poems, see Mao (gen. ed.), *Zhongguo shaoshu minzu wenxue*, vol. 2, pp. 716–21.

11 Ma Xueliang, Liang Tingwang, Zhang Gongjin et al., *Zhongguo shaoshu minzu wenxue shi*, Zhongyang minzu xueyuan chubanshe, Beijing, 1992, vol. 1, pp. 3–4. This work is a full-scale and comprehensive account of the literatures of China's minorities. Its focus is historical and literary analysis, including attention to specific works, and it is arranged by historical period.

12 Mao (gen. ed.), *Zhongguo shaoshu minzu wenxue*, vol. 3, p. 4.

13 Yang Quan, *Dongzu minjian wenxue shi*, Zhongyang minzu xueyuan chubanshe, Beijing, 1992, pp. 19–20.

14 Owen Lattimore et al., *Pivot of Asia, Sinkiang and the Inner Asian Frontiers of China and Russia*, Little, Brown and Co., Boston, 1950, AMS, New York, 1975 reprint, p. 258.

15 See the account of the Manas epic in Zhirmunsky, Victor, 'Epic Songs and Singers in Central Asia', in Nora K. Chadwick and Victor Zhirmunsky, *Oral Epics of Central Asia*, Cambridge University Press, Cambridge, 1969, pp. 304–7. Zhirmunsky claims (p. 306) that a literary document was published in 1959 testifying that the legend of Manas was known as early as the beginning of the sixteenth century. On the Manas epic, including extensive translations into Chinese, see also Mao (gen. ed.), *Zhongguo shaoshu minzu wenxue*, vol. 1, pp. 321–50.

16 There is a substantial literature on the Prince Ge sar epic. The most important contribution is that by R.A. Stein, especially *Recherches sur l'épopée et le barde au Tibet*, Presses universitaires de France, Paris, 1959, which contains a very fine bibliography on the Ge sar epic on pp. 9–42, but there has been a good deal of work done since then, much of it in the PRC.

17 Interview held on 4 September 1990 at the Languages and Literature Research Institute of Lhasa's Tibetan Social Sciences Academy, this national literary masterpiece being one of the Institute's four specialities. R.A. Stein considers that the basic cycle of the epic 'seems to have had an independent existence since the early fifteenth or late fourteenth century': see Stein, *Tibetan Civilization*, p. 279.

18 See Stein, *Recherches sur l'épopée*, pp. 43–106, where the sources and those various written versions available to Stein are discussed in considerable detail.

19 R.A. Stein has identified the places referred to in the Ge sar epic in considerable detail, reaching the conclusion that it is set in eastern Tibet: see *Recherches sur l'épopée*, pp. 183–210.

20 For a scholarly but accessible account of 'The Epic of Geser Khan' in English, see Walther Heissig, trans. D.J.S. Thomson, *A Lost Civilization, The Mongols Rediscovered*, Thames and Hudson, London, 1966, pp. 134–51.

21 See Walther Heissig, trans. Geoffrey Samuel, *The Religions of Mongolia*, Routledge & Kegan Paul, London and Henley, 1980, pp. 93–101.

22 Ma, Liang, Zhang et al., *Zhongguo shaoshu minzu wenxue shi*, vol. 2, pp. 220–21.

23 ibid., p. 464.

24 On this poem, see Yang Liangcai, Tao Lifan and Deng Minwen, *Zhongguo shaoshu minzu wenxue*, Renmin chubanshe, Beijing, 1985, pp. 143–48.

25 See Lattimore, et al., *Pivot of Asia*, pp. 250–51.

26 The general features of minorities' literatures in the late Qing and early Republic are discussed in Ma, Liang, Zhang et al., *Zhongguo shaoshu minzu wenxue shi*, vol. 2, pp. 462–65.

27 David Snellgrove and Hugh Richardson, *A Cultural History of Tibet*, Weidenfeld and Nicolson, London, 1968, p. 230.

28 Interview at the Tibetan Social Sciences Academy, Lhasa, 4 September 1990.

29 Ma, Liang, Zhang et al., *Zhongguo shaoshu minzu wenxue shi*, vol. 2, pp. 464–65.

30 Yang, *Dongzu minjian wenxue shi*, pp. 262–64.

31 On this poem, see Yang, Tao and Deng, *Zhongguo shaoshu minzu wenxue*, pp. 137–42. Although the poem is based on history, it contains some falsifications too — for instance, the depiction of Zhang Zuolin as the main opponent of the rebellion and the central Han figure robbing the Mongols of their land. Zhang Zuolin died in June 1928 before the uprising occurred. See Colin Mackerras, 'Traditional Mongolian Performing Arts in Inner Mongolia, *The Australian Journal of Chinese Affairs*, no. 10, July 1983, p. 20.

32 Quoted in *Brief History of the Mongol Nationality* Compilation Group, *Menggu zu jianshi*, Nei Menggu Renmin chubanshe, Huhhot, 1985, p. 467.

33 On the Tibetan bard as well as his social origin and status, and the occasions of performance, see Stein, *Recherches*, pp. 317–42.

34 Kanglang Shuai is a transcription of his Dai artistic name, Kanglang meaning 'a high-grade intellectual' and Shuai being the respectful form of address given him. See Yang, Tao and Deng, *Zhongguo shaoshu minzu wenxue*, p. 291.

35 Many Chinese stories and novels had been translated into Mongolian either directly from Chinese or via a Manchu version. See Jagchid and Hyer, *Mongolia's Culture and Society*, p. 219.

36 See Yang, Tao and Deng, *Zhongguo shaoshu minzu wenxue*, pp. 286–87.

37 Heissig, *Geschichte der mongolischen Literatur*, vol. 2, p. 841. See a more detailed account of Pajai's life and work on pp. 838–43. Heissig give the date of his death (p. 843) as 1960, but provides no source. The Chinese account, which gives 1962, is probably in a better position to know such a detail.

38 Yang, Tao and Deng, *Zhongguo shaoshu minzu wenxue*, pp. 291–93.

39 During a visit to Shen Congwen's birthplace in February 1992, this writer was informed by a close female relation of Shen's by marriage,

herself Han, that his mother was Miao and his father Han. Jeffrey Kinkley states in his *The Odyssey of Shen Congwen*, Stanford University Press, Stanford, 1987, p. 20, that Shen Congwen's mother was Tujia and his paternal grandmother Miao. Either version of Shen's ancestry would confirm his minority background.

40 Ranbir Vohra, *Lao She and the Chinese Revolution*, East Asian Research Center, Harvard University, Cambridge, Mass., 1974, p. 20

41 See, for example, Wang Baolin, Xie Yunmei, Wu Lide et al. (eds), *Zhongguo shaoshu minzu xiandai wenxue*, Guangxi Renmin chubanshe, Nanning, 1989, pp. 361–72.

42 Kinkley, *The Odyssey of Shen Congwen*, p. 21.

43 ibid., p. 150.

44 Helmut Martin and Jeffrey Kinkley (eds), *Modern Chinese Writers, Self-Portrayals*, M.E. Sharpe, Armonk, London, 1992, p. 289.

45 See Kinkley, *The Odyssey of Shen Congwen*, p. 21.

46 *Brief History of the Koreans* Compilation Group, *Chaoxian zu jianshi*, Yanbian Renmin chubanshe, Yanji, 1986, pp. 206–7. During an interview at Yanbian University on 28 September 1990, this writer was informed that Kim's complete works were being collected and would be published in twelve volumes.

47 *Chaoxian zu jianshi*, p. 210. For further material on specific Korean writers of the period, see Wang et al., *Xiandai wenxue*, pp. 71–87, including Kim Bong-yong, pp. 71–74.

48 See *Chaoxian zu jianshi*, pp. 209–16.

49 See Eden Naby, 'Uighur Literature: The Antecedents', in Shirin Akiner (ed.), *Cultural Change and Continuity in Central Asia*, Kegan Paul International, London and New York, in association with the Central Asia Research Forum, School of Oriental and African Studies, London, 1991, pp. 24–26.

50 Mao (gen. ed.), *Zhongguo shaoshu minzu wenxue*, vol. 1, pp. 140–55, 206–11.

51 The opening lines of the poem, this stanza was recited to me in Uygur by a young Uygur in October 1994 and translated into English.

52 See the accounts of Mutlif's short career and his work in Wang et al., *Xiandai wenxue*, pp. 189–97; Mao (gen. ed.), *Zhongguo shaoshu minzu wenxue*, vol. 1, pp. 144–49; and Yang, Tao and Deng, *Zhongguo shaoshu minzu wenxue*, pp. 283–86.

53 Zhao's biography can be found in Li, *Baizu wenxue shilüe*, pp. 330–37. On p. 337 Li sums up Zhao's career by emphasising that his poems showed anti-Japanese patriotism and love for his homeland. Li's conclusion is that Zhao's work shows not only his patriotism, but love for his nationality and people. However, to me the evidence he himself presents points far more to Zhao's love for China and the locality of his birth than to loyalty towards the Bai as an ethnic group.

54 Snellgrove and Richardson, *A Cultural History of Tibet*, p. 245.

55 Wang et al., *Xiandai wenxue*, pp. 483–84.

56 See the words of the song in Huang Xianfan, Huang Zengqing and Zhang Yimin, *Zhuangzu tongshi*, Guangxi Minzu chubanshe, Nanning, 1988, pp. 577–78.

57 Interview with Professor Ke Yang of Lanzhou University, 17 September 1990, and Xue Li and Ke Yang (eds), *Huaer xuanji*, Gansu Renmin chubanshe, Lanzhou, 1980, pp. 1–4. See a sample of the traditional love *huaer*, pp. 67–173.

58 See Snellgrove and Richardson, A Cultural History of Tibet, pp. 181, 246–47; Giuseppe Tucci, trans. Geoffrey Samuel, *The Religions of Tibet*, Routledge & Kegan Paul, London and Henley, 1980, pp. 150–51.

59 See Heissig, trans. Samuel, *The Religions of Mongolia*, pp. 81, 109 and Heissig, trans. Thomson, *A Lost Civilization*, pp. 215–16, 220.

60 For an account of the traditional dramas of China's minorities in English see Colin Mackerras, *Chinese Drama, A Historical Survey*, New World Press, Beijing, 1990, pp. 130–45.

61 R.A. Stein, *Tibetan Civilization*, p. 278, believes that the structure of Tibetan drama is of Indian origin, but with influence from Chinese drama.

62 For an summary of the Han spoken drama before 1949 see Mackerras, *Chinese Drama*, pp. 104–13.

63 Ji Yonghai and Zhao Zhizhong, *Manzu minjian wenxue gailun*, Zhongyang minzu xueyuan chubanshe, Beijing, 1991, pp. 196–99.

64 Ma, Liang, Zhang et al., *Zhongguo shaoshu minzu wenxue shi*, vol. 2, pp. 529–30.

65 See Heissig, trans. Thomson, *A Lost Civilization*, pp. 211–27.

66 Jagchid and Hyer, *Mongolia's Culture and Society*, p. 243.

67 *Menggu zu jianshi*, p. 470.

68 *Chaoxian zu jianshi*, pp. 206, 210–11, 213–15. See also Wang et al., *Xiandai wenxue*, pp. 90–92.

69 Zhang Wenxun et al., *Baizu wenxue shi, xiuding ban*, Yunnan Renmin chubanshe, Kunming, 1983, p. 326.

70 ibid., p. 342.

71 Yang, *Dongzu minjian wenxue shi*, pp. 286–87. One version of the dates suggests that the work was begun in 1911 and completed shortly after Liang Yaoting's death in 1916, but an alternative version puts his death and the subsequent completion of the work about five years later. See also *History of Dong Literature* Compilation Group, *Dongzu wenxue shi*, Guizhou Minzu chubanshe, Guiyang, 1988, p. 288, which states that Liang Shaohua arranged the drama in 1921 according to a folk legend and long lyric poem of the same name.

72 There is now a growing scholarly literature in Chinese on the *nuo* theatre, a good example being Tuo Xiuming et al. (eds), *Zhongguo nuo wenhua lunwen xuan*, Guizhou minzu chubanshe, Guiyang, 1989.

73 The writer Zhou Chufei (fl. c. 1163–80) states that 'the people of Guilin excel in the manufacture of play masks', their 'exorcism troupes' being famous in the capital Hangzhou. See the citation in William Dolby,

'Early Chinese Plays and Theater', in Colin Mackerras (ed.), *Chinese Theater From Its Origins to the Present Day*, University of Hawaii Press, Honolulu, 1983, pp. 28–29.

74 Interview with drama specialists in Guiyang on 31 October 1990. See also Qu Liuyi, 'Zhongguo ge minzu nuoxi de fenlei, tezheng ji qi "huo huashi" jiazhi', in Tuo Xiuming et al. (eds), *Zhongguo nuo wenhua lunwen xuan*, pp. 5–6.

75 Ma, Liang, Zhang et al., *Zhongguo shaoshu minzu wenxue shi*, vol. 2, p. 535.

76 Snellgrove and Richardson, *A Cultural History of Tibet*, p. 258.

77 There is a growing literature on the Tibetan drama, much of it cited in Colin Mackerras, 'Drama in the Tibetan Autonomous Region', *Asian Theatre Journal*, vol. 5, no. 2, Fall 1988, pp. 217–19. A simple account by a Tibetan in English can be found in Tiley Chodag, trans. W. Tailing, *Tibet, the Land and the People*, New World Press, Beijing, 1988, pp. 305–28.

6 Religion Among the Minority Nationalities, 1949–1995

Since the People's Republic of China (PRC) has been ruled during its entire period by the Marxist-Leninist — and thus explicitly atheist — Chinese Communist Party (CCP), there is no surprise that the overall impact of its government on religion among the minorities has been to weaken it greatly. There have been periods of strong persecution in this process, and the CCP has done all it can to make religion less socially relevant than it once was before 1949. Yet, among some of the minorities, religion retains considerable social influence — including its impact on ethnic identities — which no government can afford to ignore.

Just as before 1949, religion has exerted a far greater influence among some of minorities than others or than the Han. Several of the religions espoused by the minority nationalities continue even in the 1990s to have clergies which expect to exert powerful influences among their own nationalities. These include Islam, Tibetan Buddhism and Mahayana Buddhism. Such clergies play a strong role in the preservation and strengthening of ethnic identities among the minorities.

Policy on religion and religious freedom

For all periods other than the Cultural Revolution (1966–76), policy towards religion among the minorities has combined the two factors of autonomy for the nationalities and a degree of tolerance towards religion, but only within several clearly defined parameters. Marxism-Leninism being avowedly extremely anti-religious, the CCP early made clear its intention to ensure that religious bodies were stripped of their political and economic power. Consequently, they found implacable resistance among many religious leaders. The CCP's intent was to control religion as far as it could for its own purposes, including that among the minorities. To this end, it established government-sponsored religious organisations, which could be shown to doubters as evidence of religious freedom, but would actually assist the CCP to establish its rule.[1]

Most of the major religions — Buddhism, Daoism and Christianity — were shared among Han and minorities alike. In this respect, Islam comprised a special category. By the definitions imposed by the CCP, it was impossible to be both Muslim and Han at the same time. Those Muslims closest culturally and ethnically to the Han were identified as Hui, while the Islamic nationalities of Xinjiang were, of all the minorities, among those farthest from the Han.[2] The Chinese Islamic Association (*Zhongguo Yisilanjiao xiehui*) was formally established in May 1953 as the government-sponsored body representing Chinese Muslims.[3]

One important part of early PRC policy in general and towards religion in particular was to uproot imperialist influence and to improve relations with anti-colonial foreign countries. Western missionaries, including those in minority areas, were expelled or placed in a position where they had no alternative but to leave. In a typical statement, the Vice-Chairman of the Chinese Islamic Association, Zhang Jie, declared in 1962 that Muslims had enjoyed no religious freedom before 1949 because 'at that time, imperialism colluded with the reactionary ruling class in our country in using religion as a tool with which to consolidate their rule and oppress the people of various nationalities'.[4] The other side of opposing imperialism and colonialism was co-operation with those countries of the world most dedicated to the struggle against them. The most relevant minority religion was again Islam, because it was practised enthusiastically in so many different parts of the world, including several sympathetic or committed to the struggle against imperialism and colonialism.[5]

The United Nations' 'Universal Declaration of Human Rights' states in Article 18 that 'everyone has the right to freedom of thought, conscience and religion', including the 'freedom to change his [*sic.*] religion or belief'. Although it specifies the freedom to manifest religion 'in teaching, practice, worship and observance', it does not include the right to undertake religious propaganda.[6]

All four state constitutions of the PRC, those of 1954, 1975, 1978 and 1982, stipulate that citizens 'enjoy freedom to believe in religion and freedom not to believe in religion and to propagate atheism'.[7] In practice, freedom of religion has not been consistently implemented. At the same time, an attempt to uproot tradition and the groups which represent it should not necessarily be interpreted as persecution of religion.

There have been several important qualifications to the freedom of religious practice right from the start of the PRC. One is that religion should not interfere in politics or the legal system, and above all should not be used to split the country. These proscriptions apply not only to a religion such as the Catholic Church, with its tradition of political involvement and loyalty to a non-Chinese prelate, but also to any faith where the leaders try to split a particular part of China off from the rest of the country. This has become a serious problem among those nationalities which have made religion a strong part of politics. The main example of this is the Tibetans, but others would include Islamic minorities such as the Uygurs. Attempts to counter such trends by educating religious leaders in 'patriotism, socialism, and the unity of the nationalities' have been frequent.[8]

The second qualification on religious freedom is the ownership of property. Since the religious bodies of all nationalities in China were major landowners, land reform carried out in the early stages of PRC rule resulted in the requisition of monastic estates and lands. Tibet, which had signed a unique agreement with the central government, was initially largely exempted, but after the rebellion of 1959 the enormous landholdings of the monasteries there were also taken over by the government authorities.

Marxism-Leninism regards religion as non-productive. As a result of this policy, many temples began to be used for other purposes, especially for schools or offices. Since funds have always been short, it seemed appropriate to use already existing and perfectly adequate buildings for productive purposes such as education. Just outside the city of Xiaguan, the former capital of the Dali Bai autonomous prefecture, there is a large temple located atop a hill which dominates the surrounding countryside in a spectacular way. During a visit to the temple in 1985, this writer found that it had been taken over as the headquarters of the CCP for the area. It would be possible to cite many other similar examples.

At all stages it has been CCP policy — in line with the overall theory of autonomy — that the 'customs and habits' of the minority nationalities should be respected, as long as they are not against socialism. This policy applies also to religious practices. Muslim nationalities have always been perfectly entitled to abstain from pork. On the other hand, the custom of some communities of the Va people in Yunnan of 'sacrificing hunters' heads to the valley as entreaty for a bumper harvest'[9] was banned, even though it was part of the Va nature worship. Islamic practice did not entitle any man to have four wives. In other areas it has proven more difficult to determine a fair policy. One example is whether Muslim women should be allowed to wear the veil, a matter discussed below.

On a related question, CCP policy draws a sharp distinction between 'religious activities', which are permitted, and 'feudal superstitions', which are banned. Examples of the former are worshipping Buddha, chanting scriptures, burning incense and offering or attending the Mass. 'Feudal superstitions' include the use of their power as witch-doctors or faith healers by male sorcerers (*shenhan*) or female sorcerers (*wupo*) to harm the health of the people. Article 99 of the PRC's Criminal Code of 1979 outlaws 'making use of feudal superstitions in order to carry out counter-revolutionary activities'. Article 165 prescribes severe penalties for 'male or female sorcerers who use feudal superstitions to spread rumours or defraud people of their property'.[10]

The last qualification to mention is that freedom of religious belief does not include the right to proselytise. There is no guarantee at all that clergy may carry out pastoral work among the faithful. Religious bodies may not 'interfere in . . . school education or in social public education'.[11] Religion is allowed no positive place in the state school curriculum. On the other hand, Muslims are permitted to summon people to the mosque to worship, or to run designated schools which aim to teach aspiring clergy Arabic, the *Koran* and Islamic doctrine, practices and history.

The 1950s and early 1960s were years of formal religious tolerance but actual heavy pressure against religious bodies, including those of the minority nationalities. Propaganda was strong and consistent in opposition to religions and in support of socialism. Monastic estates were requisitioned, and many temples, mosques and churches were taken over for other purposes or even destroyed. According to one account, the worst period for the destruction of monasteries in Tibet was from 1959–61.[12]

A few figures survive from the period which, despite their shortcomings as deriving from sources hostile to religion, are consistent in showing declines in the numbers of clergy and religious buildings. A 1956 estimate claims there were about 120 000 to 150 000 lamas in Tibet, as well as some elsewhere, such as Qinghai, Gansu, Sichuan and Inner Mongolia.[13] The term 'lamas' should be interpreted as including ordinary monks and all males in the monastic estate. In Tibet, monks and nuns constituted 9.5 per cent of the total population just before the rebellion of 1959. However, the reforms which followed the uprising forced most of them to return to lay life or seek refuge abroad, so in 1960 the proportion fell drastically to 1.4 per cent.[14] In one part of Inner Mongolia, lamas and monks were claimed to make up 13.5 per cent of the population in 1956.[15] In Ningxia there were over 1600 mosques in the early 1950s, but a reform of the religious system in 1959 resulted in a sharp drop to some 900.[16]

By far the worst period for religion in the years covered by this book was the Cultural Revolution decade from 1966–76. The description of two writers on this period among the nomads of Western Tibet as 'a decade of pain and suffering' which not only took away religious freedom but 'almost destroyed their way of life'[17] would apply more or less universally among the religious minorities. The obsession with class struggle which characterised the period resulted in the forced closure of the great majority of functioning temples, monasteries, mosques and churches, as well as of all theological colleges of any religion. In 1985 and 1990 this writer visited the dGa' ldan Monastery some 60 kilometres from Lhasa in Tibet. The extent of destruction visible was enormous — so great that this once enormous and beautiful complex had obviously been dynamited.

Numerous informants in nationality areas visited in the 1980s and 1990s complained of various types of persecution during the Cultural Revolution years, ranging from the forcible return of monks to lay life as reactionary feudal remnants to the prevention of ordinary people from observing their religion or visiting temples or mosques. An old Mongol monk at the famous Wudang zhao near Baotou in Inner Mongolia whom I interviewed late in 1992 left me with the very clear impression that his community had suffered very much more intensely during the Cultural Revolution than during the Japanese occupation. The Japanese had largely left them alone, he said, whereas the Red Guards of the Cultural Revolution abused them as reactionaries, forcing them to marry and to undergo physical labour.[18]

The 1980s and 1990s have seen a return to the policies preceding the Cultural Revolution, based essentially on autonomy and conditional tolerance of formal religion, though not of feudal superstition. In March 1982, the Central Committee of the CCP issued an official communiqué entitled 'Concerning the Basic Viewpoint and Policy Towards the Question of Religion during China's Socialist Period', which summarised the PRC's policies and experiences in religion in some detail.[19] One of the points affecting the minorities raised in the document concerns members of the CCP. In general, these must believe in Marxism and hence atheism, which means that they do not enjoy the freedom of religion available to other citizens. However, the rule should not be inflexibly applied. Among minorities, religion is often an essential part of social life and customs. Moreover, among some minorities, 'nationality and religion are one and the same thing'. For this reason, they should be at least in part exempt from the rule which forbids CCP members to believe in religion or participate in religious activities.[20] In Xinjiang, CCP members may believe in Islam and attend such ceremonies as funerals, but not pray at the mosque five times a day or on Fridays. Even these limitations are not enforced rigidly. A middle-aged Tajik government worker was quite happy to tell me in October 1994 both that he was a CCP member and that he prayed frequently on Fridays and sometimes several times a day.

Despite the change in policy in the 1980s and 1990s, reports have persisted suggesting that the policy of freedom of religion has not been properly implemented in reality. Among the minorities, the most serious allegations of human rights abuses in the field of minorities' religion have been among the Tibetans. Amnesty International has regularly alleged cases of arbitrary arrest and long-term detention without charge or trial, especially of monks and nuns. One example concerns at least sixteen nuns arrested for demonstrating against the Chinese, some of whom were 'sent to labour camps without charge or trial' with others tried before imprisonment but in ways 'not believed to have satisfied international fair trial standards'.[21]

Although there has been religious persecution in China in the 1980s and 1990s, two points should be added in fairness. One is that most incidents, including among those documented by Amnesty International, in fact come under the heading of the suppression of attempted secession rather than direct persecution of religion. This issue is discussed in greater detail below, especially as it affects Tibet. The second point is that the situation has improved immeasurably when compared with the Cultural Revolution years. The suggestion that the comparative religious tolerance of the 1980s and 1990s is just for show and illusory is not borne out by my impressions or most commentators.[22]

Religious revival in the 1980s and 1990s

In the 1980s and 1990s, religion has to a large extent been revived. Buddhist, Christian and Islamic theological colleges have been opened or reopened.[23] Sympathetic research on religions is once more being undertaken. Religious associations have recommenced activities and religious buildings have been restored. Religions of various kinds once again occupy a major role in the lives of many of the minorities.

The extent of religious revival varies enormously among the different nationalities, being in general strongest among the Tibetans and the Islamic nationalities, but weakest among the Koreans. In between these two extremes are a whole series which would see the Dai of Yunnan at the upper end and the Mongols and polytheistic ancestor- and nature-worshipping groups such as the Miao at the lower. Among the various religions, the most influential in the period of reform are Tibetan Buddhism and Islam.

Tibetan Buddhism

Official figures are explicit that the Tibetan clergy was expanding in number, at least until late 1994, when the Tibetan government issued a directive circumscribing the number of monks and nuns.[24] By 1984, the proportion of the population of Tibet in the clerical order was 0.21 per cent and rising.[25] In 1992, the Chairman of the Tibet autonomous region government claimed that there were 34 000 monks and nuns — 1.5 per cent of the total population at that time.[26] My visits to the 'Bras spungs and especially the Se ra Monasteries outside Lhasa both in 1985 and in 1990 suggest that there is no shortage of young Tibetan men quite anxious to enter the monastic life, although social and political pressures are likely to prevent the proportion from regaining its pre-1966 level. At the same time, the manifestations of religion are everywhere to be seen in society. Virtually every Tibetan house in the countryside has prayer flags fluttering above it, and this applies to most of those in the urban areas as well. Each of those houses this writer was able to visit had a special room set aside for religious purposes, with battery-operated prayer wheels permanently revolving. There is widespread worship both of the Dalai Lama and the Panchen Lama, especially the former, their pictures being prominently displayed in the temples. Those monasteries and temples damaged or destroyed during the Cultural

Revolution are being systematically restored, often at considerable expense, one very good example being the great dGa' ldan Monastery some 60 kilometres outside Lhasa.[27]

The other main nationality to espouse Tibetan Buddhism is the Mongols, but among them religion is not nearly as strong as it is among the Tibetans. There are several large monasteries still open and functioning, among which the Wudang zhao near Baotou is pre-eminent, but few are major religious centres. Over the last several decades, Mongols of both Inner Mongolia and the Mongolian People's Republic have been subjected to intense anti-religious pressures. Ironically enough, even in the early 1990s, after a major religious revival had begun in the Mongolian People's Republic (renamed the State of Mongolia in 1991), Tibetan Buddhism remained weaker among Mongols there than in China. An abbot of a monastery in the Mongolian capital Ulan Bator is quoted as saying that he had visited and found much to admire and learn from in religious establishments in Inner Mongolia and Qinghai. 'They have sutras, ritual artefacts, temple architecture . . . They even have duly ordained Living Buddhas, properly selected according to the exacting criteria for recognising reincarnated lamas', all features he found lacking in his own country.[28]

Yet visits to Buddhist monasteries in Inner Mongolia and Tibet provide quite a few very stark contrasts. In Inner Mongolian monasteries, the monks, the buildings, their interiors and the courtyards are all very clean, whereas in Tibet the buildings are rather badly kept and the monks are badly dressed. In Tibet there are many pilgrims when the monasteries are open, with people lighting yak butter lamps and revolving prayer wheels. In front of the great Jo khang Temple in central Lhasa there are numerous people, especially women, prostrating themselves. At Inner Mongolian monasteries there are hardly any pilgrims, and few people either revolve prayer wheels, except for amusement, or go down in prostration; indeed, most visitors appear to come not for prayer, but for interest. In Tibet, beggars gather outside many of the big religious buildings, especially the Jo khang Temple and the Se ra Monastery. But I saw not a single beggar in any of the temples or monasteries I visited in Inner Mongolia. The contrasts can be summed up by saying that religious buildings in Tibet are centres of strong Buddhist practice and conviction, whereas those of Inner Mongolia are as much museums as places of religious worship.

Islam

Religion is a significant force among all the Islamic nationalities, especially, but certainly not entirely, among the older generation. The two most populous Islamic nationalities are still the Hui and the Uygurs. Two Islamic sources in Xinjiang told me separately in October 1994 that the number of mosques there was about 20 000 — more than in the 1950s. Official figures for the Ningxia Hui autonomous region at the end of 1985 gave the number of mosques at about 180 028 — again more than in the early 1950s.

Furthermore, considering the Islamic revival and strengthening which was obvious to this writer even in the short period between 1990 and 1992, the number has certainly grown substantially since then. In the 1980s and 1990s, Muslims in China are able to visit Mecca for the first time since 1949 and with increasing frequency. Mosques are not only numerous but, in the main Islamic areas, full on Fridays and fairly well patronised five times for prayer on each other day. In several mosques in various parts of China, including the famous ancient Najiahu Mosque near the city of Wuzhong in Ningxia in 1990 and the Tatar Mosque, the largest in Ürümqi, Xinjiang in 1994, this writer found a large crowd of worshippers of all ages during a midday Friday visit. At the great Idkah Mosque in central Kaxgar, I was assured that as many as 100 000 men attend prayer during major festivals such as Corban, spreading beyond the Mosque itself, which can contain only 20 000 people at any one time, out into the enormous square outside. Even in areas of China where Islam has never been especially strong, there are regular attendances at the mosques. An example is the city of Guiyang, where I was told that a few come five times a day for prayer.[30]

Most of those Islamic clergy attached to mosques in various parts of China whom this writer interviewed in 1990, 1992 and 1994 complained that young people no longer observed the rules against smoking and drinking. Virtually all were inclined to take a tolerant view about these *Koran*-proscribed practices, since there was nothing they could do about it. One Islamic cleric interviewed in Wuzhong in 1992 was insistent that, although young Hui men drink and smoke much more than they ought, these practices were nonetheless less pervasive among the Hui than non-Islamic nationalities. Moreover, it is quite possible that there are variations among different places and minorities. Surveys on these matters were carried out in two Uygur peasant villages in Kaxgar, Xinjiang, in 1983 and the following year among pastoral adults, both male and female, who belonged to two Kazak pastoral and peasant communities in Yili, also in Xinjiang. Even allowing for significant errors in the surveys the figures are still quite decisive in what they show, as well as unique for such areas of China. The 1983 Uygur figures showed that, among adult males, 78.7 per cent did not smoke and 99.65 did not drink alcoholic beverages. Those for the Kazaks in 1984 indicated that the rate of non-smokers was 67.27 per cent and of non-drinkers 87.83 per cent. Given the traditionally stricter influence of Islam in terms of such practices on the Uygurs than on the Kazaks, it is not surprising that fewer Uygurs drink than Kazaks, but what is really striking is how effective the traditional bans are proving to be.[31]

My observations in Ningxia, Xinjiang and other places in 1990, 1992 and 1994 suggested that older men were far more numerous among worshippers in all Islamic areas than younger. However, I heard numerous claims that young people of Islamic nationalities continue to believe in Islam, even if they do not frequent the mosques. Moreover, Islamic officials in Ningxia insist that, in the villages of the south of the autonomous region, observance of the religion is much stricter than in the cities and towns or in the north.

In the stricter and stronger Islamic regions, male circumcision still appears to be widespread — or even virtually universal — among Muslims. In Xinjiang, several informants claimed the operation as universal, at least among the Uygurs and Tajiks and, except in the big cities, almost always carried out at home, only rarely in a hospital. However, in peripheral Hui areas such as Yanbian or Guiyang, circumcision is no longer practised at all.

The Hui people have been noted for centuries for their commercial skills, and they have taken good advantage of the reform policies to use their religion for monetary advantage. At many Hui mosques visited, worshippers were making use of the gathering of crowds of men to buy and sell commodities of various kinds. The mosque in Guiyang has its own hostelry, for Muslims only. Nobody is allowed to smoke or drink on the premises and the sanitary conditions conform to the hygienic standards of the Hui people, who stand virtually at the top among China's nationalities in this respect. Every mosque of the Hui visited in the 1980s or 1990s, from Lhasa to Yanbian, from Ningxia to Guiyang, had a bath-house attached.

Mosques in Xinjiang share the emphasis on hygiene and bath-houses. The emphasis on commerce appears slighter in the sense that, in my observation, prayer is not the occasion of buying and selling. Yet there are money-oriented activities associated with mosques. At the great Idkah Mosque in Kaxgar, I learned that, although the Mosque runs no hostelry, it does operate shops nearby which sell general commodities, not including alcoholic beverages or tobacco. Visiting the Tatar Mosque in Ürümqi at Friday prayer time, I noted about a dozen beggars of all ages and both genders gathering outside the compound and moving inside to waylay the worshippers as they came out. The beggars make use of the Islamic doctrine that one should give alms to the poor, and on this occasion their efforts appeared very successful.

Other religions

Several of the peoples of Yunnan province believe in Theravada Buddhism, the Dai being the most populous of these. In numerous villages visited in 1985 outside Jinghong, capital of the Dai Sipsong Panna autonomous prefecture, newly built and well-patronised temples could be found. In one of them I witnessed a class of young boys undergoing instruction in the Buddhist sutras. Most of the Bai people, who live in the Dali autonomous prefecture in Yunnan, are Mahayana Buddhists. My experiences in Dali in 1985 suggest that the Bai, while still believers, are very much less interested in religion than the Dai. I found only a few newly built temples and no signs of major attempts to train young people in the scriptures. The Buddhist and other images in the temples are preserved, but the religious functions did not appear to obstruct the use of religious buildings for other purposes. One large one in the town of Dali was functioning not only as a temple, but as an old people's home.[32] At the other end of China, the Koreans appear to have abandoned their traditional Buddhism more or less completely.

Extensive searches in Yanbian, both in 1986 and 1990, uncovered not a single functioning Buddhist temple, and even the official account of Yanbian remarks that 'since liberation, Buddhism has gradually died out, though there are still individual old monks'.[33]

The only religion to enjoy any following at all among the Koreans of China in the 1990s is Christianity. There are Christian churches, both Catholic and Protestant, in Yanji and several other cities in Yanbian autonomous prefecture. In 1965, on the eve of the Cultural Revolution, there were still 2100 Korean Protestants and 2700 Catholics in Yanbian, numbers themselves very much lower than in the 1930s (see Chapter 2).[34] All churches were closed or destroyed during the Cultural Revolution, but the main Protestant church in Yanji was reopened in 1981, while the main Catholic one began operations in 1986. At the time of my visits in October 1990, the Catholic church conducted daily Mass (twice on Sunday), while the Protestant church held four services per week, three of them on Sunday. Both claimed good attendances, especially the Protestant church. The Catholic church was served by two priests, one of them a young Korean, the other an old Han; the Protestant church was served by an old Korean pastor. The Korean priest said he had given all Masses in the Korean language since early 1990; the Protestant pastor gave three out of his four weekly services in Korean, the other one in Chinese. In both churches the great majority of parishioners are Koreans, with a minority of Han people. The Catholic church has no direct relations with Rome. Many South Koreans visit it, but the priests there do not recognise the Catholic hierarchy of South Korea.

One of the most important of the Christian missionary centres in minority nationality areas was the British one in Weining, Guizhou province, which is now an autonomous county for the Yi, Hui and Miao peoples. Weining remains to this day the major Christian nationality area in Guizhou, with substantial congregations even in the villages. The Protestant Christian pastor in Guiyang told me that there were over 100 000 Miao Christians in Guizhou province, with very much smaller numbers among the Yi, Shui and Bai. An Yi official of the State Nationalities Affairs Commission gave me a figure of 'several tens of thousands' for Christians in Guizhou.

An aspect of Christianity in the 1980s and 1990s worth mentioning is the revival of foreign missionary work undertaken by people whose overt job is that of a teacher. In the 1980s and early 1990s, this kind of part-missionary could be found in many Chinese cities, including in the minority areas. In February 1994, the Chinese government adopted a law on religion under which this kind of missionary activity was banned, with what success was unclear as of the end of 1994.

This writer became aware of Christian teacher-missionaries especially in Yanji in 1990, when several young female students expressed great interest in, and sympathy for, Protestant Christianity, having learned of it from their American teachers of English. Several South Koreans I met in Yanji in that year told me that one of their aims in making the visit was to establish contacts with the Christian Church, in the hope of expanding its wealth and

Religion

Above: A scene at the 'Bras spungs Monastery, one of the four main monasteries of the dGe lugs pa, or Yellow Hat Sect, just outside Lhasa in Tibet.

Left: A scene in the great bKra shis lhun po Monastery in Xigaze, one of the four main monasteries of the dGe lugs pa Sect.

Left: A general crossview of the dGa' ldan Monastery outside Lhasa, one of the four main monasteries of the dGe lugs pa Sect, taken in 1985. It was heavily destroyed during the Cultural Revolution, but is now largely restored.

Below left: Two Tibetan girls with the dGa' ldan Monastery in the background.

Below: A donkey-drawn cart of the typical Tibetan style, with a general view of the town of Gyaze in the background, with the Central Hill to the right and the city's main monastery to the left.

Top left: The Jingyuan Temple, the only lamasery in the Chabchal Xibe autonomous county, in Xinjiang. It was not in use during the author's visit in October 1994, but there were plans to restore it. Some Xibes traditionally practised Tibetan Buddhism.

Left: The entrance to the Jingyuan Temple in Chabchal, with Chinese on the right and Xibe in Manchu script on the left. The Xibes are the only people in the world who still use the Manchu script, even the Manchus using Chinese. The signs say that the Jingyuan Temple is a Key Cultural Protection Unit and was formally declared so by the people's government of the Chabchal Xibe autonomous county on 9 December 1990.

Bottom left: A shrine in rural Inner Mongolia.

Below: A Buddhist temple in Jinghong, the capital city of the Sipsong Panna Dai autonomous prefecture, in Yunnan province.

Above: Front view of the Tatar Mosque in Xinjiang's capital Ürümqi, the largest and oldest in the city, with the imam standing in front (taken in 1982), used mainly by Uygurs.

Above right: Front view of the Ürümqi Theological College, built in 1987 and funded mainly by the World Islamic Development Bank and the Xinjiang government.

Below: Uygur theological students in a mosque in Turpan, which is near Ürümqi.

Below right: Old Uygur man and young Uygur girls in front of the same mosque in Turpan.

Above left: An example of ethnic harmony. These two boys are schoolmates and playmates. They are both Muslims but of different nationalities, the one on the left being Hui, the one on the right Uygur. The picture was taken at the Sulaiman Mosque in Turpan, built in the eighteenth century.

Left: After prayer at a mosque in Gulja, capital of Yili in northwestern Xinjiang, not far from the border with Kazakhstan. Only men or boys may enter a mosque in Xinjiang, although this varies throughout China.

Above: Front view of the great Idkah Mosque in central Kaxgar, southern Xinjiang.

Below: Street in front of the Idkah Mosque in central Kaxgar. Notice the woman wearing the veil which covers the whole head, even the eyes.

Bottom: People opposite the Idkah Mosque in central Kaxgar, including a female beggar wearing a veil.

Right: A traditional graveyard of the Kirgiz people in Xinjiang, who are Muslims.

Bottom right: A shrine in an ordinary Yao house in northern Guangxi.

Right: A shrine in a Zhuang house in Wuming county, Guangxi, mother and son standing in front. There they burn incense and worship their ancestors. Their surname is Lu, which is recorded on the shrine.

Below: Pastor Kim in front of the Protestant Christian Church in Yanji, capital of the Yanbian Korean autonomous prefecture. Note that the signs are in both Korean and Chinese. Pastor Kim is a Korean and almost all his services and sermons are in Korean. However, he gives one sermon a week in Chinese, on Sundays.

Education

Above: Uygur teachers at a Uygur secondary school in Gulja, the oldest 'modern' school in Xinjiang.

Left: The principal of a Uygur primary school in Ürümqi. All instruction is in Uygur and the signs in the school are in Uygur, for example the two behind her.

Top left: A very small primary school in a Zhuang village in Guangxi.

Centre left: The girls' dormitory at the Guangxi Zhuang Language School and the Guangxi Nationalities Cadre School in Wuming county, Guangxi. The two schools share one campus. They aim to train teachers who can teach Zhuang language to Zhuang people and to train cadres of the Zhuang, Yao and other minorities.

Left: A rural Miao secondary school. There are two big buildings in the school, of which this one is the older and in Miao style.

Family and gender

Top: A Zhuang weaving factory in Guangxi, staffed by women.

Above: A Yao village in Shangsi, Guangxi, the woman and baby wearing traditional Yao costume, the man and boy wearing clothing in contemporary Chinese style.

Above: The main river running through Jinxiu, a Yao town. The bridge at the end is in Yao style. The Yao wom
pride themselves on their social status by comparison with the Han and many other Chinese minorities, but t
washing of the clothes, frequently done in the river, is women's work.

Top: A Miao woman weaving in her village home near Jishou, Western Hunan. The clothes and other items she makes are generally for the use of her family.

Above: A Miao man, the husband of the woman in the top picture, making a basket. These wicker baskets are termed *beilou* in Chinese and are used very widely by the Miao of Western Hunan to carry anything from the baby to vegetables. The basket he is making will probably be sold on the open market.

Right: A Miao man in Western Hunan carries his baby in a wicker basket.

Above left: Miao girl in full traditional regalia, such as at an important courtship gathering or a festival. She is standing in front of the gate entrance to her village, which is called Langde Upper Village. It is near Kaili, Guizhou province.

Below left: Miao people at a festival gathering in Chong'an, Guizhou. Note that the women wear traditional clothing, but the men do not.

Above centre: Very old Miao woman sitting outside her village house.

Top: A Dong wedding procession in a village in Sanjiang, northern Guangxi, which is a Dong area. The procession contains people who are carrying to the bride's house the provisions which the bridegroom has paid for to give to the guests to eat. He himself does not attend the bride's family's party. He has already had drinking parties of his own the previous day.

Above: The head of the procession including the bride, front left, reaches near to her parents' house.

Left: A Kazak mother and baby near the family yurt. In the summer they live in the mountains but move down to the plains to warmer parts in the winter. This picture is very near the Heavenly Lake, itself not very far from the capital of Xinjiang, Ürümqi.

Below: The interior of a Kazak yurt, showing mother, daughter and baby. Like most of the minorities, the Kazaks are allowed more than one child. Most of the family possessions go into the big trunk to the right. The family has several rugs for the floor.

Left: A scene in the back streets of Kaxgar, southern Xinjiang, Most houses lack running water and it is still women's work to draw the water from the nearby well.

Below left: A prosperous, middle-aged Tajik couple in Taxkorgan, Xinjiang, not far from the borders with Afghanistan and Pakistan. Carpets belong more on the walls than the floor. Note that the wife is wearing traditional clothing, while the husband is not. Tajik women wear very characteristic hats and, even though I visited this family without notice and completely at random, she had a traditional hat on when I arrived.

Below centre: A Kirgiz peasant woman and her daughter at home in a village in southern Xinjiang not far from the border with Tajikistan. A very poor village, there was no electricity, but the houses had carpets both on the walls and floors, and there was a village school.

Literature and the performing arts

Above right: A Mongolian player of the horse-head fiddle, in Hohhot, capital of Inner Mongolia. This instrument is very characteristic of the Mongols.

Below right: Mr Abdurehim Utkur, the most famous Uygur literary figure alive today, shown with his daughter.

Above: The members of a Tibetan amateur folk drama troupe outside their home.

Left: The fairies in a performance of traditional Tibetan drama. The audience sits right around the players, allowing only a small space for them to go to the playing area from the greenroom.

Above: Traditional Tibetan drama normally takes place under a tent, recognisable by the design on the roof. One of its characteristics is the use of masks in animal and human forms.

Right: The Korean Fan Dance, performed in honour of the 35th anniversary of Yanbian's Finance and Trade School.

Left: An ancient, blind Uygur musician playing the stringed *satar* in one of the Twelve Mukams, the most famous items in traditional Uygur music.

Below: A Uygur orchestra of five instruments. From right to left they are the *rijek*, the *hushtar*, a bowed instrument rather like the violin in shape, the *chang*, or dulcimer, *dap*, the Uygur drum, and *rawap*, a plucked stringed instrument. Note that the player of the *hushtar* is a woman, traditionally exremely unusual for instrumental players among the Uygurs. This photograph was taken in Ürümqi, capital of Xinjiang, in a hotel, where professional players gain much of their work nowadays.

Above: The Uygur Plate Dance, performed by Uygur kindergarten children in Kaxgar, accompanied by an orchestra consisting of, among other instruments, a *rawap* and a violin.

Left: The head of the Yili Cultural Work Troupe, Saitunar Abudorkardür. Although Yili is a Kazak area, she is in fact a Uygur.

General

Above: Tibetans enjoying themselves on a festival day, screened off in the traditional way from the next family. This photograph was taken in the grounds of the Summer Palace of the dalai lamas in Lhasa.

Left: A yak in a Lhasa street. The yak is traditionally the animal most closely associated with the Tibetan people.

Above: A Tajik policeman in Taxkorgan Tajik autonomous county, Xinjiang, near the border with Afghanistan. Attempts are being made to ensure that the police belong to the nationality of the local people.

Below: An example of the scenery in Yili, not very far from the capital, Gulja.

Left: The Heavenly Lake, a scenic spot in the Kazak area of Xinjiang. The Lake is also reputed to be among the highest above sea level in the world.

Below left: A house in traditional Korean style. This house is the main part of the Korean Folk Museum in Longjing, near Yanji, Yanbian.

Below: A rural house in Korean style.

Right: A reedpipe ground in a Miao village in Rongshui county, northern Guangxi. Reedpipe grounds are places for social gathering in Miao villages, in particular for courtship. The boy traditionally plays the reedpipe to impress his partner. A reedpipe ground always has a pole with a cock atop.

Below: The 'wind and rain bridge' of the Dong people is a place for social gathering, performances, courtship and relaxation. This one in Sanjiang is a particularly large and beautiful example, but they are found in virtually all villages in Dong areas.

influence. The new kind of part-missionary is related in most cases more to the spread of Western influence in China than to a revival of identity, as well as to the intelligentsia's withdrawal of support from Marxism-Leninism, especially among the young. The fact that South Koreans visit Yanbian much more in the 1990s than was ever the case in the past springs from China's shift in foreign relations away from the Democratic People's Republic of Korea and towards the Republic.

The last kind of religion to be mentioned here is those such as polytheistic nature or ancestor worship, which are deeply embedded among the communities of many of the minorities, especially in the rural areas. There are no temples, churches or formal texts for such religions. There is no professional clergy, but there may may well be shamans or specialists who, in addition to their normal work as peasants, attempt to cure the sick through magical means and preside over ceremonies to mark the completion of a baby's first month (*manyue*), a funeral or other such event in the cycle of life and death.

Because of the lack of formal religious buildings and clergy, the reforms of the 1950s to 1970s, and especially the Cultural Revolution, affected the nature and ancestor worshipping folk religions less severely than the more highly developed ones. Although shamans, sorcerers and faith healers were condemned as reactionary and discouraged from carrying out medical or ceremonial functions, they continued their operations into the 1960s among some minorities. Alan Winnington, who carried out field work among the Va of Yunnan in the late 1950s, records that sorcerers still maintained a vested interest in keeping up the custom of decapitating enemies. In theory, the aim was to fertilise the rice with the blood from the head, but in practice Winnington found that by the late 1950s it was 'largely a method of settling clan or village blood-feuds'.[35] Yet, despite the survival of such a primitive custom in the late 1950s, pressures were already strong for its abolition and Winnington adds that 'head-cutting was on its way out'.[36]

In the 1980s and 1990s, nature and ancestor worship and shamanistic religions have, like all others, revived to some extent among China's minority nationalities. In extensive travelling in villages of the Miao, Bouyei and Shui nationalities in Guizhou in 1990, and in Zhuang, Yao, Dong, Tujia and other nationality areas in Guangxi and western Hunan in 1992, shrines and nature symbols could be found in the great majority of houses, except some cases of those newly built, as well as numerous shrines to the earth (*tudi miao*) just outside the villages. Among several of the very small nationalities of northeast China, such as the Daur and Oroqen, there are survivals of shamanistic practices in remote mountain villages.[37] In one *xiang* visited, some 100 kilometres from Duyun, capital of the South Guizhou Miao and Bouyei autonomous prefecture, up to 100 sorcerers and faith healers were said to be still working in the *xiang*, the *xiang* consisting of villages of the Miao and others of the Shui nationality. Although mainly peasants, the sorcerers still arranged funerals and other ceremonial tasks, and even tried to cure illnesses. A Shui scholar at the Guizhou Nationalities Institute in

Guiyang told me in 1990 that there were still about 1000 shamans operating in Shui villages. Inquiries in many parts of Guangxi in January 1992 suggested that sorcerers and faith healers, both male and female, were still quite active in some villages. Winnington's prediction in the late 1950s that head-cutting would shortly disappear has proved too optimistic. In January 1993 I was shown in Hong Kong a moving picture of a severed head on a pole recently taken in a Va village in Yunnan.

Religion and family planning

In general the minorities have been exempt from the family planning programs found in the PRC since 1949, and in particular from the one-child-per-couple policy implemented since the early 1980s. However, in the 1980s and early 1990s, the minorities have been encouraged more and more strongly to reduce the size of their families.[38] The impact of religion on birth control programs is a matter which has weighed heavily in many countries, but in China most religions have either been quite or very supportive of government family planning initiatives.

The Islamic community decided to support family planning in the early 1980s. Scholars found reference in the Islamic tradition that 'few children will bring prosperity, but many are a factor leading to poverty',[39] which was precisely what the government was arguing. Gladney suggests that the mosque and *ahong* have been used to disseminate policy on family planning with the result that it 'has been judged relatively successful among most Hui'.[40]

My own interviews in 1990 with Islamic clergy and laity in areas as far apart as Yinchuan, Turpan, Hohhot, Guiyang and Yanji, most of them arranged not by officials but by myself, showed only a few deviations from support for family planning. In Guiyang, several men at the mosque told me with pride that, even though the government allowed Hui people to have two children, many are in fact producing only one. This is because Muslims follow the government in believing population control to be absolutely necessary for China's economic development. A visit to Ningxia late in 1992 revealed a similar pattern, but I did hear second-hand reports that some clergy in the more conservative Muslim regions in the south of the Autonomous Region use their still strong social and political influence to oppose family planning.[41]

In Xinjiang in 1994, the line followed among all Islamic clergy I interviewed was that in such matters as family planning it was appropriate to follow the Koranic principle that one should obey government authorities. However, in Xinjiang hostility towards the Chinese government is undoubtedly much more intense than in other Islamic areas. Support for family planning is weaker and opposition stronger than elsewhere. In a mosque in Gulja, several Muslim laymen told me in very strong terms that they regarded the family planning programs of the government as a plot to reduce the Islamic population.

Catholicism is famous in many parts of the world for its opposition to birth control. However, in China the Catholic Church is not in communion with Rome and has taken a somewhat milder approach on this subject than in countries such as the Philippines or in many parts of Latin America. The Korean Catholic priest interviewed in Yanji expressed neither enthusiasm nor outright opposition in answering a question about his attitude towards birth control. He did say that his parishioners had no problem on this score. The impression he conveyed was that Korean Catholics could see the need to restrict the population and it was just not worth the political risk he himself would have to run in order to take any measures to persuade them otherwise.

In the Tibetan countryside, where as of 1994 still no restrictions applied, the issue does not arise, but I found no evidence in the cities that birth control was a specific worry for religious believers. For the polytheistic faiths involving nature and ancestor worship, birth control weighs even less as a divisive issue. Since prosperity is a major aim, there is no reason to counter government policy beyond what normal instinct would dictate, and no clergy to organise resistance.

Women and religion

It appears that the women of the minorities believe in and practise religion even more strongly than their menfolk. But in those religions with strong clergies, it is still men who dominate in terms of the power structures, and they do so to a very large extent, even to the near-total exclusion of women.

In Tibet, there are even more women than men who prostrate themselves in front of the Jo khang Temple in the centre of Lhasa and who revolve prayer wheels, either in the monasteries or elsewhere. Unlike the Tibetans, the Mongols are no longer fervent believers, but among those pilgrims and worshippers I have seen, the majority are female. Women predominate also among the small numbers of Christian Koreans, Miao, Yi and Bai who attend church.

In the case of Islam, the dominant notion and practice is still that prayer in the mosque is a male prerogative, and that women should undertake worship at home. In Xinjiang I saw or heard no evidence of women praying in mosques. On the other hand, in Ningxia I have seen women at worship relegated to one side of the rear part of the mosque, although they are not large in number. In Ningxia and a few other parts of China, the custom developed from the late 1980s and early 1990s of establishing a separate chapel to the side of some mosques especially for women to pray. These are called *qingzhen nüsi* (literally 'pure and true temples for women' or women's mosques). However, in those I have visited in Ningxia, women do not use the bathhouses which are a major feature of mosques everywhere in China.

According to government policy, women should not wear the veil. There are two main reasons for this, one being that this practice discriminates against women, placing them on a lower status than men, the other that it is impractical for working women. In the 1950s and 1960s, the rule was fairly strictly applied, while during the Cultural Revolution period of 1966–76, the wearing of veils was condemned as the height of reactionary feudal practice. Still, in the 1980s and 1990s, Muslim women do not normally wear veils, even in public. However, the practice has re-emerged to a limited extent among the Uygur, Hui and other Islamic nationalities, not only on occasions where it seems appropriate for religious reasons, but even more generally. Those women I have seen praying at the mosque, or attending an Islamic school have all been wearing a veil. In Tongxin, central Ningxia, I visited two thronging markets, at which many of the women present were wearing the veil, but by no means all. These veils cover the head, but none of the face. On the other hand, in Kaxgar quite a few women still wear veils which cover the whole head, including the eyes.

Dru Gladney writes that 'in the more conservative Muslim areas of the northwest, women are more restricted from public participation in ritual and leadership' than in Yunnan, where Southeast Asian influence may account for a more liberal attitude towards female participation in ritual and leadership.[42] This participation included both female imams and girls training to become such.[43] In Xinjiang in 1994, all my informants agreed that there were no female imams and I saw no evidence of them anywhere. During my visit to Ningxia in September 1990 and during interviews the same year with Islamic clergy and male laity in various parts of China, I gained the strong impression that while most were aware of female imams in Yunnan and some were even prepared to be tolerant about their presence, most disapproved fairly or very strongly, and none was willing to follow suit.

However, a revisit to Ningxia at the end of 1992 showed a somewhat changed situation. Although officials in Yinchuan were still denying vehemently that there were any female *ahongs* in Ningxia, explorations outside Yinchuan revealed that there were a few. Their job is to look after the women worshippers in the women's mosques. I interviewed one of them, an old women illiterate in her native Chinese, but knowing enough Arabic to read the *Koran*. She was at pains to emphasise that her beliefs were identical to those of the male imams, the only difference between her and a male counterpart lying in her social role as carer for women. She was not allowed to practise as an imam in the main part of the mosque. Moreover, the women's mosque was extremely small by comparison with the main part and would fit no more than one-tenth the number of people.

Another of her tasks was to train further female imams, of whom she had a small class, all of them young. Since the early 1990s, the women's mosques regularly include such classes, suggesting that the number of female imams is likely to grow quite rapidly in the coming years. A large mosque visited in Tongxin had a school for girls attached to it, with three classes and several female teachers. The aim of this school was not to train female imams, but to improve the religious and personal quality of the young female Muslims of the district.[44]

In Tibet, the great majority of clergy have always been male. At the same time, nunneries separate from the monasteries are nothing new. Early in September 1990 I visited a convent in the back streets of Lhasa with nearly 100 nuns, many of them novices. Conversations with a few of them revealed that, although they were happy to be able to enter a functioning nunnery again, they were very unhappy with the decline of their religion over the past few decades. I was also struck very strongly with the obvious hatred these nuns felt for the Han. While I was in Lhasa at that time, there was a demonstration by nuns in the Dalai Lama's former Summer Palace, which was small but intense. It is possible that the nuns are even more passionate concerning their religion and its role in Tibetan identity than are their male counterparts.[45]

At the higher end of the clergy, there are now a few senior nuns and a Tibetan incarnation lama (in Chinese, *huofo*, literally Living Buddha) told me in November 1992 in Hohhot that there were two female Tibetan incarnation lamas, of whom he knew one, regarding her as every bit as holy, learned and worthy as her male counterparts. In Inner Mongolia itself, the Buddhist clergy remains exclusively male. There are no nuns and, although there are a few incarnation lamas, none of them is a woman.

Religion and politics

One of the most important ramifications of the revival of religion among China's minority nationalities is the political one. Some of the nationalities regard their religion as their major hallmark, because it infuses so much of their national consciousness and national culture. The most prominent example is the Tibetans, but others include the Uygurs, Hui and Kazaks, who are Muslims and very proud of it. At least among the Tibetans and the Uygurs, pride in their nationality is very similar to pride in their religion, and the feeling extends into the younger generation. Even young Tibetans or Uygurs who may not be very religiously inclined believe in Tibetan Buddhism or Islam respectively as a way of emphasising their national identities.

The government is generally prepared, or considers it expedient, to accept this equation between religion and national identities, but with one major proviso. When it spills over to become a demand for secession or independence from China, then the Chinese authorities tread on it very firmly indeed. The most obvious example of this was in the troubles in Tibet in 1987, 1988 and 1989. These involved demonstrations in favour of independence for Tibet which were suppressed by Chinese police and troops. In March 1989, on the 30th anniversary of the 1959 rebellion, the independence demonstrations grew serious enough for the Chinese government to impose martial law in Lhasa. In its discussion of the Chinese reaction to the demonstrations, Amnesty International quotes eye-witnesses as describing 'ill-organised' police savagely beating Tibetans and 'firing indiscriminately', so that by 9 March, 'Tibetan sources estimated that over 60 people had died and more than 200 had been injured'.[46]

Both in 1959 and in the late 1980s, the Chinese authorities were convinced that the main monasteries were using religion to incite demands for independence. Considering that the Tibetan lamas and monks had always acted as a focus for anti-Chinese activities and were led by men overtly hostile to the Chinese, their conviction was no doubt soundly based. Amnesty International agrees that the demonstrations were on behalf of Tibetan independence. Certainly the belief of the Chinese that the riots were led by monks is the reason why they focused their suppression of the independence movement on the monks and lamas. Nobody who visits Lhasa can avoid being struck by the frequency of demands for pictures of the Dalai Lama, especially in the monasteries.

It appears that for the monks the Dalai Lama represents not only a religious symbol of holiness and headship of the dGe lugs pa sect of Tibetan Buddhism, but also a political one of Tibetan independence of China. One dGa' ldan Monastery monk is quoted as saying: 'Under the Chinese there will be no freedom of religion. If Tibet is independent and has freedom, then there will be freedom of religion as well. Until then there will be no freedom of religion.'[47] The link between religious freedom and independence for Tibet is absolute in this monk's mind.

When religion and politics intermingle directly, the tension between identities and integration becomes intense and freedom of religion highly controversial. Suppression of secessionist movements involving monks is regularly interpreted by commentators in the West as religious persecution or, in the case of Tibet, the suppression of culture.[48] Chinese official accounts, by contrast, present their own action as protection of Chinese unity. To imprison or beat a monk for inciting secession is not necessarily defensible, but it is not the same as religious persecution. When, late in 1994, the Tibetan government began a campaign against the influence of religion in general and the Dalai Lama in particular, its main rationale was that 'the Dalai clique' was carrying out 'divisive activities' aimed at 'undermining ethnic unity, overthrowing the people's government, splitting the motherland and restoring their ruling status in Tibet'.[49]

It is not only in Tibet that politics and religion have intermixed in the late 1980s and into the 1990s. A series of events saw Islam also take a very high political profile, but this time on a matter quite unrelated to secession and one over which the central government was quite prepared, and possibly even happy, to give the Muslims what they wanted. It was a matter rather similar to the Salman Rushdie affair which affected Western and Islamic countries at about the same time. Shortly before his death early in June 1989, Iranian leader Ayatollah Khomeini condemned Salman Rushdie to death for apostasy and insulting Islam in his novel *The Satanic Verses*. The condemnation sparked worldwide demonstrations by Muslims in support of Khomeini's decision. At the same time, many people in the West were horrified over the implications for freedom of publication, religion and other issues of a foreign leader being able to take such a decision affecting the life and writings of a novelist.

In China a similar event occurred when, early in 1989, the Shanghai Cultural Press (*Wenhua chubanshe*) published a collective academic book entitled *Sexual Customs* (*Xing fengsu*), one of the authors being a woman. Muslim leaders found the work insulting to their religion, because of a suggestion made in it that the structure of mosques was designed to resemble the male genitalia. A series of demonstrations flared in various parts of China in May, which borrowed legitimacy and vibrance from the student movement, manifesting itself in mass protests for freedom and democracy at the time. On 5 May 1989, some 20 000 Muslims demonstrated in Lanzhou demanding punishment for the authors, and a similar demonstration took place in Beijing, focusing on Muslim students from various universities and colleges there who claimed that the book was 'full of slander' against Muslims.[50] Demonstrations flared in virtually all the major Islamic regions of China.

On 18 May, several thousand Koranic students in Ürümqi joined university students, already on their second day of demonstrations in support of Beijing's Tiananmen Square hunger strikers, demanding the suppression of the book on sexual customs. They attacked the CCP headquarters and the police squads who were defending them with rocks and steel bars. A report based on a source inside the Xinjiang governor's office claims that the police had been ordered not to fight back, as a result of which some police were seriously injured. A few days later, in order to defuse the protest, the Beijing authorities banned the book everywhere in China and had it withdrawn from circulation. The Shanghai government had 95 000 copies of the book burned, the Shanghai Cultural Press was fined and went out of business, while the editor and two authors, including the woman, were arrested and charged in front of the law courts. The case came to a final conclusion in 1991; the court found in favour of the Muslims and against the Press, sentencing the editor and two main authors to varying periods of imprisonment.

In September and October 1990 and again in 1992 I had the chance to discuss this matter with Islamic male laity and clergy in various parts of China, finding an amazing similarity of views in condemnation of Rushdie and the Han authors of the book, even among Hui academics. One mullah in the main Yinchuan mosque told me in 1990 that the comparison between the British government's handling of the Rushdie affair and the Chinese government's of the book on sexual customs showed that there was more freedom of religion in China than in England. His argument in favour of this proposition was that, whereas the Chinese government had immediately acceded to the demands of the Muslims, that of Britain had dithered and done nothing to support them. When I visited the same mosque again late in 1992 and saw the same mullah again, he put forward a similar view on the matter. Moreover, a shop for selling Islamic goods had been set up, which included a display of newspaper articles on the affair, all of them in praise of the actions of the Muslims.

The reasons why the Chinese government chose to give in to the demands of the Muslims in this instance raise some interesting questions. One suspects that the notion of a woman publishing about sexual matters was deeply offensive, not only to Muslims but to the Han as well, and Chinese inhibitions about sex may have served to worsen the fate of the book and its authors. However, there were also more pressing matters concerned with politics and nationality relations. The crisis occurred at the same time as the student movement was reaching its height. For the Chinese government, a controversy over a book about sex was a mere sideshow. It was an ideal opportunity to keep the minority nationalities happy and in support of the government, with a few daring scholars a very easy sacrificial lamb. Freedom of publication was not an important or even relevant principle.

In the northern autumn of 1993, the Muslims again showed political strength over the publication, in Sichuan province, of a Taiwanese comic book in which Muslims were shown praying near a pig. Serious riots broke out in many Muslim communities in north-west China. In particular, in Qinghai province, CCP and government offices were attacked, police vehicles smashed and armed police assaulted. The authorities characteristically responded by accusing a small minority of people of trying to split China and undermine its unity. But what is most important is that they banned the comic book which had offended the Muslims, an action which seemed to have the desired effect of quietening the disorder. Their fear was that the comic book was simply a symptom of something much larger, the loyalty of the Muslim peoples to China.

During my visit to Ningxia late in 1992, several informants, including academic, religious and government, informed me of their belief that the *ahong* or imams in the villages of the autonomous region were frequently the most powerful members of their community, more influential than the government cadres.[51] If the government wants a policy implemented — for example, birth control — it must get the support of the Islamic clergy if it is to have any real chance of success. Since the villages lack law courts, the clergy usually arbitrate legal matters there, and for this reason the main Islamic theological colleges which train the clergy include courses on law. It is the state law of the PRC and the Ningxia autonomous region which they should dispense, but there is no guarantee that Islamic law will not also exercise a powerful influence in their judgments.

While in Ningxia late in 1992, it became clear to me also that the CCP's March 1982 document allowing minority Party members to believe in religion is being interpreted more and more liberally. During a visit to Ningxia in 1988, Barnett found that, although many Hui were CCP members, might call themselves Muslims, and even attend services, in fact they did not necessarily believe in religion.[52] But my own explorations suggest that with time they have gone much further back to a belief in Islam. One Hui government official told me that, as a Hui, he must believe in Islam, or he would become quite 'divorced from the masses'. 'If you don't believe in Islam, you aren't Hui,' he said flatly. When I expressed surprise that CCP members should be Islamic believers, he retorted that he himself was a member of the CCP and that what mattered was in the heart, not open formalism. In Tibet and Xinjiang, also, the CCP became more and more tolerant of religious belief among CCP members during the 1980s and 1990s. In 1980, the Qabdo Information Office published a document entitled 'Basic Study Guide No. 55', which stated that 'anyone interested in being a member of the Communist Party or Communist Youth Organisation cannot practise religion'.[53] The CCP's March 1982 decision covering not just Tibetans but all minorities clearly takes a much less restrictive view. A Tibetan incarnation lama told me in Hohhot in November 1992 that 92 per cent of Tibetan CCP members were acknowledged as religious believers. The reason for the CCP's tolerance in this matter is that any alternative course splits the Party from the people. It is a trade-off which the CCP became prepared to make in order to keep some semblance of loyalty among the religious minorities.

Another important aspect relating to politics and religion in the late 1980s and 1990s was China's relations with the Islamic countries of Southwest Asia and elsewhere. Just as in the 1950s and 1960s, Islam was the minority religion of greatest relevance to foreign relations and the Chinese government was very keen not to give offence to friendly Islamic countries. Iran and Iraq had just finished their eight-year Gulf War (1980–88), and China was concerned to maintain good relations with both countries. It was also making much progress towards establishing good relations with the conservative Islamic countries, above all Saudi Arabia. In April 1989, just the very month before the crisis over the book on the book *Sexual Customs* broke out, Saudi Arabia and China announced their decision to set up trade representatives in each other's countries, leading to full diplomatic relations the following year. What the whole series of events over the book on sexual customs demonstrated was the power of the Muslims to exert quite extraordinary political muscle in China when they really wanted to and when the circumstances were right.[54]

The improvement in relations with the conservative Islamic countries has brought tangible economic benefits to Xinjiang and to Ningxia, which many in Arab countries now know simply as 'China's Muslim province'. Arab investments and joint ventures are becoming quite numerous and, as of the early 1990s, continue to grow. The President of Ürümqi's Islamic Theological College, which is in Southwest Asian style and opened in 1987, told me in October 1994 that the Islamic Development Bank had contributed some US$1 225 000 towards its construction. The largest and most magnificent building in Yinchuan, the capital of Ningxia, is an Islamic Theological College and in Tongxin, in central Ningxia, an Arabic School. Both are also in Southwest Asian style and built with substantial funding from the Islamic Development Bank.

Conclusion

It is very clear from the foregoing that religion has contributed enormously to the regrowth of national identities among most of the minorities during the 1980s and 1990s. Naturally enough, distinctions need to be made among the various groups in determining the impact of religion on feelings of national consciousness. Among the Koreans and Mongols, religion plays a rather weak role in society and consequently in national consciousness, very much less than language or literature. Among those many nationalities of the south, the religions of which lack clergies, and specific religious texts and temples, identities are still expressed through the fact of shrines to ancestors or nature in houses and religious belief in everyday life. However, this is not a particularly powerful social force, and its manifestations are frequently influenced very strongly by the Han.

It is among the Tibetans and the Islamic nationalities that religion has played the most powerful role in identities. It is very clear from the above that religion has strengthened greatly in its influence in all aspects of social and even political life over the last few years. This contributes to ethnic identities because religion defines the essence of those nationalities to a substantial degree. Tibetans gain a strong sense of being Tibetan through their adherence to Buddhism. Islam differs from Tibetan Buddhism in that there are numerous nationalities not only in China but elsewhere which believe in it. Yet the religion remains a defining feature of Islamic nationalities in China, with the ability to arouse pride in belonging to the nationality and even to arouse political and social loyalty among members of the CCP.

The sense of 'otherness' and even antagonism towards those who do not share their religious belief is strong and a factor in identities. Many Tibetans undoubtedly feel a strong hatred for the Han, who, on their part, often harbour contempt and wariness for the Tibetans. Such feelings are not due only to difference in religious or ideological beliefs, but there can be no doubt that it exacerbates the tension. Many Uygurs hate the Han in part because they do not accept Islam. In Ningxia in 1992, this writer heard reports of social tension caused because the Hui could not tolerate the smell of pork being cooked by Han neighbours; as Muslims, they found such an odour repulsive and disgusting.

The issue of history is also relevant both to religion and ethnic identities. The fact that the Tibetans have believed in their characteristic form of Buddhism for so long, or the Uygurs in Islam, makes their religion an essential part of their national experience, which contributes so decisively towards defining their identities. The Hui cadre who told me that he must believe in Islam or could hardly claim to be Hui was saying in effect that the national tradition of the Hui put religion in so high a place that to turn one's back on Islam was tantamount to abandoning Hui identity. Nothing could better exemplify the strength of religion in identities. Yet he certainly did not consider himself disloyal to the Chinese state. There is absolutely no reason why belief in Islam should suggest to the Hui that they secede from China. In any case, such a possibility is out of the question since the Hui are spread so far and wide across the length and breadth of China.

On the other hand, in Tibet and Xinjiang there is most certainly a strong tension between the sense of ethnic identities caused by religious belief and the integration of the Chinese state. The independence movement of 1987–89 among the Tibetans was undoubtedly due, at least in part, to religion, as shown by the fact that it was the clergy who led the demonstrations. In Xinjiang, feeling on behalf of independence is probably stronger among devout Muslims than any other grouping within the population. The most passionate defence I have ever heard in China for any independence movement was for the 'East Turkestan Republic' (Xinjiang), and it came from a group of Muslim laity as we sat in a mosque in Yili after their evening prayer. The function of religion in Xinjiang against Chinese national integration can only be strengthened by the fact that the nationalities ruling the newly independent states to Xinjiang's west, such as Kazakhstan and Tajikistan, are all Islamic. The tension between identities and integration in Tibet and Xinjiang may be balanced by other factors, such as economic growth and modernisation. Yet this tension has already caused trouble to the Chinese government, which has on several occasions reacted with violence in the hope of bringing about a solution, and is sure to do so on future occasions in the coming years.

Whether the tension will become serious enough to result in the breakaway of Tibet and Xinjiang from China remains to be seen. But it is likely that the Chinese government will suppress religious and national separatism, by force if necessary, for as long as it is able. The factor with the greatest potential for the independence of Tibet or Xinjiang is not the religion or sense of national consciousness of the Tibetans or Uygurs, but the collapse of central authority in China.

Notes

1 On policy towards religion in the early years of the PRC and CCP theory on religion, see Richard C. Bush Jr, *Religion in Communist China*, Abingdon Press, Nashville and New York, 1970, pp. 15–37. Donald E. MacInnis has collected many documents relating to theory, policy and tactics concerning religion in the PRC before the Cultural Revolution, including statements by Mao Zedong and other leaders, in *Religious Policy and Practice in Communist China*, Macmillan, New York, Collier-Macmillan, London, 1972, pp. 6–89.
2 See Bush, *Religion in Communist China*, p. 264.
3 See Ali in Luo Zhufeng et al. (eds), *Zhongguo da baike quanshu, zongjiao*, Zhongguo da baike quanshu chubanshe, Beijing, Shanghai, 1988, p. 552.
4 MacInnis (comp.), *Religious Policy and Practice in Communist China*, p. 119.
5 For much more material on the foreign relations implications of China's minorities under the PRC, see Colin Mackerras, *China's Minorities: Integration and Modernization in the Twentieth Century*, Oxford University Press, Hong Kong, 1994, pp. 167–97. Bush, *Religion in Communist China*, pp. 288–96 has considered the foreign relations of Islam in the PRC's early years. For documents on 'religion and imperialism' before the Cultural Revolution, see MacInnis (comp.), *Religious Policy and Practice*

in Communist China, pp. 133–56, but there are none concerning the implications for relations with Islamic countries.

6 See, among numerous other places, Mullin and Wangyal, *The Tibetans*, p. 1.

7 Article 28 of the 1975 Constitution, cited here because it is the least liberal of the four. See *Peking Review*, vol. 18, no. 4, 24 January 1975, p. 17.

8 For example, see *Xinjiang nianjian 1993*, Xinjiang Renmin chubanshe, 1993, p. 337, which gives high priority to the strengthening of such education in Xinjiang in 1992, carried out in the interests of social stability and economic construction.

9 *Handbook on Nationalities Work* Editorial Department, *Minzu gongzuo shouce*, Yunnan Renmin chubanshe, Kunming, 1985, p. 94.

10 ibid., p. 552.

11 Luo Zhufeng and Huang Xinchuan, 'Zongjiao', in Luo et al. (eds), *Zhongguo da baike quanshu, zongjiao*, p. 7.

12 Phuntsog Wangyal in Chris Mullin and Phuntsog Wangyal, *The Tibetans: Two Perspectives on Tibetan–Chinese Relations*, Minority Rights Group, London, 1983, p. 19.

13 Ling Nai-min, Kung Wei-yang et al. (comp.), *Tibet, 1950–1967*, Union Research Institute, Hong Kong, 1968, p. 232.

14 Liu Rui et al. (eds), *Zhongguo renkou, Xizang fence*, Zhongguo caizheng jingji chubanshe, Beijing, 1988, p. 37.

15 Inner Mongolian Autonomous Region Editorial Group, *Menggu zu shehui lishi diaocha*, Nei Menggu Renmin chubanshe, Huhhot, 1985, p. 159.

16 *Outline of the Ningxia Hui Autonomous Region* Compilation Group, *Ningxia Huizu zizhi qu gaikuang*, Ningxia Renmin chubanshe, Yinchuan, 1986, p. 101.

17 Melvyn C. Goldstein and Cynthia M. Beall, *Nomads of Western Tibet, The Survival of a Way of Life*, University of California Press, Berkeley, Los Angeles, 1990, p. 140. For further detail on this period among the nomads of Western Tibet, see pp. 140–44.

18 I have developed this point also in 'Religion, Politics and the Economy in Inner Mongolia and Ningxia', in Edward H. Kaplan and Donald W. Whisenhunt (eds), *Opuscula Altaica: Essays Presented in Honor of Henry Schwarz*, Center for East Asian Studies, Western Washington University, Bellingham, Washington, 1994, pp. 444–45.

19 For a detailed summary of the document in English see Julian F. Pas, 'Introduction: Chinese Religion in Transition', in Julian F. Pas (ed.), *The Turning of the Tide, Religion in China Today*, Hong Kong Branch of the Royal Asiatic Society and Oxford University Press, Hong Kong, 1989, pp. 7–12.

20 ibid., pp. 10–11.

21 *Amnesty International Report 1990*, Amnesty International Publications, London, 1990, pp. 67–68.

22 See more discussion in Pas, 'Introduction', pp. 14–15.

23 For example, the National Seminary of the Chinese Catholic Church, *Zhongguo Tianzhujiao Shenzhe xueyuan*, was set up in September 1983 in

Beijing — see Tu Shihua in Luo et al. (eds), *Zhongguo da baike quanshu, zongjiao*, p. 551 — and the Chinese Buddhist Academy, *Zhongguo Foxue yuan*, was established in 1956 in Beijing, ceased operations in 1966 and reopened in 1980 — see Lin Ziqing in Luo et al. (eds), *Zhongguo da baike quanshu, zongjiao*, pp. 544–45.

24 The directive, which was published in the *Tibet Daily* on 23 November 1994 and included as a News Brief item in *China News Digest*, News Global, on 7 January 1995, stated that there were enough monks and nuns in the monasteries to meet Tibetans' daily needs.

25 Liu et al. (eds), *Zhongguo renkou, Xizang fence*, p. 37.

26 Cited in *Beijing Review*, vol. 35, no. 9, 2–8 March 1992, p. 16.

27 For two accounts of religion in Tibet, applying mainly to the early 1980s, see Mullin and Wangyal, *The Tibetans*, pp. 11 and 19.

28 Lincoln Kaye, 'Back to the Old Faith', *Far Eastern Economic Review*, vol. 155, no. 14, 9 April 1992, p. 20.

29 Chang Naiguang et al., eds., *Zhongguo renkou, Ningxia fence*, Zhongguo caizheng jingji chubanshe, Beijing, 1988, p. 316. The same figure is given in *Conditions in Ningxia Region* Compilation Group, *Ningxia qu qing*, Ningxia Renmin chubanshe, Yinchuan, 1988, p. 40, but without an accurate date.

30 Dru C. Gladney has discussed the Islamic and conservative revival among the Hui in several places in his path-breaking book *Muslim Chinese, Ethnic Nationalism in the People's Republic*, published by Council on East Asian Studies, Harvard University, and distributed by Harvard University Press, Cambridge, Mass. and London, 1991. See, for instance, pp. 122–31, concerning one community in central Ningxia.

31 See Zhang Yongqing, 'Dui shehuizhuyi shiqi woguo Yisilanjiao yu jingji fazhan guanxi de jidian sikao', in Zhang Yongqing (ed.), *Yisilanjiao yu jingji yanjiu wenji*, Ningxia Renmin chubanshe, Yinchuan, 1991, p. 11.

32 I have covered the question of religion among the Bai people in Yunnan in 'Aspects of Bai Culture: Change and Continuity in a Yunnan Nationality', *Modern China, An International Quarterly of History and Social Science*, vol. 14, no. 1, January 1988, pp. 54–61.

33 *General Account of the Yanbian Korean Autonomous Prefecture* Compilation Group, *Yanbian Chaoxian zu zizhi zhou gaikuang*, Yanbian Renmin chubanshe, Yanji, 1984, p. 219.

34 See Bernard Vincent Olivier, *The Implementation of China's Nationality Policy in the Northeastern Provinces*, Mellen Research University Press, San Francisco, 1993, p. 97.

35 Alan Winnington, *The Slaves of the Cool Mountains, The Ancient Social Conditions and Changes Now in Progress on the Remote South-Western Borders of China*, Lawrence & Wishart, London, 1959, p. 131.

36 ibid., p. 167.

37 Morigendi, 'Dawoer zu zhi zongjiao xinyang', in Jilin Provincial Nationalities Research Institute, *Sanman jiao wenhua yanjiu, diyi ji*, Jilin Renmin chubanshe, Changchun, 1988, p. 148.

38 I have discussed population questions among the minorities since 1949 in some detail in *China's Minorities*, pp. 234–37.

39 Liu Jinglong, 'Cong kongzhi renkou yundong kan Yisilan jiao she-huiguan de yanjin', in Composition Group for *Research Papers on Islam in China, Zhongguo Yisilan jiao yanjiu wenji*, Ningxia Renmin chubanshe, Yinchuan, 1988, pp. 427–29.

40 Gladney, *Muslim Chinese*, p. 164.

41 I have developed the Islamic attitude to population control in Ningxia in 'Religion, Politics and the Economy', pp. 454–55.

42 Gladney, *Muslim Chinese*, p. 237.

43 ibid., pp. 33, 348.

44 I have commented on the question of women in religion in Ningxia and Inner Mongolia also in 'Religion, Politics and the Economy', pp. 449–50.

45 See also Ronald D. Schwartz, *Circle of Protest, Political Ritual in the Tibetan Uprising*, Hurst & Company, London, 1994, p. 102. Schwartz refers to 'the relative powerlessness of nuns in traditional Tibetan society' and claims that the political protest of the late 1980s and 1990s has raised their status in the eyes of the people to a position similar to that of monks.

46 *Amnesty International Report*, 1990, p. 67.

47 Schwartz, *Circle of Protest*, p. 69.

48 Among numerous examples, a scholarly account with this interpretation can be found in Franz Michael, 'Non-Chinese Nationalities and Religious Communities', in Yuan-li Wu, Franz Michae et al., *Human Rights in the People's Republic of China*, Westview Press, Boulder and London, 1988, pp. 280–82.

49 *Tibet Daily*, quoted in an article reprinted in *China News*, 18 October 1994, vol. 2.

50 'Muslims Get Book Banned', *Beijing Review*, vol. 32, no. 21, 22–28 May 1989, p. 9.

51 See Carl Goldstein, 'Letter from Xinjiang', *Far Eastern Economic Review*, vol. 145, no. 31, 3 August 1989, p. 37.

52 In a speech given on 25 August 1994 at a 'National Work Conference on Exchanging Experiences in Legal System Propaganda and Education Work among 100 Counties (Cities)', the Minister of Justice Xiao Yang complained that in some areas people were using the power of religion to interfere with Party and government work and 'struggling with us to seize grass-roots political power'. See *Fazhi ribao*, 26 August 1994 as cited in *China News*, 14 October 1994, vol. 3, no. 1/3.

53 See A. Doak Barnett, *China's Far West, Four Decades of Change*, Westview Press, Boulder, San Francisco, Oxford, 1993, p. 143. On Islam in Ningxia see pp. 141–46.

54 The document is reproduced in full in English in Mullin and Wangyal, *The Tibetans*, p. 27.

55 See also the comments of Gladney in *Muslim Chinese*, pp. 1–7.

7 Minorities and the Education System, 1949–1995

The contradictions between religion and education, with their uniquely powerful ability to determine attitudes, have intensified under the PRC by comparison with the preceding period. The influence of religion over education has weakened fundamentally as compared with the first half of the century. The primary reason for this is that the CCP has succeeded in establishing a state education system which, while by no means absolutely comprehensive throughout the country, is far closer to being so than in any earlier period.

Whereas the traditional systems of education assisted ruling elites and clergies of individual minorities to get their own ideologies and points of view accepted among their own peoples, the new state system has helped to undermine the distinctions among the nationalities of China, including those between the Han and the minorities. For this reason, education has tended strongly to function as an agent of integration in China as a whole. In this important respect, it operates very differently from religion, as discussed in the previous chapter. Clearly the Chinese state wishes the people, no matter what their nationality, to regard religion as backward-looking and to seek progress in its own China-wide ideologies. This notion applies equally to the nationalism of the Guomindang and the Three People's Principles of Sun Yat-sen or of the Marxism-Leninism of the CCP. But the state has been only partly successful, the revival of religions in the 1980s and 1990s to some extent balancing the pressures produced by its education system.

In terms of national identities in the education system, the situation differs sharply from region to region. In summary, the education system allows for the consciousness of the nationalities everywhere in China in the 1980s and 1990s. But, in a few regions, it promotes such identity feelings quite strongly in several ways, such as the encouragement of language and culture survival. Prime examples are in the Korean area of Yanbian and in Xinjiang, where the education system places a strong emphasis on the use of national language for instruction at both primary and secondary levels.

Overall CCP policy on minorities education

Education is of enormous significance in the raising of future generations. Because of this, the CCP took very early steps to mould the educational system to accord with the revolutionary process it was leading. In September 1951, it held its first national conference on education among the nationalities, examined the problems and came up with some conclusions, the main ones being that education among the minorities must be in accordance with the CCP's ideology, scientific and mass-based, and also foster the special features of the nationalities.[1]

The late 1950s saw a swing back to a policy less tolerant of minority differences and more insistent on Chinese cultural unity. One sign of this was a major conference held in September 1958 on publishing among the minorities, the sponsors of which included the Ministry of Education. Although textbooks in minority languages were still allowed, the emphasis was on demanding socialist, communist and patriotic ideology, patriotism referring not to love of their own minority but to the Chinese nation as a whole. A conference of educational authorities of Yunnan, Guizhou and Sichuan in March 1963 symbolised a swing back the other way through its criticism of authorities for giving insufficient weight and recognition to minorities' and local characteristics and for allowing the education of the minorities to slide towards decline.[2]

Any improvement brought about by measures such as this was brought to an abrupt halt by the Cultural Revolution. As in so many other areas, this imposed a new, decisively different and drastically less tolerant policy on education towards the minorities. Based on the assumption that the class struggle was the main contradiction within society, the Cultural Revolution aimed to promote proletarian and socialist education among the minorities, as well as internationalism and patriotism — which as of September 1958 meant love of China as a whole, rather than relating to the individual minorities. Marxism-Leninism-Mao Zedong Thought was laid down as the appropriate ideology for study among the minorities, as for everybody else. The effects of such a policy were to downgrade the use of minority languages and to suppress any sense of minority consciousness. At no time in the twentieth century has the suppression of ethnic identities been sharper in education than during the Cultural Revolution. On the other hand, the number of schools promoting basic literacy in Chinese expanded.

In February 1981, the Ministry of Education and the State Nationalities Affairs Commission co-sponsored a further conference which confirmed and laid down policies on education in accordance with the principles of autonomy. A new Department of Nationalities Education was set up within the Ministry of Education, with corresponding organisations at various levels in relevant places throughout the country. Minorities were to be allowed to use their own languages in education, and some latitude was allowed for autonomous curricula. In addition, funds were allocated for special schools and teacher training programs for the minorities.[3]

In May 1985 the CCP Central Committee announced a series of major educational reforms, the main element being the staged introduction of universal nine-year education, six years of primary school and three for junior secondary. On 21 April 1986, the National People's Congress followed the CCP's lead and adopted the *Law of the PRC on Compulsory Education*, under which nine years' compulsory education was stipulated in the cities and developed areas by 1990 and almost everywhere in the country by the end of the century. A primary aim of these reforms was to facilitate the economic reforms and the modernisation process so central to the 1980s and 1990s.[4] Although the policy was a national one, rather than relating to the minorities in particular, it certainly applied to them as it did to the Han. However, the trend towards privatisation and the relaxation of government control in Chinese society as a whole and in education in particular have meant a widening of inequalities and allowed some parents, especially poorer ones, to keep children at home, rather than sending them to school.

At the same time, the modernisation of the country remained a key aim of education, not only in the sense of raising the level of competence for contributing to the economy of the people at large, but more specifically through training more professionals at all levels.[5] Educational authorities in minority areas have been quick with exhortations to step up the expansion of the education system to this end. In few places have such calls been more pressing than in Tibet, where levels are still recognised as dismally low and the body of professionals is far too small for effective economic growth.[6]

Structure and 'nationality schools'

The structure of the state education system is very similar throughout China. In addition to primary, secondary and tertiary institutions, there are special schools, specialised and vocational schools, and kindergartens.[7] The most advanced places — for example, Yanbian — are also served by youth palaces (*shaonian gong*), the function of which is to provide extracurricular education to young people in sport, the arts, computing and other areas.

In addition, courses in the primary and secondary schools are more or less uniform throughout China. In most cases they must use the same textbooks everywhere, including in the nationality areas. This means that, in those subjects where the government has a position to put across, all children will be taught the same ideological point of view. There is a wide range of such subjects, including not only politics, Marxist-Leninist philosophy and character building (*deyu*), but also history and geography.

China's overall policy of autonomy towards its minority nationalities means that, although secession from the PRC is absolutely forbidden, a certain degree of self-government is permitted to the minorities.[8] As it applies to education, one of the results of the policy of autonomy is the existence of 'nationality schools' and 'nationality classes' in the areas of high concentration of minorities. These are schools or classes which take in students mainly or entirely of one nationality. In some areas they are given a special subsidy by the state and enjoy the services of higher quality teachers and better equipment, entry into them being highly competitive.

In other areas it is perfectly normal for members of the minorities to attend separate schools. One such area is Xinjiang, where Uygurs, Kazaks, Uzbeks, Xibes and others have their own schools, with the Han and Hui in others. In the Uygur schools all instruction is in Uygur, but in those for Han or Hui children, it is in Chinese. At primary level, the nationality and other schools are similar in level. For the whole of Xinjiang in 1992, the rate of children as a whole entering primary school was 96 per cent, and this rate was almost the same among the minorities, 95.3 per cent. However, the Chinese-language schools appear to do better than the Uygur, Kazak and others at secondary level. This is suggested by the fact that the proportion of primary school graduates who enter lower secondary is 77.6 per cent overall but only 67 per cent for the minorities.[9]

One reason for the 'nationality schools' or 'nationality classes' is to preserve the cultures of the nationalities. As noted in the Introduction, the Law on the Autonomy of Nationality Areas of 1984 specifies that the autonomous areas may select the content of their own curricula. However, my own explorations in minority areas in 1990, 1992 and 1994 suggest that, for the main subjects, this is not followed, but on the contrary, the curricula are the same everywhere. A minority such as the Mongols, Zhuang, Uygurs or Tibetans learns the same history as any other student in China: the history of China or 'world history'. If their particular school wishes in addition to teach history with a focus on the Mongols, Zhuang, Uygurs or Tibetans, it may do so, but this will be in addition to the normal curriculum, not at its expense. A few nationalities, such as the Tibetans, have taken the trouble to compile textbook material about the history of their own nationality, but this is still an unusual pattern.

One place where history has assumed a special importance is Xinjiang. In 1992, the Xinjiang Univerity Press and Education Press published Uygur and Chinese editions of *History of the Xinjiang Region*, the compilers and editors being of various of Xinjiang's nationalities. In addition, classes were organised to enable the books to be used in Xinjiang's secondary schools. Although the authors include members of the minorities, the ideological bent of the books follows the official line strictly, its main point being that 'since ancient times Xinjiang has been an inseparable part of the motherland', namely China.[10] What this suggests is that one of the aims of the books' publication is to counter possible separatist feelings among Uygur, Kazak or other minority high school students. It is thus an attempt at promoting national integration, certainly not ethnic identities.

Although the standard China-wide curriculum gives little or no place to the history of individual minorities, some prominence is given to their literatures, arts and musics, particularly in art and music classes at primary level. In Xinjiang in 1994, I found that, whereas the history curriculum included only Chinese and world history, arts and literature had a strong component for the Uygurs or Kazaks. In Uygur schools the learning of Uygur language includes a whole year at senior secondary level which teaches the history of Uygur civilisation, mainly literature. In one high school visited in Gulja, *History of the Xinjiang Region* was used only as a supplementary text, not in the history course, but as material for the history of Uygur civilisation.

A substantial number of schools exist across China with the specific purpose of training specialised students in the arts. These should have teachers from the relevant nationalities, and stress the characteristics of their arts.[11] Having visited quite a few such schools, it appears to me that there is indeed such an emphasis, but far more among certain nationalities than others. Minorities especially keen to preserve their own arts through education include the Tibetans, Uygurs, Kazaks and Koreans. Tertiary-level education in institutions especially for members of the minority nationalities also emphasises the literature, art and culture of the relevant nationality. The Universities of Yanbian, Xinjiang and Tibet[12] have special courses and research programs teaching and researching the literature, arts and culture of the relevant nationality — that is, Koreans, Uygurs, Kazaks and Tibetans.

Availability of education

The spread of the state secular education system which replaced the religious one is reflected in the following statistics (Table 7.1), which show the number of students in thousands in several key years at all three levels of the education system among the minority nationalities in China.

Table 7.1   Minority students[13]

	Primary	Secondary	Tertiary
1952	1 474.2	92.0	2.9
1965	5 219.0	390.7	21.9
1978	7 685.6	2 526.2	36.0
1985	9 548.1	2 361.0	94.1
1988	9 835.5	2 966.5	125.4
1989	10 521.0	2 997.7	131.6
1990	10 695.2	3 128.1	136.7
1991	9 806.5	3 437.3	141.8
1992	11 223.0	3 591.1	153.0

If 1952 is taken as a base year, then these figures suggest very impressive rises in all three areas of education, the total minority population having risen from 35.32 million to 91.2 million between the 1953 and 1990 censuses.[14] Policy appears to have been to give the highest priority to primary education in the early years of the PRC, to secondary during the Cultural Revolution, but to tertiary in the decade of so after the beginning of the period of reform. In these respects, education in the nationality areas follows the trend in the country as a whole.

The figures show consistent rises except for the primary area in 1991 and the secondary in the years just after the introduction of reform. In the former case, it is possible that the population in the relevant age cohort has begun to decrease owing to the population policy and that the trend towards privatisation of education has affected intakes. Another explanation for the fall is that, in 1991, girls withdrew earlier and in greater numbers, as discussed in the section below.

As far as the secondary level is concerned, more than seven years elapsed before a recovery to the 1978 level. The disparity is even greater when we consider the rise in the population over that period, a good proportion of which was no doubt in the relevant age cohort. It is notable that the trend towards a decline in the number of enrolments at secondary level was even sharper in China as a whole during a similar period. The number of secondary students in all China reached a peak of 68.488 million in 1977 and fell every year until 1983; even by 1992, when it stood at 53.544 million, it had not even nearly recovered the 1977 level.[15]

The main reason for the decline, both among the minorities and in the country as a whole, is the attitude of various Chinese governments towards secondary education. Government policy during the Cultural Revolution had been to spread junior secondary education. One major way of accomplishing this end was to curtail primary schooling by one year but to add two-year junior secondary classes to the village primary schools. However, with the negation of the Cultural Revolution, the government quite consciously reduced the number of secondary schools. It argued that this policy had spread financial resources too thinly, with a consequent decline in the quality both of junior and senior secondary school education.[16] During the 1980s, the number of secondary schools continued to fall, although the junior secondary did so very much more slowly than in the late 1970s. The encouragement for getting rich as quickly as possible contributed even further to the decline in the number attending secondary school, because contributing directly to the economy in the villages or taking a job seemed more useful to many parents and young people than continuing education. In the light of the uneven rises in the numbers of students at secondary level in the second half of the 1980s, it seems unlikely that the targets set down in the *Law of the PRC on Compulsory Education* will be reached.[17]

In most parts of China, both Han and minority nationality, parents must pay to educate their children. Since the mid-1980s, tuition fees have gradually been introduced and there are various other additional costs to cover, such as for textbooks, pencils, pens, food and so on. Although the cost of sending a child to a state primary school was still extremely small as of the mid-1990s, it rises at junior secondary and again, sharply, at senior secondary level. In Xinjiang in 1994, costs quoted to me were RMB¥6.00 per semester at primary level in the cities, but less in the countryside, RMB¥24.00 at junior secondary and RMB¥44.00 at senior secondary level. A Uygur teacher who told me these sums added that he thought them quite excessive — quite enough to turn away the children of poor families who needed the education most. However, several other teachers interviewed defended them, arguing that very poor families are exempted, and since the schools know the families they can tell which are genuinely poor and which are not. Most cities, even in minority areas, now have universal primary school education. Among the nationality villages visited by this writer, all claimed absolutely or nearly total enrolments of the relevant age cohort for two or three years of primary school, but only a minority made the same claims for levels higher than that.

Apart from the state schools, many villages enjoy the services of popularly managed (*minban*) schools. Although these schools are expected to offer exactly the same curricula as the state schools, they are organised and largely paid for not by the government, but by the community at large. The classrooms are no worse than in the state schools, but the teaching conditions are not as good. In one Miao village near Kaili, the capital of Southeast Guizhou, Miao Dong autonomous prefecture, a Miao teacher surnamed Yang told me in 1990 that the school building of the popularly managed school where he taught had been a poor family house sold to the village for about RMB¥1000 in 1964 and made into a school. The fees were higher than in the state schools, and no 'nationality subsidies' were available.

It is perhaps fair to add that many of those in China with whom I have had the opportunity to discuss the availability of education among the minorities, whether belonging themselves to the Han or minorities, have expressed themselves seriously dissatisfied with the current situation. Especially in rural areas, there are shortages of teachers, schools, books and all other educational facilities. In Tibet, even in the city streets, I was struck by the number of children who asked me to give them a pen or pencil. Attendance is far lower than it ought to be or than levels to which officials and ordinary people aspire. The fact of general agreement that education has progressed enormously since 1949 does not mean that it has gone even nearly far enough.[18]

Inequalities and literacy

There are thus serious inequalities in terms of education between the minorities in general and the Han. Children of most of the minorities tend to go on to junior secondary school, let alone senior or university, much less than do those of the Han. The minorities are considerably less urbanised than the Han and in nationality areas, the latter tend to concentrate in the towns. There are primary schools in or within walking distance of most minority nationality villages or pastoral areas, but few secondary schools. The very poor or nonexistent transport facilities, even worse in general in the minority rural areas than in those of the Han, are among those factors which militate against the expansion of secondary school education among the great majority of the minorities.[19]

In discussing literacy among China's minorities, it is important to note that, for those nationalities with scripts, the figures mean the ability to read and write in their own language, not in Chinese. A Kazak able to read and write in Kazak would not count as illiterate, even if totally unable to read any Chinese. The distinction bears greatly on questions of identity and integration, because the preservation of one's own language is crucial for national consciousness. But at the same time, the integration of China is benefited greatly by the ability of as many of its people as possible to communicate with each other in a common language.

For those minorities without scripts, literacy rates would refer to a language with a script of widespread use. For most minorities, such a language would indeed be Chinese, but not always. For instance, the Tajiks of the far southwest of Xinjiang have no script, but use Uygur more readily than Chinese, so a Tajik who could read and write Uygur would certainly count as literate.

Illiteracy is still widespread in the nationality areas. Figures from the 1982 census show rates of education and literacy among the minorities in general to be considerably lower than in the country as a whole. Counting semi-literates and illiterates as those persons 12 years of age and over who could read or write very little or not at all, then the rate of semi-literacy and illiteracy for all China was 31.87 per cent in 1982, while the corresponding rate among the minority nationalities was 42.54 per cent. The two minority nationalities with the lowest rates of semi-literacy and illiteracy were the Tatars (8.89 per cent) and the Koreans (10.5 per cent).[20]

It is government policy to give advantages to minority students as against the Han. For instance, minority students require a lower score than their Han counterparts to gain entry into the universities and colleges. In most nationality areas, the government provides compensation against inequalities in the form of 'nationality subsidies' (minzu fei), paid to students from minority nationalities, but the size and nature vary from place to place. The subsidies are designed as a kind of affirmative action in support of minorities.[21] In Tibet, where conditions are poorest, the government of the autonomous region adopted special provisions which included free tuition in urban primary and secondary schools beginning from September 1982. Later the government introduced subsidies granting students in key primary and secondary schools free food, free clothing and free accommodation: the 'three guarantees' (sanbao).[22]

There are also great inequalities among the various minorities themselves. Among the most populous minorities, the Koreans and Tibetans stand out as presenting a strong contrast in the extent of education and literacy. It is because of Tibet's relative backwardness in this area that the government of the autonomous region has introduced special ameliorative measures. In the Yanbian Korean autonomous prefecture, over 90 per cent of Korean children already attended primary school in 1952.[23] An educational official in Yanji told me in October 1990 that Yanbian had been trying to put nine-year compulsory education into practice since 1982 and had made a great deal of progress towards implementing that goal. The proportion of children of primary school age who attended school was almost 100 per cent, the only exceptions being children who were chronically sick or had some other special condition. In Tibet in 1984, on the other hand, the proportion of children aged between 7 and 11 who attended school was only 50.4 per cent of the total.[24] Officials are quite willing to admit that among the peasants and herdsmen there are 'quite a few don't want to send their child to school but would rather send him to a monastery to become a monk'.[25] Admitting that Tibet 'has long been plagued with weak basic education', a Tibetan writer claims a goal by 'local authorities' for 'a middle school for each county, a primary school for each township and a school attendance rate of 80 per cent' in Tibet by the end of the twentieth century.[26]

The Koreans are by far the most literate of China's most populous nationalities, including the Han. According to the 1987 sample census, only 7.16 per cent were illiterate or semi-illiterate in that year,[27] this very low rate being confirmed by the 1990 census, which showed 7 per cent.[28] The same count showed that 822.54 per thousand of Koreans had graduated from primary school or higher, this being by far the highest of any nationality in China and including much the highest rate of senior secondary graduates among any nationality (175.58 per thousand) and the highest in university graduates among the more populous nationalities (22.71 per thousand).[29] Educational officials in Yanbian argue that one of the main reasons for the excellent record of the Koreans in this field is because the people of that nationality have placed a special emphasis on education for well over a century; even during the period of Japanese rule, parents tried as far as possible to give their sons some education, however poor they might be.[30]

In Tibet, on the other hand, illiteracy was over 95 per cent in 1950. Counting a semi-literate or illiterate as a person of 12 years or over who knew no or few written words, the 1982 census found that 74.31 per cent of Tibetans throughout China fell into that category. The 1990 census showed a fall in illiteracy to about 68 per cent.[31] However, it also confirmed that the Tibetans were doing very badly among the nationalities in their education. Their rate of graduation from primary school or higher was the lowest of the most populous nationalities (only 264.7 per thousand) including one of the lowest proportions of primary school graduates of any nationality in China (194.02 per thousand).[32]

Language and education

A highly significant issue in minority education is the language of instruction. If education is to play any kind of role in retaining ethnic identities, instead of merely trying to eradicate the differences among the minorities, it must pay due regard to the cultural and language sensitivities of the minorities. Already in the September 1951 national conference on education among the nationalities, the use of indigenous languages in minority primary and secondary schools was emphasised.[33] The *Law on Nationalities* of 1984 states that in schools where most students are from the minority nationalities, one 'ought to use textbooks in the relevant minority language and use that minority language as the medium of instruction'.[34] It is quite possible for Han students to attend classes taught in, for example, Mongolian, but in fact few elect to do this because it is not really necessary in today's China for Han people to know Mongolian, even if they live in Inner Mongolia or another Mongolian area. The converse does not hold true. It is useful for everybody in China to know Modern Standard Chinese and necessary in all the cities, whether in nationality areas or Han. As a result, quite a few members of the minorities attend Han classes or schools.

Since the normal primary and secondary schools must cover the national curriculum set down, the textbooks stipulated by the central State Education Commission are used everywhere in China. Some nationalities, including the Tibetans, Mongols, Koreans, Uygurs, Kazaks, Zhuang, Dong and Yi of Liangshan have translated the textbooks into their own languages for use in their schools, as is their specific right under the 1984 *Law on Nationalities*. As of January 1992, the Zhuang books were still being used on an 'experimental basis'. Textbooks using Yi script were in use everywhere in Liangshan. The Dong textbooks were in use in Guizhou schools, but in Sanjiang Dong Autonomous county, Guangxi, they were only for adults. The authorities intended to introduce them into schools there as well, but only when there were enough teachers competent in the Dong written language to make it worthwhile.

Other than Xinjiang, where the whole idea of 'nationality schools' is based mainly on the language of instruction and textbooks, one minority area where the local national language is used especially widely and effectively is Yanbian. From the time the CCP controlled the Korean areas of China, the schools were very active in teaching Korean children in their own language. In August 1988, the autonomous prefecture promulated specific regulations on Korean language work, among which Articles 18, 19 and 20 laid down the compulsory usage of the Korean language in all Korean schools at the primary and secondary levels. There are numerous schools where almost all instruction is in Korean, and Korean translations of the standard textbooks are well developed.[34] One of the primary tasks of the Yanbian People's Press is to publish textbooks in the Korean language. However, classes for Chinese language are taught in Chinese. Modern Standard Chinese is taught from lower primary on and all students take it. The reason is that, although the Koreans are trying very hard and successfully to preserve their own language, especially in the areas where they are most concentrated, they also realise that it is essential for them to know Chinese. Bilingualism is extremely widespread among the Koreans of China. However, among Koreans living in areas where the great majority of the people are Han, the use of the Korean language is much weaker and in decline. For example, in Harbin, the capital of Heilongjiang, only about one in three of the city's more than 30 000 Koreans speak Korean fluently, one in three understand the language to a limited extent, and the remaining one-third know only Chinese.[36]

In those parts of China where several minority nationalities live close to each other, very little attempt is made to instruct the students in the language of their own nationality. One example is Guizhou province. In the Miao areas, some primary schools in rather remote areas use the Miao language for instruction for a couple of years, but then increasingly transfer to Modern Standard Chinese. Moreover, even the 'nationality schools' teach overwhelmingly in Chinese. During a discussion with officials of the State Nationalities Affairs Commission in Guiyang in November 1990, it became plain that any use of Miao for instruction in Miao areas was aimed at convenience so that the students could understand, not at preserving the language of the relevant nationality.

In Guangxi there are several special schools for teaching the Zhuang language, of which the main one is that in Wuming county. At senior secondary specialist level, it is designed to train teachers and cadres who will be able to use the Zhuang language in their work. It also offers instruction in Zhuang culture as well as the standard curricula available elsewhere. The great majority of the graduates are Zhuang, but from time to time a cohort of Yao students is taken in. However, only for the Zhuang language and culture classes is any instruction undertaken in the Zhuang language, and even in those some Chinese is used as well. All other courses are given in Chinese only. In every school I came across in Guangxi, including many in the villages, it was obvious that instruction was almost entirely in Chinese, although in first year primary, teachers of the minorities are very willing to assist children who find difficulty in understanding the class. However, a Dong cadre in Sanjiang informed me that in remote villages it is customary to use the Dong language in the first three years of primary school.

Other than at Xinjiang University, where there are separate Uygur and Chinese classes for most courses, the universities in the nationality areas generally use Chinese for instruction, except in the departments concerned with the language and literature or arts of the relevant nationality. For instance, at the University of Tibet in Lhasa, the Arts Department, which focuses specifically on Tibetan arts, uses Tibetan as its medium of instruction, whereas the other departments use Chinese. On the other hand, the research carried out in the branches of the Social Sciences Academy located in the nationality areas virtually all focus their major or exclusive attention on the nationality of the particular area. Moreover, the personnel belong largely, or overwhelmingly, to that nationality.

Encouraging the preservation of national languages has been official policy since the early years of the PRC. However, reality and policy have frequently been different, especially during the Cultural Revolution. Tibet is an important illustrative example. By the end of the Cultural Revolution in 1976, Chinese had become the more or less universal language of instruction from lower secondary level upwards and even in primary most instruction was in Chinese.[37] In the 1980s the situation improved greatly in the primary schools, with Tibetan being increasingly introduced as the language of instruction, but progress has been much slower at secondary level. A document referring to the late 1980s acknowledges that 'there was a properly formed system from primary school up to university only for Chinese-language instruction', with a comparable availability of Tibetan-language classes only at primary level.[38]

Early in 1989, the government of the Tibetan autonomous region issued a rule that from 1993 on, all Tibetan classes in the three years of lower secondary schools throughout Tibet must use Tibetan as the medium of instruction in class. From 1997 the same rule applies also to the three years of upper secondary school. When I visited the autonomous region in August and September 1990, both scholars and school principals informed me that the process of adopting Tibetan in secondary schools was already well underway at that time, but the opportunities for actually checking this claim in practice were limited.

Another area illustrating the tension between policy and reality is Guizhou. One Dong writer complained in the late 1980s that cadres and intellectuals had not been particularly supportive of promoting nationality languages, with policy-makers and leaders not giving nearly enough attention to the matter. As a result, Guizhou had been quite slow in developing nationality languages, especially in the educational system. Because of inadequate implementation of CCP policy in this area, 'we have witnessed the phenomenon of the loud sound of thunder but with only meagre rain, and even of the tiger's head but the snake's tail', all talk but very little action.[39]

It is quite clear that some of the minority nationalities, especially those with their own scripts, are making great efforts to use the education system to preserve and further the use of their own languages, and they enjoy support from governments in so doing. Certainly such a practice assists the heightening of their ethnic identities. There is, however, a problem. Government leaders have at times encouraged Han people living among minority nationalities to learn the language of the relevant nationality and, in the case of the Yanbian Korean autonomous prefecture, the August 1988 regulations compel the cadres among them to do so by law.[40] Yet, in practice, the effort and time involved are such as to dissuade even the more willing of learners. But on the other hand, if the members of the minority nationalities do not learn Modern Standard Chinese, they will find all the opportunities that society has to offer barred to them. This means that whereas the Han need know only one language, the members of the minorities must know two if they wish to preserve their own language. In Inner Mongolia I met a Mongol incarnate lama (Living Buddha, *huofo*) at the end of 1992 who told me that he taught Mongolian language in a nearby secondary school. He expressed himself to me very unsure about the value of his endeavours: 'There isn't much use in the modern world in knowing Mongolian,' he said.

In today's world, more and more people are becoming aware of the advantages of knowing a foreign language such as English. In most parts of China, a foreign language is a regular part of the high school curriculum, English being far more prevalent than any other. If a minority wishes to maintain its own language, then it must either be trilingual or not learn any language of countries outside China. This puts them at a disadvantage as against the Han people. In Xinjiang, several Uygur teachers told me simply, 'For us Chinese is the foreign language. It's the national language, so our students must know it. But it means they can't learn English.' Only at university or specialised secondary level can Uygur students in Xinjiang learn English. It was not China which determined the value of English in the world of the late twentieth century, and there is merit in allocating such efforts to maintaining minority languages. Nevertheless, the problems created in terms of knowing an international language such as English are very real for China's minority nationalities.

There is gender inequality in the knowledge of languages. In almost every minority area visited, this writer learned that women were learning Chinese much less readily than men and maintaining the use of their own language more persistently. This was especially the case in the rural areas, where Chinese quite frequently proved useless for communication, especially with women. Since Chinese is taught as part of the curriculum from the earliest grades, it follows that those girls who drop out from school early will get to know comparatively little Chinese language. Ironically, this may mean that, at least in respect of language, women will end up as a more important repository of ethnic identities than men.

Although it is generally true that minority females know much less Chinese than their male counterparts, there are great variations among the nationalities. Among the Tibetans, very few rural girls or women speak any but their own language. On the other hand, among the Koreans, it is only older rural women who cannot speak any Chinese. These two minorities probably represent extremes among those nationalities with written and spoken languages carrying strong traditions. However, it should be noted also that two of the most populous minorities, the Manchus and the Hui, are entirely or almost entirely Chinese-speaking, as a result of which the issue does not arise.

Female secular education

The issue of women and language use raises the more general question of how minority females have fared in the secular education system of the PRC. Certainly, the position and participation rate of girls is incomparably higher than in the first half of the twentieth century. Moreover, girls and boys normally attend the same schools under the PRC. This is in contrast to the preceding period, when the norm was to separate the sexes into different schools. Literacy is certainly beneficial for women, as for men, and though some educational theorists favour the retention of some schools especially for girls, most would favour a general pattern of coeducation. Despite the great advances for girls under the PRC, gender equality in education is neither a reality nor on the horizon.

According to the 1982 census, the number of minority semi-literates or illiterates was just over 6.9 million among men but nearly 12.7 million among women.[41] The 1987 sample census showed the rate of semi-literacy or illiteracy among males of the minorities at 24.02 per cent and among females at 47.6 per cent.[42] Both years reveal a very large difference between the two sexes. The 1982 census showed the incidence of illiteracy and semi-literacy to be higher among women than men in every single nationality. Minorities where the gap in illiteracy or semi-literacy is more than 20 per cent between the rate in the whole population of 12 years of age and over and that among women in the same age group include the Bouyei (55.53 per cent for the population as a whole, 77.69 per cent for women) and the Dong (comparable proportions being 44.59 and 65.84 per cent). The nationalities with the lowest illiteracy and semi-literacy rates among women of twelve and over were the Tatars (11.16 per cent), the Xibes (15.65 per cent) and the Koreans (16.07 per cent).[43] In the Chabchal Xibe autonomous county, near Gulja in Xinjiang, I was informed in October 1994 that girls there generally did better than boys at primary level, though not at secondary.

The 1990 census showed some improvements but still with a great distance to go. For instance, Tibetan women of 12 years of age or over were no less than 86.78 per cent illiterate or semi-literate in 1982 and 81.25 per cent in 1990, as against 60.88 and 55.5 per cent in the same respective years for men. Better records came from several other populous nationalities. Among women of child-bearing age, only 0.9 per cent of Koreans were still illiterate or semi-literate according to the 1990 census, while other minorities with rates better than the Han included the Manchus, Kazaks and Uygurs.[44]

Among the Bai people of Yunnan, and the Bouyei and Miao of Guizhou and Western Hunan, which are typical in this respect, primary school education is more or less universal for two to three years, but the girls then begin to withdraw from school. The imbalance becomes more and more serious in the remaining years of primary school and upward.[45] In junior middle schools, boys outnumber girls by about three to one. In a very poor Yao village this writer visited in Shangsi county, Guangxi, in January 1992, every child was educated up to the third grade, but only 70 per cent went on to higher grades, the ones who withdrew being overwhelmingly girls. An official of the Guizhou State Nationalities Affairs Commission told me in November 1990 that in the Sandu Shui autonomous county in Guizhou there was a district (*qu*) where, among a total of 33 primary schools, the students are all boys in fourteen. The reason is that all parents send their sons to school but some keep their daughters at home, perhaps after a very short education, to look after younger brothers or acquire traditionally feminine skills, such as cooking, housework and the embroidery of the relevant nationality. In several Miao villages, both in Guizhou and Western Hunan, it was explained to me that a major reason why girls often get less education than boys is because of the old tradition of 'making much of the male but light of the female' (*zhongnan qingnü*).

The Islamic minorities show enormous variation in attitudes towards female education. It is possible that some Hui parents may be driven by traditionalist religious views to prefer their children, and especially their daughters, to learn the *Koran* and other matters connected with religion rather than the curricula available at the state schools. Dru Gladney cites parents in one place as expressing doubts about the value of learning Chinese and mathematics.[46] It could be that such subjects are seen as even less appropriate for girls than boys. One effect of this continuing emphasis on traditional religious knowledge may be that they will learn a little Arabic even before Chinese or their own language.

In Xinjiang in October 1994, I found a definite enthusiasm for female education, greater than in any other part of China. In all those schools visited, girls were claimed to be as keen or keener on education as boys. In one Uygur secondary school in Gulja, figures for students showed 672 girls and 422 boys. The reason given for the imbalance — 61.4 per cent girls to only 38.6 per cent boys — was that, with the introduction of fees and the money-oriented society, poor parents preferred their sons to go out and make money as soon as possible and they could do this better than their sisters. In several rural Kazak families chosen at random, the wife was better educated than her husband.

It may be added that generally six years of primary schooling is universal in the cities of China, whether for minority or Han, and that there are many rural nationality areas in which six-year primary education is universal for both boys and girls. Moreover, gender differentials favouring boys are common in Han rural areas as well as those of the minorities, with the possible exception of Xinjiang. Especially in poor areas, 'education seems to be a privilege exclusive to sons; daughters must stay at home to help their parents'.[47] However, there was some increase in the overall Chinese primary female education during the 1980s. Statistics indicate that 44.6 per cent of all primary school students were female in 1980, but 45.9 per cent in 1989.[48]

In the late 1980s, a series of programs was begun to prevent girls, and especially those of the minority nationalities, from dropping out of school. One specific official report concerned a township in Guangxi's Rongshui county, inhabited by people of the Miao, Yao, Dong and several other minorities, with the claim that special courses in embroidery and cloth weaving had been begun in 1988 to attract girls, because of a belief among many minorities that if a young women does not possess these skills nobody will marry her. Rural girls in Shaanxi and Ningxia were given classes in the evening after they had finished the day's housework.[49]

During a visit to Rongshui in January 1992, I inquired about developments in education for girls and learned of an investigation the previous year to check on the measures to prevent girls dropping out of school. Some good results had been claimed, with expansion in the number of special classes for girls, including an increase in the range of courses beyond those simply confirming the gender stereotypes of female labour, such as embroidery and cloth weaving. Among the Yao, the fundamental problem uncovered was that some communities still maintained a long-standing tradition forbidding girls to leave their house after reaching the age of 13 or 14. The investigation of 1991 had found that to overcome this notion enough to enable the girls to continue education required not only consistent pressure, but also funds to pay for their textbooks, food and other requirements. Tuition might be free, but some parents still refused point blank to continue their daughters' education if they had to pay for the other necessities of education. According to my informants in Rongshui in January 1992, the county government had indeed expended the money, as recommended by the 1991 investigation team, but nobody was claiming a basic solution to the more basic question of changing the attitudes of conservative people. That is bound to be a long and time-consuming process, with one or two specific programs being no more than a minor beginning. The problem of ensuring education for girls is somewhat less severe among the Miao than the Yao, but still serious enough. A visit to a Miao village in Rongshui in 1992 showed universal education for the first three years of primary school, but significant dropouts among girls after that.

Minority teachers

One of the main problems in promoting minority education is the shortage of minority teachers. Table 7.2 shows official figures for the number of full-time minority teachers in primary and secondary schools in selected years, together with the respective proportion at either level of all primary and ordinary secondary school teachers in China.

Table 7.2   Minority teachers in China[50]

Year	Primary teachers	Percentage	Secondary teachers	Percentage
1953	59 800	3.8	5 435	3.9
1965	133 200	4.7	14 635	3.2
1978	310 200	5.9	112 261	3.5
1985	397 800	7.4	125 560	4.7
1986	421 300	7.8	139 210	5.0
1987	436 800	8.0	150 474	5.2
1990	458 700	8.2	197 800	6.5
1991	464 100	8.4	219 500	7.1
1992	476 000	8.6	229 200	7.3

What the figures show is a consistent rise both in the absolute numbers of minority teachers at both primary and secondary levels and in the per-

centage of all teachers in China. A period of great increase is the 1980s —
no doubt at least in part due to the extra effort and money allocated to solving the problem[51] — and this improvement appears to have continued into
the 1990s. In the case of primary school teachers, the proportion has actually overtaken the minority population, for according to the 1990 census,
minorities took up 8.04 per cent of the total population, lower than the proportion of minority primary school teachers to all teachers in China shown
in the table.

The signs evident from my travels in minority areas suggest that indeed
the numbers of minority teachers are growing, but that many contribute
significantly more to the integration of the minorities with the Han than to
any strengthening of their feelings of national identity, with the situation differing from region to region. In Kaili, Guizhou province, I visited a teacher
training school, where the students were half Miao, 30 per cent Dong and
the remainder Han. However, the teachers were mostly Han and there was
not much Miao content in what they were teaching. In a primary school I
visited at random in a Miao township outside Kaili, the teachers were all
Miao except for the principal, who was Han. The school buildings were in
Miao style, but very old and not in good repair.

In Tibet, attempts to increase education were initially carried out mainly by Han teachers from outside. However, a Tibetan writer claims that, as
of early 1994, 'locally trained Tibetan teachers supported by the state are
dominant'.[52] In 1990, Tibetan and Han scholars at the University of Tibet
informed me that, in the villages, a substantial majority of the teachers at that
time were Tibetan, and that it was in the countryside at primary level that
the Tibetan dominance was greatest, although they made no claims about
where they were trained. Unfortunately I was unable to check how many
rural primary teachers were Tibetan, although the limited number of village teachers of whom I became aware were indeed so. In the main primary school in Lhasa, of 103 teachers and staff, 68 were Tibetans, the remainder
being Han, while two of the three principals and the Party Secretary were
Tibetan. On the other hand, in the main secondary school in Lhasa, only
45 per cent of teachers were Han, with three of the four principals being
Tibetan. In both schools, Tibetans were about 70 per cent of the students. Just
as the figures in the table suggest, secondary school teachers are less likely
to belong to the local minority than primary teachers.

In the Korean areas, especially in Yanbian, minority teachers are far more
dominant and apparently better trained. In the whole of Jilin province —
where most of the Koreans live in Yanbian — there were 706 primary or
middle schools for minority nationalities in 1987, of which 640 were Korean,
40 Mongol and the others Hui or Manchu, and in addition some mixed
nationality schools with special classes for minority students. Provincial
government figures show that in all these schools and classes there were
190 980 students, of whom 165 728 were Koreans, and 9531 were Mongols.
Among the staff there were 16 434 people, of whom Koreans were 14 292,
or 87 per cent, and 696 Mongols.[53] What this shows is that virtually all teach-

ers of Korean students are now Korean. Certainly this was corroborated by my explorations in Yanbian in 1990. I visited several primary and secondary schools in Yanji and Tumen, where all teachers were Koreans, even though a few of the students were Han. Moreover, in the secondary schools, there were very substantial signs of Korean identity, with Korean symbols and pictures, and notices in Korean but not in Chinese.

Since the main feature of 'nationality schools' in Xinjiang is the use of the relevant minnority language for instruction, it follows that teachers must know the language of the school where they work. The result is that minority teachers approximately reflect the national proportions of the population as a whole. In a Uygur primary school visited in Ürümqi in October 1994 about four-fifths of the teachers were Uygurs, most of the rest being Hui, while in the Uygur secondary school in Gulja mentioned earlier, nearly all the 100 or so teachers were Uygurs, with just a few Uzbeks and others.

In some places, the standard of living of teachers is extremely low. The Miao teacher surnamed Yang interviewed in a Miao village outside Kaili, Guizhou, had taught at the same school consistently since it was founded but complained that the salary the government gave him, much less than at the state schools, was not nearly enough to live on. While he acknowledged being able to supplement the government salary through the students' fees, he had still been so poor all his life that he had never been able to afford to marry. The only positive factor in what he said was that his school had been hardly affected at all by the Cultural Revolution.

Despite many advances, education was in crisis in the 1980s and 1990s all over China, and not merely among the minority nationalities. One of the main reasons for this was that, while salaries may have risen considerably, they were still extremely low by comparison with the rise in the cost of living. At the same time, making money not only resulted in a good standard of living but also a high social status. In many cities, including in nationality areas, it was possible to earn over ten times more than a teacher with far less training, less work and less pressure by driving a taxi or, where they still existed (as in Lhasa), a pedicab. The result was that falling numbers of good and intelligent people went into the teaching profession. The problem of insufficient and poor-quality teachers may have been unusually severe in Tibet because of the vastness, backwardness and sparse population of the region, but it was actually a nationwide one.

Education and religion

One measure of crucial importance which has followed from the strengthening of the secular system of education has been to overturn the old systems. Among many of the minority nationalities, the old system was dominated by religious organisations and their clergies. So, together with the land base of the old monastic estates, the CCP attempted to destroy the religious education systems. The clergies themselves might survive, but not the land or ideological base which gave them power and influence. Since freedom of religion did not imply the right to proselytise or spread religion (see Chapter 6), the CCP could argue that this policy was well within the bounds of the Chinese Constitution.

In some nationality regions, the policy was carried out reasonably easily. Among many of the southwestern nationalities such as the Zhuang, Bouyei and Miao, the main education system of the pre-1949 period was that established by the Guomindang, although Christian missionaries exercised considerable influence in particular places. Among some nationalities, resistance to the CCP's secular education was strong. Although the Cultural Revolution meant the total elimination of religious influence in education, the revival of the 1980s and 1990s affected education.

In Tibet, for example, the lama temple schools retained substantial influence several decades after the rise to power of the CCP. One official authority, in a book published as late as 1989, acknowledged that even in the late 1980s, many people remained unconvinced of the value of the state school education 'because of the deep influence of the Buddhist education in the lama temples over thousands of years'. He continued that, according to his own analysis, 'it is not only now that the religious question exercises an impact on the development of Tibetan education, but it will continue to have a strong influence into the future'.[54]

In my visits to several mosques and schools in Xinjiang in October 1994, it became clear that no religious instruction at all is allowed in the state education system. All officially sponsored Islamic clergy told me they either approved or accepted that the *Koran* had no place in the state system. On the other hand, one group of laymen in a mosque in Gulja told me in no uncertain terms that they saw it as equivalent to suppression of Islam to forbid the teaching of the *Koran* and Islamic doctrine to children in the schools and bitterly resented the proscription.

Despite the overwhelming importance of the state education system, religious bodies are still allowed to operate schools which train members of their clergies or otherwise assist them to develop. In Islamic regions such as Ningxia and Xinjiang, there are, in addition to the ordinary primary and secondary schools,[55] quite a few schools attached to the main mosques which aim to teach religious matters, the *Koran* and the Arabic language to selected young people. It is important to note that the students of these schools also attend, or have attended, normal state schools, so that their religious training is in addition to, not instead of, their normal secular education. In addition, there are theological colleges with the special function of training further imams.

In 1990 a Han official in Lhasa informed me that some temples still run schools, which teach Buddhist sutras and morals. He said that sometimes the peasants and pastoralists preferred these schools to those belonging to the government system because of the influence of religion. Some parents sent one child to the temple school and another to the government school, and perhaps a third not to school at all.

In the late 1980s and early 1990s, the practice has also begun for clerical people to work within the state education system as a way of maintaining the language and to some extent the identity of their particular minority. A case in point was the Mongol incarnate lama I met late in 1992 who thought fit to teach Mongolian in a state secondary school; he said that only his classes were conducted in Mongolian, the rest in the school being in Chinese, and the standard of Mongolian language was not high. However, in the Islamic areas of Ningxia and Xinjiang I did not hear of Muslim clerics actually teaching in schools belonging to the state system.[56]

The CCP is well aware that in places such as Tibet and the Islamic areas it will have to confront religious influence on education for the indefinite future. Its members and leaders realise that the ethnic identities which have reasserted their influence along with religion in the 1980s are inimical to their own education system and to Chinese national cohesion.

Conclusion

The demonstrations in favour of Tibetan independence which took place from 1987–89 have been the most important secessionist movement in China of the reform period since 1978. It is therefore important to ask whether the education system in Tibet contributed to or opposed such demonstrations. During a visit to Tibet in 1990 I asked at a major secondary school if any students had been involved in these demonstrations. The answer was that the secessionist movement had for a short time exercised some influence, but not to a serious extent. The school authorities, themselves mostly Tibetans, were firmly against independence at all stages and strongly discouraged any students from taking part in the demonstrations. Even religious believers in the school, whether teachers or students, were of the belief that the future lay with a China in which a materialist philosophy would prevail.

Given the political situation, these answers were hardly surprising. But they do not represent the only point of view. This was shown clearly when an article published in an official newspaper in Tibet late in 1993 called the situation there 'extremely grim', and complained about the influence of the Dalai Lama and his followers, especially among the youth. The article called on the education system to 'strengthen anti-splittist education in the schools' in order to develop a 'patriotic spirit', meaning one dedicated to the unity of the PRC, not to Tibetan independence. What this demand indicated was that the Dalai Lama does indeed retain influence not only in Tibet as a whole, but even in the schools there.[57]

Yet I suspect strongly that politics has influenced the education system, rather than the other way around. The independence movement and the demonstrations were a political phenomenon led by monasteries and convents, in which the education system played only a minor or even negligible role. The Chinese authorities are happy to put Tibetans in charge of the schools, but only those Tibetans, such as those I was able to interview at the secondary school in 1990, who are not likely to influence their students in favour of secession. Where they find their opponents in positions of educational influence, they take remedial action if they can.

There are great difficulties in the way of using the state education system anywhere in China to foster feelings of national identity among the minorities strong enough to desire secession from China. The curricula are the same all over the country, in particular in a subject such as history which exemplifies national identity above all others. Although Tibetans, to cite but one minority, were entitled to mount their own curricula in history, they did so only through specific measures and had to be content for Tibetan history to be taught outside the normal curriculum and in addition to it. This shows that the government was interested in education far more for what it could contribute to national integration and the integration among the various nationalities than to what it might mean for the feelings of national consciousness of individual minorities.[58]

Although language remains a sensitive issue in education and society as a whole in the minority areas, it has so far been contained reasonably well in China. The policy of allowing the use of local languages in certain minority areas has produced some worthwhile results. Certainly nationalism based on language has been notably absent in China by comparison with, for instance India or Canada. This writer shares the impression of A. Doak Barnett from a visit to many of China's western regions in 1988 in doubting 'that problems rooted in linguistic nationalism are likely to develop soon into explosive political issues'.[59] Even in Tibet, the contentious issues revolve far more around religion than language.

There is an important gender issue involved in education. The more educated women and girls become, the more they will learn the PRC's national curriculum and, above all, the Chinese language, which will inevitably integrate them better into the life of the PRC. That would lead to a decline in a sense of national identities among women even if, as seems likely, they retain the use of their own languages indefinitely, at least within rural homes and, among some minorities, still more widely.

Everywhere the dominant aim of the government has been to bring about a modern and integrated Chinese national culture in which the minority peoples would accept the prevailing socialist ideology and state, even if they believed in a religion which was hostile to socialism. At the same time, the policy of unified national curricula does not necessarily mean that minority cultures and languages are suppressed. Among those nationalities with strong traditional scripts and cultures, the trend in the 1980s and 1990s was undoubtedly in the direction of using the education system to develop the use of minority languages and preserve their cultures.[60] But the focus was different for those nationalities without strong written language traditions, among whom the trend was to use the education system to learn the language and culture not of their own specific minority but of China as a whole, which in effect means those of the Han.

Notes

1   Xie Qihuang, *Minzu jiaoyu gailun*, Guangxi Minzu chubanshe, Nanning, 1984, p. 15. For more detail on the conference see Gerard A. Postiglione, 'The Implications of Modernization for the Education of China's National Minorities', in Ruth Hayhoe (ed.), *Education and Modernization, The Chinese Experience*, Pergamon Press, Oxford, 1992, pp. 313–14.

2   *Chronology of Nationalities Work in Contemporary China Editorial Department, Dangdai Zhongguo minzu gongzuo da shiji, 1949–1988*, Minzu chubanshe, Beijing, 1990, pp. 123, 173.

3   See Postiglione, 'The Implications of Modernization', pp. 314–15.

4   See Linda A. Reed, *Education in the People's Republic of China and U.S.–China Educational Exchanges*, National Association for Foreign Student Affairs, Washington DC, 1988, pp. 9–10 and Colin Mackerras, Pradeep Taneja and Graham Young, *China Since 1978, Reform, Modernisation and 'Socialism with Chinese Characteristics'*, Longman Cheshire, Melbourne, 1994, pp. 168–69.

5   See, for example, the 'Decision of the CPC Central Committee on Some Issues Concerning the Establishment of a Socialist Market Economic Structure', adopted by the Third Plenum of the CCP's Fourteenth Central Committee on 14 November 1993. See *Beijing Review*, vol. 36, no. 47, 22–8 November 1993, pp. 26–28.

6   See, for instance, Dainzin, 'Reform and Growth of Tibetan Education', *China's Tibet*, vol. 5, no. 2, 1994, pp. 14–16.

7   The structure of China's education system is discussed at length in Reed, *Education in the People's Republic of China*, pp. 19–42.

8   I have discussed this policy in some detail in *China's Minorities: Integration and Modernization in the Twentieth Century*, Oxford University Press, Hong Kong, 1994, pp. 139–66.

9   See these figures in *Xinjiang nianjian 1993*, Xinjiang Renmin chubanshe, 1993, p. 276.

10 Xinjiang Uygur Autonomous Region Education Commission Higher Education History Teaching Material Compilation Group, *Xinjiang difang shi*, Xinjiang daxue chubanshe, Ürümqi, 1992, 'Qianyan', p. 1. See also *Xinjiang nianjian 1993*, p. 276.

11 Xie, *Minzu jiaoyu gailun*, pp. 81–87.

12 Interviews with officials of the Universities of Tibet and Yanbian in September 1990 showed the proportion of Tibetan and Korean students at 70 per cent at the two universities respectively. On Yanbian University and the Yanbian tertiary education system in general, see Chae-Jin Lee, *China's Korean Minority, The Politics of Ethnic Education*, Westview Press, Boulder and London, 1986, pp. 124–37. According to officials of Xinjiang University interviewed in October 1994, just over 60 per cent of the students at that time belonged to the minority nationalities.

13 The figures are based on *Zhongguo tongji nianjian 1990*, Zhongguo tongji chubanshe, Beijing, 1990, p. 80 and *Zhongguo tongji nianjian 1993*,

Zhongguo tongji chubanshe, Beijing, 1993, p. 72. For further educational statistics, see also Postiglione, 'The Implications of Modernization', pp. 316–21.

14 For much more detail and discussion on minority population problems as a whole, see Mackerras, *China's Minorities*, pp. 233–59.

15 See the figures in *Zhongguo tongji nianjian 1993*, p. 710. See also Mackerras, Taneja and Young, *China Since 1978*, pp. 173–75.

16 See Suzanne Pepper, 'Chinese Education After Mao: Two Steps Forward, Two Steps Back and Begin Again?', *The China Quarterly*, no. 81, March 1980, p. 12.

17 According to official figures, the number of children in primary schools throughout China reached a peak of 150.941 million in 1975 but stood at only 122.013 million in 1992, having declined in most of the years in the intervening period. See the figures in *Zhongguo tongji nianjian 1993*, p. 711.

18 See also the comments in A. Doak Barnett, *China's Far West, Four Decades of Change*, Westview Press, Boulder, San Francisco, Oxford, 1993, pp. 606–7, which puts forward an impression very similar to my own.

19 See also Liu Mingshan, Chen Chen et al., *Minzu diqu caizheng gailun*, Guangxi Renmin chubanshe, Nanning, 1989, p. 52.

20 See Research Institute of All China Women's Federation Research Office of Shaanxi Provincial Women's Federation (comp.), *Zhongguo funü tongji ziliao (1949–1989)*, Zhongguo tongji chubanshe, Beijing, 1991, pp. 62, 67–68; and Julia Kwong (ed.), *Education of Minorities*, issue of *Chinese Education*, vol. 22, no. 1, Spring 1989, pp. 95–97.

21 See also the comments of Barnett in *China's Far West*, in particular p. 607.

22 Liu Qinghui, 'Xizang minzu jiaoyu shiye de chuangban he fazhan', in Geng Jinsheng and Wang Xihong (eds), *Xizang jiaoyu yanjiu*, Zhongyang minzu xueyuan chubanshe, Beijing, 1989, pp. 114–15.

23 Lee, *China's Korean Minority*, p. 68.

24 Investigation Group in Tibet on Topics in Nationality Education, 'Xizang jiaoyu xianzhuang yu duice, Xizang jiaoyu diaocha baogao', in Geng and Wang, *Xizang jiaoyu yanjiu*, pp. 34–35; Zhang Tianlu, 'Zhongguo shaoshu minzu renkou', in Deng Zhixian (ed.), *Minzu renkouxue sanlun*, Guizhou Renmin chubanshe, Guiyang, 1990, p. 47.

25 'Xizang jiaoyu xianzhuang yu duice', in Geng and Wang (eds), *Xizang jiaoyu yanjiu*, p. 42.

26 Dainzin, 'Reform and Growth of Tibetan Education', p. 15. According to *Renmin ribao* of 1 November 1994 (see *China News*, 23 November 1994, vol. 2), the school enrolment rate had risen to 67 per cent of school-age children at that time, mainly as a result of Tibet Education Year in 1993.

27 Zhang Tianlu, 'Zhongguo shaoshu minzu renkou', in Deng Zhixian (ed.), *Minzu renkouxue sanlun*, Guizhou Renmin chubanshe, Guiyang, 1990, p. 47.

28 Chen Qiuping, 'Progress Seen in Minority Population', *Beijing Review*, vol. 36, no. 29, 19–25 July 1993, p. 15.

29 *Zhongguo tongji nianjian 1993*, pp. 91–92. Other nationalities with good rates of graduation from primary school or higher are the Xibes (785.38

per thousand), the Russians (784.59 per thousand) and the Manchus (763.17 per thousand). The Han trail somewhat behind these minorities with 706.66 per thousand.

30 For a detailed analysis of the reasons for the great attention the Koreans of China give to education, see Lee, *China's Korean Minority*, pp. 141–50.

31 See *Zhongguo funü tongji ziliao*, p. 67 and Chen, 'Progress Seen in Minority Population', p. 15. Writing in 1994, Dainzin, 'Reform and Growth of Tibetan Education', p. 14 claims that about 44 per cent of the population of Tibet above the age of 15 are either illiterate or semi-literate. The figure shows a much better situation than the census and is probably too low, even allowing for several differences in the precise population to which reference is made, such as that the lower age limit is three years different.

32 *Zhongguo tongji nianjian 1993*, pp. 91–92. According to 1990 figures, the only nationalities in China with proportions of primary school graduates lower than the Tibetans were the Salar (188.39 per thousand) the Bonan (162.12 per thousand), the Monba (141.5 per thousand) and the Dongxiang (121.71 per thousand).

33 Postiglione, 'The Implications of Modernization', p. 313.

34 *Zhonghua renmin gongheguo falü huibian, 1979–1984*, Renmin chubanshe, Beijing, 1985, p. 548.

35 For an account of Korean education in China, with a strong focus on the issue of the use of the Korean language in education, see Bernard Vincent Olivier, *The Implementation of China's Nationality Policy in the Northeastern Provinces*, Mellen Research University Press, San Francisco, 1993, pp. 239–50. For an earlier but more detailed discussion of the nationality schools and classes, and the education system in general in Yanbian in the period of reform, see Lee, *China's Korean Minority*, pp. 105–24.

36 See Olivier, *The Implementation*, p. 238.

37 See also Chris Mullin and Phuntsog Wangyal, *The Tibetans: Two Perspectives on Tibetan–Chinese Relations*, Minority Rights Group, London, 1983, p. 11.

38 'Xizang jiaoyu xianzhuang yu duice', in Geng and Wang (eds), *Xizang jiaoyu yanjiu*, p. 40.

39 Shi Jinhong, 'Mantan Guizhou minzu yuwen fazhan huanman de yinyou ji ying caiqu de cuoshi', in Office for Nationality Spoken and Written Languages of the Guizhou Provincial Nationality Affairs Commission, *Guizhou shuangyu jiaoxue lunwen ji*, Guizhou Minzu chubanshe, Guiyang, 1989, p. 109.

40 Article 5 of the August 1988 regulations on Korean language work promulated in Yanbian stipulates that all cadres of non-Korean nationality must learn the Korean language. See Olivier, *The Implementation*, p. 235.

41 Zhang, 'Zhongguo shaoshu minzu renkou', p. 46.

42 He Xiangwei, Yuan Jianhua and He Lin, 'Shaoshu minzu renkou xianzhuang fenxi', in Ma Bin et al., *Zhongguo renkou kongzhi: shijian yu duice*, Zhongguo guoji guangbo chubanshe, Beijing, 1990, p. 310.

43 See the figures for illiteracy and semi-literacy of those 12 years of age

and over among the total populations of all the minorities and among women in particular in *Zhongguo funü tongji ziliao*, pp. 67–68.

44 Chen, 'Progress Seen in Minority Population', pp. 15–16.
45 See Colin Mackerras, 'Aspects of Bai Culture, Change and Continuity in a Yunnan Nationality', *Modern China, An International Quarterly of History and Social Science*, vol. 14, no. 1, January 1988, p. 67.
46 See Dru C. Gladney, *Muslim Chinese, Ethnic Nationalism in the People's Republic*, published by Council on East Asian Studies, Harvard University, and distributed by Harvard University Press, Cambridge, Mass., and London, 1991, p. 126.
47 *China Daily*, 28 November 1990, p. 4.
48 *Zhongguo renkou tongji nianjian 1990*, Kexue jishu wenxian chubanshe, Beijing, 1991, p. 664.
49 *China Daily*, 3 December 1990, p. 3.
50 The figures come from State Nationalities Affairs Commission Finance and Economic Section, *Minzu gongzuo tongji tiyao, 1949–1987*, n.p., 1988, pp. 93–94, 85–86 and *Zhongguo tongji nianjian 1993*, pp. 72, 709.
51 Postiglione, 'The Implications of Modernization', p. 324.
52 Dainzin, 'Reform and Growth of Tibetan Education', p. 15.
53 *Jilin nianjian (1988)*, Jilin sheng renmin zhengfu bangongting and Jilin sheng difang zhi bianzuan weiyuanhui, Changchun, 1989, p. 462.
54 Wang Xihong, 'Yi shehuizhuyi chuji jieduan lilun wei zhizhen dui Xizang jiaoyu teshuxing jinxing zairenshi', in Geng, Wang et al. (eds), *Xizang jiaoyu yanjiu*, p. 23.
55 As of the end of 1987 there were, according to official figures, seventeen secondary schools especially for Hui students in the Ningxia Hui autonomous region, and 100 primary schools: *Conditions in Ningxia Region* Compilation Group, *Ningxia qu qing (Conditions in Ningxia Region)*, Ningxia Renmin chubanshe, Yinchuan, 1988, p. 463.
56 For more detail on religious education in Inner Mongolia and Ningxia in the 1990s, see Colin Mackerras, 'Religion, Politics and the Economy in Inner Mongolia and Ningxia', in Edward H. Kaplan and Donald W. Whisenhunt (eds), *Opuscula Altaica: Essays Presented in Honor of Henry Schwarz*, Center for East Asian Studies, Western Washington University, Bellingham, Washington, 1994, pp. 447–49.
57 *Tibet Daily*, 11 October 1993, cited from Beijing by Reuter, 21 October 1993, and published in *China News Digest* (News Global), 22 October 1993, item 2.
58 On education among the minorities and national integration, see also Postiglione, 'The Implications of Modernization', pp. 329–32.
59 Barnett, *China's Far West*, p. 608.
60 The comment by Phuntsog Wangyal in 1983 that 'the disappearance of the written [Tibetan] language is almost accomplished' (*The Tibetans*, p. 18) is belied by my observations in 1985 and 1990 in Tibet, which suggest that precisely the opposite to what he expected has actually happened.

8 Some Gender Issues, Marriage and Divorce, 1949–1995

In the early period after it came to power, the CCP was active in its support for improving the status of women and girls. The Marriage Law of 1950 is generally acknowledged as having been 'uniquely significant' as an instrument of family change, including relations between the sexes. Its first article banned 'the supremacy of man over woman', along with arranged marriages, and stipulated a new marriage system based on 'equal rights for both sexes'.[1]

All four Constitutions of the PRC, those of 1954, 1975, 1978 and 1982, lay down equality between men and women among 'the fundamental rights and duties of citizens', with that of 1982 specifying in Article 48 that the state 'trains and selects cadres from among women',[2] cadres being people holding positions of public responsibility or professional expertise. Although in legal terms this was an improvement over the preceding constitutions, in fact the period of reform since 1978 has seen a conflict between the imperatives of economic growth and the needs of women. Margery Wolf has coined the term 'revolution postponed' to describe the position of women in China since the end of the Cultural Revolution.

Hers is one of several divergent views to emerge among feminist scholars in the West over the intentions of Mao Zedong and his followers in the CCP leadership concerning the position of women. She argues that, despite good intentions, their 'patriarchal lenses' ruled out real equality.[3] However, other scholars are less willing to acknowledge progressive motives. For instance, Judith Stacey claims that from the beginning the CCP wanted nothing more for women than a stable family life in the traditional patriarchal style,[4] making socialism and patriarchy mutually co-operative. Neither view denies improvements for women under the PRC, but both paint a very bleak picture indeed of the impact of the policies of the reform period on the status of women, and of the prospects for women to fight on their own behalf against patriarchy.[5] There have undoubtedly been many changes in the position of women within society, but there are also major continuities with the past, and these have become more and more obvious since the period of reform began in 1978.

The substantial changes for women in the early days of the PRC affected the minorities, as they did the Han. The overthrow of the property-owning classes inevitably created some impact on women, and their relationships with men. The entry of women into a production system dominated by a Marxist-Leninist approach could not fail to affect their status in society, especially in the cities. Individual women of the minorities have attained to significant positions in the professions and in society.

At the same time, the special exemptions allowed to the minorities left their traditional values regarding women generally even stronger than among the Han. One example to illustrate the point is that when the CCP adopted a policy encouraging reproduction control in 1953, the primary reason was to promote the health and protection of mothers and children, and possibly to assist in women's development.[6] The fact that the minorities were exempt from the policy meant that any advantages for Han women failed to accrue to those of the minorities.

Gender issues were a concern for the PRC right from its establishment. For instance, on International Women's Day (8 March) 1953, a preparatory committee for the Women's Friendship League was set up in Lhasa, one PRC writer describing this as 'a step forward of great historical significance' because it was the first organisation in Tibet designed to safeguard women's interests and work for equality between the sexes.[7] Yet gender issues do not appear to have been given a particularly high priority in PRC nationalities policy as a whole. This is evident from the fact that the first Conference on Women's Work in the Minority Nationality Regions did not take place until September 1987. Organised jointly by the Women's Federation and and the State Commission for Nationalities, the conference was held in Ürümqi and discussed a range of topics relevant to minority women, including the preservation of the rights of women and children, the training of female cadres and the strengthening of organisation among women. Among the main tasks the conference set for women's work in the new period were 'the enhancement of the quality of minority nationality women and the powerful development of their production of commodities'.[8]

Earlier chapters have considered gender issues as they concern religion and education among the PRC's minority nationalities. The present chapter focuses attention on other gender issues such as the political participation of women and especially marriage.

Labour and political participation among women

The extent of female participation in the working life of a nation, and espe-cially in places of political power, is generally regarded as a criterion of the status of women. In China, official policy considers it desirable that they should work and involve themselves in politics equally with men, the inclu-sion in the 1982 Constitution of reference to training female cadres being evidence of an affirmative action notion. As noted above, the Ürümqi Conference of 1987 also took up this matter as a priority. However, imple-mentation has been very patchy.

Figures from the 1982 census show that labour patterns by gender among the minorities are changing only very slowly indeed in the countryside, although in some areas of commercial, labouring and professional work the women of some of the minorities are adopting a more substantial role than in the past. However, everywhere in China it appears that the more respon-sible a job becomes, the less likely a woman is to hold it.[9] Despite official rhetoric to the contrary, the holding of power among the minority national-ities is still regarded mainly as a male prerogative, just as it is among the Han.

There are, however, differences among the minorities in this respect. This is shown through some figures from the 1982 census, concerning the main power-holding category of employment, called 'State or Party organisations, or responsible people in enterprises and units'. This group includes 'cadres', but is) much more exclusive, with groups like professionals or technicians being counted as 'cadres' but not in the category 'State or Party organisa-tions'. The figures show that in 1982, there were 37 486 women from all the minorities holding positions in the exclusive power-holding categories, or just under one in ten of the 377 176 minority members occupying such posi-tions. Among the 37 486, by far the best represented minority was the Hui, with 10 333 women, or 16.5 per cent of all the 62 525 Hui people, in such positions. The only other minorities with more than 2000 women in such political or power-holding posts, together with the percentage of all those of their nation-ality in such positions in parentheses were the Manchus with 6223 (12.2 per cent), the Mongols with 3931 (10.6 per cent), the Tibetans with 3153 (12.7 per cent), the Zhuang with 2871 (5.6 per cent) and the Koreans with 2666 (9.7 per cent).[10] In these proportions, the southwestern minorities do not come off particularly well, with even the Yi, traditionally noted for equality in gender relations, showing quite a low proportion of women in the main power-hold-ing or decision-making positions.

Throughout China, the Women's Federation provides opportunities for some political participation for women. Although such participation is new for most of the nationalities, it is government-controlled, so that in fact polit-ical involvement mainly means serving official organs. For instance, any polit-ical participation the Women's Friendship League might enable to Tibetan women is on behalf of Chinese rule, not against it. Official statistics claim that in 1993, in the Tibet autonomous region, women constituted 30 per cent of all cadres, although only 13.33 per cent at the higher autonomous region level.[11]

In Guangxi in January 1992, this writer learned of an officially sponsored target that women should hold about one-third of 'cadre' positions. The Zhuang School in Wuming county (see Chapter 7) takes in about twice as many male students as female, to accord with that objective. My own observations in Guangxi and western Hunan in January and February 1992 suggested that the proportion of women at that time was very much lower than one-third. Women do well among intellectuals, but in government positions they are rather less well represented. Although some of the elected village committees include up to a third of women, the great majority contain only one woman out of at least five members, and she is likely to be responsible for women's affairs. Even among the Yao, a minority still proud of its tradition of gender equality, there is very little female participation in the political process. When I visited the Jinxiu Yao autonomous county in Guangxi in 1992, there were hardly any women in leading government positions at that time, and not many lower down either. In neither of the two villages which I saw were there any women at all elected to the village committees.

Grassroots observations on women and gender relations

In terms of social attitudes, the notion mentioned in Chapter 5 of 'making much of the male but light of the female' persists stubbornly among a great many of the nationalities, including the Han, even in the 1990s, and is one of the reasons why women are moving so slowly into positions of political influence. Quite a few Miao village members visited were quite frank in conversation that such a view remained very strong among them. Several female Miao cadres in leading local positions in Guizhou and Western Hunan merely shrugged their shoulders over its persistence, remarking that it was something they had to live with.

The notion of 'making much of the male but light of the female' brings with it two matters related to female participation and social attitudes. One is that the great majority of the nationalities, including the Han, regard the upbringing of children as the task of females, who therefore should not expect to take part in the urban labour force equally with males. The same logic extends much less to the countryside, where training for the job is through upbringing and tradition, not through formal education. This writer has found such views on the relationship between child-rearing and equality more or less universal in China, among both men and women.

Most of the minorities prefer sons over daughters, but to a weaker degree than the Han. One writer, blaming the attitude of 'making much of the male but light of the female' for a high incidence of female infanticide in a county in Han-inhabited Anhui province in the late 1970s, goes on to point out that 'a few of our country's minority nationalities have the good custom of equality between male and female'. Among these minorities, the one with the best reputation for gender equality is the Tibetans, who 'consider that the birth either of a boy or girl can bring the family joy',[12] a viewpoint which the writer obviously considers not nearly as widespread in China as it should be.

Although the writer probably exaggerates the extent of gender equality among the minorities, and in particular among the Tibetans, the suggestion that they are less apt to prefer sons over daughters than are the Han is probably well taken. There are two reasons for this. The first is that the minority traditions are generally less biased in favour of sons, as explained in much more detail in Chapter 5. The other is that on the whole they are much less bound by restrictions on population growth than the Han. Although policy and practice during the 1980s and 1990s have moved increasingly in favour of curbing birth rates, most of the minorities are still not subject to the policy of allowing one child only per couple.[13] What this implies is that the option of 'trying again' if the first, or even second, child is female is more likely to be open to the great majority of minorities than to the Han.

The southern nationalities of Guangxi, Guizhou and Yunnan traditionally accord a greater degree of equality to women than do those with Confucianist or Islamic traditions. These marks of cultural identities remain observable even in the 1990s, despite the changes occasioned by the various revolutions of the twentieth century.

One minority which draws attention to its degree of equality between the sexes is the Yao. The allocation of rural labour is relatively equal, and women can accept their husband into their own family or *vice versa*, as convenience dictates. Among most of the nationalities, men drink and smoke quite heavily, but women hardly at all. Yet Yao women drink along with men not only at festivals, but also quite frequently in the evening after the day's work. Among most nationalities of the south, one sometimes sees a man with a baby on his back, but among the Yao this is perhaps an even more common sight.

At the same time, there are definitely limits to equality between the sexes among the Yao. The low degree of female political participation among the Yao was already noted. In domestic matters, women are often forced to stay at home after reaching the age of 13 or 14. The housework and cooking appear to fall largely or entirely on women. Women may drink a bit, but they do not smoke. Among the Yao, as among almost all China's nationalities, the man with the cigarette hanging out of his mouth or fingers is an extremely common sight, but in the Yao regions I never once saw a Yao woman smoking, even older ones.

In Xinjiang, all families visited and interviewed in 1994, both in rural and urban areas, claimed that their daughters enjoyed opportunities for education and employment as good as their sons' and that the attitude of 'making much of the male but light of the female' was dying or dead. Certainly urban Uygur and other minority women are entering business and the professions to a greater extent that ever before, with younger men accepting this trend fairly readily. I heard that the richest person in Xinjiang was a Uygur woman, who had done brilliantly in business.[14] However, in the

Uygur, Kazak and Tajik families visited, I was struck by the fact that it was always the husband who did the talking, answering even questions addressed to the wife. When the husband was not at home at the start of the interview, he generally took it over once he appeared. In several cases the wife or sister simply disappeared either at the beginning of or during an interview. Moreover, most of Xinjiang's minorities are still Muslims and the continuing proscription on females even to enter mosques there, let alone the clergy, can only hinder the breakdown of traditional attitudes towards women.

A very general observation among minority women is that their age, profession and temperament are every bit as important a source of their demeanour and overall confidence, or the lack of it, as their gender. Professional women of the minorities I have met, including Zhuang, Miao, Tujia, Bai, Hui, Mongol, Xibe, Uygur, Kazak and Tibetan, are quite definitely trying to make their way in the world, and are being encouraged to do so by official policy, even though reality and social tradition often obstruct them. It is undoubtedly easier for a man to advance in the professions and in power positions than it is for a woman, and younger married women feel the pressures of family responsibilities more than men do, even when child-care provisions are very good.

Women become much more confident as they grow older. I have been struck with this phenomenon in all minority areas, ranging from Tibet to Yanbian, Xinjiang to Guangxi, Inner Mongolia to Yunnan. One Dong woman in her fifties who I met in a village outside Sanjiang was more than happy and able to dominate conversation before lunch, even though, as custom demanded, she withdrew when lunch was actually served. Two middle-aged Xibe women in Chabchal, just outside Gulja City in northern Xinjiang, both of them members of the Chinese Communist Party and proud of it, fairly exuded the confidence of the belief that what they did and thought mattered to their society. The Uygur head of the main Kazak performing troupe in Yili displayed great pride and enthusiasm for her work, with a self-assuredness that crossed any gender boundaries. Miao girls are not encouraged to dominate, and mostly do not, but as they grow older they gain and often display confidence. Young Tibetan women appear to me to be rather more self-assured than their counterparts in other comparable nationalities, and in particular than the Mongols — a nationality with which the Tibetans are readily compared because both share a Tibetan Buddhist tradition. Hui women struck this writer as very similar to the Han, with ideological differences occasioned by their religion being minimal for practical purposes nowadays. Rural Hui women are much less confident than their urban counterparts, just as is the case with the Han.

The minority among whom modernisation has progressed furthest is probably the Koreans. In modern urban society, a degree of sophistication is emerging among women which rivals or surpasses that of their Han counterparts. My experiences in Yanbian and elsewhere gave some inkling about the similarities and differences between Korean and Han women in the same place, and comparisons with several other minorities. In Longjing, Yanbian, a Korean family visited at random on 1 October 1990 — that is, Chinese National Day — was having a celebration lunch for the occasion, with the men eating at one table and the women at another. The women did all the preparation of the food and all the housework. Moreover, as I left, the men were about to settle down to a game of mahjong, while the women were preparing to clean up. It should be added that such practices are by no means confined to the Koreans: as obvious from an earlier comment, it is still practice among the Dong and many other minorities of the south and elsewhere for men only to sit at table when guests are invited, the women preparing the meal but not taking part in eating it until the guests are gone. Rural Mongol women customarily serve out the immense quantities of wine consumed by their menfolk but imbibe none themselves.

In Yanbian, young people, both male and female, expect that the men will get the better jobs, and reality usually proves them right. Good opportunities are open just as much to Koreans as to Han nowadays, but among those encountered in good jobs, almost all were men, while people in the service roles, such as in restaurants and shops, were all women. On the other hand, the high number of female taxi drivers in Yanji — at least one in three, according to my observations — shows a confidence that they will not be molested or otherwise harmed, which reflects well on their society.

Korean women in Yanbian are more deferential and polite towards people in general, and to men in particular, than are Han women there. They dress better and take more trouble over their personal appearance than do their Han counterparts. In the families visited, the style of the women, including even the way they sat on the floor, showed great elegance. Han influence has made but little difference to their posture and manners, which remain much more like what I have seen in both North and South Korea than they are like those of Han women.

A Korean male professor told me that, in Yanbian, Korean women are considered rather submissive on the whole, but if committed to a cause of any kind can become very determined, even stubborn, and able to get their way. This feature became more pronounced as they gained confidence with age. He said that Korean women could make very good fighters, much better than their Han counterparts. His are very broad generalisations, but my own observations in Yanbian, and indeed in both North and South Korea, suggest they may have enough validity to make them worth reporting.

One Han scholar points out some important negative factors in the position of rural Korean women:

> The attitude is to make much of the male but light of the female. The status of women in the family and society is low. They have to bear the responsibility for all domestic labour, as well as much of the onerous labour in the fields. Even when preganant, including up to a few days before delivery, they do not get enough attention in terms of food and drink and even have to go to the paddy fields to transplant rice seedlings, spray insecticide, gather in the harvest and so on.[15]

Considering the same writer is at pains to note the general sophistication and high degree of education of the Koreans by comparison with other
nationalities in China, this can only be taken as a rather bleak picture. Yet
the material in this section shows clearly that differences persist among the
various minorities in terms of gender relations and the position and behaviour of women, suggesting that these factors still exercise a bearing in ethnic identities, even if not a strong one.

Marriage

Marriage and divorce are areas relevant to gender relations in which traditions have proved themselves very tenacious in many societies, even when
modernising processes have gathered substantial momentum. Despite some
commonalities among various societies, they also display enormous differences and for that reason are highly relevant to issues of national identities.

Among the great majority of China's nationalities, very few people remain
single all their lives, especially women. Yet figures applying to 1982 show
that, in the age brackets from 30 years and over, there are more minority
women who have never been married than Han.[16] Of the most populous
minorities, it is only among the Tibetans that substantial numbers of people never marry. In Sichuan province, where several nationalities are significantly represented, the Tibetans stand out for the number of people,
including both men and women, who do not marry.[17]

There are several reasons for the differing marriage conditions among
the Tibetans. One is the continuing influence of Tibetan Buddhism, which
still induces some Tibetan men into the clerical order, although incomparably fewer than in the past (see Chapter 2). A second reason is the persistence of polyandry and polygyny, discussed below. It is notable that, among
China's provinces and autonomous regions, the 1990 census showed Tibet
to have the lowest sex ratio, which could account for a slightly lower marriage rate among Tibetan women than those of other nationalities.[18]
However, the main reason why the proportion of Tibetans who never marry
is higher than of the Han or most other minorities is because the registration process is very much less strict in Tibetan areas than other parts of
China. Most people in the rural peasant and pastoral areas still do not reg-
ister marriages with the authorities,[19] and so will not show up in official
figures. Many may, in fact, consider themselves married, even if they are not
registered as such.

Courtship

It is part of the rhetoric of the modernising China that young people should
court their own spouses, meeting them in the course of their work or social
activities of various kinds. This principle applies both to the Han and the
minorities. The extent to which policy matches reality depends less on

nationality than on whether it is the urban or rural areas that are under discussion. In the cities nowadays, young people — no matter what their nationality — tend to follow progressive practice and look for their own spouses. My explorations in minority areas suggest that there has been substantial change in the countryside as well, but it is very much less thorough-going than in the cities, and old patterns cling with remarkable tenacity.

Under the PRC, the reed-pipe gatherings prevalent among the minorities of Yunnan, Guizhou and Guangxi have have generally been maintained with relatively little major change. They constitute a prime example of minority mass customs which are not anti-socialist or anti-people, and which never depended mainly on the richer classes for their popularity. Only during the Cultural Revolution, with its homogenising obsession with class struggle, were any serious attempts made to eliminate them as feudal survivals, but in the 1980s and 1990s they have revived strongly, or in some cases been reinvented. It is quite likely that many young people still depend on them to find spouses.

On the other hand, my inquiries in Miao areas in November 1990 lead strongly to the belief that quite a few young men would prefer to marry girls they meet in the normal course of their work rather than at festival gatherings. This applies especially to urban areas, but also to some extent to the villages. With the changing tastes in the arts, many young Miao men are not interested in learning to play the reed-pipe, let alone well enough to use the skill for so important a matter as finding a life-long partner. This form of courtship is tending to decline in the modern age as a primary function of large-scale gatherings.

In November 1990 I attended a festival gathering near Chong'an, a small town in a Miao area of Southeast Guizhou. About 30 000 people of all ages came to take part in the festivities, many of them having walked quite long distances. The women, and especially the young ones, wore traditional Miao dresses, but the men normal clothing which is nowadays the same among virtually all the nationalities of China. Family members came to share in the fun as unities, but with the young men and women in separate groups, some of them hoping to find friends of the opposite sex. On the same evening, the men sang folk songs in groups, to which the women responded in the same way, suggesting that some of them had been successful. At the same time, persistent searching and listening uncovered very little evidence of the reed-pipe's use for courtship.

The decline of arranged marriages

Closely allied with the issue of courtship is that of parental arrangement of their children's marriages. The CCP banned arranged marriages as early as 1950 through the Marriage Law of that year. Since that time, the incidence appears to have been much reduced. The pattern among the Han in the 1980s and 1990s is that young urban people determine their own marriage partner, but require their parents' consent, whereas in the countryside it is the parents who take the initiative to find a spouse for their offspring but require the agreement of the young people. This is a substantial advance on the pre-1949 period when the consent of the bride and bridegroom was not usually required.

Official sources of the 1980s and 1990s are generally cautious about claiming that arranged marriages have disappeared among the minorities. In 1983 the Nationalities Research Institute of the Xinjiang Social Sciences Academy undertook a survey of 130 Uygurs working in a factory in Kaxgar in southwestern Xinjiang and found that free marriages made up 57.7 per cent, those through introduction by somebody other than parents 8.6 per cent and arranged marriages 33.8 per cent.[20] These figures do not show whether the young people were free to refuse the parents' arrangements. A small sample, they may not be very reliable. Moreover, although they strongly suggest that marriage is considerably freer than it was before 1949, they give no indication whether the trend in the 1980s is still away from parentally arranged marriages, since the time of the wedding is not shown. But it is extremely likely that the rate of arranged marriages in rural Xinjiang is higher than in the Kaxgar factory, which would lead to the general conclusion that arranged marriages remain surprisingly widespread in Xinjiang as a whole.

In Tibet, according to a very well informed but officially sanctioned writer, 'rural areas and remote regions still lag behind the towns' in the matter of replacing the 'unfair forms of the past' with 'marriage based on love'.[21] An official account of Sandu Shui autonomous county, the main centre of the Shui population, is prepared to claim that arranged marriages 'have been greatly reduced, and the number of free marriages for love is increasing day by day',[22] but not that arranged marriages have disappeared.

My own interviews with a range of urban and rural Tibetan, Korean, Hui, Miao, Bouyei, Dai, Zhuang, Yao, Qiang and Shui families and township heads found only one exception to the claim that marriage partners were now chosen freely by the young people themselves. The exception was in a fairly remote Miao and Shui township about 60 kilometres from Duyun in Guizhou, where the head informed me that totally free marriages were very much in the minority. However, she added that the young people could always refuse their parents' choice. Professor Pak Changuk of Yanbian University told me in October 1990 that Zhu Xi's Confucian family rules still exercised some influence in remote Korean villages, though this was incomparably weaker in general than in the old days. A fair conclusion would be that under the PRC there has been substantial change in the direction of allowing young people to determine their own marriage partner, but it is nowhere near absolute and is marked by differing rates of advance in the various nationality areas of China.

Particular marriage survivals

The practice found among many of the nationalities of Guizhou, Yunnan, Guangxi and Sichuan whereby the wife does not live with her husband until she gets pregnant (*buluo fujia*) can still be found, especially among the rural communities of the less well integrated nationalities.[23] Authorities generally regard this as an antiquated, and therefore undesirable, practice, but in the 1980s and 1990s they have preferred to allow it to die out, rather than actively trying to eliminate it. It may have the great advantage of postponing the relevant couple's first birth and thus function as a kind of late marriage.[24] One source claims that, 'following the development of society', the custom has 'already essentially disappeared'.[25] My inquiries at various levels in Guizhou in 1990 and Guangxi in 1992 suggest that, while it is not completely dead, the practice has weakened sharply in its old form and may not last long.

However, among the Yi of Liangshan in Sichuan, brides still go home for a period after the wedding ceremony, although they do not necessarily wait until pregnancy to move in with their husband. The Dong people still practise a variation of the custom of *buluo fujia* very widely in the rural mountain areas. On the day of the wedding, the bride goes home not with her husband but to her own family. She walks at the end of a procession which includes people carrying the provisions for a wedding feast. The husband or his family pays for the provisions, but does not take part in the celebrations at his wife's house, having earlier held a drinking party with his relations and friends. The Spring Festival is a standard time for such marriages, and only a couple of months later, at the time of the seed transplanting, does the wife move in to live with her husband.[26]

The 'walking marriages' of the Mosuo people, who live near the Lugu Lake between Sichuan and Yunnan provinces and are classified by PRC authorities as a branch of the Naxi, may well have declined in importance compared with the pre-1949 society. However, research carried out in the PRC indicates that in the early 1960s the great majority of people in some Mosuo communities around the Lugu Lake had been through a stage in their lives when 'walking marriages' were their preferred option, the average number per person being over seven. One man of 21 years old had already had eight lovers or 'walking marriages', and commented: 'Having only one lover all through life is like a crow's keeping a dead dog — it has no prospects'. Younger people of both sexes agreed with such a view, expressing the general desire to change partners reasonably frequently. On the other hand, older people preferred to move towards longer term relationships.[27] During the Cultural Revolution, the authorities tried to suppress these walking marriages as a feudal remnant, and forced the Mosuo to adopt the more conventional marriages of the PRC. However, as of 1980, the matrilineal forms of family in which walking marriages were either exclusive or common remained dominant among over 400 surveyed and researched Mosuo families of the region.[28] Even in the 1990s, 'walking marriages' show no sign of dying out.

Field work carried out in the Jingpo areas of Yunnan in the late 1950s revealed strong persistence of the traditional patterns found before 1949, such as the free love communal houses and marriage by capture (see Chapter 4).[29] Alan Winnington's research at about the same time suggested that the old ways were beginning to break down, but rather slowly. One Jingpo girl whom he interviewed showed herself progressive enough to have read the Chinese Marriage Law of 1950, but added that it was not yet widely known among the Jingpo, let alone followed. Conditions had changed enough that she was able successfully to resist being married off by involuntary abduction to an opium-smoking 'lazybones' over 30.[30] The Cultural Revolution certainly stamped on such 'feudal' practices. Sources from the 1980s suggest that changes had been very extensive by then and a list of certain ancient customs which had survived did not include either communal houses or marriages by abduction.[31] That they had weakened substantially by then is perfectly credible, but the evidence from the Mosuo suggests strongly that the official account underestimates the degree of survival of ancient national customs.

Article 8 of the 1980 Marriage Law states that, after marriage, 'the woman may become a member of the man's family, or the man may become a member of the woman's family', as the couple agrees.[32] Despite this, it is extremely rare for a man to marry out among the great majority of China's nationalities, including the Han, Miao, Dong, Bouyei and Islamic minorities. Two which stand out as exceptional are the Tibetans and the Yao. In a visit to the Jinxiu Yao autonomous county in the Da Yaoshan Mountains, Guangxi, in January 1992, I was informed that it was actually more common there for men to marry out than the converse. The random cases of which I became aware — two each way — may have been statistically inadequate, but did point in the general direction of equality on this score.

As noted in Chapter 4, marriages between close relations and in particular those between people of the same surname, have always been regarded with particular disgust by the Han people. On the other hand, although the *Koran* lays down strict prohibitions on marriage or sexual intercourse with persons of certain close relationships, there are some which do not come under the bans, such as first cousins. These marriages have always been very much commoner among Islamic nationalities than among Tibetans, Mongols, Han and others. Although the PRC is as hostile to any forms of such marriage as preceding Chinese states, marriage with close relations such as first cousins remains fairly frequent among Muslim minorities. A survey carried out in 1985 in several regions of southern Xinjiang among 8093 Uygur, Tajik, Uzbek, Hui and Kirgiz couples found quite a few close-relationship marriages, especially among the less populous nationalities. Specifically, of 3493 Uygur couples, 17.7 per cent were closely related, of 1325 Tajik pairs the rate was 42.8 per cent and among 2863 Kirgiz couples, no less than 45.2 per cent were of close relationship.[33]

Age of marriage

The age of marriage has tended to rise since 1949, both in the whole country and among the minority nationalities, but certainly the rise has been more pronounced among the Han than among the great majority of the minorities. The PRC Marriage Law of 1950 specified 20 as the minimum marriage age for men and 18 for women, but the 1980 Marriage Law raised both ages by two years, to 22 for men and 20 for women. It also allows the people's congresses and their standing committees in national autonomous areas to 'enact certain modifications or supplementary articles . . . in conformity with the actual conditions prevailing among the minority nationalities of the locality in regard to marriage and family relations', as long as they are 'in keeping with the principles' of the Marriage Law and are ratified by the standing committee of the relevant provincial or regional people's congress. They must also be submitted to the Standing Committee of the National People's Congress 'for the record', but do not require its formal approval. According to a group of minority cadres in the Guizhou State Nationalities Affairs Commission interviewed on 15 November 1990, the relevant standing committees usually accept a request for such variation in the PRC law. These 'modifications' frequently include the age of marriage, varying it downwards by two years.

One Chinese researcher found that the age of women at first marriage was 18.39 among the minorities in 1949 and 18.46 among the Han, reaching over 20 for the first time among minority women in 1975, as against 21.73 among the Han, with the 1982 figures being respectively 20.96 and 22.81. In other words the gap in the age of first marriage for women between the minority nationalities and Han had actually widened between 1949 and 1982. Even though both had shown rises, that of the Han was substantial, while that of the minorities was less impressive.[34]

The tendency for women's marriage ages to rise among minorities, although with a widening gap in the case of the Han, is reflected in the figures in Table 8.1. Comparing the minorities with 'All China', these show the percentages of early marriages, defined as those before the age of 18, and late marriages, defined as those of women who have completed their 23rd year. Since the minority nationalities took up only 8.04 per cent of the total population according to the 1990 census, the category All China overwhelmingly represents the Han.

Table 8.1   Percentages of early and late marriages[35]

Year	Minority nationalities		All China	
	Early marriages (%)	Late marriages (%)	Early marriages (%)	Late marriages (%)
1950	37.14	11.19	48.3	7.2
1955	31.79	11.79	37.3	6.6
1960	24.52	15.48	32.0	11.0
1965	22.67	14.98	28.5	12.0
1970	21.29	14.81	18.6	13.8
1975	11.95	30.82	7.8	31.0
1980	13.28	41.55	5.2	52.8
1981	13.75	37.81	4.5	50.9

Whereas early marriages were actually much more numerous among the Han than the minorities in 1950, and late marriages less so, the precise opposite was the case by 1981. A major reason is that minority people are allowed by law to marry earlier than Han. Another feature of the figures is that the proportion of early marriages among the minorities actually started increasing again in the early 1980s. The Cultural Revolution had pushed strongly to promote later marriages for people of all nationalities, but the revived autonomy among the minorities from the late 1970s on would certainly go some way towards explaining the increased proportion of early marriages among the minorities.

An important aspect of the rise in age of first marriage is the near disappearance of child brides aged between 12 and 14. These reached a peak of 11.96 per cent of the total among the minorities in 1951, but declined fairly steadily after that to not far from vanishing point in the 1980s.[36] On the other hand, brides aged between 15 and 19 are still far too numerous. In 1950, 64.71 per cent of all minority nationality brides were in that age group, the lowest proportion being 21.75 per cent in 1979, but in the early 1980s the proportion rose steeply again, being 31.65 per cent in 1981 and 38.08 per cent in 1982.[37] The accuracy of these figures is suspect, but they do suggest a striking tenacity of early first marriage among minority women. The 1990 census showed that, among China's nationalities with a population of more than one million, there were, in no less than eight of them, women between the ages of 15 and 19 who had given birth to three or four children.[38]

The Guizhou State Nationalities Affairs Commission cadres interviewed in November 1990 claimed that, at least in Guizhou, it was rare for people to marry earlier than allowed by the law of their particular autonomous place. It is true that quite a few of the minority areas of the province have taken advantage of their autonomous status to lower the minimum marriage age by two years.[39] Marriage is counted from the time it is registered, not from the time the couple actually start living together, and the two may be different in those cases where the wife moves in with her husband only after she becomes pregnant. The incidence of marriage below the legal age may well have declined between 1982 and 1990, as implied by the claim of the Guizhou Commission's cadres. On the other hand, the heads of several villages visited in 1990 acknowledged that a few girls still married below the legal age, and among the Yao people even as young as 15.

The law of the Ningxia autonomous region permits marriage for Hui men at the age of 20 and for women at the age of 18, two years lower than the 1980 PRC Marriage Law. Samplings from the 1982 census showed that there were some 24 580 married people below the age of 20, of whom about 4000 were men and the remainder women.[40] What this shows is that even official figures acknowledge quite a few people married illegally in Ningxia, including the 4000 men and at least as many women and probably more.

There are very considerable differences among the various minorities in the age of first marriage, influenced by factors such as economic and educational level, employment, religion and custom. Two advanced nationalities in this respect, as in quite a few others, are the Koreans and Mongols. Among the Koreans, the average age of marriage for women was 19.17 in the 1950s, 21.43 in the 1960s, 22.80 in the 1970s and 23.47 in the 1980s, this last figure being 0.63 years older than the national average for Han women.[41] In the first half of the 1950s, the average age of first marriage of the Mongols in Inner Mongolia was 18.13, but this rose nearly four years to 22.08 by 1980.[42]

The 1987 sample census included data on the age of first marriage among minority women who were already married in 1987. Admittedly the data do not say when they had married, and some may have done so many years before 1987. Moreover, only 1 per cent of China's total population was covered and the proportion of communities remote from the eastern seaboard, which would include many minorities, was no doubt even smaller. The figures may not be completely accurate, but they are nevertheless unique and detailed and the trends they show are probably reasonably close to reality.

Of the main nationalities, the one to show the highest proportion of marriages between the ages of 20 and 24 was the Koreans (58.13 per cent), with 29.81 per cent having married younger than 20. Similar to the Koreans were the Bouyei, among whose married women, 56.66 per cent had married between 20 and 24, and 26.77 per cent before reaching 20. In other words, the figure in the age bracket 20 to 24 was a bit less than for the Koreans, but so were the before-20s, from which it follows that the women who had married at 25 or over were more numerous among the Bouyei than among the Koreans.

At the other end of the spectrum, the nationality with the highest proportion of youthful brides was the Uygurs, 3.61 per cent of whose women had married before reaching the age of 15, and 82.55 per cent of whom had done so between 15 and 19, meaning that no less than 86.16 per cent had married before reaching the age of 20. Only 12.41 per cent had married from 20 to 24. Corresponding figures showed that, apart from the Uygurs, Hui women were the earliest marriers, with 51.57 per cent wedded before reaching 20 and 37.73 per cent between 20 and 24.[43] The continuing power of cultural traditions, especially those associated with Islam, may well be a major reason why early marriage persists so strongly among the Uygurs and Hui. A major reason for the difference between the Uygurs and Hui is because the Uygurs are much less urbanised. In Xinjiang, where most of the Uygurs live, it was still very common in the late 1980s to find young married men of 18 or 19 and married women of 16 or 17 in the agricultural or pastoral rural areas among Islamic minorities such as the Uygurs, Kazaks, Kirgiz, Tajiks or Uzbeks.[44]

Intermarriage among nationalities

Intermarriage among different ethnic groups has the potential to break down the barriers between them, and also opens the possibility for the more populous to integrate and even assimilate the less numerous. In the 1990s, Jews in the United States and Britain have expressed fears that their numbers would reduce and their ethnic identity be weakened by too much intermarriage with non-Jews. Some older Jews actively discourage young Jews from marrying people of non-Jewish background as a way of preserving Jewish identity.

In China, authorities argue in favour of marriage between persons of different nationalities on the grounds of being 'beneficial to exchange and unity among the nationalities'.[45] It has been suggested that when the policy of intermarriage between Han and minority was promoted in the late 1950s, its aim was 'the complete assimilation of the minority groups',[46] but to this writer such a view is exaggerated and ethnic harmony would seem a more likely goal, especially given the government's exemption of the minorities from the most restrictive population policies applied to the Han even in the 1950s.[47] An official interviewed in the government of the Jinxiu Yao autonomous county early in 1992 pointed to the rise in intermarriage as one factor showing how good relations among the nationalities were. In the great majority of mixed marriages between a member of a minority and a Han, the couple may follow the family planning policy of the minority partner. However, although there are no legal or official obstacles, quite strong social pressures survive against intermarriage.

Among a few very well integrated nationalities, intermarriage is becoming quite widespread, especially in the cities. The Zhuang of Guangxi intermarry fairly readily with the Han or other peoples of their region.[48] In Inner Mongolia, about 15 per cent of married Mongols have non-Mongol spouses, almost all of them Han. Mongols who marry people of other nationalities are about half and half male and female. Marriage between Han and Manchu is also widespread. The obstacles against such intermarriage were already breaking down in the nineteenth century. After the fall of the Manchu Qing dynasty in 1911, many Manchus called themselves Han and increasingly adopted Han customs, as a result of which larger numbers of Manchus sought spouses among the Han.[49] By contrast, intermarriage is very rare in Tibet by comparison with most other minority areas.[50]

It is far commoner for urban people of different ethnic groups to marry than rural. In the vast majority of villages, the people still belong to a single nationality. Even in the Miao and Shui township visited about 60 kilometres from Duyun in Guizhou, the inhabitants of all individual villages are either Miao or Shui, there being no villages with both Miao and Shui families. As a result, young people cannot easily meet suitable partners of another nationality. It is true that the courtship gatherings, or *huaer hui*, of parts of Gansu and Qinghai are still very much alive in the 1980s and 1990s and involve young people of various nationalities, including the Han, Hui, Salar, Bonan, Dongxiang and Tibetans.[51] However, in the great majority of nationality areas, people who attend courtship gatherings all belong to the same nationality. In the countryside, the societies of most of the minorities still favour finding a marriage partner of one's own nationality. For these reasons, it is generally difficult for young people to get to know prospective marriage partners from any nationality other than their own, or to marry such partners with parental blessing.

Marriage between Muslims and non-Muslims is fraught with problems. Normally in a mixed marriage of this sort, the non-Muslim will be expected to convert to Islam, since the *Koran's* proscription on marriage to unbelievers remains valid. Marriages between Hui men and Han women are less uncommon than the other way around.[52] A Han women who marries a Hui man often resents the need to change to Islam or is subjected to heavy pressures from her family to prevent her from doing so. In Xinjiang, the proportion of inter-nationality marriages is very low, and when they occur, family breakups frequently follow.[53] It is quite possible that the fairly high rate of close-relationship marriages among such minorities as the Tajik and Kirgiz, mentioned above, is due at least in part to reluctance to marry outside their own nationality, even if a Muslim.

In noting extensive intermarriage between the Bai and Han immigrants into Bai territory, David Wu suggests that this trend could actually contribute to Bai identity, as well as to more rapid acculturation with Han culture.[54] On the other hand, Stevan Harrell contrasts two communities in Panzhihua City in far south Sichuan province, almost on the border with Yunnan, both of which are classified by the state as Yi. One is very different culturally from the neighbouring Han, and with a pronounced ethnic identity; the other is highly integrated, with strong absorption of Han culture. Among the former community, intermarriage with the Han is rare, but very common indeed among the latter.[55] This would suggest a negative correlation between the extent of identity and intermarriage.

What is most striking to this writer is that the greatest resistance to intermarriage is among the Islamic nationalities, where a religion inimical to the Han still plays a major role, and those minorities which resent the Han most, such as the Tibetans. In general, therefore, a strong feeling of identity seems to prevent intermarriage rather than encourage it. Put the other way around, intermarriage tends to point more strongly in the direction of integration of minorities with the Han than towards ethnic identities.[56]

Polygyny and polyandry

Both Marriage Laws of the PRC, those of 1950 and 1980, stipulate one man, one wife and outlaw polygyny. Although the autonomous places may vary the minimum age of marriage, they must forbid a plurality either of wives or husbands. This has occasioned a family revolution among the minority nationalities, as among the Han, since the wealthy classes of virtually all China's nationalities practised polygyny in the past.

The incidence of polygyny has declined drastically over the history of the PRC. The Koranic practice of allowing up to four wives for one man is now outlawed everywhere in China. Muslims never admit to its persistence, but in widely separated Islamic areas state that specific social conditions should dictate how many wives a man should be allowed to keep. In other words, if there are far more women than men, then polygyny should be permitted; the example of the Korean War was raised on several independent occasions.

But in China at present there could be no justification for any man to marry more than one wife because the gender imbalance in the relevant age group is not nearly great enough. Muslims I interviewed in various parts of China declared themselves quite happy with the existing law allowing only one wife per man — even one group of bitterly anti-Chinese Uygurs I met in Yili who were making no secret of their hope for independence.

However, there are parts of China where even official sources acknowledge the persistence of polygyny or polyandry. One example is the Yi of Sichuan, among whom the 1982 census found a small number of polygamous marriages, each wife being equal in position with her own small part of the house and family.[57] In Tibet, both polygyny and polyandry are less prevalent than they once were, but are not by any means extinct.

Both marriage patterns were outlawed by the Tibetan Marriage Law of 1981, which stipulated, however, that any such marriages which were contracted before the law came into effect should be maintained unless one of the parties concerned applied for a divorce.[58] The reduction in the prevalence both of polygyny and polyandry has been far more rapid in some areas than others, and in particular far quicker and more thorough in the cities than in the countryside. PRC figures from 1958, the year before the rebellion and reform in Tibet, show that in one part of a county in the Shannan region to the southeast of Lhasa, ten marriages out of 141, or 7 per cent, were still polyandrous, five of them with brothers sharing a wife and three of them with father and son doing so. Polygamous marriages were somewhat fewer. The figures in this particular place are described as 'more or less the same as other regions in Tibet'.[59] However, one place in the Gyaze region to the southwest of Lhasa revealed 26 polyandrous marriages out of 104 in the same year, or 25 per cent, very similar to the proportions of the pre-1950 period. Government statistics from the main part of Lhasa showed 0.45 per cent of marriages were polyandrous in 1980 and virtually zero in 1985, but in a district of one county about 60 kilometres east of Lhasa, the corresponding figures for the two years were 1.68 and 1.63 per cent. Perhaps even more striking was that, according to a survey carried out among 53 Tibetan students of the University of Tibet in the 1980s, 64.2 per cent believed that polyandrous or polygamous marriages were good both for family harmony and work co-operation, while only 28.3 per cent regarded them as backward marriage forms.[60] With views of this kind prevalent even among students, it would be foolhardy to predict the imminent demise either of polyandry or polygyny among the Tibetans, despite the law of 1981. It is also quite possible that such opinions are an expression of Tibetan identity.

Among the Monba people of southern Tibet, marriages in a typical village with 42 households in the post-1976 period were shown as 85.72 per cent monogamous, 9.52 per cent polyandrous, and 4.76 per cent polygamous. Monogamy had always been the overwhelmingly prevalent form, with polyandry being regarded, at least by CCP cadres, as 'a remnant of primitive collective marriages'.[61] Although the extent of polyandry had declined since the 1950s, authorities in the 1980s still acknowledged change as slow.[62]

Divorce

The PRC is not a country especially afflicted with divorce. Both the Marriage Laws of 1950 and of 1980 devote space to the question of divorce, but the 1980 law makes it somewhat easier than that of 1950.

In the 1980s and 1990s, the incidence of divorce has tended to rise in China, especially in the main cities. Moreover, it was in general higher among the minorities than among the Han. Figures applying to 1982 show a larger percentage of divorced people in all age groups among the minorities than the Han. In particular, in the 20 to 24 age group 1.17 per cent of minority people were divorced but the corresponding figure for the Han was only 0.07 per cent.[63] In 1991 and 1992, the ratio between the number of registered divorcing and marrying couples was highest in Xinjiang (34.9 and 35.2 per cent respectively), with Qinghai (18.7 and 17.4 per cent) and Tibet (17.6 and 12.7 per cent) also showing among the highest proportions of divorce in the whole country, all three being regions with very significant minority populations. For the sake of comparison, it may be added that in 1991 and 1992 the proportions in China's two most sophisticated cities, Beijing and Shanghai, both fell — in the former case from 17.5 to 16.8 per cent and in the latter from 18.5 to 17.7 per cent. Yet the fact that the national ratio between the number of registered divorcing and marrying couples rose slightly from 8.7 per cent in 1991 to 8.9 per cent in 1992 still highlights the frequency of divorce in the most sophisticated cities and in certain minority areas.[64] The point made earlier concerning poor registration practices in Tibet may affect the reliability of the Tibetan percentages, especially since the two years given are so different, but does not change the overall thrust of the argument, since figures from Sichuan referring to 1982 show the Tibetans with a far higher divorce rate than any of the other nationalities in that province.[65]

The reason why Xinjiang heads the list for its divorce rate is because of the extreme instability of marriage relationships among Uygurs in the south of the autonomous region. Data from the three first decades of PRC rule suggest most strongly that the Uygurs divorce much more readily than the Han in Xinjiang.[66] They also confirm the trend noted before 1949 by which the Uygur rate of divorce was unusually high among the Islamic minorities. Informants have stressed to me the difference between northern Xinjiang, where marriage is quite stable, and the south, where relations between Uygur men and women are very fluid. One told me of a friend of his who had married no less than 43 times, remaining with most wives only a few months. A survey taken among Uygur women in a county near Kaxgar in southwest Xinjiang in 1982 reveals a general trend towards a rising proportion of divorcees as the age bracket falls, suggesting a growing instability in marriage among the Uygurs.[67]

On the other hand, a precisely opposite trend operates among the Hui, who are also Muslims. Not only are divorce rates among them very low indeed by comparison with the Uygurs, but the general direction over the

PRC period is downwards. Comparing Hui women in Jingyuan county in the extreme south of Ningxia with the Uygur women of the county near Kaxgar, we find that, among those over 60 years old, the proportion of divorcees among the former was some ten times that of the latter, but for the age bracket 20 to 24, over fifteen times, while in the 15 to 19 years age group there were hardly any Hui divorcees, but a significant number of Uygur ones.[68]

Two sets of Mongol communities, one in Inner Mongolia, the other in Qinghai, show a differing pattern in one respect, but a similar one in another, from surveys undertaken in 1982. The difference is that the divorce rate in the Qinghai community is five times higher than that of the Inner Mongolian for women in the 50 to 59 age bracket, who would have married in the late 1940s and 1950s, and considerably higher even than that in all other other age brackets, meaning that the gap between the two has widened considerably over the PRC period. As noted in Chapter 4, divorce was common in some Mongol communities, but not others, a pattern which appears to have been maintained under the PRC. The convergence between the Inner Mongolian and Qinghai communities lies in the fact that divorce rates have fallen very substantially in both over the period, possibly in part because of the general decline in arranged marriages.[69]

It may be possible to extrapolate some of the reasons for the higher divorce rates among the minorities than the Han from material provided by the Lhasa Municipal Government in the mid-1980s, applying to the main city area of Lhasa, where most of the people are Tibetans. The reasons given for divorce for 1983 were drunken beating (32.35 per cent), lack of understanding because of too short an acquaintance before marriage (26.72 per cent), disagreement over allocation of housework (21.26 per cent), incompatible lifestyles between husband and wife (7.68 per cent), living apart (3.60 per cent), poor sex life (3.51 per cent), escape from parentally arranged marriages (2.10 per cent), and other reasons (2.78 per cent).[70]

Two points are notable about the first and most important of these reasons: drunken beating. Firstly, it rose from 26.76 per cent of all answers in 1981, and 28.12 per cent in 1982, thus showing a consistent upturn.[71] The second is that the seekers of divorce on such grounds are more likely to be women than men. Extensive travelling in minority areas in the 1980s and 1990 indicated to me that heavy drinking by husbands is not only traditional, but on the increase among them. Moreover, drinking is overwhelmingly a male habit among almost all the nationalities, especially among the young. The rising prosperity of the period of reform has given people more money to spend on alcoholic drink, and individual companies can make very large sums of money from manufacturing it. In a small township visited in a Miao area, this writer was very struck to find that the owners of the local wine venture, which was privately operated, could make four times more each month than doctors in the clinic opposite their factory. I suspect that surveys among most of the minority areas would show precisely the same main reason for divorce as among the Tibetans. Moreover, it could be the main reason why divorce is now more prevalent among the minorities than among the Han. Although many Han men are adequate performers at the bottle, in my experience they cannot compete with most of the minorities. Several Koreans and Mongols — nationalities in so many respects equal to or ahead of the Han — have acknowledged to me the enormous damage which excessive drinking does to many of their menfolk.

The other reasons listed for the Tibetans of Lhasa, which actually have a rather modern ring about them, no doubt apply to a greater or lesser extent to other nationalities. There may also be reasons special to the societies of the nationalities themselves which may help account for the higher divorce rates. The excessively low marriage age of women and continuing arranged marriages among the Uygurs may easily be a far more important factor contributing to divorce in the changed society of the 1980s than it was in the past. In those nationalities of Guangxi, Guizhou and Yunnan among which young people meet at courtship gatherings but do not actually live together until after the wife gets pregnant, young married couples may drift apart during a crucial period of their marriage, especially since both continue to lead their own social lives and attend courtship gatherings.[72]

Conclusion

National consciousness is less clearly reflected in women's affairs than in religion or several other aspects. Yet they are definitely relevant to issues of identity. To take but one example, I have on several occasions heard a comment like: 'Women get a better deal among us Yao than among the Han or even Zhuang, which shows we are different' — and, perhaps it is even implied, superior. It was my clear impression that Tibetans consider their women have a higher status than their Han sisters and they are proud of that. On the other hand, a number of men and women of the Miao, Korean and several other nationalities, including the Han, gave me separately to understand that they regarded it as in accord with 'human nature' that men should dominate in positions of power.[73]

The developments in the area of marriage and divorce definitely point to a more integrated society in China, but with the minorities retaining features which identify them as special. Autonomy allows the marriage laws to vary one from another, but the trend is towards more uniform minimum marriage ages and divorce practices. Although many minorities retain particular marriage forms, such as the *buluo fujia* of the Dong or the 'walking marriages' of the Mosuo, they are tending to wither in favour of the more socially acceptable 'modern' form.

One aspect of marriage not covered elsewhere in this book is wedding celebrations. In the cities, these retain their old flavour and practices, but with a far greater likelihood of the use of such modern amenities as the motor car for transport. In the countryside, wedding celebrations have changed little under the PRC, with any destructions carried out during the Cultural

Revolution being balanced by revival during the 1980s and 1990s. The manner of wedding celebrations differs sharply from nationality to nationality and is a factor demonstrating ethnic identities. Weddings are possibly the most important of all occasions, during which the women of the minorities wear traditional national garb, another important social factor emphasising identity, with the men mostly wearing suits in the international style.

The discussions of marriage suggest that, while there have been very substantial changes under the PRC, including the beginnings of a modernisation process, continuities with the past are also very easy to find. In a range of areas connected with marriage, official rhetoric conflicts with reality. The tenacity of outlawed customs like polyandry among the Tibetans and polygyny among the Yi are major illustrative examples, even though the scale on which they persist is much smaller than it used to be.

In marriage, divorce and the status of women, change and the decline of traditions have been very much more rapid in the cities than the countryside. Three points should be made here.

The first is that most of the minorities are still considerably more rural than the Han. The extent of urbanisation has been slower and even those towns or cities that do exist show Han influence in terms of commerce, society and architecture much more strongly than the countryside. The towns in the minority areas generally lack the sophistication of the main Han cities, and most are not too different from the rather backward Han towns found all over China.

The second is that the material in this chapter bears out the differing status of women in the countryside and cities. The age of first marriage has risen and arranged marriages declined, but much less thoroughly in the countryside than the cities, the pace of change affecting the status of women more than that of men. This is because old traditions tend to weaken much more slowly and against greater resistance in the rural than urban areas.

Finally, the more rapid social change in the cities than the countryside applies to the Han as it does to the minorities. Han marriage patterns have changed far more slowly in the rural areas than in the urban. Survivals keeping the status of Han women lower than of men are far stronger in the villages than the cities.

The slighter the changes, the smaller is the extent of integration, but correspondingly the greater the remaining sense of national identity. The urban women of the minorities have accepted modern values more readily than their rural sisters. This is largely because they are much more in contact with the modernised economy, with its televisions, radios and mass-produced clothes.

Yet integration is beginning to come also to the villages. Except among a few of the minorities, such as the Tibetans and Kazaks, most rural women nowadays wear the traditional clothing of their nationality only on special occasions such as weddings and festivals. Convenience for women and a rise in their standard of living may point more towards the integration of China than the ethnic identities of particular minorities.

Notes

1 See Penny Kane, *The Second Billion, Population and Family Planning in China*, Penguin, Ringwood, Victoria, 1987, p. 19.

2 'Constitution of the People's Republic of China', 1982, *Beijing Review*, vol. 18, no. 52, 27 December 1982, p. 18.

3 Margery Wolf, *Revolution Postponed, Women in Contemporary China*, Stanford University Press, Stanford, 1985, p. 261.

4 Judith Stacey, *Patriarchy and Socialist Revolution in China*, University of California Press, Berkeley, 1983, pp. 155–57.

5 Wolf, *Revolution Postponed*, pp. 260–73 and Stacey, *Patriarchy and Socialist Revolution*, pp. 268–80.

6 See Kane, *The Second Billion*, pp. 64–65.

7 Tiley Chodag, trans. W. Tailing, *Tibet, the Land and the People*, New World Press, Beijing, 1988, p. 231.

8 *Chronology of Nationalities Work in Contemporary China* Editorial Department, *Dangdai Zhongguo minzu gongzuo da shiji, 1949–1988*, Minzu chubanshe, Beijing, 1990, p. 556.

9 Labour and gender questions are discussed in Colin Mackerras, *China's Minorities, Integration and Modernization in the Twentieth Century*, Oxford University Press, Hong Kong, 1994, pp. 217–23.

10 Research Institute of All China Women's Federation Research Office of Shaanxi Provincial Women's Federation (comp.), *Zhongguo funü tongji ziliao (1949–1989)*, Zhongguo tongji chubanshe, Beijing, 1991, p. 308.

11 Huang Wei, 'Female Participation in Government', *Beijing Review*, vol. 36, no. 29, 19–25 July 1993, p. 26.

12 Song Qixia,'Tantan shenger yunü', *Minzu tuanjie*, no. 3, 15 March 1983, p. 47.

13 For much more detail on this subject, see Mackerras, *China's Minorities*, pp. 233–59.

14 Her name is Mrs Rebiya Kader; see also Kathy Chen, in *The Wall Street Journal*, 21 September 1994, as reproduced in *China News Digest*, News Global, 1–2 October 1994, item 3.

15 Zhang Tianlu, 'Zhongguo shaoshu minzu renkou', in Deng Zhixian (ed.), *Minzu renkouxue sanlun*, Guizhou Renmin chubanshe, Guiyang, 1990, p. 74.

16 ibid., pp. 58–59.

17 Liu Hongkang et al. (eds), *Zhongguo renkou, Sichuan fence*, Zhongguo caizheng jingji chubanshe, Beijing, 1988, p. 348.

18 According to *Zhongguo renkou tongji nianjian 1990*, Kexue jishu wenxian chubanshe, Beijing, 1991, p. 64, the 1990 census showed 1 098 694 male and 1 097 316 female long-term registered residents in Tibet. The sex ratio, or number of males for every hundred females, was thus 100.13.

19 Liu Rui et al. (eds), *Zhongguo renkou, Xizang fence*, Zhongguo caizheng jingji chubanshe, Beijing, 1988, p. 268.

20 Zhang Tianlu, Song Zhuansheng and Ma Zhengliang, *Zhongguo Musilin renkou*, Ningxia Renmin chubanshe, Yinchuan, 1991, p. 49.
21 Tiley Chodag, *Tibet*, p. 231.
22 *Survey of the Sandu Shui Autonomous County* Compilation Group, *Sandu Shuizu zizhi xian gaikuang*, Guizhou Renmin chubanshe, Guiyang, 1986, p. 60.
23 Huang Xianlin, Mo Datong et al. (eds), *Zhongguo renkou, Guangxi fence*, Zhongguo caizheng jingji chubanshe, Beijing, 1988, pp. 330–31.
24 Pan Zhifu et al. (eds), *Zhongguo renkou, Guizhou fence*, Zhongguo caizheng jingji chubanshe, Beijing, 1988, p. 382.
25 Huang Xianfan, Huang Zengqing and Zhang Yimin, *Zhuangzu tongshi*, Guangxi Minzu chubanshe, Nanning, 1988, p. 699.
26 This material on the Dong is based on observations and enquiries in rural Sanjiang Dong autonomous county at Spring Festival time 1992. See also *Survey of the Sanjiang Dong Nationality Autonomous County* Compilation Group, *Sanjiang Dongzu zizhi xian gaikuang*, Guangxi Minzu chubanshe, Nanning, 1984, p.19, which notes the persistence of the custom of *buluo fujia*, but claims that it 'has undergone some reform'.
27 Yan Ruxian and Song Zhaolin, *Yongning Naxi zu de muxi zhi*, Yunnan Renmin chubanshe, Kunming, 1983, pp. 93–97.
28 Yan Ruxian, trans. Xing Wenjun, 'A Living Fossil of the Family — A Study of the Family Structure of the Naxi Nationality in the Lugu Lake Region', *Social Sciences in China*, vol. 3, no. 4, December 1982, pp. 60–71. See also the study of Mosuo marriage customs in Yang Zhiyong et al., *Yunnan shaoshu minzu hunsu zhi*, Yunnan Minzu chubanshe, Kunming, 1983, pp. 133–46.
29 Among Chinese sources see, for instance, Song Enchang, *Yunnan shaoshu minzu yanjiu wenji*, Yunnan Renmin chubanshe, Kunming, 1986, pp. 455–56.
30 Alan Winnington, *The Slaves of the Cool Mountains, The Ancient Social Conditions and Changes Now in Progress on the Remote South-Western Borders of China*, Lawrence & Wishart, London, 1959, p. 180.
31 See Yang et al., *Yunnan shaoshu minzu hunsu zhi*, p. 157.
32 The text of the Marriage Law of the PRC, adopted on 10 September 1980, and coming into force on 1 January 1981, is contained in English translation in *Beijing Review*, vol. 24, no. 11, 16 March 1981, pp. 24–27. For the Chinese original, see *Zhonghua renmin gongheguo falü huibian, 1979–1984*, Renmin chubanshe, Beijing, 1985, pp. 203–9.
33 Zhang, Song and Ma, *Zhongguo Musilin renkou*, pp. 30–31.
34 Zhang, 'Zhongguo shaoshu minzu renkou', p. 52.
35 The table is taken from Yang Yixing, Zhang Tianlu and Xiong Yu, *Zhongguo shaoshu minzu renkou yanjiu*, Minzu chubanshe, Beijing, 1988, p. 158.
36 The table in Zhang, 'Zhongguo shaoshu minzu renkou', pp. 54–55 shows the proportion of marriages of girls aged from 12 to 14 as 0.69 per cent in 1980 and 0.65 per cent in 1981 among the minority nationalities, and 0.04 per cent in 1980 and 0.03 per cent in 1981 among the Han. It gives

a dash for both under 1982. A Chinese source, *Renkou yanjiu*, no. 3 of 1982, cited by Erika Platte, 'China's Fertility Transition: The One-Child Campaign', *Pacific Affairs*, vol. 57, no. 4, Winter 1984–85, p. 665, claims that marriage still occurred as young as 12 or 13 among certain ethnic groups in Yunnan.

37 Zhang, 'Zhongguo shaoshu minzu renkou', pp. 53–55. The figure for 1981 is based on *Zhongguo funü tongji ziliao*, p. 357, the comparable proportion of first marriages among Han women in 1981 in the age group 15 to 19 being 12.55 per cent.

38 Chen Qiuping, 'Progress Seen in Minority Population', *Beijing Review*, vol. 36, no. 29, 19–25 July 1993, p. 16.

39 Pan et al. (eds), *Zhongguo renkou, Guizhou fence*, pp. 381–82.

40 Chang Naiguang et al. (eds), *Zhongguo renkou, Ningxia fence*, Zhongguo caizheng jingji chubanshe, Beijing, 1988, p. 312.

41 Zhang, 'Zhongguo shaoshu minzu renkou', pp. 51, 53.

42 Song Naigong et al. (eds), *Zhongguo renkou, Nei Menggu fence*, Zhongguo caizheng jingji chubanshe, Beijing, 1987, p. 375.

43 Zhang, 'Zhongguo shaoshu minzu renkou', pp. 56–57.

44 Zhou Chongjing et al. (eds), *Zhongguo renkou, Xinjiang fence*, Zhongguo caizheng jingji chubanshe, Beijing, 1990, p. 305.

45 Yang Yixing and Wang Yanxing, 'Renzhen guanche shaoshu minzu renkou zhengce, nuli cujin ge minzu gongtong fanrong', in Deng (ed.) *Minzu renkouxue sanlun*, p 102.

46 Judith Banister, *China's Changing Population*, Stanford University Press, Stanford, 1987, p. 319.

47 See discussion of this question in Colin Mackerras, *China's Minorities*, pp. 233–34.

48 Huang, Mo et al. (eds), *Zhongguo renkou, Guangxi fence*, p. 330.

49 Song et al.(eds), *Zhongguo renkou, Nei Menggu fence*, pp. 372–75.

50 See Rong Ma, 'Han and Tibetan Residential Patterns in Lhasa', *The China Quarterly*, no. 128, December 1991, p. 817.

51 Interview with Professor Ke Yang of Lanzhou University, and Xue Li and Ke Yang (eds), *Huaer xuanji*, Gansu Renmin chubanshe, Lanzhou, 1980, p. 1.

52 Dru C. Gladney, *Muslim Chinese, Ethnic Nationalism in the People's Republic*, published by Council on East Asian Studies, Harvard University, and distributed by Harvard University Press, Cambridge, Mass., and London, 1991, pp. 209–11, and on intermarriage between Han and Hui, see also pp. 244–45.

53 Zhou et al. (eds), *Zhongguo renkou, Xinjiang fence*, p. 311.

54 See David Y.H. Wu, 'Chinese Minority Policy and the Meaning of Minority Culture: The Example of Bai in Yunnan, China', *Human Organization*, vol. 49, no. 1, Spring 1990, p. 8.

55 Stevan Harrell, 'Ethnicity, Local Interests, and the State: Yi Communities in Southwest China', *Comparative Studies in Society and History, An International Quarterly*, vol. 32, 1990, especially pp. 529, 532–33.

56 See also the general comments of Banister in *China's Changing Population*, pp. 319–20.
57 Liu et al. (eds), *Zhongguo renkou, Sichuan fence*, p. 351.
58 See *Beijing Review*, vol. 24, no. 20, 18 May 1981, p. 6.
59 See Tibetan Social and Historical Investigation Materials Series Editorial Group, *Zangzu shehui lishi diaocha, Er*, Xizang Renmin chubanshe, Lhasa, 1988 pp. 156–58.
60 Liu et al. (eds), *Zhongguo renkou, Xizang fence*, pp. 275–76.
61 *Brief History of the Monba Nationality* Compilation Group, *Menba zu jianshi*, Xizang Renmin chubanshe, Lhasa, 1987, p. 71.
62 ibid., p. 73.
63 See the figures in Zhang, 'Zhongguo shaoshu minzu renkou', p. 59.
64 The proportions for 1991 are based on the figures given in *Zhongguo tongji nianjian 1992*, Zhongguo tongji chubanshe, Beijing, 1992, p. 802 and for 1992 on those in *Zhongguo tongji nianjian 1993*, Zhongguo tongji chubanshe, Beijing, 1993, p. 811. The total number of marriages in all China in 1992 was 9 545 047 and of divorces 849 611.
65 Liu et al. (eds), *Zhongguo renkou, Sichuan fence*, p. 345.
66 See Zhou et al. (eds), *Zhongguo renkou, Xinjiang fence*, p. 268.
67 Zhang, Song and Ma, *Zhongguo Musilin renkou*, pp. 47–48.
68 ibid.
69 ibid.
70 Liu et al. (eds), *Zhongguo renkou, Xizang fence*, pp. 270–72.
71 ibid., p. 272.
72 See, for example, Huang, Mo et al. (eds), *Zhongguo renkou, Guangxi fence*, p. 336.
73 One official opinion has it that women 'are not psychologically adapted to participation in administration'. The evidence is a questionnaire administered by the Shanghai Federation of Women among 208 female cadres, which found that 93 per cent lacked motivation and interest in an administrative career. See Huang, 'Female Participation in Government', p. 28.

9 Literature and the Performing Arts, 1949–1995

Under the PRC, the arts of the minorities have received far more government patronage than was ever the case in the past. State-sponsored artistic and literary creation hardly existed before 1949 but became quite important under CCP rule, while at the same time the folk arts have persisted and even done quite well, except for the Cultural Revolution decade (1966–76). As in other areas, policy has not been consistent in the arts, the Cultural Revolution decade being probably the bleakest in the century, with virtually no freedom and not much creativity.

In terms of the arts, autonomy for the minorities means that the special features of style and content should be maintained and developed, but only as long as they contain nothing hostile to socialism or the people. The policy introduced through several key government-sponsored conferences in the 1950s and early 1960s was to collect, rearrange, translate and publish minority literary and artistic works.[1] The four processes had major implications. The government requested the assistance of old folk artists who knew the works by heart to recite and sing stories, long poems and other items, while trained amanuenses wrote them down. This meant that many minority literary works were for the first time accessible outside their own particular area. The term 'rearrange' implied that the original works were changed to enhance the mass nature and the ethnic qualities of the items collected. Many were translated into Chinese and other languages and then published, as a result of which they were for the first time available for appreciation to a very much wider audience than had ever been the case before.

Article 3 of the 1954 Constitution laid down the right of all the nationalities to 'use and develop their own spoken and written languages'. However, at the time the CCP came to power, although a number had obsolete or obsolescent scripts, only 21 still used their own written languages on a regular basis. The CCP devised scripts for several of the southern minorities, such as the Zhuang and Miao, based on the international phonetic script, but on the whole writers have not found them useful and most Zhuang and Miao written literature is in Chinese. In 1960 the international phonetic script was introduced to write the Uygur and Kazak languages, even though the two minorities already had a perfectly satisfactory script in the form of Arabic.[2] This experiment proved quite long-lasting, but eventually met with successful resistance. Beginning in 1982 the Arabic script was progressively reintroduced for newspapers and other publications, and within about three years was in more or less universal use for written Uygur, Kazak and other Turkic and Iranian languages of Xinjiang.

The PRC government established a whole series of official bodies to look after literature and the arts. Foremost among them was the Federation of Literature and Art Circles of China, set up in July 1949, even before the PRC itself. It included minority literature and arts within its purview. In addition, the government set up the professional Central Nationalities Song-and-Dance Troupe in Beijing in September 1952 and a whole range of arts troupes in the various minority regions, as well as schools to train potential members. Old folk artists were invited to join these troupes and to assist in the training of the next generation of artists. The result was a strong trend towards professionalisation of the minority folk arts. Artists received a much better and more secure livelihood and their status within society rose enormously.

For the literatures and arts of the minorities, there was one powerful advantage in these processes: for the first time, a national government was prepared to take the arts of the minorities seriously and to include them as part of China's artistic treasury. Part of the official policy, repeated on numerous occasions, was that the artistic items should illustrate the characteristics peculiar to the minorities. Because earlier governments had made no secret of their contempt for the arts of the minorities, this policy could only contribute to a feeling of pride and ethnic identity among the minorities.

This encouragement of ethnic identity most certainly did not imply the right to propagate secession from China through the arts. On the contrary, what these arts were enjoined to advocate was the 'unity of the motherland'. Authorities have kept a sharp eye out to forestall even the slightest suspicion that the 'special features of the minorities' should cross the border into advocating independence or 'splitting the unity of the motherland'.

It follows that the most obvious disadvantage of official patronage of the minority literatures and arts has always been government control. Certain themes were encouraged, especially revolutionary ones, while others were banned — in particular those which explicitly showed the former ruling classes in a favourable light or demeaned the masses. Any new creations must gain the approval of CCP authorities or censors before they could be published, while even folk arts had to be careful to avoid offending the new political order.

During the Cultural Revolution decade of 1966–76, the positive aspects of the CCP's policies collapsed, while the main negative one was greatly intensified. The traditional and folk arts of the minorities, and indeed also of the Han, became anathema, while Mao Zedong's wife Jiang Qing went about uprooting China's cultural heritage. Strong restrictions were placed on writing or publishing in minority languages, with the number of new book titles published in them, other than textbooks, declining from 560 in 1965 to only 134 in 1970.[3] Quite a few distinguished poets, dramatists and fiction writers were killed or hounded to suicide by Red Guards and other representatives of the Cultural Revolution, by far the most important being the Manchu Lao She. Many minority works were castigated as 'poisonous weeds' and criticised as 'traitorous literature'. Bans were savage and long-lasting, including almost everything outside Jiang Qing's extraordinarily narrow canons of value. The Cultural Revolution had the effect of suppressing ethnic identity, not encouraging it.

The aftermath of the Cultural Revolution and Deng Xiaoping's accession to power brought a further drastic change of policy, initially back to what it had been before 1966. Late in 1979 the Fourth Congress of the Federation of Literature and Art Circles of China, the first since 1960, established a Nationalities' Literature Committee within the Association of Chinese Writers.[4] In July the following year, the first All-China Minority Nationality Literatures Creation Conference took place in Beijing. Along with the standard rhetoric about strengthening CCP leadership over the minority literature and arts, it also called for greater efforts to train more practitioners and far greater variety and freedom in style and theme.[5] The message was absolute reversal of the Cultural Revolution stereotypes which had been so devastating to minority arts.

The 1984 Law on the Autonomy of Nationality Areas articulated several of the policies on minority arts. Other than advocating literature and arts in the forms and with the characteristics of the individual minorities, it repeated several themes familiar from the 1950s. The second paragraph of Article 38 calls on the autonomous organs 'to collect, rearrange, translate and publish the books of the nationalities, protect the scenic spots, historical sites and precious cultural objects of the nationalities and their important historical and cultural relics'.[6] The number of newly published books in minority languages, other than textbooks, more than doubled from 689 in 1978 to 1532 nine years later in 1987.[7]

The strong implication of these policies is to encourage members of the minorities to preserve their own heritage on the one hand, but to develop it in new ways on the other. What has happened is that scholars, writers and artists of all kinds have taken up this cue by analysing and reprinting works from their own traditions as well as creating new items.[8] In general, the minorities have carried out their tasks enthusiastically, but also cautiously. Their enthusiasm is for dealing with their own nationality, and writing works reflecting its problems. Their caution has been due to the danger of political interference and recriminations if they step too far out of line and fail to predict some political movement or other. If the comparison is with the Han writers and theatre practitioners, then the extent of freedom in terms of content has been greater, with one major exception: that advocacy of secession through literature or the arts is impermissible.

The CCP's patronage and control of the arts has meant that organisations have been set up to study the minorities' arts as well as train professionals. The number of writers belonging to the minorities who publish literary works has therefore expanded greatly, with some of them attaining reputations in literary circles all over the country. Measures were taken to train poets and fiction writers belonging to the minorities who would put forward the viewpoint of the CCP.

One of the respects in which artists and literary figures have been encouraged to promote the identity of their own nationality has been to absorb elements of the content and style of the folk arts of their own nationality into their work. The long poem was part of the literary heritage of a great many of the minorities, whereas only a few had produced novels or short stories. Newly trained poets or novelists were able to borrow extensively from the long folk poems for their style, even though the particular item they were creating was set in the present.

Apart from finding its way into the professionalised literature and theatre of the present age, the folk literature has generally remained intact in its own right. Although the leaders of the Cultural Revolution, and especially Jiang Qing, tried to discredit this literature, their actions merely produced a backlash of revival in the 1980s. The 1990s show a continuing strength of particular folk literary arts, but since these are not in accord with the money-making thrust of society since the 1980s, the likelihood is for them to weaken in the coming years.

Literature

In order to enable a continuity of treatment from Chapter 5, the present section focuses attention on two genres of literature, namely poetry and fiction. Both are major exemplars of the processes of continuity and change in literature under the PRC. They are also important for what they show about ethnic identities and integration in literature.

Poetry

Folk poetry and folk songs have persisted into the PRC period, the forms including short lyrics about love, labour or homeland, among other topics, or very long epic poems of the sort discussed in Chapter 5. These folk poems were collected and published, one of the main bases for selection of individual poems being revolutionary content.

One of numerous illustrative examples is the long poem, 'Ghada Merin', mentioned in Chapter 5. There have been quite a few versions of short and long poems in the PRC on the theme of this famous revolutionary Mongol hero. In 1950, oral sung traditions were published in Chinese translation in the form of a long narrative poem of about 600 lines. From 1959–63, scholars collected further material and rearranged a longer and more complex version, in which the characters were drawn more sharply than in the original with the aim of creating clear-cut revolutionary images. What emerged was a poem of more than 2000 lines, but it was not actually published until 1980, because of the criticisms levelled during the Cultural Revolution against anything produced during the period 1949–66.[9]

Any folk culture changes and develops. So, despite the persistence of the traditional folk poems and songs among the minorities, there has been a great deal of room for new content. Not surprisingly, this showed strongly socialist themes in the early days of the PRC, including praise for the CCP and its leaders, the misery of the past and love of labour. This trend strengthened still further during the Cultural Revolution, with traditional themes of all kinds being banned. However, the tendency since the late 1970s has been for new poems and songs to reflect the changed rural life of the time, with people becoming more and more tired of revolutionary politics with the passage of time.

One example of a category of new and rearranged folk poem was the 'new song' (xin'ge) of the Dong people, termed gal meik in Dong language. According to one authority, 'the most prominent feature of the new song is to reform the old tunes of the traditional folk songs of the Dong nationality which mainly sang of love into new songs reflecting Dong social life comprehensively'.[10] What that meant was that poems were especially written which followed the style of the traditional Dong poetry but expressed horror of past oppression or praise for a specific political movement or notion, such as the 'four modernisations' in the late 1970s. These folk poems were mostly in Dong, but there were some in Chinese or in a mixture of both languages. A typical illustration was 'Becoming a Soldier under Feudal Oppression' (in Dong, 'Fongh jeenl yac beec bail dangh bienh'), which became popular in eastern Guizhou in the early days of the PRC. In form, the poem has seven syllables to a line; in content, it deals with the sufferings of a Dong family in the old society, leading to their joy at liberation.[11]

The folk poems of the minorities were normally sung rather than recited, which is why the terms 'poem' and 'song' are more or less interchangeable for this particular genre. Moreover, under the PRC they have frequently been performed by folk artists or subjected to reform as short items for performance by professionals. In such form they belong to the performing arts and are considered briefly in the section on that subject below.

In contrast to the folk poetry, the PRC has seen the growth of a more formal literature among the minority nationalities. This formality is characterised by becoming known to its target through publication, for although much folk literature has in fact been published under the PRC, it is by recitation or performance that it normally first reaches its audience. The writer of 'formal' literature is virtually always known, whereas folk authors are usually anonymous.

The minority nationalities have produced a few non-folk poets under the PRC. Apart from those few with established reputations during the Republican period, a new group emerged during the 1950s and another even larger generation in the 1980s. The minorities to excel most in the production of published or non-folk poetry include the Tibetans, Uygurs, Mongols, Koreans, Hui, Bai and Miao. As with the Han, the poetry of the 1980s and 1990s has been very much less ideologically driven than in earlier times.

An example of the generation of minority poets who began writing in the 1950s was the Korean Kim Chul. His long epic *The Story of Morning Star* (*Chinsong-jon*) is a highly politicised love poem about Morning Star, the daughter of a poor family, set against the background of a peasant uprising in the 'feudal' period. Morning Star's father is executed for taking part in the rebellion, but Morning Star and her fiancé seize and bury the corpse, after which they marry and both redouble their efforts in organising rebellion. The villain of the piece belongs to the land-owning classes and attempts to suppress the rebellion as well as to seize Morning Star for himself. In the end he shoots Morning Star's husband with an arrow, but she blocks it with her own body and is killed.[12]

The writing and publishing of poetry in the Uygur language has proliferateded greatly under the PRC, especially in the 1980s and 1990s. The literary journal *Tarim* (*Tarim*) is among several featuring a range of Uygur-language poetry, as well as short stories and essays. There is also a literary journal called *Springs* (*Bulak*), which reproduces items of classical literature and research articles about it.

Two poets are especially worth mentioning. Both write in Uygur, with mastery of the traditional poetic style of their people. The first is Abdurehim Utkur, probably the foremost literary figure in Xinjiang in the 1980s and 1990s. Although a prolific and distinguished poet, his main works are historical novels, so he is considered in the section on fiction below.

The second is Kurban Barat, who was born into a peasant family in Artush in 1946. In 1962 he graduated from the Literature Department of Xinjiang Normal College and worked on the *Xinjiang Daily* as a correspondent and editor. After 1980 he worked in the Xinjiang People's Press as an editor for *Bulak*. His first poem, 'Cuckoo Bird' ('Kakkuk'), dates from 1956 and, as of 1993, he had published some 400 poems and ten epics.[13]

In the 1980s and 1990s he put out several volumes of poems, one of them being entitled *Snow Flower* (*Karguli*), which contains poems written from 1966–93. The title of the book derives from one of the poems, written in 1966, which opens:

A snow flower can grow even through the coldest winter.
And still maintain its brightness.
Its roots strike on the ice-covered peaks
And blossoms though white snows cover the entire earth.

It grows and gives hope to the heart,
With the tears of the land watering the flower.

The snow flower is a metaphor for the Uygur people, praising them for their ability to bend but never lose hope or succumb to final defeat. Despite the poem's strong patriotic Uygur ring, it is not explicitly anti-Chinese. It is easy to read the hope for independence into its message, but such an interpretation is neither spelled out nor clear enough to prevent the book's publication in 1993 and sale.[14] Yet this kind of poetry is certainly symbolic of the identity of the Uygurs.

Fiction

The most significant departures from tradition have occurred in the field of fiction, which can be divided into three categories, long and short novels and short stories. The kind of novel which deals with a single core struggle, and rises to a climax and denoument is essentially an import from the West, but in China the tradition was initially far stronger among the Han than any other nationality. The minority novels of the PRC are the brainchild more of the socialist state as a whole than of any particular nationalities. Only a few have written novels in their own language, the Koreans and Uygurs being pre-eminent, with the Tibetans, Mongols, Kazaks and others also making some worthwhile contributions.

Given that the novel was not a form of literature favoured by many of the minorities, it comes as no surprise that they have produced far more short and long novels and short stories under the PRC than during any other period. There have been basically three generations. The first is the older writers with already established reputations when the CCP came to power in 1949. The second is the new generation who gained prominence in the 1950s and the third is those who entered on the main part of their career after the Cultural Revolution, mainly from the late 1970s and early 1980s. The late 1950s and early 1960s were a particularly good period for minority novels, but this period was succeeded by a very bleak one during the Cultural Revolution. The 1980s saw a definite revival, with new and creative departures, and attempts to find new ways of expressing the changes in society. However, the new wave of creativity appears to have run out of steam by the late 1980s, even before the suppression of the student movement in Beijing and elsewhere in the middle of 1989.

One official account of minorities literature in the year 1988, itself written by a member of the minorities, complained that the middle-aged and young writers had lost their enthusiasm for production and entered upon a dry period. He suggested two reasons for this. The first was that the writers were trying to push against the trends of the times: their 'original literary conceptions have been relentlessly proclaimed as out of date, with even their nationality patterns, despite having survived since ancient times, being in conflict with the current situation'. The second was the commercialisation of literature, which he believed had led to vulgarity.[15]

The author is giving expression, from an official point of view, to distress over a process taking place in China throughout the 1980s and, on the whole, continuing in the 1990s. This was a loss of belief in socialism of any kind by the people as a whole, and especially by writers. Instead, the principle valued by society was the glory of getting rich, in some places coupled with a return to tradition. The first suggestion implies that literary figures had given up their sense of national identity by the end of the 1980s. This was no doubt the case among some minorities, such as the Miao, Bai or Zhuang, whose literature was in Chinese and not much different from that of the Han. But it is also possible that by the end of the 1980s, national consciousness had begun taking forms very unwelcome to the government, as exemplified in the 1987 demonstrations for independence in Tibet. No literary figure who wanted to support such openly secessionist feelings of national identity through writing would have had a hope of getting such work published unless through an underground press. The commercialisation to which reference is made was happening in all the arts all over China. The result was that artists created what they thought the people would buy, not what the government imposed as ideologically correct.

One nationality with a particularly strong secular literary culture as well as its own script is the Koreans. Since, in addition, this nationality has for long had a higher literacy rate than virtually any other minority, there is no surprise in finding that the Koreans have been among the most productive of all minorities in terms of literature, including both poetry and fiction. In the first three decades after 1949, Korean writers produced more than ten long and short novels and numerous short stories.[16]

The three generations of Korean writers down to the 1990s follow patterns similar to those elsewhere in China. The first is the old revolutionaries, of whom a very good example is Kim Ch'ang-gul, already mentioned in Chapter 5 as having worked in resistance to the Japanese. The full-length novel *Tiger Cliff* (*Noho ae*), by Yi Kun-chon, is set in the late 1940s and concerns the Korean movement to liberation under the CCP.[17] It is clearly strong in propaganda content.

The second generation of writers places somewhat more emphasis on tradition and shows less foreign influence than the third. Just as in other parts of China, Western and other foreign influence has grown enormously in literary Korean circles since the late 1970s, two major figures being Jean-Paul Sartre (1905–80) and Bertolt Brecht (1898–1956) and specific countries being France, Germany, the United States, Japan and South Korea. From the mid- to late 1980s, both South Korean and Japanese writers have expressed considerable interest in the work of the Yanbian Korean authors.

Two notable long Korean novels of the 1980s are *Snowy Nights* (*Sol ya*), by Yi Chi-kil, and *Spring Waves* (*Chun cho*), by Yu Chi-mu. Both concern life in the peasant villages, including changes in the family system and the relationships between the generations and sexes. Both are based more on life vignettes, states and conditions than on plot or story. Yet, despite the progressive structure and content, the language of Korean fiction of the 1980s tends to be traditional, rather than colloquial. Although the emphasis on the psychological and the 'stream of consciousness' brings these two nov-

192 CHINA'S MINORITY CULTURES: IDENTITIES AND INTEGRATION SINCE 1912

els into line with trends in the Han areas of China at the same time, neither has been translated into Chinese.

These two novels are typical in being written in Korean, for of all minorities in China, the Koreans are, together with the Uygurs, probably the one to insist most on the use of their own language in literary creation. It is true that books in Chinese are still much more readily available than those in Korean, even in Yanbian, yet there are quite a few literary magazines in northeast China which are in Korean and make a special point of encouraging Koreans to publish literary works in their own language.[18] The main advantage of this course is that the Korean identity is enhanced through literature, but there is a major disadvantage too, namely that their writings are not available to most readers in China, which means that their works tend to remain outside the mainstream of PRC literature. In general, very little of their work is translated into Chinese. Yet, at the same time, the Korean writers are subject to pressures rather similar to those of Beijing, Shanghai and other Han cities, such as the same ideological dictates. However, since the late 1970s they have also been enthusiastic to experiment with new literary ideas of the sort which can help them break out of rigid Marxist-Leninist stereotypes. From this point of view, the Koreans rank very high in sophistication among all the minority authors.[19]

If the test is contribution to national identity, however, the Uygurs are in no sense inferior. In the 1980s and 1990s, an unsurpassed figure among them is Abdurehim Utkur. Born in the early 1920s, his family, and he himself, were closely bound up with the history of the exciting but bloody and tragic period of Xinjiang's history in the present century. When I interviewed him in October 1994, he had completed three volumes of novels concerning the history of Xinjiang from 1907–45 and was planning a fourth which would take the story up to 1949. The novels are *Traces of the Explorer* (*Iz*), published by the Xinjiang People's Press in 1985 and *The Wakened Land* (*Oyghangan Zimin*), of which the two volumes so far had been published by the same Press in 1988 and 1994. *Traces* takes Xinjiang's history from 1907–13, while the two volumes of *The Wakened Land* go to 1945. Abdurehim told me that he sees these novels as about 60 to 70 per cent factual history and the remainder fiction. They are very definitely intended to put forward real history as told by one who actually experienced most of the events or heard about them from those who did. He has also done a good deal of research into written records.

Two points are of particular interest concerning the national identity inherent in these novels. The first is that they are written in Uygur and not yet published in Chinese. Abdurehim told me that there had been bureaucratic problems with the publication in Chinese, no doubt stemming from sensitivity that they may support secessionist tendencies, but he remains confident that this will follow eventually. In the meantime, he has found readers in various parts of the Turkic world, including Turkey itself, Kazakhstan, Kyrgyzstan and other states of what used to be the Soviet Union. Parts of *Traces* were actually published in a Turkish newspaper.

The second point is the importance of history in identity. Abdurehim told me that he regards his novels as politically essentially neutral, and does not believe that there was ever a realistic chance that the various uprisings of the 1930s and 1940s could ever have led to independence for Xinjiang. At the same time, his point of view is determinedly Uygur and concerned to put forward a point of view reflecting that of the Uygur people. One of his main aims in writing the novels was to educate the Uygur youth and intelligentsia concerning their own modern history. Because the novels are in Uygur, the readership quite definitely belongs to the Uygur nationality, or those nationalities with languages close to Uygur, such as the Kazaks, Uzbeks or Kirgiz.

The overwhelming majority of minorities have written their fiction in Chinese. The most distinguished minority novelists of the Republican period continued their work under the PRC. These were Lao She and Shen Congwen, both of them already famous during the Republican period and discussed briefly in Chapter 5. Lao She returned to China from abroad when the CCP came to power and initially did very well under the new government. In 1956 he was even designated a labour model in literature and the arts. However, he fell a victim to the Cultural Revolution and died, by drowning himself, on 24 August 1966. He continued to write fiction after 1949, but his main work written under the PRC period is drama and is considered below.

Shen Congwen continued to be prolific in the early years of the PRC, although his writings are extremely different in character from those of the years before 1949, with stress on the factual rather than fiction. Like all but a few other writers, he was sharply criticised and humiliated during the Cultural Revolution. Yet, in contrast to Lao She, he did at least survive the terrors of those years and in 1979–80 was rehabilitated, enjoying a good reputation as a literary figure since then, both in China and overseas. His works were republished in a twelve-volume edition and research was undertaken about his life and work.[20] In particular, for the first time in the 1980s, Shen was prepared to be completely open about his Miao and Tujia ethnic background.[21] People of the Miao and Tujia minorities in Western Hunan are very proud of having produced a literary figure with stature recognised throughout the world. It is doubtful whether this means that he can be taken to have furthered minority identities through his post-1949 writings, but it is possible to reread what he wrote before 1949, including his sympathy for downtrodden peoples, with an attitude more attuned to minority problems, and to interpret the enthusiasm for them in the 1980s and 1990s in China as expressions of identity in the current age.

One of the most important minority writers of the PRC period has been Li Qiao. Belonging to the Yi minority, Li was born in 1909 in Yunnan and was able to gain an education. As a young man, he came under the influence of the works of leftist writers such as Guo Moruo. He went to Shanghai in 1930 where he contacted the left-wing literary movement there, even producing a novel which, however, was not published due to the outbreak of the war against Japan.

Despite the strong influence of Han literature on him, Li Qiao remained very strongly committed to the Yi nationality. The great majority of his works deal with the history or present circumstances of the Yi people of Liangshan in Sichuan. Among them, the one to receive the most publicity is the long novel *Merry Jinsha River* (*Huanxiao de Jinsha jiang*), which is a trilogy, the three parts of which were published in 1956, 1962 and 1965 respectively. All are set in the very recent past, dealing with the changes wrought by the initial three or four years of CCP rule in the Yi areas of Liangshan.[22] Although silenced and denounced by the Cultural Revolution, he wrote several further novels in the late 1970s and 1980s.[23]

Despite the strong Yi atmosphere in this novel — and indeed in Li Qiao's other works, two factors militating against his expression of Yi identity should be mentioned. One is that *Merry Jinsha River* is extremely thick in propaganda content. The whole point of the novel is to put forward the CCP's line on the social processes taking place among the Yi people. Although all the main characters belong to the Yi nationality and the trilogy is set in Yi territory, the characterisation and ideological principles underlying the novels are more characteristic of the PRC as a whole than of the Yi people in particular. Most of the main characters appear in all three parts of the trilogy and the way they are developed, showing the way their thinking changes over time, fulfils more CCP criteria than anything specific to the Yi people.

The other factor goes to the language of the novel, which is Chinese. The Yi people of Liangshan are among those which have their own script, but before the Cultural Revolution it was replaced by romanised writing, although it has revived since the late 1970s.[24] For a Yi novel to be written in any language but Chinese would exclude it from the mainstream of contemporary Chinese literature and make it completely inaccessible to any people but the small number of Yi people who still know the old Yi written language — a dwindling minority.

The Tibetans produced no novels in the early period of CCP rule. Indeed, the modern novel is a Han import into Tibet which was not taken up by Tibetan writers until the 1980s. During that decade, a group of seven long novels was produced, all of them dealing with differing periods among the Tibetans themselves, leading one commentator to note that 'together they make up a chronicle of modern Tibetan history' from the British–Tibetan battle over Gyaze in 1904 to the end of the Cultural Revolution.[25] The ideological line of the novels follows the conventional politically correct stereotypes of the 1980s.

In addition to these long novels, and more innovative and interesting than them, the Tibetans of the 1980s have produced a fine body of short stories and short novels. The most important representative figure is bKra shis zla ba (also romanised as Tashi Dawa), who was born in 1959. His father was a Tibetan CCP cadre from Batang, a Tibetan area of Sichuan, who worked in Lhasa and Xigaze in Tibet. bKra shis zla ba spent most of his childhood in his mother's home in Chongqing, Sichuan, but travelled frequently to Tibet. Although he is Tibetan, he writes in Chinese. Some of his stories are set in Tibet at a time roughly contemporary with their composition, but others span modern Tibetan history. The main protagonists are Tibetans, which means that his work reflects Tibetan society.

In 1985, bKra shis zla ba published a short story entitled *Tibet— A Soul Tied to a Leather Cord (Xizang — Xizai pisheng koushang de hun)*[26] followed soon after by *Tibet — The Mysterious Years (Xizang — yinmi suiyue)*.[27] Both are composed of vignettes of Tibetan life, with little plot, and both reflect clearly the fact that Tibet has been governed by the CCP since 1951, with what that means in terms of economic and social development, but are essentially neutral on the merits or faults of Chinese rule. Both reflect the continuing influence of religious belief and practices in Tibetan life. The first of the two stories is set in 1984 and concerns the day-to-day lives of a Tibetan couple, ending with the death of the man. The second and longer is actually a chronicle of Tibet, revolving around the lives of ordinary Tibetans, with the first section entitled '1910–1927' and the last '1953–1985'.

What is so special about these two works is the influence exerted on them by the literary device known as 'magic realism'. Developed by the Colombian novelist and short story writer Gabriel García Márquez (b. 1928) in his 1967 novel *One Hundred Years of Solitude*, the essence of 'magic realism' is that the author expresses his own thoughts and fantasies, and hence human myth and experience, against a background of realism. What bKra shis zla ba has done for Tibet is to combine the psychology and mysticism of the Tibetan people with their historical experience to form a Tibetan 'magic realism', just as Gabriel García Márquez did for Colombia. The influences on him are not merely Tibetan and Chinese, but also Latin American.[28] He represents not only Tibetan integration with China, but also Tibetan identity. It is, however, not an identity which lauds tradition above all, as is still very common in Tibet, but a modernised identity which is willing to accept outside influences. In terms of the ideas, style and content of his stories, as well as of his role in innovative Chinese and minority literature, bKra shis zla ba is among the most significant of all China's minority writers of the 1980s.

The performing arts

We turn next to another major branch of the arts, the performing arts, specifically song and dance and drama.

In the PRC, the traditional forms of song and dance and theatre have in the main persisted and, except during the Cultural Revolution, generally thrived quite well by comparison with the first half of the century. Folk songs and dances have remained very much in vogue among ordinary people of the minorities and, during the 1980s and 1990s, are especially popular on festival days or at a special occasion like a wedding. In 1990 this writer heard unaccompanied courtship folk songs being sung late at night on a festival day in the township of Chong'an in Guizhou province. In every minority visited, emphasis was placed on the role which song and dance play in special festivities, to an extent hardly less than before the CCP came to power. On the other hand, such pure folk literature may be among those non-modern forms to weaken as the twentieth century gives way to the twenty-first and modernisation takes root.

Among folk drama forms to survive into the 1990s, the strongest appears to be the Tibetan drama, which is performed in its original unreformed form regularly on festival days or other special occasions. A very popular site since the 1980s, as in the old days, is the former Summer Palace of the Dalai Lama. There are also several other forms of folk drama which have survived in their unreformed state since the 1980s, one example being the Dong drama — of which this author saw a performance of a little-known example at the time of the Spring Festival in 1992. The performance occurred on a stage in a drum tower built in traditional style in the centre of a township near Sanjiang, Guangxi.

One form of highly traditional drama which has revived since the 1980s is the *nuo*, discussed briefly in Chapter 5. As of the early 1990s, it is still found in quite a few parts of China, with the strongest province being Guizhou. Among Guizhou's minorities where *nuo* is still perform are the Dong, Yi, Miao, Tujia and Gelao. *Nuo* was at one time primarily a ritual form, and this tradition survives strongly among the Zhuang as an expression of national identity. However, as a general rule, this writer's explorations reinforce a Han Chinese scholar's suggestion that *nuo* in the late 1980s and into the 1990s is strongest as folk entertainment theatre.[29] Its site of performance varies, but is not much changed from ancient times, meaning that it is normally in the open air. However, this writer has seen a *nuo* performance given by an amateur folk troupe consisting of members of several different nationalities on an old stage in Fenghuang county, western Hunan.

Apart from the largely untouched traditional items are those which have undergone reform at the behest of officials and the CCP. As in other parts of China, the traditional songs, dances and dramas of the minorities have been selected out by the CCP as examples of folk art favoured by the masses and hence as desirable. At the same time, they have been subjected to a rigorous reform process.

There are several aspects to this reform. The first is that only those traditional folk items which show correct or 'healthy' content have been allowed to survive, while even they have been changed to improve them from a political point of view. The second point is that, whereas the folk theatre was performed under a tent in the case of the Tibetan version, or on stages attached to temples or other community buildings, as with the Dong or Bai, or in the open air, under the PRC modern theatres were built to perform both them and songs and dances. Third, professional troupes were especially established by the state to perform the reformed traditional folk songs, dances and dramas.

A two-hour professional presentation of minority performing arts contains reformed folk songs and dances, and sometimes a very brief drama item as well. The items feature the repertory of the particular nationality (or nationalities) from which the professional troupe is drawn or show its style in some way or another. Over the years, the content has followed patterns familiar in other arts in China, whether Han or minority. Traditional themes, including love of a member of the opposite sex or of homeland, were popular during the 1950s and early 1960s, but suppressed during the Cultural Revolution period, only to make a comeback more strongly than ever from the late 1970s. Political themes, pushed in the 1950s and 1960s along with traditional themes, turned exclusive during the Cultural Revolution, but have become less and less fashionable and increasingly boring to the people since the late 1970s.

One of innumerable songs or dances among more or less any of the minorities to illustrate the processes of reform of tradition is the Mongol dance, *Andai*. Its basic structure is the waving of handkerchiefs with accelerating foot movement rising to an exciting climax. The vigorous waving of the handkerchief was originally part of a religious ritual which aimed to drive evil spirits away from a sick person and so effect a cure, but in the course of time came to represent any plea to the spirits, such as sending drought-breaking rain. The reformed and professionalised *Andai* dance retains the handkerchief waving and the exciting climax, but disposes of the religious significance. It is performed by both male and female dancers in concert, with the costumes and music modernised and professionalised and designed to be visually and aurally pleasing at the same time as retaining some Mongol flavour.[30]

Visits to minority areas in the 1990s suggest the acceleration of a trend already underway for some time which is highly inimical to the minority song and dance forms as they are presented by professionals. More and more the professional troupes target their performances not at their own people, but at tourists and people from outside their own region. They perform on demand for foreigners' hotels, which pay them quite well for their services. During an interview in October 1994 I learned that the Kaxgar Song and Dance Troupe contracts out no less than 70 per cent of its annual performances to organisations such as tourist hotels. The good troupes go abroad as much as they can or spend quite a bit of time in areas of China other than those where they live. Less and less do they perform in the ordinary theatres of their home city or town. The professionalised traditional song and dance forms of the minorities are thus tending to become reduced to a tourist attraction.

Traditional drama is also to some extent subject to the demands of the tourist, but very much less so than song and dance, simply because it is much less accessible. On the other hand, professionalisation and reform have affected the drama just as much as song and dance. The Dong drama *Julang and Nyangmui*, discussed in Chapter 5, was rearranged and reformed several times. One version was translated into Chinese and published in January 1960, the first time any Dong drama script had actually been published. In the same year, the item was even adapted as a Guizhou drama (*Qianju*), which is a Han style, performed in a theatre in Guiyang, the capital of Guizhou, and also made into a film.[31]

Reformed theatre can coexist with purely traditional, Tibetan drama being a prime case in point. The stories, costumes and music may be similar to the more authentic and traditional theatre, but there are great changes too. Religious content is reduced or excluded, with attempts to bring out the ideologically correct aspects of the plots, such as those which side with the masses against the ruling class. Masks are still used, but far less than in the authentic tradition. The orchestra is expanded beyond the simple Tibetan percussion to include stringed and wind instruments, even some Western ones. The performance takes place in a theatre and lasts only an evening, not two or three full days.

A further aspect of reform is the creation of completely new forms of the performing arts. Since the establishment of the PRC, the authorities have actually got artists from the minorities to forge new styles from their own literature, songs and dances. Two examples are Yi drama and Miao drama, both dating from the 1950s. Apart from the just-discussed *nuo*, there were no full-fledged drama traditions among either of these two nationalities. On the other hand, both had their own folk poems, songs, stories, legends, music and various performance techniques.[32] It was based on these that artists were able to develop the new drama forms by adding the features essential to drama, especially impersonation by performers of particular characters in a story. Most of the features of the new drama style are clearly special to the Yi or Miao, but the forms themselves were created in a way characteristic of Han drama history.

There are also several forms which are to a large extent a creation of left-wing artists. One example is the song drama (*geju*), which was found only among a few of the minorities before 1949, but spread throughout the country under the PRC. As noted in Chapter 5, the first full-length item was actually Uygur, not Han. In the field of the song drama (*geju*), the Uygurs have remained pre-eminent during the PRC period, their works being based mainly on local stories, either of the past or present, and their own traditional musical style.[33]

Among all the minorities, the best-known specific example of song drama is probably *Liu Sanjie*, which concerns a much loved eighth-century singer of Guangxi able to defeat the blandishments of a landlord wanting to take her as a concubine through her intelligence and skill in singing. The item was created by a team of artists including Huang Yongcha, a Zhuang, and Bao Yutang, a member of the Gelao minority. From 1958, the team collected an enormous amount of Liu Sanjie material in the field and then presented it in the form of a small-scale northern Guangxi regional style called *caidiao* at a festival of *Liu Sanjie* items held by the Guangxi Zhuang autonomous region in 1960. They then revised the *caidiao* version into a song drama.[34]

The spoken drama (*huaju*) had a good tradition in Han China during the Republican period, and it began to spread to a few of the minorities, such as the Manchus, Koreans and Mongols. But under the PRC, spoken dramas have become a recognised part of the repertoire everywhere in urban China, even though they are not always particularly popular.

The most distinguished spoken drama writer under the PRC who was a member of a minority was the Manchu Lao She, who wrote 23 play-scripts, mostly in the form of spoken dramas, before his suicide in 1966. By far his best play, and one which to this writer has as good a claim as any to be called the finest spoken drama produced under the PRC for its conception, style and sensitivity to the social environment it portrays, is *Teahouse* (*Chaguan*), premiered in 1958. The play is set in a single teahouse in Beijing and thus conforms to the principle of unity of place. But the three acts take place in widely separated times, and give a microcosm of China's historical and social development from the end of the Qing dynasty to the eve of the CCP's victory.[35]

Among the numerous characters in *Teahouse*, only very few are identified as Manchu, with one of them, Fourth Elder Chang, expressing what is close to shame that the Manchus once ruled China. The Manchu Qing dynasty 'deserved to collapse', he states. 'I'm a Bannerman [Manchu] myself, but I must speak the truth . . . Bannermen are Chinese too!'[36] A positive but tragic figure, one of his last sentences expresses his patriotism but disillusionment: 'I love my country, but no one gives a damn about me.'[37] It is possible, as has been suggested by one writer, that 'it was important to Lao She to say, loud and clear, that not all Manchus were traitors' to China,[38] but although *Teahouse* shows remarkable local sensitivity to Beijing, there is very little in it of relevance to nationality issues. Very much in the mainstream of Chinese and not minority spoken drama, it can hardly be interpreted overall as an expression of Manchu identity.

As in the Republican period, the Koreans are in the forefront of spoken drama production among the minorities. An interview with a leader of the Yanbian Spoken Drama Troupe in October 1990 emphasised two major points. One was the claim that virtually all performances are given in Korean, even though the troupe members are bilingual. The same rule applies both for plays originally written in Korean and those translated from Chinese. The reason for the practice is in order to maintain the Korean identity of the troupe and its audiences. The second point to flow from the interview was that in fact the content of Korean spoken dramas of the 1980s and 1990s, although mostly about Koreans, is rather similar to those found in Beijing, Shanghai and other major Chinese cities in that they are challenging traditional social and political norms, probably more adventurously than any other minority.[39]

The Uygurs have produced some worthwhile spoken dramas in their own language. One which gained great popularity in the mid-1990s is very interesting for its social content, even if not necessarily outstanding as literature. It is *The Way of Death* (*Olüm yuli*), which deals with the heroin problem, my informants claiming that there were about 30 000 addicts in Xinjiang in 1994, most of them Uygurs. The drama was produced by the Kaxgar Spoken Drama Troupe, members of which told me in October 1994 that the play had been shown all over Xinjiang, and several times on television, and had netted the company some ¥20 000 profit. Several Uygurs of my acquaintance had seen and been impressed by the play.

There are two drug-traffickers in the item, one of them a woman. They entice two young men into drug addiction. The sister of the female trafficker is the Party member, but though she is clearly a positive character, she does not dominate. In the end, both the traffickers are arrested, the Party member helping the police against her own sister. But in the meantime, one of the addicts has killed his sister by mistake. The play is thus a tragedy, with neither addict solving his heroin problem. There is a propaganda content against the evils of heroin, but it is on behalf of a cause which all would support, whatever their attitude to current rule in Xinjiang.

The Inner Mongolian autonomous region has witnessed the rise of a new revolutionary theatre, including spoken drama. Possibly the most famous of the Mongol playwrights is Tsogtnarin. Born in 1925, he became active in revolutionary drama in the late 1940s. His most productive period was from 1959 to the eve of the Cultural Revolution, but that campaign effectively silenced him. In 1979 he produced two more dramas and then became active as a writer of film scripts — for instance, one for the film *Ghada Merin* (1980) and for *Chinggis Khan* (1984).

Most of Tsogtnarin's work deals with the Mongols, their history and revolution. His best known piece is named after its hero, *Burkut*, meaning literally *Golden Eagle*. Written in the Mongolian language, it concerns a Mongol herdsman and his struggle against the feudal princes at the end of the Qing dynasty. Burkut is arrested by a prince who wants to abduct his beloved, but is released by mass action and arrives at the head of a rebel army in time to save her. Tsogtnarin claims that the drama's content is based on stories and people he actually met and talked to while researching to write the drama.[40]

The spoken drama is a much later implant for the Tibetans than for the Koreans, going back only to 1960, when some Tibetan students were sent to Shanghai to study drama and returned to form the Tibetan Spoken Drama Troupe in 1962. The Troupe's members are bilingual but most of their dramas are in Tibetan. One which this author saw in 1985 was called *Yid rong ma* by Tshe ring rdo rje, perhaps Tibet's leading contemporary dramatist, and others. The play is titled for its main character and is based on an eighteenth-century Tibetan novel-like tract in which she refuses the marriage her father has arranged for her. The play shows her as a fighter for freedom and against feudal marriage practices. This item exemplifies both Tibetan identity and integration with the Han. Its Tibetan identity derives from its being in the Tibetan language and based on a classical Tibetan work, in which all main characters are Tibetans. It also shows strong Han influence in the fact that the spoken drama form is a direct implant from Shanghai. The scenery, stage properties and acting style show very strong Han influence, as does the ideology behind the rearrangement of the drama and the characterisation of the central characters.[41]

Conclusion

A consolidated PRC account of Chinese literature and theatre produced since 1949 was not really possible until the 1980s. One major such treatment, published in 1985 and dealing with the years 1949–82, includes a chapter on the minorities, which praises their contributions for expressing ethnic characteristics so well. It goes on:

> Because the authors of the fraternal nationalities take the life of their own nationality as their source, they can always express its life and fate against the strong background of its natural scenery and customs ... Since the authors are fully familiar with the history and life of their own nationality and understand the characteristics of its people's ideas, feelings, psychology and temperament, they can delineate typical characters of their own people deeply and vividly, and accurately reflect their national personality, temperament and special features.[42]

The passage does not use words like 'identity', let alone phrases such as 'ethnic identities'. Yet it appears that the kind of ethnic identity of concern to the present book is precisely what is under discussion in the above passage, even down to details such as psychology and temperament. It also needs to be added that the passage is expressing an official view on the question of the nature of minorities literature, including theatre. What is apparent is that government opinion believes that minorities literature and theatre both *should* express ethnic identities and have indeed done so under the PRC, and especially in the 1980s.

Have the minorities' literature and theatre in fact intensified their ethnic identities in China since 1949? The answer in some ways is yes, but in others no. A comparison between the PRC and Republican periods shows far more minority writers and performers, far more books published in minority languages, far more troupes, both professional and folk, in the PRC. The content of the short stories, novels and plays is generally set among the nationality itself, with the authors and performers, as well as the main characters depicted, generally belonging to it. In the case of those nationalities with long-standing and powerful literatures, such as the Koreans, the Tibetans and the Mongols, at least some writers use their own languages, although with others, like the Miao, Zhuang and Bouyei, authors more or less always write in Chinese, since the PRC-imposed scripts have proved to be of limited use only. With regard to the theatre, the written script is much less relevant, since performance is what matters most. The minorities troupes are generally able to perform both in their own language and Chinese, but when their audience is mainly made up of their own people, it is their own language that they use. The Koreans are remarkable for the strength of their retention of cultural identity through literature and the arts. Their novelists write in Korean and it has even been observed that the Yanbian Korean community has preserved some traditional Korean folk songs, dances and games more successfully than in South Korea itself.[43]

There are also respects in which identities have actually weakened in ethnic literature under the PRC. One is that the system of training is socialist and follows similar patterns all over the PRC, as a result of which there is a certain consonance of style and aim even for different nationalities. All forms of literature, including theatre, have undergone reform under the

PRC, and although the nature of the reform has differed from period to period, the long-term impact has been considerable.

The whole issue of identities nowadays depends on state-imposed categories. A poem or song attributed to a recognised minority by a publisher might in fact come from the hands of a person or group claiming membership of subgroups or even a totally different unrecognised nationality. One American scholar claims that some Yi collaborators told him that a collection of songs attributed to the Yi were in fact created by people from various Yi subgroups with traditions quite different from his Yi collaborators.[44] It becomes difficult to say which group's identity is represented in each of the songs.

Another issue is form. Although the traditional forms of literature and theatre have been maintained among the minorities, several new ones have been added which are actually implants from outside China. Examples include the modern long novel, the spoken drama and the dance-drama. These were hardly found at all among the minorities when the CCP came to power, but had become established, if not necessarily universally popular, among all the minorities by the 1990s. The traditional forms of poetry and theatre remain strong among the minorities, but even these are beginning to suffer from the impact of modernisation, which may mean the whittling away of major differences of style among the various nationalities.

In those minority areas visited by this writer, young people are beginning to adopt and love the international culture expressed through American pop, disco and karaoke. Every minority area visited in the 1990s proved to have at least one karaoke bar. One young Bouyei man told me he regarded such culture as 'Hanised and modernised' (Hanhua xiandaihua) and that was an advantage in his mind, though his father told me he thought such a view was a pity and hostile to the culture of the Bouyei people. The 'Hanised and modernised' culture is available through television which now reaches most parts of China, and has penetrated even some of the most remote minority areas.

Another important reservation to be placed on the strength of ethnic identities in the literature and theatre of the minorities is the ideological one. For most of the period of the PRC, newly written fiction and drama among the minorities have tended strongly to follow ideological dictates from the CCP. These are by no means necessarily inimical to ethnic identities. A Tibetan play like Yid rong ma, based on a Tibetan tract of the eighteenth century, may intensify Tibetan identity, even if it is politically correct according to the canons of the 1980s. But most of the drama, fiction and poetry written under the PRC has been more closely politicised than this particular item.

The ideological factor is designed by the authorities to militate in favour not only of socialism but of Chinese unity, and thus against any hint of secession. It is not surprising that published authors among the minorities have tended to be those in favour of 'the unity of the nationalities' rather than against. What this means is that the literature and theatre of the minorities under the PRC have generally benefited both the integration of the Chinese state and the integration of the nationalities with one another rather than the converse.

It is my impression that, among some minorities, this may be changing. In Xinjiang in October 1994, I became aware that young Uygur intellectuals look for the 'hidden meaning' in their own contemporary literature to find hostility to the Chinese and even support for independence. The Chinese themselves have a very long tradition of skill at hiding their real meaning, but those censors who would try to uncover the hidden meaning in Uygur literature may experience great difficulty, since they usually do not know the language very well at all, let alone understanding its nuances.

One perceptive observer has written that the minorities 'sing, they dance, they twirl, they whirl. Most of all, they smile, showing their happiness to be part of the motherland'. The minorities he describes as colourful, himself using colourful language to emphasise the colour.[45] His argument is that the professionalised songs and dances of the minorities have become very much part of the state propaganda which helps create the identity not so much of each of the minorities themselves but of the Han majority and the Chinese state. It is an interesting and appealing notion, but one which does not to this writer detract from the genuine artistic skills and creativity of the performers nor even from their desire to maintain their own traditions. Apart from the professionalised and televised performances, certain places have been specifically set up even to show folk performances to Han or foreign tourists and others. Yet, having attended folk performances without plans in several parts of China, it is evident to me that at least a portion of the authentic folk arts are genuine revivals.

Generally speaking, the main expressions of ethnic identities among the minorities are in such revivals of tradition rather than in the reformed or professionalised performances or in expressions of open hostility to the unity of the Chinese state. A very good example to illustrate the point is the drama of the Tibetans in the late 1980s and early 1990s. During a visit to Tibet in 1985, this writer was able to see the reformed traditional fairy story *vGro ba bzang mo* and a recently written spoken drama in Tibetan. But on his return in 1990, with the pro-independence disturbances having separated the two visits, there were ample performances of pure and unreformed traditional drama, but no amount of hunting uncovered any spoken dramas or reformed traditional theatre.

If the comparison is with the Republican period, the field of literature and theatre displays a substantial but inconsistent rise in ethnic identities among China's minorities over the period 1949 to the mid-1990s. This has gone hand in hand with a growing integration of the minorities into the Chinese state and with each other. This is still tension between ethnic identities and integration. But it is the kind of tension which is more likely to express itself in conservative revivals of traditions than in violence serious enough to lead to successful secession.

Notes

1 See Wu Zhongyang, *Zhongguo dangdai minzu wenxue gaiguan*, Zhongyang minzu xueyuan chubanshe, Beijing, 1986, p. 21.

2 For more detail on the languages of Xinjiang see S.A. Wurm et al., *Language Atlas of China*, Longman on behalf of the Australian Academy of the Humanities and the Chinese Academy of Social Sciences, Hong Kong, 1987, p. C4 and map C4.

3 State Nationalities Affairs Commission Finance and Economic Section, *Minzu gongzuo tongji tiyao, 1949–1987*, (n.p., 1988), p. 55.

4 Wu, *Minzu wenxue gaiguan*, p. 23.

5 *A Chronology of Nationalities Work in Contemporary China* Editorial Department, *Dangdai Zhongguo minzu gongzuo da shiji, 1949–1988*, Minzu chubanshe, Beijing, 1990, p. 309.

6 *Zhonghua renmin gongheguo falü huibian, 1979–1984*, Renmin chubanshe, Beijing, 1985, p. 548.

7 *Minzu gongzuo tongji tiyao*, p. 55.

8 For some discussion of two Uygur anthologies published in the 1980s, see Eden Naby, 'Uighur Literature: The Antecedents', in Shirin Akiner (ed.), *Cultural Change and Continuity in Central Asia*, Kegan Paul International, London and New York, in association with the Central Asia Research Forum, School of Oriental and African Studies, London, 1991, pp. 20–26.

9 Colin Mackerras, 'Traditional Mongolian Performing Arts in Inner Mongolia', *The Australian Journal of Chinese Affairs*, no. 10, July 1983, p. 20.

10 *History of Dong Literature* Compilation Group, *Dongzu wenxue shi*, Guizhou Minzu chubanshe, Guiyang, 1988, p. 403.

11 For extracts from the poem, both in Dong and Chinese, see ibid., pp. 405–7.

12 For a brief exposition of the story and some excerpts, in Chinese, see Mao Xing (gen. ed.), *Zhongguo shaoshu minzu wenxue*, Hunan Renmin chubanshe, Changsha, 1983, vol. 2, pp. 324–26.

13 See brief biographical notes on the poet in Kurban Barat, *Karguli*, Xinjiang Halk nashriyati [Renmin chubanshe], Ürümqi, 1993, pp. 1–2.

14 See the poem in ibid., pp. 15–16. The opening lines were translated and the sense of the poem explained to me by a Uygur friend in Xinjiang.

15 Aikebaier Mijiti, 'Shaoshu minzu wenxue', *Zhongguo baike nianjian 1989*, Zhongguo da baike quanshu chubanshe, Beijing, Shanghai, 1989, p. 408.

16 Jin Dongxun, 'Jianlun jianguo hou Chaoxian zu de xiaoshuo chuangzuo', in Yanbian Literature and Art Research Institute, *Chaoxian zu wenxue yishu gaiguan*, no publisher or place, 1982, p. 30.

17 ibid., pp. 41–42.

18 See Bernard Vincent Olivier, *The Implementation of China's Nationality Policy in the Northeastern Provinces*, Mellen Research University Press, San Francisco, 1993, pp. 252–53. Olivier gives figures on p. 252 showing

that in the Yanji Municipal Library there were 230 000 books in 1981, of which 30 800 or 13.4 per cent were in Korean, while in 1989 there was a total of 310 000 books, of which about 50 000, that is approximately 16 per cent, were in the Korean language.

19 Based on an interview held in October 1990 with a Korean representative of the Yanbian Branch of the Association of Chinese Writers, *Zhongguo zuojia xiehui*, which was itself set up in August 1956.

20 Jeffrey C. Kinkley, *The Odyssey of Shen Congwen*, Stanford University Press, Stanford, 1987, pp. 269–74.

21 ibid., p. 20.

22 For a detailed discussion of Li Qiao and his works, especially *Huanxiao de Jinsha jiang*, see Wu, *Minzu wenxue gaiguan*, pp. 264–75.

23 Wang Baolin, Xie Yunmei, Wu Lide et al. (eds), *Zhongguo shaoshu minzu xiandai wenxue*, Guangxi Renmin chubanshe, Nanning, 1989, p. 267.

24 In the late 1970s a regularised (*guifan*) version of the traditional Liangshan Yi script was developed, and became used for books of folk poetry, literature, agricultural methods and even scholarship, as well as for school textbooks.

25 Wu, *Minzu wenxue gaiguan*, p. 302.

26 It came out in the first issue of the periodical *Xizang wenxue* (*Tibetan Literature*) and was republished as a book in Tianjin the following year by the Hundred Flowers Literature and Arts (Baihua wenyi) Press. See the original Chinese version in Feng Liang (ed.), *Xizang xin xiaoshuo*, Xizang Renmin chubanshe, Lhasa, 1989, pp. 1–23. It has been translated into English, under the title 'A Soul in Bondage', by David Kwan, in Tashi Dawa, *A Soul in Bondage, Stories from Tibet*, Panda Books, Beijing, 1992, pp. 13–40.

27 Liu Shicong has translated the story into English under the title 'Tibet: the Mysterious Years' in Tashi Dawa, *A Soul in Bondage*, pp. 41–106.

28 The material on Bkra-shis zla-ba is based mainly on Zhang Jun, 'Ru mo de shijie — lun dangdai Xizang xiaoshuo', in *Xizang xin xiaoshuo*, pp. 445–50 and Dondrup Wangbum's 'Preface' to Tashi Dawa, *A Soul in Bondage*, pp. 5–11.

29 See Qu Liuyi, 'Zhongguo ge minzu nuoxi de fenlei, tezheng ji qi "huo huashi" jiazhi', in Tuo Xiuming et al. (eds), *Zhongguo nuo wenhua lunwen xuan*, Guizhou Minzu chubanshe, Guiyang, 1989, p. 3.

30 See further commentary on the Mongol dance *Andai* in Mackerras, 'Traditional Mongolian Performing Arts', pp. 22–23.

31 *Dongzu wenxue shi*, p. 438.

32 See more detail in Colin Mackerras, 'Integration and the Dramas of China's Minorities', *Asian Theatre Journal*, vol. 9, no. 1, Spring 1992, pp. 18–19.

33 For more detail see Colin Mackerras, *Chinese Drama, A Historical Survey*, New World Press, Beijing, 1990, pp. 193–94.

34 On Liu Sanjie, including commentary and short selections from the text, see Yang Liangcai, Tao Lifan and Deng Minwen, *Zhongguo shaoshu minzu wenxue*, Renmin chubanshe, Beijing, 1985, pp. 278–83.

35 See also Mackerras, *Chinese Drama*, pp. 155–56.
36 Lao She, trans. John Howard-Gibbon, *Teahouse, A Play in Three Acts*, Foreign Languages Press, Beijing, 1980, pp. 33–34.
37 ibid., p. 75.
38 Ranbir Vohra, *Lao She and the Chinese Revolution*, East Asian Research Center, Harvard University, Cambridge, Mass., 1974, p. 163.
39 For more detail on the spoken drama among the Koreans, see Mackerras, 'Integration and the Dramas of China's Minorities', pp. 22–23.
40 On Tsogtnarin and *Burkut*, see especially Wu, *Minzu wenxue gaiguan*, pp. 325–30.
41 For more detail on the Tibetan spoken drama, including *Yid-rong-ma*, see Colin Mackerras, 'Drama in the Tibetan Autonomous Region' *Asian Theatre Journal*, vol. 5, no. 2, Fall 1988, pp. 206–10.
42 Wang Huazao et al., *Zhongguo dangdai wenxue jianshi*, Hunan Renmin chubanshe, Changsha, 1985, p. 576.
43 Pyong Gap Min, 'A Comparison of the Korean Minorities in China and Japan', *International Migration Review*, vol. 26, no. 1, Spring 1992, p. 9.
44 Mark Bender, 'Approaching the Literatures of China's Minority Nationalities', *China Exchange News*, vol. 21, nos 3 and 4, Fall–Winter 1993, p. 14.
45 Dru C. Gladney, 'Representing Nationality in China: Refiguring Majority/Minority Identities', *The Journal of Asian Studies*, vol. 53, no. 3, February 1994, especially p. 95.

10 Conclusion

For the entire period since 1912, most of China's currently recognised minority nationalities have seen themselves as distinct from the Han, but with the feeling very much weaker among the southwestern peoples of Guangxi, Guizhou and Yunnan than in the far west of China, notably Xinjiang and Tibet. With some significant exceptions, such as Xinjiang in the 1930s and 1940s, the strength of these ethnic identities has been greater during the 1980s and 1990s than in any previous decade. Although national cultural consciousness among China's minorities does not loom large as a particular general factor for the first half of the twentieth century or during the Cultural Revolution, it became a highly significant and widespread force during the 1980s and has remained so during the 1990s, creating an impact which has not hitherto received as much attention as it deserves. In very general terms, religion has been the most important cultural site of these feelings of national consciousness, with a resurgence of local languages and a revival but also modernisation of national literatures and arts occupying a significant location as well.

Over the present century, China has experienced ups and downs in terms of political integration as well as in terms of the integration of the minorities with the dominant Han people. In general, the PRC period has seen a higher level of integration in both senses of the term. During the Republican period, China was fragmented and the great majority of minority populations remote from central control. Under the PRC, central control has generally been very much stronger and the nationalities better integrated, despite the formal autonomy enjoyed by the minority areas. However, the degree of control of the centre appears to have eroded to some extent everywhere in the country since the late 1980s. This process is the result of the increasing tendency of the prosperous southern provinces such as Guangdong to make economic decisions independently of the central government. The nationality regions have to some extent been affected by this increasing autonomy, but the southern areas of greatest prosperity are virtually all Han.

It has been suggested that the minorities played a significant role in the formation of the Chinese nation by Sun Yat-sen, not because of their objective importance but because they played the role of Other to the Han and therefore in 'essentialising the Han'.[1] The minorities may well still play such a role in the increasing nationalism of China as a whole in the 1990s. An argument of this kind attaches importance to the minorities, but it also places them in a very low position by comparison with the Han, because they become merely the foil against which the Chinese nation as a whole can be promoted and strengthened. Although it is an interesting notion, it does not tell us anything about the identities of the minorities themselves.

Ethnic identities and integration: Specific cultural factors

The site of the present book is not politics, but culture. Yet those specific factors of culture which are defined as the focus of the present book in the Introduction do not necessarily point in precisely the same direction as one another in terms of what they tell us about ethnic cultural identities and the extent of integration of nationalities in China.

Religion

Throughout the twentieth century, the most powerful force favouring ethnic identities among those minorities with strong clergies has been religion. This is because it has, of all factors, been the one most likely to be a source of pride in the particular nationality and, in general, of resentment against those with different points of view. Throughout the century, to be a Tibetan has always been nearly synonymous with belief in Tibetan Buddhism, with Tibetans feeling very little difference between pride in being Tibetan and in believing in their own particular form of Buddhism. If the Han were the opposition, then the Muslim nationalities have also seen some kind of confluence between pride in their own ethnic or local grouping and intense belief in Islam. As far as the south of China is concerned, the Dai people have always been devout Theravada Buddhists and quite ready to see their pride in their religion as equivalent to that in their nationality.

In the Republican period, Islam in Xinjiang generally militated against the integration of China and of the Han with the minorities. There were many secessionist rebellions among the Turkic peoples of Xinjiang, and especially the Uygurs, which caused enormous bloodshed and resentment against the Han and against the anti-religious ideologies which they held.

At the same time, it is notable that the Hui, who are also Muslims, were not so keen to split China. On several occasions in the 1930s they actually sided with the forces they believed loyal to the central Nanjing government to suppress Muslim-led secessionist rebellions. They were generally happy to unite with the Han people against the Japanese. Many people among the Hui came to support the nationalism of China as a whole. Moreover, this was a period of generally improving relations between the Han and Hui, even if tensions remained.

In the PRC period, religion has been much weaker among the minorities than under the Republic, largely because the state has been stronger and on the whole more anti-religious. During the Cultural Revolution, religions of all kinds were persecuted savagely, and since the minorities included the most dedicated religious believers, they reacted with the most acute resentment, although much less with the armed rebellion characteristic of Xinjiang in the 1930s. The Cultural Revolution may have been able to suppress opposition effectively, but the religious persecutions certainly promoted identities because they caused the sense of 'otherness' to stick to the Han Communists most intensely.

In the 1980s and 1990s, religion is generally stronger among the minorities than it was in the 1950s, let alone the 1960s. It is also a sign of national feeling. A young Uygur is likely to adhere to Islam for this reason, even if he or she is not very devout, or not at all enthusiastic about Islamic doctrines or faithful in following Muslim practices. The feeling that to be a Dai means to believe in Theravada Buddhism has grown again with considerable power, the reaction against the Cultural Revolution merely serving as an intensifier. On the other hand, there is little doubt that religion is not nearly as potent a social force as it was before the CCP's accession to power. Clergy no longer own property or estates and do not control the political process, as they once did among many of the nationalities. The numbers entering the monasteries of Tibet and especially Inner Mongolia are minimal by comparison with what they once were.

In some areas, religion in the 1980s and 1990s has achieved not only social power, but also political power. Islam has revived in influence, even within the CCP and the central government. This was shown in particular in 1989, when the Muslims of China were able to have banned a book they found insulting to their religion. Later on the publisher was forced to close down and the editor and authors of the book were charged in law and punished. Indeed, the Muslims of China secured the political result they wanted far more effectively and quickly than happened in the case of the Salman Rushdie affair in other parts of the world at a similar time.

In the case of the Tibetans, it is notable that it was the clergy who took the lead in the separatist demonstrations of 1987 to 1989, and there have been Islam-led secessionist movements among the minorities of Xinjiang as well. Certainly, these movements militated strongly against good relations between Han and the minorities. What this suggests is that religion is still sometimes a force operating against integration in China. This would hold

true no matter which of the two senses of the term 'integration' is used —
the cohesion of China or harmonious relations between nationalities.

At the same time, it is necessary to add that there are quite a few minorities in China among which religion functions weakly or not at all as a source
of ethnic identity. This would apply to those peoples of Guizhou, Guangxi
and Yunnan and western Hunan with their own or Han-imported folk religions which have no or very weak clergies. It would also cover peoples like
the Koreans who have little time for religion despite a strongly developed
sense of identity.

Education

On the whole, the effects of education systems among the minorities in China
from 1912–95 were far more integrative and modernising than those of religion, and conversely their effects generally acted against feelings of distinct
ethnic identities among the minorities. During the Republican period, the traditional systems maintained some hold, especially the religious ones. But the
direction, no doubt very haltingly and unevenly, was clearly in favour of
China's integration. In the case of only a few minorities could it be said that
education caused individual national consciousness to grow stronger by 1949
than it had been in 1912, with decline being a very much commoner pattern.

In terms of education, from 1912–49 the Koreans and Uygurs show interesting similarities and contrasts. Both were subject to extreme foreign influence, the Koreans from Japan and the Uygurs from the Soviet Union through
Sheng Shicai's government. Both benefited from the experience if modernisation, literacy and numeracy were the criteria. But both reacted very
strongly indeed against the foreign imposition. That kind of hostility to outsiders which often heightens a sense of identity was common to both, but
the results were very different. In the case of the Koreans, the defeat of the
Japanese may actually have assisted the integration of the Koreans with the
Han and with China, because of the reaction against the attempts of the
Japanese education system to suppress Korean culture. Among the Uygurs,
there was only a short interregnum before the CCP established its education system and the hiatus over the period from the 1930s to the 1950s was
not particularly drastic. Unlike the Japanese in Jilin, the Soviet-influenced
education system in Xinjiang was not aiming to turn the Uygurs or other
minorities against China or the Han Chinese.

The policy of the CCP in education is similar to the Guomindang's in
that it aims to foster national unity. But it is far more tolerant towards the
preservation of the cultures of the nationalities. Perhaps more important is
the fact that, among the minority nationalities, state education never extended nearly as far among the ordinary people as has happened under the PRC.
This suggests that the degree of national integration due to education under
the PRC has been very extensive indeed.

It is not surprising that the CCP's dominant educational aim has always
been to bring about an integrated Chinese national culture in which the

minority peoples would accept the prevailing socialist ideology and state, even if they believed in a religion which was hostile to socialism. Its policy to promote unified nationwide curricula does not necessarily mean that minority cultures and languages are suppressed, although it may mean that they tend to lose force. Among those nationalities with strong traditional scripts and cultures, the trend in the 1980s and early 1990s was undoubtedly in the direction of using the education system for cultural and language preservation. The insistence on using Uygur language and emphasising Uygur arts in schools for Uygurs in Xinjiang is a very good illustrative example. But the focus was different with those nationalities without strong written language traditions. Among them, the trend was towards using the education system to learn the language and culture not of their own specific minority but of China as a whole, which in effect meant those of the Han.

Literature and the arts

One sphere of culture which normally illustrates ethnic identities with particular clarity is literature and the arts. Contrary trends have been evident over the period 1912–93, but while there are signs of the national identity of individual nationalities, they are scarcely prominent enough to outweigh the integration of China. The overall trend has been in the direction of an integrated culture but with strong regional and national characteristics.

During the Republican period, the major literary figures worked in favour of unified Chinese culture, even if they belonged to the minorities. Lao She hardly even mentioned his Manchu identity, let alone emphasised it. At the same time, the Republican period was one when the local national traditions were generally in decline, and in some cases even moribund. Even the Tibetan literary and dramatic tradition, one of the strongest among China's minorities, was long past its high point and produced virtually nothing new in the first half of the twentieth century.

A few of the minorities were influenced by modern trends, mainly from the left. In Xinjiang, Uygur and Kazak literary and theatrical figures came under Soviet influence, especially in the 1930s during the period of Sheng Shicai's ascendancy. The Koreans of Yanbian reacted strongly against Japanese occupation which, attempting to crush their culture, ended up forcing them to a more modern but still very clearly Korean literature and theatre. Neither in Xinjiang nor in Yanbian did literature or drama assist the integration of the minorities with the Han or into the Chinese state.

Under the PRC, the impact of socialism from the 1950s to the late 1970s was definitely integrative for the literatures and theatres of the minorities, because it imposed such clear ideological goals which were the same everywhere, and artistic forms which had formerly been used mainly by the Han and more integrated minorities spread among all the peoples of China. At the same time, in the 1950s and early 1960s, the CCP encouraged the minorities to revive and emphasise their national theatres, a process which was initially successful but which was cut short totally by the eruption of the Cultural Revolution in 1966.

In the 1980s and 1990s a more interesting process has been at work. On the one hand, all the artistic and literary traditions of China have revived, with a strong negative reaction against the assimilative policies of the Cultural Revolution evident, and the resurgence has manifested itself strongly in expressions of ethnic identities. But on the other hand, this has been a period of rapid economic development and modernisation all over China. The result is new ideas and modes of expression in literature and the arts. The artistic styles favoured by young people tend towards a very modern and Western-influenced ring, and are the same all over China, no matter what the nationality to which the relevant people belong.

The Tibetans are a people with an extremely strongly rooted script and written language. It is not surprising to find, then, that much contemporary Tibetan fiction and drama is written or performed in Tibetan. But it is notable that bKra shis zla ba, whose works are a good illustration of Tibetan identity combined with strong outside influences and modernity, writes entirely in Chinese. Although some of his work has been translated into Tibetan, he himself does not write Tibetan and his audience is thus not his own people at all. Since the modern novel is an implant on to Tibetan culture and does not use Tibetan language exclusively, its contribution to Tibetan identity is limited, even though the characters and setting of the novels and short stories are Tibetan.

In Xinjiang, the contemporary novel of the 1980s and 1990s actually places a heavier emphasis on national identity even than in Tibet. Authors there insist on writing in their own language. A literary figure such as Abdurehim Utkur not only writes in Uygur, but emphasises the modern history of his own people through his novels. His stand is passionately pro-Uygur and the positive figures in his novels are Uygur.

Dru Gladney has pointed out the eroticisation and exoticisation of the Han visual arts in the 1980s in the sense that a portion of them focus on minority women as sexual objects where they would not dare to do so with Han counterparts. He observes that paintings of nude women are almost always of minorities, not Han, adding that this objectifies the minorities and subordinates them with respect to the Han.[2] The eroticisation and exoticisation of literature and the arts begins to bear on feelings of ethnic identities among the minorities, rather than on Han images of the minorities, only when the minorities themselves begin to protest against this attitude. That this has indeed begun to happen is acknowledged by Gladney, at least as far as the Muslim nationalities are concerned.[3] This writer has become aware of examples among the nationalities of the southwest. A particularly famous case of protest came at the instance of the Tibetans early in 1987 as part of a campaign against 'bourgeois liberalisation', or Western influence perceived as detrimental to the rule of the Communist Party. Pressures from the Tibetans persuaded the relevant leaders to dismiss Liu Xinwu, the editor of China's foremost official literary periodical, *Chinese Literature* (*Zhongguo wenxue*), for carrying a long story dealing with Tibetan incest and sexual abuse. In addition, Liu was asked to make a public self-criticism. The grounds for the dismissal and self-criticism were that the story vilified Tibetan culture and customs.[4] Although both the nationalities and the authorities thus show sensitivities to cultural differences, it seems to me fair to add that the kind of thinking which emphasises sexist or racist slights against the minorities on the part of Han literary figures or artists is not yet strong in China. It is very easy to read such notions into the works of Chinese artists because reactions of this kind have become so fashionable in the West.

Marriage, family, gender

The family is an aspect of 'culture' under the definition of that term offered in the Introduction, and it has something to tell us about ethnic identities and the integration of the minorities both with the Han and with China as a whole. It is, for instance, clear that the overwhelming majority of minority women resisted the Han practice of foot-binding. The Han looked down on many of them for their rather free-wheeling and anti-Confucian approaches to relations between the sexes.

Clothing is one of the most obvious features of difference among the various nationalities.[5] The gradual adoption of international or Han clothing styles by the great majority of men and most women of the minority nationalities in preference to their own traditional clothing definitely indicates a decline in ethnic identities. The revival of traditional festivals in the 1980s brought back the traditional clothes for women and children of the minorities, but for most of them only on such special days. The 1980s also saw a revival of traditional family patterns among the minorities, examples being the courtship gatherings of the Miao and other southern minorities and polyandry among the Tibetans. Although modernisation may eventually lead to another withering of these practices, it is not likely that they will die out completely in the short term.

In some respects, women have maintained their ethnic identities more strongly than their menfolk and been slower and probably more reluctant to integrate with the Han. Clothing is more or less entirely the responsibility of women among China's peoples. Among some peoples with strong feelings of identity, such as the Tibetans, Uygurs, Kazaks and Yi, rural and even many urban women still wear traditional garb, while men do so much less or not at all. In the 1980s it has been mainly women who wear traditional clothes during festivals or special occasions. Generally, the women have been slower to learn Chinese than the men, even under the PRC. In many minority areas, this writer found that in the countryside the number of women who did not learn Chinese was greater than the number of men. The retention of national diets of the minorities, another quite clear trend of the 1980s and 1990s, is to a very large extent in the hands of women.

Though matters connected with family and women have some relevance for ethnic identities and integration with the Han, they do not appear to be

214 CHINA'S MINORITY CULTURES: IDENTITIES AND INTEGRATION SINCE 1912

nearly as important as several other aspects of culture, or of politics. In the demonstrations of 1989 over the publication of *Sexual Customs* and in those in Lhasa for Tibetan independence, women took part, but they did so more as representatives of their nationality or believers in their religion than as women. It was men who took the lead in all cases. What the demonstrators cared about was religion and national consciousness, gender and family issues never being more than marginal. It follows that the theoretical parallel between ethnic minorities and women as groups suffering discrimination, which is noted by Western feminists,[6] is not yet a feature of the Chinese scene.

Reasons for the rise in ethnic identities

Why is it that feelings of national cultural identity among China's minorities have experienced a resurgence during the period of reform in the 1980s and 1990s?

The main reason for the expansion of ethnic identities among China's minority nationalities in the 1980s is reaction against the savage assimilation with China and with the Han practised during the Cultural Revolution. It was signalled in the Introduction that the feeling of marginalised otherness was a major factor sparking pride in one's own culture and feelings of identity because '*we* are different', along with bitter resentment of domination by a majority which gives itself the airs of superiority. The Cultural Revolution was extremely repressive against minority cultures, probably even more than the Japanese were, because of the obsession held by its main leaders regarding the importance of class struggle and consequent downgrading of national struggle and ethnic identities. The Chinese government during the Cultural Revolution itself was politically powerful enough to suppress any latent ethnic identities among the minorities, but once the clamps were lifted in the early 1980s, the sense of national consciousness blossomed like flowers in spring.

Two scholars have aptly summed up this process of cultural revitalisation among the 'nomads of Western Tibet'.

> Compelled to abandon the traditional beliefs and symbols that gave meaning to the world around them and to actively embrace a new 'communist' culture consisting of norms and values that they considered repugnant, they experienced a crisis of morality and meaning. This was further exacerbated when they had to put the new morality into practice by persecuting and physically punishing the newly defined 'class enemies,' many of whom were friends, spouses, and kinsmen. China's new post-1980 policies created conditions wherein individual Tibetans were able to resurrect a more satisfying culture by readopting traditional components of their cognitive and affective systems and discarding components of the 'revolutionary' culture they had been forced to profess. They had done this not just with religion, but with all facets of their way of life.[7]

This comment leads directly to another reason for the growth of ethnic identities, namely the rising prosperity of the 1980s and 1990s, coupled with the loss of faith everywhere in China in Marxism-Leninism. This has left a vacuum in the minds of many people, which religion and attachment to ethnicity have tried to fill, to some extent successfully. Just as in the West, many young Chinese require more than material goods and values to give meaning to their lives. It is a very common phenomenon everywhere that traditional ideas move in to fill voids created by disillusionment with 'modern' philosophies. It is therefore quite natural that national consciousness should accompany religious revival.

The revival or reinvention of national identity feelings in China should be set in the context of a worldwide trend in favour of such a sense of ethnic consciousness. Given the enormous improvements in communications everywhere, it would come as no surprise that ideas found in one part of the world would spread also to others.

In those parts of the world which had once formed part of the Soviet Union, as well as in the countries of Eastern and Central Europe, the sense of national identity was both a reason for, and a result of, the collapse of the Marxist-Leninist governments. Lenin and his followers had been able to establish powerful states which held together peoples of very different cultures. Political reform in these states led to the disintegration of political centres strong enough to be able to hold their diverse peoples together.

At the same time as these states declined and collapsed, the world has seen the revival of religions, a prime cultural source of ethnic identities. Among the religions to benefit from this trend, Islam has been at the forefront. It was in 1979 that the Ayatollah Khomeini began his ten-year-long ascendancy in Iran, a major factor in the rise of Islamic fervour in many other parts of the world.

The religious revival of the 1980s and 1990s in China has brought with it the growth of a worldwide culture in which indigenous people everywhere have played a major role. In the West, a significant strand of this culture has been a new spirituality in which indigenous religions from many parts of the world have vied with Christianity for the hearts and minds of people, and especially of youth, and on occasion even overtaken it. Education systems in the Western world, and even Christians themselves, have been happy to allocate affirmative action principles in favour of indigenous cultures, even at the expense of traditional Western ones. Among the indigenous cultures of China, the Tibetans have received by far the most attention, with the Dalai Lama and his supporters establishing a major worldwide industry in favour of Tibetan Buddhism, other features of Tibetan culture and advocacy for the political independence of Tibet.

Imagined communities?

I have found these feelings of identity in virtually all China's minorities in the 1980s and 1990s, although they are vastly weaker among some peoples than others. At the weakest end, even the Zhuang, who are noted for the extent of their acculturation with the Han, have taken steps to revive the use of their own language and knowledge of their own history and culture. At the strongest end stand the Tibetans, Uygurs and Koreans, who have loomed so large in this book. Yet it is fair to add that, apart from the Tibetans and Uygurs, the regrowth of ethnic identities is not leading to that kind of passionate resentment against domination or demands for empowerment which is found in some quarters in the West.[8]

It is legitimate to ask how genuine these revived cultures of the minorities in China are. David Wu has suggested that, while the Bai have reasserted their 'subjective "minority" identity', this 'strong Bai identity is not built on a distinct cultural identity as a total way of life' but is rather 'an expression of subjective sentiment activated recently by official promotion'.[9] In other words, it is more a culture 'reinvented' or imagined for political purposes than a genuine revival of something old.

It is true not merely in China but everywhere that nationalists are able to reinvent a past and imagine an identity to suit political or cultural purposes.[10] Some of the newly formed states of what was the Soviet Union had long histories of independence before the Bolshevik Revolution of 1917, but others were in fact new states without histories as such at all. It was the Soviet Union itself which gave birth to such republics as Tajikistan, Kyrgyzstan and Turkmenistan. Even for a state such as China, with its long history of unity under a single emperor, it has been suggested that the notion of the Chinese as a *nation* is actually quite recent, not predating the twentieth century. At least in one sense it is, then, an 'imagined' nation.[11]

It appears to follow from the material in this book that, while some of the minority cultures were 'reinvented' or 'imagined', others were partly so and yet others not at all. There is sometimes only a very hazy distinction between outright reinvention, or recovery of something either buried deeply or lost altogether, and modern or contemporary adaption and strengthening of readily available cultural phenomena. Those minorities without strong cultures, expressed above all in a rich literature written in a national language, underwent very strong Han influence which came close to extinguishing the national culture. The revival of the 1980s and 1990s was partly based on very real past features, but part was certainly an invention which owed as much to the needs of the present as to the creativities of the past. The Bai are a very good example of this trend, and others would include the Zhuang, the Bouyei and the Tujia.

There are also examples of minorities which once had much stronger cultures but had already been weakened well before the fall of the Qing dynasty. A succession of wars and suppressed rebellions over several centuries had done great damage to the political significance and culture of the Miao by the end of the nineteenth century. The Manchus ruled China from 1644–1911 but it is one of the great ironies of history that this very fact brought with it the long-term result of undermining their culture and language. The Miao and the Manchus are two peoples among those in China which perhaps had rather more to 'reinvent' or 'imagine' from the past than in fact they have done.

A people with a fairly strong culture, including traditional script, literature and tradition of anti-Chinese resistance is the Yi of Liangshan. Their script and many other features of their culture were lost during the 1950s to 1970s, but then recreated, in an adapted form, in the 1980s. The culture prevalent among the Yi in the 1990s is different from that of the 1940s, but it certainly has enough in common with its predecessor to be unmistakably and recognizably Yi.

Another group of the minorities comprises those with very strong cultures, fine literatures and arts and pervasive religions with clergies which once held powerful social and political influence. The most obvious examples are the Tibetans, Mongols and Uygurs. Among these, a sense of national identity is currently very much stronger among the Tibetans and Uygurs than the Mongols, but none of these three would need to 'reinvent' a tradition in the way that might apply to the Bai. The clergies, monasteries and mosques were ample repositories of these traditions.

In the case of the Uygurs and other Turkic peoples of Xinjiang, loyalty was traditionally much more to Islam and to local princes than to ethnicity. In particular, the Uygurs 'shared a long a close relationship with what is today Uzbek culture'.[12] The culture was certainly strong, but its uniqueness to the Uygurs was not obviously identifiable. Even the term 'Uygur' itself was 'reinvented' at a conference of Turkic peoples held in Tashkent in 1921, after a break of some thousand years, and reintroduced through Central Asia and Xinjiang in the 1920s.[13]

Moreover, even for these nationalities with very strong cultures based on their own scripts, it is possible to manufacture a picture of past glories which accord more with current political needs than with realities. One major example is the Tibetans. Because of the strong appeal of the Dalai Lama and his religion in the West, it has proved possible for his supporters to get accepted there a much rosier view of old Tibet and its society than is warranted by historical records. One does not have to read Chinese propaganda to find oppression in the government and religion of pre-1950 Tibet.

Identity versus integration: Prospects for the future

The two themes of ethnic identities and integration are in many ways dichotomous to each other. The more tightly integrated a nation-state becomes, the more one would generally expect hostilities among ethnic groups to fade. If pride in a particular nationality grows, pressures towards its secession might grow. But at the same time, it was pointed out in the Introduction that identity does not necessarily mean statehood. It should be within the ingenuity of contemporary leaders to 'find new kinds of regional standing for national communities that have no state of their own'.[14] It is possible for one people's feelings of national identity to survive and even prosper within a larger nation-state populated mainly by the members of another nationality.

What is extremely ironic in the case of China is that the feelings of identity and cultural integration among the minorities both appear to have strengthened in the 1980s and 1990s, at precisely the same period. David Wu has suggested that 'acculturation into Chinese culture and the resurgence of a minority identity are occurring at the same time'.[15] He is referring specifically to one of China's more integrated minorities, the Bai of Yunnan, but his comments may be valid in a more general sense for the great majority of China's minority peoples.

Another factor bearing on the interplay between ethnic identities and integration is modernisation. This is especially the case in a large and historically centralised state such as China. I have argued elsewhere that economic and political modernisation has contributed to the integration of the minorities with the Han in China over the twentieth century, including in the 1980s and early 1990s.[16] Modernisation refers to those processes which have tended to accompany industrialisation in other countries in the past. In effect, this meaning of the term is not very different from Deng Xiaoping's 'four modernisations' of industry, agriculture, national defence and science and technology.

There has been much debate about the long-term survival of minority cultures in China, especially that of the Tibetans which has aroused the greatest interest among all the minorities. Many have suggested that Tibetan Buddhism, arts, family life, architecture, language and other cultural features will disappear unless Tibet quickly gains political independence. That view appears to this writer to be far too pessimistic, and to underrate both the honesty of Chinese policy and the determination of the Tibetan people to retain their own culture. I saw no sign that the Chinese authorities are currently trying to suppress Tibetan or other minority cultures. Quite the contrary: the revival of ethnic identities all over China points in precisely the opposite direction.[17] In the unlikely event that Chinese authorities ever again tried to suppress minority cultures in the near to intermediate future, the overwhelming likelihood is that they would strike the same reaction as during the Cultural Revolution, namely antagonism and resistance — probably leading to a further resurgence in ethnic identities. Just as last time, this would not necessarily be equally strong among all minorities, but the Tibetans, Uygurs and Koreans are likely to be in the forefront of resistance because theirs are traditionally the strongest of the minority cultures.

On the other hand, modernisation tends all over the world to whittle away differences among cultures. The Chinese government currently follows a firm policy of modernisation and is likely to do so for the foreseeable future. The process of modernisation has affected China's minority areas in the present century, especially in the 1980s and 1990s, even though it remains tentative and weak in some places. Its effect has been generally an integrative one throughout China with the main cities of the eastern seaboard, such as Shanghai, Guangzhou and Beijing, taking the lead and spreading their influences throughout the country. Although the minority areas have been much slower to modernise than the main cities, they have quite clearly begun to feel the impact of modern trends. This has been felt in virtually all areas of life, including ideas, politics, the economy and culture.

In the case of Tibet and Xinjiang, the peoples are still extremely attached to their traditional culture, including language, arts and other social forms. But there are very clear signs of modernisation too. Literary, artistic and ideological trends elsewhere in the PRC and the world cannot help but influence what happens in Tibet and Xinjiang. Young people in the cities would sooner dance and sing disco and karaoke than adopt the traditional forms of culture.

The Koreans are the most 'modern' of China's minorities. They are also a people with a strong culture and tradition, as well as their own homeland. Even though it is currently divided, the heart of Korean culture lies in Korea itself, certainly not in China. Yet precisely because there are Korean communities in various parts of the world, this people can serve as an example illustrating degrees in the strength of ethnic identity and of modernisation. The Korean American writer Pyong Gap Min has drawn attention to the higher degree of ethnic awareness among the Koreans of China than those of Japan, giving three reasons: China's policy of autonomy; the fact that, in contrast to Japan, the Koreans live in a specific and identifiable territory in China; and the fact that the cultural influences from Korea itself are stronger among the Koreans of China than those of Japan.[18] The basic conclusions accord with my own observations and I find the first two reasons valid enough. Pyong Gap Min's argument concerning cultural influence from Korea focuses mainly on family exchange and other influence from North Korea. But in two visits to Yanbian, in 1986 and 1990, what struck me most strongly was how little influence came from the North. There is family exchange, certainly, but very few other Koreans now visit Yanbian from North Korea. On the other hand, cultural influence from South Korea is now quite extensive. Ironically, it is more modern and international than Korean in texture, including music in the modern pop idiom, knowledge of economic and other theory and — though to a very much lesser degree — Christianity.

Although I have argued here that ethnic identities and integration are both important features of contemporary Chinese minority society, there are very strong differences in the extent of each among the nationalities. It is for this reason that the identities of each particular nationality have to be distinguished from those of the others. That is why, as appropriate, this book discusses identities in the plural, with the singular used mainly to apply to individual peoples. Even within particular minorities, sharp variations occur. In his study of those people classified as Yi by the state, Stevan Harrell has drawn attention to three specific communities which show extremely different degrees of national identity and consequently of integration with each other and the Han.[19]

So, assuming that ethnic identities and the integration of the minorities into the Chinese state are both generally strong and rising, even if to different degrees depending on the locality, and assuming that they point in different directions, which of the two is likely to prove the stronger? If the tension between them moves to an open and protracted clash, a victory for ethnic identities could tear China apart, but conversely the forces of integration are more likely to hold it together. The future of China as a single nation-state is likely to depend on a range of political, economic and other factors which lie well outside the scope of this book.[20] However, it would follow from the material presented here that, in cultural terms, the forces tending towards integration are stronger than those towards ethnic identities at present. This would likely change only if the Chinese economy underwent a prolonged and severe recession and if political power struggle within the CCP were to lead to long-term and serious instability. While fragmentation in China is undoubtedly possible, it does not appear to this writer to be either inevitable or desirable. The model of Yugoslavia, the Soviet Union and Ethiopia would suggest that prolonged and violent conflict would either precede or accompany such a fragmentation.

Another possibility is for the forces of integration to prevail for some minorities, but for those of identity to do so for others. Among the vast bulk of the minorities, feelings of identity do not imply the wish for secession.[21] But could the areas where ethnic identities are strongest, Tibet and Xinjiang, secede from China, leaving the rest of the country united? Visits to a great many minority areas show that the wish for independent states is strong among the Uygurs and Tibetans, weak among a few others such as the Mongols and nonexistent among the great majority of the peoples of China. Such secessionist feelings as exist in China depend not only on culture, but on politics and other factors as well. Peoples like the Tibetans and Uygurs may feel a right to statehood on many grounds, including loss of control over their land and hatred of a perceived occupying force, in this case the Chinese.

The question of independence for Tibet and/or Xinjiang is more a political and economic question than a cultural one. Although such a scenario is possible, it seems unlikely. The reason is because Chinese policy under governments of all political persuasions have for well over two centuries insisted so strongly on the unity of China that only the collapse of the central state would allow for independence of any of its current territories. And that would more likely bring on a general fragmentation, just as happened with the Soviet Union and Yugoslavia, than the secession of one or two territories.

Could a successor government to the one led by Deng Xiaoping agree to independence for Tibet or Xinjiang? Although this possibility cannot be ruled out, history points against it. Unlike the Soviet Union or Yugoslavia, China's population belongs overwhelmingly to one nationality, namely the Han. China is also a country in which a dislike of 'chaos' (luan) and a strong central government ruling over a unified country both have a very long tradition.

The emerging cultures of the minorities hold very strong traditional characteristics, but they are also changed from the past. That is both inevitable and desirable, because a living culture is a changing culture. It is both unrealistic and unreasonable to expect any culture to remain completely unchanged. Nor is outside influence necessarily bad. In the case of China's minority cultures, the impact of modernity carries some unfortunate features, among which this writer would include the spread of an international style of Western-dominated pop music and American television programs, but it is inevitable and dominantly positive. The main issue does not seem to me to be freedom, because very few peoples choose the cultures available to·them, whether or not they control their own nation-states. What matters most is whether features essential to the traditional cultures of particular minorities survive or not. Fortunately the assimilation of minorities does not appear to be in the offing in the case of China. On the other hand, a modernised and integrated China, in which the minorities maintain their own recognisable cultures — some of them powerfully — appears quite possible. If fragmentation and ethnic conflict are the alternative, then it is certainly also desirable.

Notes

1 See Dru C. Gladney, 'Representing Nationality in China: Refiguring Majority/Minority Identities', *The Journal of Asian Studies*, vol. 53, no. 3, February 1994, especially pp. 98–99.

2 ibid., pp. 114–16.

3 See, for instance, ibid., p. 114.

4 The story, by Ma Jian, was carried in the first two 1987 issues of *Zhongguo wenxue*. For a report on the comments on the case by He Jingzhi, Deputy Head of the Propaganda Department of the Chinese Communist Party's Central Committee, see *Beijing Review*, vol. 30, no. 21, 25 May 1987, p. 28.

5 Stevan Harrell, 'Ethnicity, Local Interests, and the State: Yi Communities in Southwest China', *Comparative Studies in Society and History, An International Quarterly*, vol. 32, 1990, p. 527 calls women's clothing the 'most obvious' of 'cultural markers' distinguishing one of the Yi communities he studied from the Han.

6 See, for instance, Nancy Hartsock, 'Rethinking Modernism: Minority vs Majority Theories', in in Abdul R. JanMohamed and David Lloyd (eds), *The Nature and Context of Minority Discourse*, Oxford University Press, New York, Oxford, 1990, p. 17.

7 Melvyn C. Goldstein and Cynthia M. Beall, *Nomads of Western Tibet, The Survival of a Way of Life*, University of California Press, Berkeley, Los Angeles, 1990, p. 151.

8 See, for instance, Abdul R. JanMohamed and David Lloyd, 'Introduction: Toward a Theory of Minority Discourse: What Is To Be Done?', in JanMohamed and Lloyd (eds), *The Nature and Context of Minority Discourse*, especially pp. 1–2, 7, 13–16, and the papers of the 1986 Conference of which the cited article is the Introduction to the published version.

9 David Y.H. Wu, 'Chinese Minority Policy and the Meaning of Minority Culture: The Example of Bai in Yunnan, China', *Human Organization*, vol. 49, no. 1, Spring 1990, p. 9.

10 See Benedict Anderson, *Imagined Communities, Reflections on the Origin and Spread of Nationalism*, Verso, London, New York, 1983; rev. edn 1991, especially pp. 5–6. To be fair, Anderson himself does not distinguish communities 'by their falsity/genuineness, but by the style in which they are imagined' (p. 5). He is talking about nationalism in general, rather than that kind of ethnonationalism which leads to the breakup of large states. But the idea of 'imagined communities' appears to me to apply in both situations.

11 Gladney, 'Representing Nationality in China', pp. 98–99.

12 Eden Naby, 'Uighur Literature: The Antecedents', in Shirin Akiner (ed.), *Cultural Change and Continuity in Central Asia*, Kegan Paul International, London and New York, in association with the Central Asia Research Forum, School of Oriental and African Studies, London, 1991, p. 14.

13 See Linda Benson, *The Ili Rebellion, The Moslem Challenge to Chinese Authority in Xinjiang, 1949–1949*, M.E. Sharpe, Armonk, London, 1990, p. 30.

14 Gidon Gottlieb, 'Nations Without States', *Foreign Affairs*, vol. 73, no. 3, May/June 1994, p. 112.

15 Wu, 'Chinese Minority Policy and the Meaning of Minority Culture', p. 10.

16 See Colin Mackerras, *China's Minorities: Integration and Modernization in the Twentieth Century*, Oxford University Press, Hong Kong, 1992, especially pp. 260–73.

17 Compare the comments of Goldstein and Beall in *Nomads of Western Tibet*, especially p. 183.

18 See Pyong Gap Min, 'A Comparison of the Korean Minorities in China and Japan', *International Migration Review*, vol. 26, no. 1, Spring 1992, pp. 4–21, especially, for the 'factors contributing to differential levels of ethnicity', pp. 13–19.

19 Harrell, 'Ethnicity, Local Interests, and the State', especially pp. 541–48.

20 I have discussed this question in some detail in *China's Minorities*, especially pp. 274–77.

21 Right at the beginning of one autobiographical study by a member of the Bai, the notion of identity with no wish for secession is expressed strongly as follows: 'I am, of course, Chinese; however, I should like to add one more word: I am Bai Chinese. I belong not to the great Hans of Central China but to the Bai National Minority. At home we speak Bai, not the official language of my country, Mandarin.' See He Liyi, with Claire Anne Chik, *Mr. China's Son, A Villager's Life*, Westview Press, Boulder, San Francisco, Oxford, 1993, p. 3.

References

Books and articles

Aikebaier Mijiti, 'Shaoshu minzu wenxue', 'Minority Nationalities' Literature', *Zhongguo baike nianjian 1989 (Encyclopedic Yearbook of China 1989)*, Zhongguo da baike quanshu chubanshe, Beijing, Shanghai, 1989, p. 408.

Ali, Abdullah Yusuf (trans. and ed.), *The Holy Qur-an, Text Translation and Commentary*, Khalil Al-Rawaf, Riyadh, Saudi Arabia, 1946; The Islamic Center, Washington, 1978.

Anderson, Benedict, *Imagined Communities, Reflections on the Origin and Spread of Nationalism*, Verso, London, New York, 1983; rev. edn 1991.

Aris, Michael, with the assistance of Booz, Patrick and contributions by Sutton, S.B. and Wagner, Jeffrey, *Lamas, Princes, and Brigands, Joseph Rock's Photographs of the Tibetan Borderlands of China*, China House Gallery, China Institute in America, New York City, 1992.

Banister, Judith, *China's Changing Population*, Stanford University Press, Stanford, 1987.

Barnett, A. Doak, *China on the Eve of Communist Takeover*, Frederick A. Praeger, New York, 1963.

—— *China's Far West, Four Decades of Change*, Westview Press, Boulder, San Francisco, Oxford, 1993.

Bell, Sir Charles, *The People of Tibet*, Clarendon Press, Oxford, 1928.

Bender, Mark, 'Approaching the Literatures of China's Minority Nationalities', *China Exchange News*, vol. 21, nos 3 and 4, Fall–Winter 1993, pp. 9–16.

Benson, Linda, *The Ili Rebellion, The Moslem Challenge to Chinese Authority in Xinjiang, 1949–1949*, M.E. Sharpe, Armonk, London, 1990.

Black, Cyril E., Dupree, Louis et al., *The Modernization of Inner Asia*, M.E. Sharpe, Armonk, New York and London, England, 1991.

Border Education Section of the Ministry of Education, *Bianjiang jiaoyu gaikuang, (The General Condition of Border Education)*, Jiaoyu bu Bianjiang jiaoyu si, Chongqing, 1943.

Brief History of the Dong Nationality Compilation Group, *Dongzu jianshi (Brief History of the Dong Nationality)*, Guizhou Minzu chubanshe, Guiyang, 1985.

Brief History of the Koreans Compilation Group, *Chaoxian zu jianshi (Brief History of the Koreans)*, Yanbian Renmin chubanshe, Yanji, 1986.

Brief History of the Monba Nationality Compilation Group, *Monba zu jianshi (Brief History of the Monba Nationality)*, Xizang Renmin chubanshe, Lhasa, 1987.

Brief History of the Miao Nationality Compilation Group, *Miaozu jianshi (Brief History of the Miao Nationality)*, Guizhou Minzu chubanshe, Guiyang, 1985.

Brief History of the Mongol Nationality Compilation Group, *Menggu zu jianshi (Brief History of the Mongol Nationality)*, Nei Menggu Renmin chubanshe, Hohhot, 1985.

Brief History of the Shui Nationality Compilation Group, *Shuizu jianshi (Brief History of the Shui Nationality)*, Guizhou Minzu chubanshe, Guiyang, 1985.

Bush, Richard C. Jr., *Religion in Communist China*, Abingdon Press, Nashville and New York, 1970.

Chan, Wing-tsit, *Religious Trends in Modern China*, Columbia University Press, New York, 1953; Octagon Books, New York, 1969.

Chang Naiguang et al. (eds), *Zhongguo renkou, Ningxia fence (China's Population, Ningxia Volume)*, Zhongguo caizheng jingji chubanshe, Beijing, 1988.

Chen Qiuping, 'Progress Seen in Minority Population', *Beijing Review*, vol. 36, no. 29, 19–25 July 1993, pp. 14–17.

Chronology of Nationalities Work in Contemporary China Editorial Department, *Dangdai Zhongguo minzu gongzuo da shiji, 1949–1988 (Chronology of Nationalities Work in Contemporary China, 1949–1988)*, Minzu chubanshe, Beijing, 1990.

Conditions in Ningxia Region Compilation Group, *Ningxia qu qing (Conditions in Ningxia Region)*, Ningxia Renmin chubanshe, Yinchuan, 1988.

Dainzin, 'Reform and Growth of Tibetan Education', *China's Tibet*, vol. 5, no. 2, 1994, pp. 14–16.

Das, Sarat Chandra, edited by W.W. Rockhill, *Journey to Lhasa and Central Tibet*, Murray, London, 1902.

Diamond, Norma, 'The Miao and Poison: Interactions on China's Southwest Frontier', *Ethnology, An International Journal of Cultural and Social Anthropology*, vol. 27, no. 1, January 1988, pp. 1–25.

Ding Zhipin, *Zhongguo jin qishi nian lai jiaoyu jishi (Chronology of Chinese Education over the Last Seventy Years)*, Guoli bianyi guan, Nanjing, 1933.

Dolby, William, 'Early Chinese Plays and Theater', in Colin Mackerras (ed.), *Chinese Theater From Its Origins to the Present Day*, University of Hawaii Press, Honolulu, 1983, pp. 7–31.

Dorjee, Tashi, trans. Dhondup, K., 'Education in Tibet', *The Tibet Journal*, vol. 2, no. 4, Winter 1977, pp. 31–37.

Dreyer, June Teufel, *China's Forty Millions, Minority Nationalities and National Integration in the People's Republic of China*, Harvard University Press, Cambridge, Mass. and London, 1976.

Erikson, Erik H., 'Identity, Psychosocial', in Sills, David L. (ed.), *International Encyclopedia of the Social Sciences*, 18 vols, The Macmillan Company and The Free Press, New York, 1968–79, vol. 7, pp. 61–65.

Etherton, P.T., *In the Heart of Asia*, Houghton Mifflin, Boston and New York, 1926.

Evans, Grant (ed.), *Asia's Cultural Mosaic, An Anthropological Introduction*, Prentice Hall/Simon & Schuster (Asia) Pte Ltd., Singapore, 1993.

Feng Jiasheng et al. (comp.), *Weiwuer zu shiliao jianbian, xiace, (Concise Collection of Historical Materials on the Uygurs)*, vol. 2, Minzu chubanshe, Beijing, 1981.

Feng Liang (ed.), *Xizang xin xiaoshuo (New Tibetan Fiction)*, Xizang Renmin chubanshe, Lhasa, 1989.

Fitzgerald, C.P., *The Tower of Five Glories, A Study of the Min Chia of Ta Li, Yunnan*, The Cresset Press, London, 1941; Hyperion Press, Westport, Connecticut, 1973.

Forbes, Andrew D.W., *Warlords and Muslims in Chinese Central Asia, A Political History of Republican Sinkiang 1911–1949*, Cambridge University Press, Cambridge, 1986.

Fox, Robin, *Kinship and Marriage, An Anthropological Perspective*, Penguin Books, Harmondsworth, 1967; 1976.

Fu Xiruo, 'Lun Xinjiang sheng jiaoyu' ('On Education in Xinjiang Province'), in Gansu Provincial Library Bibliography Department, comp., *Xibei minzu zongjiao shiliao wenzhai (Xinjiang fence), (Digest of Historical Materials on Nationalities and Religions of the Northwest) (Xinjiang Volumes)*, 2 vols, Gansu sheng tushuguan, Lanzhou, 1985, vol. 2, pp. 948–56.

General Account of the Yanbian Korean Autonomous Prefecture Compilation Group, *Yanbian Chaoxian zu zizhi zhou gaikuang (General Account of the Yanbian Korean Autonomous Prefecture)*, Yanbian Renmin chubanshe, Yanji, 1984.

Gladney, Dru C., *Muslim Chinese, Ethnic Nationalism in the People's Republic*, published by Council on East Asian Studies, Harvard University, and distributed by Harvard University Press, Cambridge, Mass. and London, 1991.

—— 'Representing Nationality in China: Refiguring Majority/Minority Identities', *The Journal of Asian Studies*, vol. 53, no. 3, February 1994, pp. 92–123.

Gibb, H.A.R. and Kramers, J.H., *Shorter Encyclopaedia of Islam*, Cornell University Press, Ithaca, NY, 1953.

Goldstein, Carl, 'Letter from Xinjiang', *Far Eastern Economic Review*, vol. 145, no. 31, 3 August 1989, p. 37.

Goldstein, Melvyn C. and Beall, Cynthia M., *Nomads of Western Tibet, The Survival of a Way of Life*, University of California Press, Berkeley, Los Angeles, 1990.

Gottlieb, Gidon, 'Nations Without States', *Foreign Affairs*, vol. 73, no. 3, May/June 1994, pp. 100–12.

Goulart, Peter, *Forgotten Kingdom*, John Murray, London, 1957.

Graham, David Crockett, *Folk Religion in Southwest China*, Smithsonian Press, Washington DC., 1961.

Guizhou Provincial Editorial Group, *Miaozu shehui lishi diaocha, Yi, Er (Social and Historical Investigations on the Miao Nationality, One and Two)*, Guizhou minzu chubanshe, Guiyang, 1986 and 1987.

Han Woo-keun, trans. Lee Kyung-shik, *The History of Korea*, Eul-yoo Publishing Company, Seoul, 1970; 1981.

Handbook on Nationalities Work Editorial Department, *Minzu gongzuo shouce (Handbook on Nationalities Work)*, Yunnan Renmin chubanshe, Kunming, 1985.

Harrell, Stevan, 'Ethnicity, Local Interests, and the State: Yi Communities in Southwest China', *Comparative Studies in Society and History, An International Quarterly*, vol. 32, 1990, pp. 515–48.

Harrer, Heinrich, trans. Graves, Richard, *Seven Years in Tibet*, Rupert Hart-Davis and the Book Society, Britain, 1953; J.P. Tarcher, Los Angeles, 1982.

Harris, Marvin, *Culture, People, Nature, An Introduction to General Anthropology*, 2nd edn, Harper & Row, New York, 1975.

Hartsock, Nancy, 'Rethinking Modernism: Minority vs. Majority Theories', in Abdul R. JanMohamed and David Lloyd (eds), *The Nature and Context of Minority Discourse*, Oxford University Press, New York, Oxford, 1990, pp. 17–36.

He Liyi, with Chik, Claire Anne, *Mr. China's Son, A Villager's Life*, Westview Press, Boulder, San Francisco, Oxford, 1993.

He Xiangwei, Yuan Jianhua and He Lin, 'Shaoshu minzu renkou xianzhuang fenxi' ('Analysis of the Present Condition in the Populations of the Minority Nationalities'), in Ma Bin et al., *Zhongguo renkou kongzhi: shijian yu duice (China's Population Control: Practice and Countermeasures)*, Zhongguo guoji guangbo chubanshe, Beijing, 1990, pp. 305–11.

Heissig, Walther, trans. Thomson, D.J.S., *A Lost Civilization, The Mongols Rediscovered*, Thames and Hudson, London, 1966.

—— *Geschichte der mongolischen Literatur*, 2 vols, Otto Harrassowitz, Wiesbaden, 1972.

—— trans. Samuel, Geoffrey, *The Religions of Mongolia*, Routledge & Kegan Paul, London and Henley, 1980.

History of Dong Literature Compilation Group, *Dongzu wenxue shi (History of Dong Literature)*, Guizhou Minzu chubanshe, Guiyang, 1988.

Hu, Chang-tu, in collaboration with Chu, Samuel C., Clark, Leslie L., Lo, Jung-pang and Wu, Yuan-li, ed. Hsia Hsiao, *China, Its People, Its Society, Its Culture*, HRAF Press, New Haven, 1960.

Huang Wei, 'Female Participation in Government', *Beijing Review*, vol. 36, no. 29, 19–25 July 1993, pp. 25–28.

Huang Xianfan, Huang Zengqing and Zhang Yimin, *Zhuangzu tongshi (General History of the Zhuang Nationality)*, Guangxi Minzu chubanshe, Nanning, 1988.

Huang Xianlin, Mo Datong et al. (eds), *Zhongguo renkou, Guangxi fence (China's Population, Volume on Guangxi)*, Zhongguo caizheng jingji chubanshe, Beijing, 1988.

Inner Mongolian Autonomous Region Editorial Group, *Menggu zu shehui lishi diaocha (Social and Historical Investigations on the Mongolian Nationality)*, Nei Menggu Renmin chubanshe, Hohhot, 1985.

Investigation Group in Tibet on Topics in Nationality Education, 'Xizang jiaoyu xianzhuang yu duice, Xizang jiaoyu diaocha baogao' ('The Present Condition and Countermeasures of Tibetan Education, Investigation Report on Tibetan Education'), in Geng Jinsheng and Wang Xihong (eds), *Xizang jiaoyu yanjiu (Studies on Tibetan Education)*, Zhongyang minzu xueyuan chubanshe, Beijing, 1989, pp. 27–49.

Jagchid, Sechin and Hyer, Paul, *Mongolia's Culture and Society*, Westview Press, Boulder, 1979.

JanMohamed, Abdul R. and Lloyd, David, 'Introduction: Toward a Theory of Minority Discourse: What Is To Be Done?', in Abdul R. JanMohamed and David Lloyd (eds), *The Nature and Context of Minority Discourse*, Oxford University Press, New York, Oxford, 1990, pp. 1–16.

Ji Yonghai and Zhao Zhizhong, *Manzu minjian wenxue gailun (Outline of Manchu Folk Literature)*, Zhongyang minzu xueyuan chubanshe, Beijing, 1991.

Jiahefu Mierzhahan, trans. Nabijian Muhamudehan and He Xingliang, *Hasake zu (The Kazaks)*, Minzu chubanshe, Beijing, 1989.

Jiang Yingliang, *Daizu shi (History of the Dai)*, Sichuan Minzu chubanshe, Chengdu, 1983.

Jin Donghe, trans. from Korean to Chinese by the Research Room for the History of the Youth Movement of the Communist Youth League's Yanbian Prefectural Committee, *Yanbian qingnian yundong shi (History of Yanbian's Youth Movement)*, Yanbian Renmin chubanshe, Yanji, 1989.

Jin Dongxun, 'Jianlun jianguo hou Chaoxian zu de xiaoshuo chuangzuo' ('On the Creation of Korean Nationality Fiction after the PRC's Founding'), in Yanbian Literature and Art Research Institute, *Chaoxian zu wenxue yishu gaiguan (General Survey of Korean Literature and Arts)*, n.p., 1982, pp. 30–65.

Kane, Penny, *The Second Billion, Population and Family Planning in China*, Penguin, Ringwood, 1987.

228 CHINA'S MINORITY CULTURES: IDENTITIES AND INTEGRATION SINCE 1912

Kaye, Lincoln, 'Back to the Old Faith', *Far Eastern Economic Review*, vol. 155, no. 14, 9 April 1992, p. 20.

Kinkley, Jeffrey C., *The Odyssey of Shen Congwen*, Stanford University Press, Stanford, 1987.

Kurban Barat, *Karguli*, Xinjiang Halk nashriyati [Renmin chubanshe], Ürümqi, 1993.

Kwong, Julia (ed.), *Education of Minorities*, issue of *Chinese Education*, vol. 22, no. 1, Spring 1989.

Lang, Olga, *Chinese Family and Society*, Yale University Press, New Haven, 1946.

Lao She, trans. Howard-Gibbon, John, *Teahouse, A Play in Three Acts*, Foreign Languages Press, Beijing, 1980.

Lattimore, Owen, *Manchuria, Cradle of Conflict*, rev. edn, Macmillan, New York, 1935, AMS, New York, 1975 reprint.

—— et al., *Pivot of Asia, Sinkiang and the Inner Asian Frontiers of China and Russia*, Little, Brown and Co., Boston, 1950, AMS, New York, 1975 reprint.

Lee, Chae-Jin, *China's Korean Minority, The Politics of Ethnic Education*, Westview Press, Boulder and London, 1986.

Li Zuanxu, *Baizu wenxue shilüe (Outline of the History of the Literature of the Bai)*, Zhongguo minjian wenyi chubanshe (Yunnan ban), Kunming, 1984.

Liang Oudi, 'Guizhou de Miaomin jiaoyu' ('Education among the Miao People of Guizhou'), *Bianzheng gonglun (Border Politics Forum)*, vol. 3, no. 2, February 1944, pp. 51–60.

Lin Xinnai (ed.), *Zhonghua fengsu daguan (Compendium of Chinese Customs)*, Shanghai Wenyi chubanshe, Shanghai, 1991.

Ling Nai-min, Kung Wei-yang et al. (comp.), *Tibet, 1950–1967*, Union Research Institute, Hong Kong, 1968.

Liu Hongkang et al. (eds), *Zhongguo renkou, Sichuan fence (China's Population, Volume on Sichuan)*, Zhongguo caizheng jingji chubanshe, Beijing, 1988.

Liu Jinglong, 'Cong kongzhi renkou yundong kan Yisilan jiao shehuiguan de yanjin' ('A Look at the Evolution of Islam's Social View through Population Control'), in Composition Group for *Research Papers on Islam in China, Zhongguo Yisilan jiao yanjiu wenji (Research Papers on Islam in China)*, Ningxia Renmin chubanshe, Yinchuan, 1988, pp. 416–29.

Liu Mingshan, Chen Chen et al., *Minzu diqu caizheng gailun (An Introduction to the Finances of the Nationality Areas)*, Guangxi Renmin chubanshe, Nanning, 1989.

Liu Qinghui, 'Xizang minzu jiaoyu shiye de chuangban he fazhan' ('The Establishment and Development of the Tibetan Nationality Education Cause'), in Geng Jinsheng, Wang Xihong et al. (eds), *Xizang jiaoyu yanjiu*, Zhongyang minzu xueyuan chubanshe, Beijing, 1989, pp. 109-22.

Liu Rui et al. (eds), *Zhongguo renkou, Xizang fence (China's Population, Volume on Tibet)*, Zhongguo caizheng jingji chubanshe, Beijing, 1988.

Luo Jiansheng, *Wuzibieke zu (The Uzbeks)*, Minzu chubanshe, Beijing, 1990.

Luo Zhufeng et al. (eds), *Zhongguo da baike quanshu, zongjiao (China Encyclopedia, Religion)*, Zhongguo da baike quanshu chubanshe, Beijing, Shanghai, 1988.

Luo Zhufeng and Huang Xinchuan, 'Zongjiao', in Luo Zhufeng et al. (eds), *Zhongguo da baike quanshu, zongjiao*, Zhongguo da baike quanshu chubanshe, Beijing, Shanghai, 1988, pp. 1–9.

Ma Cibo, 'Huijiao yu Huizu bian' ('Debate on the Hui Religion and the Hui Nationality'), in Gansu Provincial Library Bibliography Department (comp.), *Xibei minzu zongjiao shiliao wenzhai (Gansu fence) (Digest of Historical Materials on Nationalities and Religions of the Northwest) (Gansu Volume)*, Gansu sheng tushuguan, Lanzhou, 1984, pp. 225–36.

Ma Fulong, 'Yisilan zai Ningxia' ('Islam in Ningxia'), in Gansu Provincial Library Bibliography Department (comp.), *Xibei minzu zongjiao shiliao wenzhai (Ningxia fence) (Digest of Historical Materials on Nationalities and Religions of the Northwest [Ningxia Volume])*, Gansu sheng tushuguan, Lanzhou, 1986, pp. 215–28.

Ma Hetian, 'Qinghai zhi zongjiao' ('The Religions of Qinghai'), in Gansu Provincial Library Bibliography Department (comp.), *Xibei minzu zongjiao shiliao wenzhai (Qinghai fence) (Digest of Historical Materials on Nationalities and Religions of the Northwest [Qinghai Volumes])*, 2 vols, Gansu sheng tushuguan, Lanzhou, 1986,vol. 2, pp. 621–28.

Ma, Rong, 'Han and Tibetan Residential Patterns in Lhasa', *The China Quarterly*, no. 128, December 1991, pp. 814–35.

Ma Xueliang, Liang Tingwang, Zhang Gongjin et al., *Zhongguo shaoshu minzu wenxue shi (History of the Literatures of China's Minority Nationalities)*, 2 vols, Zhongyang minxu xueyuan chubanshe, Beijing, 1992.

Ma Yin et al. (eds), trans. Liu Qizhong et al., *China's Minority Nationalities*, Foreign Languages Press, Beijing, 1989.

MacInnis, Donald E. (comp.), *Religious Policy and Practice in Communist China*, Macmillan, New York, Collier-Macmillan, London, 1972.

Mackerras, Colin, 'Traditional Mongolian Performing Arts in Inner Mongolia', *The Australian Journal of Chinese Affairs*, no. 10, July 1983, pp. 17–38.

—— 'Education in the Guomindang Period, 1928–1949', in David Pong and Edmund S.K. Fung (eds), *Ideal and Reality, Social and Political Change in Modern China, 1860–1949*, University Press of America, Lanham, New York, London, 1985, pp. 153–83.

—— 'Aspects of Bai Culture, Change and Continuity in a Yunnan Nationality', *Modern China, An International Quarterly of History and Social Science*, vol. 14, no. 1, January 1988, pp. 51–84.

—— 'Drama in the Tibetan Autonomous Region', *Asian Theatre Journal*, vol. 5, no. 2, Fall 1988, pp. 198–219.

—— *Chinese Drama, A Historical Survey*, New World Press, Beijing, 1990.

—— 'Integration and the Dramas of China's Minorities', *Asian Theatre Journal*, vol. 9, no. 1, Spring 1992, pp. 1–37.

—— *China's Minorities: Integration and Modernization in the Twentieth Century*, Oxford University Press, Hong Kong, 1994.

—— 'Religion, Politics and the Economy in Inner Mongolia and Ningxia', in Edward H. Kaplan and Donald W. Whisenhunt (eds), *Opuscula Altaica: Essays Presented in Honor of Henry Schwarz*, Center for East Asian Studies, Western Washington University, Bellingham, Washington, 1994, pp. 437–64.

Mackerras, Colin, Taneja, Pradeep and Young, Graham, *China Since 1978, Reform, Modernisation and 'Socialism with Chinese Characteristics'*, Longman Cheshire, Melbourne, 1994.

Manduertu, 'Zhongguo beifang minzu de saman jiao' ('The Shamanism of China's Northern Nationalities'), in Jilin Provincial Nationalities Research Institute, *Saman jiao wenhua yanjiu, diyi ji (Research on Shamanistic Culture, Volume I)*, Jilin Renmin chubanshe, Changchun, 1988, pp. 1–9.

Mao Xing (gen. ed.), *Zhongguo shaoshu minzu wenxue (The Literatures of China's Minority Nationalities)*, 3 vols, Hunan Renmin chubanshe, Changsha, 1983.

Martin, Helmut and Kinkley, Jeffrey (eds), *Modern Chinese Writers, Self-Portrayals*, M.E. Sharpe, Armonk, London, 1992.

McKhann, Charles F., 'The Naxi and the Nationalities Question', in Harrell, Stevan (ed.), *Cultural Encounters on China's Ethnic Frontiers*, University of Washington Press, Seattle and London, 1995, pp. 39–62.

Michael, Franz, 'Non-Chinese Nationalities and Religious Communities', in Wu Yuan-li, Franz Michael et al., *Human Rights in the People's Republic of China*, Westview Press, Boulder and London, 1988, pp. 268–86.

Min, Pyong Gap, 'A Comparison of the Korean Minorities in China and Japan', *International Migration Review*, vol. 26, no. 1, Spring 1992, pp. 4–21.

Ministry of Education Advisers' Room, *Jiaoyu faling (Laws and Decrees on Education)*, Jiaoyu bu, Chongqing, Nanjing, 1946.

Morigendi, 'Dawoer zu zhi zongjiao xinyang' ('The Religious Beliefs of the Daur Nationality'), in Jilin Provincial Nationalities Research Institute, *Saman jiao wenhua yanjiu, diyi ji (Research on Shamanistic Culture, Vol. 1)*, Jilin Renmin chubanshe, Changchun, 1988, pp. 136–48.

Mullin, Chris and Wangyal, Phuntsog, *The Tibetans: Two Perspectives on Tibetan–Chinese Relations*, Minority Rights Group, London, 1983.

Naby, Eden, 'Uighur Literature: The Antecedents', in Shirin Akiner (ed.), *Cultural Change and Continuity in Central Asia*, Kegan Paul International, London and New York, in association with the Central Asia Research Forum, School of Oriental and African Studies, London, 1991, pp. 14–29.

Norbu, Thubten Jigme and Turnbull, Colin M., *Tibet, Its History, Religion and People*, Chatto & Windus, London, 1969; Penguin, Harmondsworth, 1987.

Olivier, Bernard Vincent, *The Implementation of China's Nationality Policy in the Northeastern Provinces*, Mellen Research University Press, San Francisco, 1993.

Outline of the Ningxia Hui Autonomous Region Compilation Group, *Ningxia Huizu zizhi qu gaikuang (Outline of the Ningxia Hui Autonomous Region)*, Ningxia Renmin chubanshe, Yinchuan, 1986.

Pan Zhifu et al. (eds), *Zhongguo renkou, Guizhou fence (China's Population, Volume on Guizhou)*, Zhongguo caizheng jingji chubanshe, Beijing, 1988.

Pas, Julian F., 'Introduction: Chinese Religion in Transition', in Julian F. Pas (ed.), *The Turning of the Tide, Religion in China Today*, Hong Kong Branch of the Royal Asiatic Society and Oxford University Press, Hong Kong, 1989, pp. 1–24.

Pepper, Suzanne, 'Chinese Education After Mao: Two Steps Forward, Two Steps Back and Begin Again?', *The China Quarterly*, no. 81, March 1980, pp. 1–65.

Platte, Erika, 'China's Fertility Transition: The One-Child Campaign', *Pacific Affairs*, vol. 57, no. 4, Winter 1984–85, pp. 646–71.

Postiglione, Gerard A., 'The Implications of Modernization for the Education of China's National Minorities', in Ruth Hayhoe (ed.), *Education and Modernization, The Chinese Experience*, Pergamon Press, Oxford, 1992, pp. 307–36.

Prasithrathsint, Amara, 'The Linguistic Mosaic', in Grant Evans (ed.), *Asia's Cultural Mosaic, An Anthropological Introduction*, Prentice Hall Simon & Schuster [Asia] Pte Ltd., Singapore, 1993, pp. 63–88.

Qiu Pu, trans. Wang Huimin, *The Oroqens, China's Nomadic Hunters*, Foreign Languages Press, Beijing, 1983.

Qu Liuyi, 'Zhongguo ge minzu nuoxi de fenlei, tezheng ji qi "huo huashi" jiazhi' ('The Categories, Features and Value as a "Living Fossil" of the Chinese *Nuo* Drama of Every Nationality', in Tuo Xiuming et al.(eds), *Zhongguo nuo wenhua lunwen xuan (A Selection of Papers on China's Nuo Culture)*, Guizhou minzu chubanshe, Guiyang, 1989.

Reed, Linda A., *Education in the People's Republic of China and U.S.–China Educational Exchanges*, National Association for Foreign Student Affairs, Washington DC, 1988.

Research Institute of All China Women's Federation Research Office of Shaanxi Provincial Women's Federation (comp.), *Zhongguo funü tongji ziliao (1949–1989) (Statistics on Chinese Women [1949–1989])*, Zhongguo tongji chubanshe, Beijing, 1991.

Richardson, H.E., *A Short History of Tibet*, E.P. Dutton, New York, 1962.

Schwartz, Ronald D., *Circle of Protest, Political Ritual in the Tibetan Uprising*, Hurst & Company, London, 1994.

Seymour, James D., *China, The Politics of Revolutionary Reintegration*, Thomas Y. Crowell, New York,1976.

Shi Honggui, 'Xiangxi Miaozu kaocha ji (zhailu)' ('Explorations of the Miao of Western Hunan [Summary]'), in Zhang Ermu et al. (eds), *Xiangxi wenshi ziliao, di shijiu ji, Miaojiang guzhen (Materials of the Culture and History of Western Hunan, Vol. 19, Old Towns of the Miao Borderlands)*, *Xiangxi wenshi ziliao* bianji bu, Jishou, 1990, pp. 139–52.

Shi Jinhong, 'Mantan Guizhou minzu yuwen fazhan huanman de yinyou ji ying caiqu de cuoshi' ('On the Slow Development of the Nationality Spoken and Written Languages in Guizhou and the Measures which Ought to be Adopted'), in Ofice for Nationality Spoken and Written

Languages of the Guizhou Provincial Nationality Affairs Commission, *Guizhou shuangyu jiaoxue lunwen ji (Papers on Two-Language Education in Guizhou)*, Guizhou minzu chubanshe, Guiyang, 1989, pp. 107–12.

Shi Qigui, *Xiangxi Miaozu shidi diaocha baogao (Report of an On-the-Spot Investigation of the Miao of Western Hunan)*, Hunan Renmin chubanshe, Changsha, 1986.

Singer, Milton, 'The Concept of Culture', in David L. Sills (ed.), *International Encyclopedia of the Social Sciences*, 18 vols, The Macmillan Company & The Free Press, United States of America, 1968–79, vol. 3, pp. 527–43.

Skrine, C.P. and Nightingale, Pamela, *Macartney at Kashgar, New Light on British, Chinese, and Russian Activities in Sinkiang, 1890–1918*, Methuen, London, 1973; Oxford University Press, Hong Kong, Oxford, 1987.

Snellgrove, David and Richardson, Hugh, *A Cultural History of Tibet*, Weidenfeld and Nicolson, London, 1968.

Song Enchang, *Yunnan shaoshu minzu yanjiu wenji (Collection of Studies on the Minority Nationalities of Yunnan)*, Yunnan Renmin chubanshe, Kunming, 1986.

Song Naigong et al.(eds), *Zhongguo renkou, Nei Menggu fence (China's Population, Volume on Inner Mongolia)*, Zhongguo caizheng jingji chubanshe, Beijing, 1987.

Song Qixia,'Tantan shenger yunü', *Minzu tuanjie*, no. 3, 15 March 1983, pp. 46–47.

Sorensen, Clark W., 'Asian Families, Domestic Group Formation', in Grant Evans (ed.), *Asia's Cultural Mosaic, An Anthropological Introduction*, Prentice Hall/Simon & Schuster [Asia] Pte Ltd, Singapore, 1993, pp. 89–117.

Spicer, Edward H. 'Acculturation', in David L. Sills (ed.), *International Encyclopedia of the Social Sciences*, 18 vols, The Macmillan Company & The Free Press, United States of America, 1968–79, vol. 1, pp. 21–27.

Stacey, Judith, *Patriarchy and Socialist Revolution in China*, University of California Press, Berkeley, 1983.

State Nationalities Affairs Commission Finance and Economic Section, *Minzu gongzuo tongji tiyao, 1949–1987 (Summary of Nationalities Work Statistics, 1949–1987)*, n.p., 1988.

Stein, R.A., *Recherches sur l'épopée et le barde au Tibet*, Presses universitaires de France, Paris, 1959.

—— trans. Stapleton Driver, J.E., *Tibetan Civilization*, Faber and Faber, London, 1972.

Sun Hanwen, 'Qinghai minzu gaiguan' ('Survey of Qinghai's Nationalities'), in Gansu Provincial Library Bibliography Department, comp., *Xibei minzu zongjiao shiliao wenzhai (Qinghai fence) (Digest of Historical Materials on Nationalities and Religions of the Northwest) (Qinghai Volumes)*, 2 vols, Gansu sheng tushuguan, Lanzhou, 1986, vol. 1, pp. 290–315.

Survey of the Sandu Shui Autonomous County Compilation Group, *Sandu Shuizu zizhi xian gaikuang (Survey of the Sandu Shui Autonomous County)*, Guizhou Renmin chubanshe, Guiyang, 1986.

Survey of the Sanjiang Dong Nationality Autonomous County Compilation
Group, *Sanjiang Dongzu zizhi xian gaikuang (Survey of the Sanjiang Dong
Nationality Autonomous County)*, Guangxi Minzu chubanshe, Nanning,
1984.

Sutton, S.B., 'Joseph Rock: Restless Spirit', in Michael Aris, with the assistance of Patrick Booz and contributions by S.B. Sutton and Jeffrey
Wagner, *Lamas, Princes, and Brigands, Joseph Rock's Photographs of the
Tibetan Borderlands of China*, China House Gallery, China Institute in
America, New York City, 1992, pp. 22–27.

Tashi Dawa, *A Soul in Bondage, Stories from Tibet*, Panda Books, Beijing, 1992.

Thompson, John B., *Ideology and Modern Culture, Critical Social Theory in the
Era of Mass Communication*, Polity Press, Cambridge, 1990.

Tibetan Social and Historical Investigation Materials Series Editorial Group,
*Monba zu shehui lishi diaocha, Er (Social and Historical Investigations of the
Monba Nationality, Two)*, Xizang Renmin chubanshe, Lhasa, 1988.

Tibetan Social and Historical Investigation Materials Series Editorial Group,
*Zangzu shehui lishi diaocha, Er, San, (Social and Historical Investigations of
the Tibetan Nationality, Two and Three)*, Xizang Renmin chubanshe, Lhasa,
1988 and 1989.

Tiley Chodag, trans. W. Tailing, *Tibet, The Land and the People*, New World
Press, Beijing, 1988.

Tucci, Giuseppe, trans. Geoffrey Samuel, *The Religions of Tibet*, Routledge
& Kegan Paul, London and Henley, 1980.

Tucci, Giuseppe, trans. J.E. Stapleton Driver, *Tibet, Land of Snows*, London,
Elek, Stein and Day, New York, 1967.

Tuo Xiuming et al. (eds), *Zhongguo nuo wenhua lunwen xuan (A Selection of
Papers on China's Nuo Culture)*, Guizhou minzu chubanshe, Guiyang, 1989.

Tylor, Edward B., *Primitive Culture: Researches into the Development of
Mythology, Philosophy, Religion, Language, Art, and Custom*, 2 vols.,
J. Murray, London, 1871.

Vohra, Ranbir, *Lao She and the Chinese Revolution*, East Asian Research Center,
Harvard University, Cambridge, Mass., 1974.

Vreeland, Herbert Harold III, *Mongol Community and Kinship Structure*, HRAF
Press, New Haven, 1962; Greenwood Press, Westport, Conn., 1973.

Waardenburg, Jacques, 'Islam in China: Western Studies', in Shirin Akiner
(ed.), *Cultural Change and Continuity in Central Asia*, Kegan Paul
International, London, 1991, pp. 306–43.

Walker, J.T. and De Lacouperie, A. Terrien, 'Tibet', in *The Encyclopædia
Britannica, A Dictionary of Arts, Sciences, and General Literature, Ninth Edition,
Volume XXIII*, Adam and Charles Black, Edinburgh, 1888, pp. 337–48.

Wang Baolin, Xie Yunmei, Wu Lide et al. (eds), *Zhongguo shaoshu minzu
xiandai wenxue (The Modern Literatures of China's Minority Nationalities)*,
Guangxi Renmin chubanshe, Nanning, 1989.

Wang Duanyu, 'Lama jiao yu Zangzu renkou' ('Lamaism and the Population
of the Tibetans'), *Minzu yanjiu (Nationality Studies)*, no. 2, 20 March 1984,
pp. 44–57.

Wang Huazao et al., *Zhongguo dangdai wenxue jianshi*, Hunan Renmin chubanshe, Changsha, 1985.

Wang Wenhan, 'Qinghai Meng Zang renmin zhi zongjiao xinyang' ('The Religious Beliefs of the Mongol and Tibetan Peoples of Qinghai'), in Gansu Provincial Library Bibliography Department (comp.), *Xibei minzu zongjiao shiliao wenzhai (Qinghai fence) (Digest of Historical Materials on Nationalities and Religions of the Northwest) (Qinghai Volumes)*, 2 vols, Gansu sheng tushuguan, Lanzhou, 1986, vol. 2, pp. 632–36.

Wang Xihong, 'Yi shehuizhuyi chuji jieduan lilun wei zhizhen dui Xizang jiaoyu teshuxing jinxing zairenshi' ('A Reconsideration of the Special Features of Tibetan Education on the Basis of the Theory of the Primary Stage of Socialism'), in Geng Jinsheng and Wang Xihong (eds), *Xizang jiaoyu yanjiu (Studies on Tibetan Education)*, Zhongyang minzu xueyuan chubanshe, Beijing, 1989, pp. 16–26.

Winnington, Alan, *The Slaves of the Cool Mountains, The Ancient Social Conditions and Changes Now in Progress on the Remote South-Western Borders of China*, Lawrence & Wishart, London, 1959.

Wolf, Arthur P. and Huang, Chieh-shan, *Marriage and Adoption in China, 1845–1945*, Stanford University Press, Stanford, 1980.

Wolf, Margery, *Revolution Postponed, Women in Contemporary China*, Stanford University Press, Stanford, 1985.

Wu, Aitchen K., *Turkistan Tumult*, Methuen, London, 1940.

Wu, David Y.H., 'Chinese Minority Policy and the Meaning of Minority Culture: The Example of Bai in Yunnan, China', *Human Organization*, vol. 49, no. 1, Spring 1990, pp. 1–13.

Wu Zhongyang, *Zhongguo dangdai minzu wenxue gaiguan (Outline of China's Contemporary Nationalities Literatures)*, Zhongyang minzu xueyuan chubanshe, Beijing 1986.

Wulanshaobu, 'Zhongguo Guomindang de dui Meng zhengce (1928–1949)' ('The Mongolia Policies of China's Nationalist Party 1928–1949'), in CCP Inner Mongolian Regional Party History Research Institute of the Inner Mongolian University and Inner Mongolian Recent and Modern History Research Institute of the Inner Mongolian University (eds), *Nei Menggu jindai shi luncong, di sanji (Papers on Recent Inner Mongolian History, Volume 3)*, Nei Menggu Renmin chubanshe, Hohhot, 1987, pp. 188–317.

Wurm, S.A. et al., *Language Atlas of China*, Longman on behalf of the Australian Academy of the Humanities and the Chinese Academy of Social Sciences, Hong Kong, 1987.

Xie Qihuang, *Minzu jiaoyu gailun (Introduction to Nationality Education)*, Guangxi Minzu chubanshe, Nanning, 1984.

Xinjiang Social Sciences Academy's Nationalities Research Institute, *Xinjiang jianshi, dier ce*, Xinjiang Renmin chubanshe, Ürümqi, 1980.

Xinjiang Uygur Autonomous Region Education Commission Higher Education History Teaching Material Compilation Group, *Xinjiang difang shi (History of the Xinjiang Region)*, Xinjiang daxue chubanshe, Ürümqi, 1992.

Xue Li and Ke Yang (eds), *Huaer xuanji (Selection of Huaer)*, Gansu Renmin chubanshe, Lanzhou, 1980.

Yan Ruxian, trans. Xing Wenjun, 'A Living Fossil of the Family — A Study of the Family Structure of the Naxi Nationality in the Lugu Lake Region', *Social Sciences in China*, vol. 3, no. 4, December 1982, pp. 60–83.

Yan Ruxian and Song Zhaolin, *Yongning Naxi zu de muxi zhi (The Matriarchy of the Naxi of Yongning)*,Yunnan Renmin chubanshe, Kunming, 1983.

Yang Hanxian, 'Xi'nan jizhong zongzu de hunyin fanwei' ('The Range of Marriage among Some Southwestern Clans'), *Bianzheng gonglun (Border Politics Forum)*, vol. 3, no. 6, June 1944, pp. 48–51.

Yang Liangcai, Tao Lifan and Deng Minwen, *Zhongguo shaoshu minzu wenxue (The Literatures of China's Minority Nationalities)*, Renmin chubanshe, Beijing, 1985.

Yang Quan, *Dongzu minjian wenxue shi (A History of Dong Folk Literature)*, Zhongyang minzu xueyuan chubanshe, Beijing, 1992.

Yang Yixing and Wang Yanxing, 'Renzhen guanche shaoshu minzu renkou zhengce, nuli cujin ge minzu gongtong fanrong' ('Earnestly Carry Out the Minority Nationalties Population Policies and Energetically Push Forward the Common Prosperity of Every Nationality'), in Deng Zhixian (ed.), *Minzu renkouxue sanlun (Articles on the Demography of Nationalities)*, Guizhou Renmin chubanshe, Guiyang, 1990, pp. 75–103.

Yang Yixing, Zhang Tianlu and Xiong Yu, *Zhongguo shaoshu minzu renkou yanjiu (Studies on the Populations of China's Minority Nationalities)*, Minzu chubanshe, Beijing, 1988.

Yang Zhiyong et al., *Yunnan shaoshu minzu hunsu zhi (Marriage Customs of Yunnan's Minority Nationalities)*, Yunnan Minzu chubanshe, Kunming, 1983.

Ye Dabing, Wubing'an et al. (eds), *Zhongguo fengsu cidian (Dictionary of Chinese Customs)*, Shanghai cishu chubanshe, Shanghai, 1990.

Yunnan Provincial Editorial Committee of the *Five Series on Nationalities Problems, Baizu shehui lishi diaocha (Explorations in the Society and History of the Bai Nationality)*, Yunnan Renmin chubanshe, Kunming, 1983.

Zhang Juling, *Qingdai Manzu zuojia wenxue gailun (Survey of Manchu Authored Literature in the Qing Dynasty)*, Zhongyang minzu xueyuan chubanshe, Beijing, 1990.

Zhang Jun, 'Ru mo de shijie — lun dangdai Xizang xiaoshuo' ('A World Like Magic — On Contemporary Tibetan Fiction', in Feng Liang (ed.), *Xizang xin xiaoshuo (New Tibetan Fiction)*, Xizang Renmin chubanshe, Lhasa, 1989, pp. 431–68.

Zhang Tianlu, *Xizang renkou de bianqian (Changes in Tibetan Population)*, Zhongguo Zangxue chubanshe, Beijing, 1989.

Zhang Tianlu, 'Zhongguo shaoshu minzu renkou' ('The Populations of China's Minority Nationalities'), in Deng Zhixian (ed.), *Minzu renkouxue sanlun (Articles on the Demography of Nationalities)*, Guizhou Renmin chubanshe, Guiyang, 1990, pp. 1–74.

Zhang Tianlu, Song Zhuansheng and Ma Zhengliang, *Zhongguo Musilin renkou (China's Muslim Populations)*, Ningxia Renmin chubanshe, Yinchuan, 1991.

Zhang Wenxun et al., *Baizu wenxue shi, xiuding ban (History of Bai Literature, Revised Edition)*, Yunnan Renmin chubanshe, Kunming, 1983.

Zhang Yongqing, 'Dui shehuizhuyi shiqi woguo Yisilanjiao yu jingji fazhan guanxi de jidian sikao' ('Some Reflections on the Relationship between Economic Development and Islam in Our Country in the Socialist Period'), in Zhang Yongqing (ed.), *Yisilanjiao yu jingji yanjiu wenji (Research Papers on Islam and the Economy)*, Ningxia Renmin chubanshe, Yinchuan, 1991, pp. 5–17.

Zhirmunsky, Victor, 'Epic Songs and Singers in Central Asia', in Nora K. Chadwick and Victor Zhirmunsky, *Oral Epics of Central Asia*, Cambridge University Press, Cambridge, 1969, pp. 269–339.

Zhou Chongjing et al. (eds), *Zhongguo renkou, Xinjiang fence (China's Population, Xinjiang Volume)*, Zhongguo caizheng jingji chubanshe, Beijing, 1990.

Zhu Jielin, *Zangzu jinxiandai jiaoyu shilüe (Outline History of the Modern Education of the Tibetan Nationality)*, Qinghai Renmin chubanshe, Xining, 1990.

Zuo Yingfan, 'Hasake lisu' ('Kazak Etiquette and Customs'), in Gansu Provincial Library Bibliography Department (comp.), *Xibei minzu zongjiao shiliao wenzhai (Xinjiang fence) (Digest of Historical Materials on Nationalities and Religions of the Northwest) (Xinjiang Volumes)* 2 vols, Gansu sheng tushuguan, Lanzhou, 1985, vol. 2, pp. 991–95.

Newspapers, periodicals, yearbooks, compendia, etc.

Amnesty International Report 1990, Amnesty International Publications, London, 1990.

Beijing Review, weekly published in Beijing.

China Daily, daily published in Beijing.

China Handbook, 1937–1944, A Comprehensive Survey of Major Developments in China in Seven Years of War, Chinese Ministry of Information, Chungking, 1944.

China News, available several times daily through electronic mail.

China News Digest, available approximately daily through electronic mail.

Dierci Zhongguo jiaoyu nianjian (Second China Education Yearbook), 4 vols, Ministry of Education, Nanjing, 1948.

Jilin nianjian (1988) (Jilin Yearbook 1988), Jilin sheng renmin zhengfu bangongting and Jilin sheng difang zhi bianzuan weiyuanhui, Changchun, 1989.

Peking Review, weekly published in Beijing, renamed *Beijing Review* from the beginning of 1979.

The Japan–Manchoukuo Year Book 1936, Cyclopedia of General Information and Statistics on the Empires of Japan and Manchoukuo, The Japan–Manchoukuo Year Book Co., Tokyo.

The Japan–Manchoukuo Year Book 1939, Cyclopedia of General Information and Statistics on the Empires of Japan and Manchoukuo, The Japan–Manchoukuo Year Book Co., Tokyo.

Xinjiang nianjian 1993 (Xinjiang Yearbook 1993), Xinjiang Renmin chubanshe, Ürümqi, 1993.

Zhongguo renkou tongji nianjian 1990 (China Population Statistical Yearbook 1990), Kexue jishu wenxian chubanshe, Beijing, 1991.

Zhongguo tongji nianjian (China Statistical Yearbook), Zhongguo tongji chubanshe, Beijing, annual.

Zhonghua renmin gongheguo falü huibian, 1979–1984, Renmin chubanshe, Beijing, 1985.

Index